G000066607

A Tragedy of Errors

BAR QAMTZA AND THE FALL OF JERUSALEM

A Tragedy of Errors

BAR QAMTZA AND THE FALL OF JERUSALEM

Amram Tropper

HEBREW UNION COLLEGE PRESS

HEBREW UNION COLLEGE PRESS

© 2022 Hebrew Union College Press

Cover design by Elena Barschazki

Set in Arno Pro by Raphaël Freeman MISTD, Renana Typesetting

Library of Congress Cataloging-in-Publication Data

Names: Tropper, Amram D., author.

Title: A tragedy of errors : Bar Qamtza and the fall of Jerusalem / Amram
Tropper.

Description: Cincinnati : Hebrew Union College Press, [2022] | Includes
bibliographical references and index. | Summary: "The story of Bar
Qamtza is one of the most famous stories in all rabbinic literature. In
this tragic tale, a private feud at a Jerusalem banquet triggers a
series of events which eventually culminates in the destruction of the
Second Temple in Jerusalem. Until the Holocaust, Jews commonly viewed
the razing of the Second Temple as the greatest calamity in all Jewish
history, and for many Jews through the ages, the story of Bar Qamtza
explained why it had happened. In time, the story also became emblematic
of the internal strife and divisive infighting which have troubled
Jewish communities time and again across the generations"-- Provided by
publisher.

Identifiers: LCCN 2021060735 (print) | LCCN 2021060736 (ebook) | ISBN
9780878201969 (hardback) | ISBN 9780878201976 (adobe pdf) | ISBN
9780878201976 (adobe pdf)

Subjects: LCSH: Jerusalem--History--Siege, 70 A.D.--Sources. | Temple of
Jerusalem (Jerusalem)--History. | Hate--Religious aspects--Judaism. |
Jerusalem--In rabbinical literature.

Classification: LCC BM518.J4 T76 2022 (print) | LCC BM518.J4 (ebook) |
DDC 270.1--dc23/eng/20211223

LC record available at https://lccn.loc.gov/2021060735

LC ebook record available at https://lccn.loc.gov/2021060736

The stunning late antique Roman mosaic displayed on the book cover depicts
an extravagant banquet in a Roman dining room (or *triclinium*) with nine
reclining and inebriated banqueters (some in various states of undress), seven
attentive servants, and remnants of the banquet's courses scattered across the
messy floor of the unswept room (or *asarotos oikos*). The captivating mosaic
is currently housed in the Château de Boudry in Neuchâtel, Switzerland
and the image of the mosaic is courtesy of Phoenix Ancient Art.

למרים האהובה,

"וַתַּעַן לָהֶם מִרְיָם שִׁירוּ לַה׳"

Contents

Abbreviations

Ab urbe cond.	*Ab urbe condita* (*From the Founding of the City / History of Rome*)
Avod. Zar.	Avodah Zarah
ad loc.	*ad locum* (at the place discussed)
Ag. Ap.	*Against Apion* (*Contra Apionem*)
AJP	*American Journal of Philology*
ANDRL	*Archive of the New Dictionary of Rabbinic Literature*
Ant.	*Jewish Antiquities*
Arak.	Arakhin
b.	Bavli (Talmud Bavli/Babylonian Talmud)
B. Bat.	Bava Batra
B. Metz.	Bava Metziʿa
B. Qam.	Bava Qamma
Bacch.	*Bacchides* (*The Two Bacchises*)
Bek.	Bekhorot
Bell. Iug.	*Bellum Iugurthinum* (*The War with Jugurtha*)
Ber.	Berakhot
Brut.	*Brutus*
Cat. Maj.	*Cato Major* (*Cato the Elder*)
CBR	*Currents in Biblical Research*
Compot.	*De compotatione* (*Symposia*, Oration 27)
Dan	Daniel
De arch.	*De architectura* (*On Architecture*)
Deipn.	*Deipnosophistae* (*The Learned Banqueters*)
Deut	Deuteronomy
Dial. d.	*Dialogi deorum* (*Dialogues of the Gods*)
DSD	*Dead Sea Discoveries*

Ep.	*Epistulae (Letters)*
Epigr.	*Epigrammata* (Epigrams)
Epit.	*Epitome*
Eruv.	Eruvin
Esth	Esther
Exod	Exodus
Ezek	Ezekiel
Gen	Genesis
Git.	Gittin
Hist.	*Histories*
Hist. Rom.	*Historiae Romanae (Roman History)*
Hos	Hosea
HTR	*Harvard Theological Review*
HUCA	*Hebrew Union College Annual*
Ḥul.	Ḥullin
Il.	*Iliad*
ICS	*Illinois Classical Studies*
Isa	Isaiah
JQR	*Jewish Quarterly Review*
JBL	*Journal of Biblical Literature*
JJS	*Journal of Jewish Studies*
JMS	*Journal of Mediterranean Studies*
JSIJ	*Jewish Studies, an Internet Journal*
JSJ	*Journal for the Study of Judaism*
JSJF	*Jerusalem Studies in Jewish Folklore*
JSRS	*Judea and Samaria Research Studies*
JTR	*Journal of Textual Reasoning*
J.W.	*Jewish War*
Ketub.	Ketubbot
Kipp.	Kippurim
Lam	Lamentations
Lam. Rab.	Lamentations Rabbati *(Midrash Eikhah Rabbah)*
LCL	Loeb Classical Library
Legat.	*Legatio ad Gaium (The Embassy to Gaius)*
Lev	Leviticus
Lev. Rab.	Leviticus Rabbah *(Midrash Wayyikra Rabbah)*

Lucil.	*Ad Lucilium* (*Letters to Lucilius*)
m.	Mishnah (cited according to *Faksimile Ausgabe des Mischnacodex Kaufmann*)
Mal	Malachi
Matt	Matthew
Mekh.	Mekhilta de-Rabbi Ishmael
MHJ	*Melbourne Historical Journal*
Men.	*Menaechmi* (*The Two Menaechmuses*)
Menah.	Menahot
Merc. cond.	*De mercede conductis* (*Salaried Posts in Great Houses*)
Mic	Micah
Midr. Mish.	Midrash Mishle
Midr. Rab.	Midrash Rabbah
Nat.	*Naturalis historia* (*Natural History*)
Od.	*Odyssey*
Paed.	*Paedagogus* (*The Instructor*)
Par.	*De parasito* (*The Parasite*)
Pers.	*Persae* (*The Persian*)
Pesah.	Pesahim
Pesiq. Rab.	Pesiqta Rabbati
Phars.	*Pharsalia* (*De bello civili/The Civil War*)
Pirk. B. Azz.	Pirke Ben Azzai
Prob.	*Quod omnis probus liber sit* (*Every Good Person Is Free*)
Prov	Proverbs
Ps	Psalms
Qidd.	Qiddushin
Qoh. Rab.	Qohelet Rabbah (*Midrash Kohelet Rabbah*)
Qoh. Zuta	Qohelet Zuta (cited according to Kiperwasser, "Addenda: Kohelet Zuta Synopsis")
Quaest. conv.	*Quaestionum convivialum* (*Table Talk*)
Resp.	*Respublica* (*The Republic*)
Rev	Revelation
s.n.	*sine nomine* (without name [of publisher])
s.v.	*sub verbo* (under the word)
s.vv.	*sub verbis* (under the words)
Shabb.	Shabbat

Sanh.	Sanhedrin
Sat.	*Satires*
Saturn.	*Saturnalia*
Satyr.	*Satyricon*
Shevu.	Shevuʿot
Sen.	*De senectute* (*On Old Age*)
Sept. sap. conv.	*Septem sapientium convivium* (*Symposium of the Seven Sages*)
Sheqal.	Sheqalim
Sert.	*Sertorius*
Sir	Ben Sira (*Sefer Ben-Sira Ha-shalem*)
Song Rab.	Song of Songs Rabbah
Suas.	*Suasoriae*
Symp.	*Symposium*
t.	Tosefta
Taʿan.	Taʿanit
Trad. ap.	*Apostolic Tradition* (cited according to *La Tradition Apostolique*)
VT	*Vetus Testamentum*
y.	Yerushalmi (Jerusalem/Palestinian Talmud cited according to *Talmud Yerushalmi According to Ms. Or. 4720 (Scal. 3) of the Leiden University Library with Restorations and Corrections*)
Yevam.	Yevamot
Zevaḥ.	Zevaḥim
ZAW	*Zeitschrift für die alttestamentliche Wissenschaft*
1 Chr	1 Chronicles
1 Cor	1 Corinthians
1QS	Serek Hayaḥad (Rule of the Community)
1QSa	Rule of the Congregation
1 Sam	1 Samuel

Texts and Translations

The central rabbinic texts cited below are rendered as they appear in the high-resolution photographs of medieval manuscripts supplied by the manuscripts' home libraries, The National Library of Israel or The Friedberg Jewish Manuscript Society. Some less central rabbinic texts were also copied from photographs while others were either drawn from transcriptions of the manuscripts (provided by Ma'agarim of The Academy of the Hebrew Language, The Sol and Evelyn Henkind Talmud Text Databank, Hachi Garsinan of The Friedberg Jewish Manuscript Society or Torat Hatannaim of Bar-Ilan University) or from the editions of the rabbinic works listed in the Bibliography.

Unless otherwise stated, translations of rabbinic texts are my own (though often devised in consultation with previous translations) and biblical translations stem from the *JPS Hebrew-English Tanakh*. The New Testament is cited according to *The Greek New Testament* and Ben Sira according to *Sefer Ben-Sira Ha-shalem*; both are translated in accordance with *The New Oxford Annotated Bible: New Revised Standard Version with the Apocrypha: An Ecumenical Study Bible*. Unless otherwise indicated, classical texts in Greek and Latin as well as their translations are quoted according to the editions and translations listed in the Bibliography.

Introduction

In the early centuries of the Common Era, Jewish sages in Palestine and Babylonia composed countless stories that were preserved for posterity in rabbinic literature, and the story of Bar Qamtza stands out as one of the best known. The story tells of a private feud at a Jerusalem banquet which triggered a series of events that culminated in the destruction of the Second Temple in Jerusalem. Until the Holocaust, Jews commonly viewed the razing of the Second Temple as the greatest calamity in all Jewish history, and, for many Jews down through the ages, the story of Bar Qamtza explained why it had happened.

For two thousand years, Jews have looked back nostalgically at the period of the Second Temple, which spans from the return of the Judean exiles from Babylonia to Zion during the late sixth century BCE until the temple's destruction in 70 CE. For much of this period, the Jews of Yehud/Judaea/Palestine enjoyed some measure of political autonomy and worshipped in the Jerusalem temple. During the early Second Temple period a Jewish temple also flourished on the Egyptian island of Elephantine, and later on in Second Temple times a temple was founded in the Egyptian city of Heliopolis, but these two temples only served relatively small local populations.[1] By contrast, the temple in Jerusalem, which Herod famously revamped, was the sole legitimate cultic site in the eyes of most ancient Jews the world over. Unlike the Greeks and Romans, who worshipped their gods in multiple temples,

---

1. See Amram Tropper, *Simeon the Righteous in Rabbinc Literature: A Legend Reinvented* (Leiden: Brill, 2013), 160–62.

most Jews believed that their sacrificial offerings should only be brought in the Jerusalem temple. Hence, by late Second Temple times, the Jerusalem temple was the primary Jewish pilgrimage site. Not merely a busy place of worship, the temple was also a thriving economic hub, an illustrious edifice, and a monumental symbol of corporate Jewish identity and political autonomy. The Second Temple, burnt to the ground as Jerusalem fell during the first Jewish revolt against Rome (66–73 [or 74] CE), was never rebuilt, and Jewish autonomy did not return to the region for almost two thousand years. The destruction of the Second Temple has thus long signaled the end of a glorious era in Jewish history. As the moment when Jewish sacrificial worship was terminated and the ultimate symbol of Jewish corporate identity was tragically demolished in a failed rebellion, the destruction of the temple gradually emerged as the paradigmatic catastrophe in the historical consciousness of the Jews. For countless Jews in medieval and modern times, the story of Bar Qamtza explained how it unfolded.

Today, we learn about the fall of Jerusalem, the destruction of the Second Temple, and the first-century Jewish revolt against Rome from archaeological remains, ancient non-Jewish writings, and, most importantly, Josephus Flavius's account of the revolt. Josephus was a Jewish officer during the revolt who was captured by the Romans and eventually wrote a history of the war (and much more) while living in Rome during the late first century CE. Over the course of the last two thousand years, however, most Jews did not learn about the revolt from Josephus's work (or from its medieval adaptation called *Josippon*), but from rabbinic literature. A handful of rabbinic texts address, in various ways, the backdrop to the destruction of the Second Temple, but the story of Bar Qamtza eventually emerged as perhaps the most prominent Jewish account of the ultimate causes of the conflict.[2] This short didactic story is a literary tour

---

2. Many rabbinic reflections on the destruction of the temple are general statements, but a good story, like the story of Bar Qamtza, has far more emotional power. See Chapter 7, n. 10 below. Furthermore, rabbinic works, such as Lamentations Rabbati, Avot de-Rabbi Nathan, and the Bavli, tell other stories about the destruction of Jerusalem and its temple, such as the tale of Rabban Yohanan ben Zakkai's escape from the besieged city. Few other famous stories, however, relate the ultimate causes of the conflict.

de force with a moral sting, and its prominent place at the opening of the
Babylonian Talmud's (or Bavli's) "legends of destruction" helped ensure
its popularity through the ages.[3] As the rabbinic work most studied over
the centuries, the Bavli has made an indelible impact on numerous facets
of Jewish life – including imaginings of the Jewish past – and through
its "legends of destruction" it has imprinted the story of Bar Qamtza on
many hearts and minds.

Some time ago I started researching the story of Bar Qamtza, and
the more I explored the story the more I recognized that only a book
would do it justice. Like most rabbinic stories, however, the story of
Bar Qamtza is short and, so far as I know, no one has written an entire
book about a single rabbinic story. Despite this, I believe there are three
compelling reasons for writing a book-length examination of the story
of Bar Qamtza.

First, the story of Bar Qamtza is not just any old story; it is one of
the rabbis' most renowned tales. The story not only relates to the most
cataclysmic event in ancient Jewish history, but for centuries on end it
has been emblematic of fraternal strife – of the divisive and unnecessary
infighting which has repeatedly troubled Jewish communities (like
most communities) throughout history.[4] Since the story attained such
an eminent place in Jewish historical discourse across the centuries and
since it still resonates strongly with many contemporary Jews, I believe
that it warrants its own book.

Second, a book about the story of Bar Qamtza offers an excellent
opportunity to illustrate the methods and tools of modern talmudic
scholarship which are not always well known beyond the small cadre
of talmudic specialists and ancient historians. For example, modern
approaches to the study of a rabbinic story include (lower) criticism
of the story's textual witnesses, a philological analysis of its language,
a close reading of its narrative and literary context, a (higher) critical

---

3. On the prominent location of the story in the Bavli, see Abraham Weiss,
Studies in the Literature of the Amoraim (על היצירה הספרותית של האמוראים), (New
York, NY: Horeb, Yeshiva University, and The Lucius N. Littauer Foundation,
1961–1962), 262–63.

4. See, for example, Ruth R. Wisse, *Jews and Power* (New York, NY: Schocken,
2007), 128.

analysis of its sources of inspiration, an intertextual reading of its themes, a critical assessment of its historical credibility, a broad contextual interpretation which considers the ambient non-Jewish cultural setting, the comparison of Palestinian and Babylonian textual parallels, a search for traces of social forces and political tendencies, and an examination of the story's social constructions and cultural conventions. Although commentators over many centuries have written thoughtful and incisive analyses of our story, the tools of modern scholarship open up new vistas for exploration and identify new ways to read the story. An author, editor, audience, or readership always experiences a story through the mediation of particular frames of reference and interpretive lenses, and the new approaches of modern scholarship help us reconstruct the ancient frames of reference and interpretive lenses of our story's creators and early audiences.[5]

Third and perhaps most important, although this book is heavy on literary interpretation, literary analysis is less an ultimate goal and more a tool in the writing of a *microhistory of sorts*.[6] Microhistory's most prominent feature is its high-resolution thick description of a single episode, person, or locale, and this study is a *microhistory* in the

---

5. On the formative role of our frames of reference for interpretation, see Willard V.O. Quine, "Two Dogmas of Empiricism," *The Philosophical Review* 60 (1951): 39–43; Thomas S. Kuhn, *The Structure of Scientific Revolutions* (Chicago, IL: University of Chicago Press, 1962), 77–91; Stanley Fish, *Is There a Text in This Class? The Authority of Interpretive Communities* (Cambridge, MA: Harvard University Press, 1980), 338–55. Our frames of reference, however, are constrained by the texts themselves. While an author's thoughts, not evident in a text, do not dictate the meaning of the text (see William K. Wimsatt and Monroe C. Beardsley, "The Intentional Fallacy," *Sewanee Review* 54 [1946]: 468–88), the text itself expresses or encodes the author's message or intent along with much more that is presumed or unconscious. See Jay Clayton and Eric Rothstein, "Figures in the Corpus: Theories of Influence and Intertextuality," in *Influence and Intertextuality in Literary History*, ed. Jay Clayton and Eric Rothstein (Madison: The University of Wisconsin Press, 1991), 3–37.
6. For a brief overview of microhistory, see Carlo Ginzberg, "Microhistory: Two or Three Things that I Know about It," *Critical Inquiry* 20 (1993):10–35. Note also Ginzberg's comment on p. 22: "In reducing the scale of observation, that which for another scholar could have been a simple footnote in a hypothetical monograph on the Protestant Reformation in Friuli was transformed into a book."

sense that it enlists one short narrative, the story of Bar Qamtza, as a springboard for the exploration of ancient Jewish history.[7] As a window into the world of its authors and early audiences, the story reveals ancient Jewish social ideals and cultural practices, religious beliefs and literary trajectories, historical imaginings and political inclinations, systemic structures and institutional realities.[8] In other words, the famous story of Bar Qamtza serves as a platform from which to explore the interplay between the minutiae of everyday life in antiquity and the overarching architecture of ancient Jewish society.

This study is a microhistory *of sorts* because the story of Bar Qamtza is fictional. Unlike the majority of microhistories, which generally focus on credible historical materials, the story of Bar Qamtza did not actually happen.[9] Nonetheless, even as fiction, our story serves as an excellent springboard for social and cultural microhistory. Whereas the story teaches us little about the actual events leading up to the destruction of the temple, it teaches us a great deal about the world of its authors and audiences a few centuries later.

In this microhistory of sorts, we will encounter, through the story of Bar Qamtza, a Jewish variation on a central social institution in Greek, Roman, and Persian antiquity which was fraught with the potential for conflict, that is, the banquet. While ancient banquets were designed to foster a sense of brotherhood and fellowship, they also drew the line between insider and outsider as they defined a community's boundaries. Over the course of our investigation we will also discover how the story of Bar Qamtza adopted widespread features of Greek and Roman banquet narratives and adapted them to the local Jewish context,

---

7. See Clifford Geertz, *The Interpretation of Cultures: Selected Essays* (New York, NY: Basic, 1973), 3–30.

8. On the potential historical value of sources like the story of Bar Qamtza, see Elizabeth A. Clark, *History, Theory, Text: Historians and the Linguistic Turn* (Cambridge, MA: Harvard University Press, 2004), 77; Peter Burke, *History and Social Theory*, 2nd edition (Ithaca, NY: Cornell University Press, 2004), 38–43.

9. The materials studied by microhistorians, however, are not always as straightforward as microhistorians imagine. See Clark, *History, Theory, Text*, 77–79. See also Catherine Gallagher and Stephen Greenblatt, *Practicing New Historicism* (Chicago, IL: University of Chicago Press, 2000), 1–19.

transforming a critique of abuses in Roman reciprocal relations into a critique of a fractured Jewish solidarity. We will see how our story gave narrative form to earlier non-narrative sayings and drew literary inspiration from non-rabbinic historical materials. We will discern how our story imagines Second Temple Jerusalem ultimately falling not because of any systemic conflict between Jerusalem and Rome, but because the Jewish leadership of the time was ethically flawed. We will learn how our story promotes a positive view of the overarching Roman imperial regime as it signals its preference for peaceful accommodation over armed resistance. We will chart the evolving faces of the story of Bar Qamtza, tracing its recasting in the rabbinic study houses of Sasanian Persia as well as the gradual process of its rabbinization.

Although I have categorized the story of Bar Qamtza as fiction, most talmudic scholars would have viewed it quite differently until rather recently. The story of Bar Qamtza is a "sage story" (and historical legend), and scholars have traditionally viewed such stories as embroidered historical accounts. Presuming the stories to be genuine and credible – assuming that the stories ultimately stemmed from trustworthy and reliable eyewitness testimonies – scholars generally accepted the authenticity of the stories and the veracity of their contents just so long as there were no local or immediate reasons for doubt. All the supernatural, fantastic, anachronistic, impossible, and implausible elements of the stories were viewed as mere literary embellishments, as husks to be peeled away in the hopes of recovering the stories' pristine historical kernels.

Half a century or so ago, however, scholars came to realize that classifying rabbinic sage stories as ornamented historical reports was an error. With a newfound sensitivity to rabbinic literature's literary qualities, scholars understood that sage stories are better classified as didactic fiction and dramatic narrative, artistic literary genres which do not necessarily stem from eyewitness testimonies or rest on credible facts. Instead of presuming that the stories faithfully preserve the reliable accounts of eyewitnesses, scholars now focus on the stories' literary qualities rather than on their possible or questionable historical veracity. While the rabbis surely incorporated many credible events and details into their sage stories, we often lack any rational method for distinguishing fact from fiction. Moreover, once we consider the late date of the stories relative to the early events they depict, once we better appreciate the stories' pervasive and thick artistic qualities, and once we identify the stories' underlying literary sources of inspiration (whose existence renders unnecessary the unfounded traditional presumption that the stories evolved from historical kernels), we can often conclude that the stories are most likely fictitious.[10] In our case, there is no reason to presuppose that the story of Bar Qamtza preserves a genuine and credible account of late Second Temple history. The story's late date, artistic design, and underlying sources of inspiration establish that the story is most likely a fictional tale.

Although I have been referring to the story of Bar Qamtza in the singular, the truth is that rabbinic literature has preserved two similar yet distinct versions of our story. Our story appears, with significant variations, in Lamentations Rabbati, which was edited in Byzantine Palestine sometime during the fifth or sixth century CE, and also in the Bavli, which was edited in Babylonia sometime in the sixth or seventh century CE.[11] Scholars have long debated the relationship between these two versions: some view Lamentations Rabbati's version as early and primary and the Bavli's version as late and secondary;[12] others view the

---

10. For an overview of the shift in historical scholarship outlined here, see Amram Tropper, *Rewriting Ancient Jewish History: The History of Jews in Roman Times and the New Historical Method* (London: Routledge, 2016), 106–33.

11. On the date of Lamentations Rabbati, see Paul Mandel, "'Tales of the Destruction of the Temple': Between the Land of Israel and Babylonia" ("אגדות החורבן: בין ארץ ישראל לבבל"), in *Center and Diaspora: The Land of Israel and the Diaspora in the Second Temple, Mishna and Talmud Periods*, ed. Isaiah M. Gafni (Jerusalem: Zalman Shazar Center, 2004), 142. On the date of the Bavli, see H.L. Strack and Günther Stemberger, *Introduction to the Talmud and Midrash*, trans. Markus Bockmuehl (Minneapolis, MN: Fortress Press, 1996), 2–7.

12. See, for example, Joshua Efron, "Bar-Kokhva in the Light of the Palestinian and Babylonian Talmudic Traditions" ("מלחמת בר־כוכבא לאור המסורת התלמודית־ הארצישראלית כנגד הבבלית"), in *The Bar-Kokhva Revolt: A New Approach*, ed. Aharon Oppenheimer and Uriel Rappaport (Jerusalem: Yad Ben Zvi, 1984), 91n211; Daniel R. Schwartz, "More on 'Zechariah ben Avkules: Humility or Zealotry?'" ("עוד לשאלת 'זכריה בן אבקולס: ענוותנות או קנאות?'"), *Zion* 53 (1988): 313n3; Anat Yisraeli-Taran, *The Legends of the Destruction* (אגדות החורבן: מסורות החורבן בספרות התלמודית), (Tel Aviv: Hakibutz Hameuchad, 1997), 17–18n25;

Bavli's version as early and primary and Lamentations Rabbati's version as late and secondary;[13] and yet others maintain that both versions evolved independently out of a common core.[14] In my opinion, which is summarized in Appendix I below, a thorough comparison of the parallel stories demonstrates that Lamentations Rabbati has preserved the earliest extant version of our story, which was recast later on in the Bavli. In light of the relative chronology of the story's two versions, Part I of this book focuses on the primary version preserved in Lamentations Rabbati and Part II on the Bavli's later and secondary rendition.

In my analysis of both versions of the story of Bar Qamtza, I divide the story into two acts with three scenes per act. Both the broad division into acts and the narrow split into individual scenes trace natural literary fissures in the text, though the terminology employed – "act" and "scene" – stems from the world of theater, not short stories. Although the story of Bar Qamtza is a story and not a play, I have enlisted some theater terminology not only because it is a helpful way to refer to the different segments of the story, but also because the story, with just a few changes of scenery, a small cast of characters, and some typical traits of ancient plays, can easily be imagined as a play. Picturing the story playing out on stage not only helps bring it to life, but also encourages us to flesh out the narrative, helping us spot lacunae in the plotline and elements left unstated. While immersing ourselves in the theatrical atmosphere

---

Jeffrey L. Rubenstein, *Talmudic Stories: Narrative Art, Composition, and Culture* (Baltimore, MD: Johns Hopkins University Press, 1999), 172–73; Yair Furstenberg, "Qamtza and Bar Qamtza, 55b–56a," ("קמצא ובר קמצא, נה ע"ב - נו ע"א"), in *Five Sugyot from the Babylonian Talmud*, ed. Shamma Friedman (Jerusalem: The Society for the Interpretation of the Talmud, 2002), 111; Mandel, "Tales of the Destruction," 150–55; Meir Ben Shahar, "The Abolishment of the Sacrifice on Behalf of the Emperor" ("ביטול הקרבן לשלום הקיסר"), in *Josephus and the Rabbis*, ed. Tal Ilan and Vered Noam (Jerusalem: Yad Ben-Zvi, 2017), 595n124.

13. See, for example, Anthony J. Saldarini, "Varieties of Rabbinic Response to the Destruction of the Temple," *Society of Biblical Literature 1982 Seminar Papers* (Chico, CA: Scholars Press, 1982), 454–55; David Rokéaḥ, "Zechariah ben Avkules: Humility or Zealotry?" ("זכריה בן אבקולס: ענוותנות או קנאות?"), *Zion* 53 (1988): 55–56.

14. See, for example, Richard Kalmin, *Jewish Babylonia between Persia and Roman Palestine* (Oxford: Oxford University Press, 2006), 48–49.

of the story of Bar Qamtza, I hope we will be rewarded with a glimpse of the society, culture, and religion of the story's authors, editors, and early audiences.

If there is a central puzzle in the story of Bar Qamtza, it is how a local quarrel at a private banquet, triggered by a humorous mishap, transitioned to the international arena and was believed to lead to a national calamity. How a minor altercation between two Jerusalemites brought about the destruction of the temple is the mysterious crux of the story to which we shall return time and again. In other words, why would rabbinic authors imagine that the fall of Jerusalem ultimately stemmed from an everyday sort of feud? While a wide variety of issues will emerge over the course of our microhistory, this fundamental enigma will have much to teach us about ancient Jewish culture and society.

Part I

Bar Qamtza in Lamentations Rabbati

"No room! No room! they cried out when they saw Alice coming.

"There's *plenty* of room!" said Alice indignantly, and she sat down in a large arm-chair at one end of the table.

"Have some wine," the March Hare said in an encouraging tone.

Alice looked all round the table, but there was nothing on it but tea. "I don't see any wine," she remarked.

"There isn't any," said the March Hare.

"Then it wasn't very civil of you to offer it," said Alice angrily.

"It wasn't very civil of you to sit down without being invited," said the March Hare.

Lewis Carroll, *Alice's Adventures in Wonderland*, 109–10.

"מהרסיך ומחריביך ממך יצאו" (ישעיהו מט:יז): המהרסים והמחריבים אותך
יצאו ממך, רוצה לומר הרשעים שבקרבך הם סבבו ההריסה והחורבן ולא
מאתי יצאה הרעה.

Those who ruined you and destoyed you shall go forth from you (Isa 49:17): Those who ruined and destroyed you shall go forth from you, that is to say, the wicked from your midst are the cause of the ruin and the destruction, for the tragedy did not come from me.

David and Yechiel Hillel Altschuler,
Metzudat David on Isaiah 49:16.

Chapter 1

The Text

The story of Bar Qamtza appears for the first time in Lamentations Rabbati, a rabbinic work edited within the cultural climate of Byzantine Palestine.[1] Since the story was authored by rabbinic sages of Byzantine Palestine, the Jewish community in Palestine as well as the overarching cultural setting in the Greek-speaking east of the Roman Empire supply us with crucial interpretive lenses for the story, lenses which are deployed throughout Part I. The ambient Greek and Roman settings offer us important frames of reference for our story because the rabbis and their Jewish contemporaries in Palestine were Roman provincials who absorbed, adapted, adjusted, manipulated, and subverted countless facets of the surrounding cultures.[2] While we

---

1. Lam. Rab. 4:2 (*Midrash Eikhah Rabbah,* ed. Salomon Buber [Vilna: Romm, 5659], 142–43).
2. See Hayim Lapin, *Rabbis as Romans: The Rabbinic Movement in Palestine, 100–400 CE.* (Oxford: Oxford University Press, 2012); Annette Yoshiko Reed and Natalie B. Dohrmann, "Rethinking Romanness, Provincializing Christendom," in *Jews, Christians, and the Roman Empire: The Poetics of Power in Late Antiquity,* ed. Annette Yoshiko Reed and Natalie B. Dohrmann (Philadelphia: University of Pennsylvania Press, 2013), 1–21; Burton L. Visotzky, *Aphrodite and the Rabbis: How the Jews Adapted Roman Culture to Create Judaism as We Know It* (New York, NY: St. Martin's Press, 2016); Tropper, *Rewriting Ancient Jewish History,* 33–50; Ishay Rosen-Zvi, "Is the Mishnah a Roman Composition?" in *The Faces of Torah: Studies in the Texts and Contexts of Ancient Judaism in Honor of Steven Fraade,* ed. Michal Bar-Asher Siegal, Tzvi Novick, and Christine Hayes (Göttingen: Vandenhoeck & Ruprecht, 2017), 487–508.

cannot trace direct paths of influence between the Greek and Roman texts and practices discussed below and our Jewish story, the substantive similarities between the Jewish and classical materials, in tandem with their geographical and temporal proximity, strongly suggest that these practices stem from a shared discursive space and intercultural network populated by entwined pathways of habits and practices, themes and ideas, literary materials and folk creativity.[3] Before embarking on a detailed analysis of Lamentations Rabbati's version of our story, however, let us survey the text of the story from beginning to end.

Although Lamentations Rabbati was edited in the fifth or sixth century CE, the work's earliest extant textual witnesses – that is, its earliest manuscripts, fragments from the Cairo Genizah, and printed editions – were written hundreds of years later. Over the course of Lamentations Rabbati's transmission, whether orally or in writing, the text was changed both intentionally and accidentally, and, as a result, variations among the textual witnesses of Lamentations Rabbati's story of Bar Qamtza are numerous and substantial. Since these variations include alterations that were made many centuries after the text's original formation, they pose a challenge to anyone who wishes to read the original text from Byzantine Palestine. In truth, like many rabbinic texts, the precise wording of the original text of our story may well be unrecoverable.

In order to approximate the original text as best we can, we will focus on the textual tradition which seems to have preserved the earliest extant reading. As spelled out in Appendix II below, a comparison of Lamentations Rabbati's textual witnesses suggests that branch **B**, characterized by Paul Mandel as the conservative branch of manuscripts, has preserved the earliest extant reading of our story. Since the scribes

---

3. See Peter Schäfer, "Introduction," in *The Talmud Yerushalmi and Graeco-Roman Culture*, ed. Peter Schäfer, vol. 1 (Tübingen: Mohr Siebeck, 1998), 14–16; Galit Hasan-Rokem, *Web of Life: Folklore and Midrash in Rabbinic Literature*, trans. Batya Stein (Stanford, CA: Stanford University Press, 2000), 1–8, 67–69. See also Michael Satlow, "Beyond Influence: Toward a New Historiographic Paradigm," in *Jewish Literatures and Cultures: Context and Intertext*, ed. Anita Norich and Yaron Z. Eliav (Providence, RI: Brown University Press, 2008), 37–54; Tropper, *Simeon the Righteous*, 215–16; Shai Secunda, *The Iranian Talmud: Reading the Bavli in Its Sasanian Context* (Philadelphia: University of Pennsylvania Press, 2013), 110–43.

and copyists of branch **B** tended to transmit the text they received with minimal alterations, while those of branch **A** modified the text more freely, branch **B** more closely approximates the original text. In line with this conclusion, Lamentations Rabbati's story of Bar Qamtza is cited here according to Oxford 102, a faithful representative of branch **B**.

Lamentations Rabbati's original text of our story should not be confused with the original story itself. Earlier versions of the story, whether oral or written, may have existed prior to Lamentations Rabbati, but so long as we lack evidence for the existence of these hypothetical versions of the story they need not concern us. In two instances, however, philological considerations will enable us to peel away a late and secondary layer of the text, thereby revealing an earlier version of our story hidden within Lamentations Rabbati.

1 ד'א "בני ציון היקרים" (איכה ד:ב):

2 מה היתה יקרותן?

3 לא היה אחד מהם הולך לסעודה עד שהיה נקרא ונשנה.

4 מעשה באדם אחד בירושלם שעשה סעודה.

5 אמר לשלוחו: לך והבא לי בן קמצא רחמי; אזל ואייתי ליה בר קמצא שנאיה.

6 על[4] ויש̇ב בין האורחים; עאל ואשכחיה ביני ארסטטיה.

7 אמר ליה: [את]5 שנאי ואת יתיב בגו ביתאי, קום ופוק לך מגו ביתאי!

8 אמר ליה: לא תבסרני ואנא יהיב לך טימי מגוסי.

9 אמר ליה: לית את מסובי הכא.

10 אמר ליה: לא תבסרני ואנא יהיב לך דלא אכיל ולא שתי.

11 אמר ליה לית את מסובי הכא.

12 אמר ליה: אנא יהיב לך טימי הדה סעודתא.

13 אמר ליה: קום פוק ליך!

---

4. On the basis of the other textual witnesses, I have corrected Oxford 102, which reads here "עלה," "he went up."

5. The word "את," "you," appears here (or following the word "שנאי," "my enemy,") in all the other textual witnesses and was apparently omitted from Oxford 102. In citations of texts and their translations, square brackets surround words which I have interpolated on the basis of other textual witnesses and round parentheses surround words which I have inserted to enhance the translation.

14 והיה שם זכריה[6] בן אבקולס והיה ספק בידו למחות ולא מיחה.

15 מאן דנפק ליה, אמר בנפשיה: מה אלין מסבין יתבין בשלותהון?!

16 מה עשה?

17 הלך לו אצל השילטון,

18 אמר[7]: אלין קורבניא דאת משלח אינון אכלין יתהון ומקרבין אחרנין בחילופין.

19 נזף ביה; עאל לגביה תוב,

20 אמר ליה: כל אלין קורבניא דאת משלח אינון[8] אכלין להון ומקרבין אחרנין בחלופיהון

21 ואין לית את מהימן לי, שלח עמי חד אפרכוס וקורבניא עמיה ואת ידע.

22 כי אתי בשבילא עד דאפרכוס דמיך,

23 קם בליליא ועשאן בעלי מומין [בסתר].[9]

24 כיון שראה הכהן אותן הקריב אחרים תחתיהן.

25 אמ׳ ליה: למחר אנא קריב להון.

26 אתא יומא אחרינא, אמר ליה: לית את מקריב להון.

27 אמר ליה: למחר.

28 אתא יומא תליתאה ולא קריבהון.

29 שלח ואמר למלכא: ההיא מילתא דיהודייא קושטא הוא!

30 מיד סלק וחרב בי מקדשא,

31 הדא היא דבריתא אמרין: בין קמצא לבין קמצא חריב בי מקדשא.

32 א״ר יוסי: ענוותנותו של ר׳ זכריה בן אבקולס שרפה את ההיכל.

1 Another teaching: *The precious children of Zion* (Lam 4:2):

2 What was their preciousness?

3 Not one of them would attend a banquet until he was invited and (then) invited again.

---

6. Save for Parma 2559, the other textual witnesses refer to Zechariah as "Rabbi Zechariah."

7. The phrase "מרדו בך יהודאי," "the Jews have rebelled against you," was interpolated here into Casanatense H 3112 and Parma 2559 due to the influence of the Bavli.

8. I have omitted the word "משל" which apparently was accidentally written here in Oxford 102, perhaps in an unwitting repetition of the word "משלח."

9. The phrase "בדוקין שבעין," "on the white of its eye," was interpolated into Oxford 102 and Parma 2393 due to the influence of the Bavli. London 27089 reads here "בסתר," "secretly."

4 A story of one man in Jerusalem who made a banquet.

5 He said to his messenger: Go and bring me Ben Qamtza my friend; he (the messenger) went and brought him Bar Qamtza his enemy.

6 He (Bar Qamtza) entered and sat among the guests; he (the host) entered and found him (Bar Qamtza) among the banqueters.

7 He said to him: [You] are my enemy and (yet) you sit within my home! Get up and get yourself out of my home!

8 He said to him: Do not shame me and I will pay you the cost of my meal.

9 He said to him: You are not reclining here.

10 He said to him: Do not shame me and I will pay you without eating or drinking.

11 He said to him: You are not reclining here.

12 He said to him: I will pay you the cost of the banquet.

13 He said to him: Get up and get yourself out!

14 Zechariah ben Avqulas was present and he had the opportunity to protest but did not protest.

15 When he (Bar Qamtza) went out he said to himself: How do they (dare) recline and sit at ease!

16 What did he do?

17 He went to the ruler

18 (and) said: Those offerings that you send, they eat them and offer up others in their stead.

19 He reprimanded him. (Nonetheless,) he (Bar Qamtza) came to him (the ruler) again.

20 He said to him: All those offerings that you send, they eat them and offer up others in their stead

21 and if you do not believe me, send with me an officer and offerings with him and you will know.

22 While they were traveling on the path, the officer fell asleep.

23 He (Bar Qamtza) got up in the night and [secretly] made them (the animals) blemished.

24 When the priest saw them, he offered up others in their place.

25 He (the priest) said to him (the officer): Tomorrow I will offer them up.

26 The next day came and he (the officer) said to him (the priest): You are not offering them up.

27 He said to him: Tomorrow.

28 The third day came and he did not offer them up.

29 He (the officer) sent (a message) to the king saying: The statement of the Jew is true![10]

30 Immediately he rose up and destroyed the temple

31 hence people say: Between Qamtza and Qamtza the temple was destroyed.

32 Rabbi Yose said: The meekness of Rabbi Zechariah ben Avqulas burnt down the sanctuary.

Writ large, the story of Bar Qamtza is made up of two acts: Act I – the banquet, and Act II – Bar Qamtza's revenge. The story opens in Act I scene 1 with a banquet invitation gone wrong: in lieu of the intended guest, Bar Qamtza is accidentally invited. In scene 2, Bar Qamtza negotiates with the banquet host who wishes him gone, hoping to convince the host to allow him to remain at the banquet; scene 3 concludes Act I with Bar Qamtza's furious indignation over his ejection from the banquet. When no other banqueter protests his expulsion, Bar Qamtza is appalled and his revenge then plays out in Act II. In Act II scene 1, Bar Qamtza sets his diabolical plot in motion: he convinces the Roman ruler to check whether the Jews offer up Roman sacrificial animals and then he blemishes the animals sent by the ruler in order to ensure that the Jerusalem priests will refuse to sacrifice them. Scene 2 tells of an extended negotiation between the Roman ruler's representative, sent to verify Bar Qamtza's slanderous report, and the Jewish priest who refuses to offer up the Roman animals. Scene 3 then concludes Act II with the furiously indignant Romans demolishing the temple in Jerusalem in revenge for the rejection of their sacrifices.

If we extend the scope of our viewpoint beyond the story of Bar

---

10. Alternatively one might translate: "The matter of the Jews is true."

Qamtza proper to include its literary context, we find that Lamentations Rabbati situates the story within its exposition of Lamentations 4:2. Since this local context erects a literary backdrop which paints the story in a particular light, we turn now to Lamentations Rabbati's discussion of Lamentations 4:2.

Chapter 2

The Literary Context

Mourning the "precious children of Zion" who were slaughtered indiscriminately during the destruction of the First Temple, Lamentations 4:2 reads as follows:

בני ציון היקרים המסלאים בפז, איכה נחשבו לנבלי חרש מעשה ידי יוצר.
The precious children of Zion; once valued as gold – alas, they are accounted as earthen pots, work of a potter's hands!

Lamentations Rabbati, which often interprets the biblical Book of Lamentations vis-à-vis the destruction of the Second Temple, illustrates at length the phrase "בני ציון היקרים," "the precious children of Zion" in its exposition of Lamentations 4:2.[1] At first, Lamentations Rabbati reveals how "the precious children of Zion," understood as the invaluable youth of Jerusalem, were quite literally "once valued as gold." When brides and grooms of Jerusalem wedded non-Jerusalemites, they would receive their weight in gold. On the heels of this remarkable expression of the high valuation of Jerusalem's youths, Lamentations Rabbati offers a second illustration of "the precious children of Zion," focusing this time not only on the high monetary value of Jerusalem youth but also on the considerate or "precious" practice of Jerusalem grooms. When Jerusalem grooms married brides of a higher social standing, they invested more in their wedding banquet than in their domestic furnishings, but when they married brides of a lower social standing, they did the reverse. The

---

1. Cf. Ben Shahar, "Abolishment of the Sacrifice," 578, 592.

prominent role of weddings in these two illustrations and the reference in the latter to wedding banquets in particular form a natural bridge to Lamentations Rabbati's ensuing discussion of the exquisite banquet practices and manners of the "precious" Jerusalemites. The portrait of the Jerusalemites' banquet customs, which interprets "precious" in terms of character rather than monetary value and no longer limits "children" to the youth, also serves as the backdrop for Lamentations Rabbati's story of Bar Qamtza.

Six Banquet Customs of "The Precious Children of Zion"

In bridging the gap between the two noted illustrations of "the precious children of Zion" and the story of Bar Qamtza, Lamentations Rabbati further develops its exposition of Lamentations 4:2 with the help of six banquet customs ascribed to the "precious" Jerusalemites of the Second Temple period:

1: ד״א "בני ציון היקרים" (איכה ד:ב): מה היתה יקרותן? בשעה שהיה אחד מהם מזומן לסעודה, היה הופך בית יד אונקלי השמאלית שאם יבא אחר לזמנו, יהיה יודע שהוא מזומן לסעודה ולא יטעננו טענת חנם.

2: ד״א "בני ציון היקרים" (איכה ד:ב): מה היתה יקרותן? בשעה שהיה אחד מהם עושה סעודה היה צר כל מיני סעודה במפה מפני האסטניסין, שלא יאכל אחד מהם דבר שלא הגון לו ונזיק.

3: ד״א "בני ציון היקרים" (איכה ד:ב): מה היתה יקרותן? שלא היה אחד מהם נכנס לסעודה עד שהוא יודע מי הם המסובין עמו, ומי ומזוגו ומי משמשו, ולא חותם בנייר עד שהוא יודע מי הם החותמין עמו, משום "אל תשת ידך עם רשע" (שמות כג:א).

4: ד״א "בני ציון היקרים" (איכה ד:ב): מה היתה יקרותן? תני רבן שמעון בן גמליאל: מנהג גדול היה בירושלם, שבשעה שהיה אחד מהם עושה סעודה, היה תולה המפה על פתחו; כל זמן שהיה מפה פרוסה היו האורחים נכנסין לביתו, העביר את המפה לא היה רשות ליכנס.

5: ועוד מנהג אחר היה שם שכל זמן שהיה אחד מהם עושה סעודה היה מוסר את הסעודה לטבח שאם נתקלקל דבר בסעודה יבא על ראשו; ואם היו מוצאין דבר מקולקל בסעודה היו מענישין הטבח, הכל לפי כבוד בעל הבית ולפי כבוד האורחים.

6: ד"א "בני ציון היקרים" (איכה ד:ב): מה היתה יקרותן? לא היה אחד מהם
הולך לסעודה עד שהיה נקרא ונשנה.

1: Another explanation of *The precious children of Zion* (Lam 4:2):
What was their preciousness? Whenever one of them was invited
to a banquet, he would turn over his left shoulder clasp (or the left
sleeve of his undergarment) so that if someone else should come to
invite him, he would know that he was (already) invited to a banquet
and would not extend a wasted invitation.[2]

2: Another explanation of *The precious children of Zion* (Lam 4:2):
What was their preciousness? Whenever one of them made a banquet,
he would wrap up all the courses of the banquet in a cloth because
of the fastidious ones, so that none of them should eat something
unfitting for him and harmful.[3]

3: Another explanation of *The precious children of Zion* (Lam 4:2):
What was their preciousness? Not one of them would enter a banquet
until he knew who his fellow-recliners were to be, and who would
pour for him and who would serve him and he would not sign a
document until he knew with whom he was signing because of that
which is said: "you shall not join hands with the guilty to act as a
malicious witness" (Exod 23:1).

4: Another explanation of *The precious children of Zion* (Lam 4:2):
What was their preciousness? Rabban Simeon ben Gamaliel taught:

---

2. See Jacob Nahum Epstein, "Midiqduqei yerushalmi" ("מדקדוקי ירושלמי"),
Tarbiz 5 (1934): 271; Saul Lieberman, *Tosefta Ki-Fshuṭa* (תוספתא כפשוטה), 12
vols. (New York, NY: The Jewish Theological Seminary of America, 1955–1988),
vol. 1, 63; Daniel Sperber, "Melilot 5" ("מלילות ה'"), *Sinai* 91 (1982): 272–73;
Richard S. Sarason, *The Talmud of the Land of Israel: A Preliminary Translation
and Explanation: Demai* (Chicago, IL: University of Chicago Press, 1993), 143;
Michael Sokoloff, *A Dictionary of Jewish Palestinian Aramaic of the Byzantine
Period* (Ramat-Gan: Bar Ilan University Press, 2017), 12.
3. Alternatively, perhaps the meaning is that he would draw ("צר") pictures of
the foods on a cloth. See Lieberman, *Tosefta Ki-Fshuṭa*, vol. 1, 62–63. Cf. T-S C
1.69 + T-S AS 78.27 (cited in Appendix 11 below) where the courses are wrapped
in bread. On the Roman practice to use bread as a napkin, see R. Alan Streett,
An Analysis of the Lord's Supper under Roman Domination during the First Century
(Eugene, OR: Pickwick, 2013), 14.

There was a fine custom in Jerusalem that whenever one of them made a banquet, he would hang a cloth over its entryway; so long as the cloth was spread guests would enter there, but once it was removed, none had permission to enter.

5: And another custom was there that any time one of them made a banquet he would entrust the banquet to a cook so if anything spoiled at the banquet, it was on his head; and if they found anything spoiled at the banquet, they would punish the cook, everything according to the honor of the host and according to the honor of the guests.

6: Another explanation of *The precious children of Zion* (Lam 4:2): What was their preciousness? Not one of them would attend a banquet until he was invited and (then) invited again.[4]

The banquet practices listed here were apparently designed to regulate the invitation process, assist the fastidious, ensure a banquet's sense of fellowship, and maintain a banquet's order and decorum. Whether turning over one's left shoulder clasp to signal that one was already invited out to dine, carefully wrapping up banquet foods within cloths out of consideration for fastidious eaters, ascertaining the identity of one's fellow banqueters before entering a banquet, signaling with a cloth over the banquet doorway whether guests were still welcome to enter, entrusting the responsibility of the banquet to a cook, and attending a banquet only after receiving both an invitation and a confirmation, the "precious" Jerusalemites' banquet practices emerge as dignified and urbane communal regulations.[5]

Save for the practice of waiting for a confirmation of the original invitation, all the other banquet practices cited here appear, with only slight variations, in earlier rabbinic literature. The transfer of the shoulder clasp is portrayed as a Jerusalemite custom in a passage found, with only minute differences, in y. Demai 4:4, 24a and y. Avod. Zar. 1:3, 39c:

---

4. Lam 4:2 according to Oxford 102. The translation is mine but is indebted to A. Cohen, trans. *Midrash Rabbah: Lamentations* (London: Soncino, 1977), ad loc.
5. On the practice of signaling with a cloth, see Lieberman, *Tosefta Ki-Fshuṭa*, vol. 1, 62. More generally, see Alan Mintz, *Ḥurban: Responses to Catastrophe in Hebrew Literature* (New York, NY: Columbia University Press, 1984), 65.

וּבִירוּשָׁלֵם הֲוָה מָפֵיךְ מְפֵיךְ פֵיבְלֵיהּ דִּשְׂמָאלָא לִימִינָא.

And in Jerusalem one would turn over his left (shoulder) clasp to the right (to indicate that he was provided for and not available for a banquet).[6]

The practice of wrapping up the courses in a cloth for the benefit of the guests is ascribed to a king within a parable already found in y. Avod. Zar. 3:1, 42c:

לְמֶלֶךְ שֶׁעָשָׂה סְעוּדָה וְצָר כָּל מִינֵי סְעוּדָה בְּמַפָּה. כֵּיוָן שֶׁנִּכְנְסוּ הָאוֹרְחִין רָאוּ
אוֹתָן וְנַפְשָׁם שְׂבֵיעָה וִישֵׁנוּ לָהֶן.

It may be compared to a king who made a banquet and wrapped up all the courses of the banquet in a cloth (apparently for display purposes). When the guests entered, they saw them, their souls were satiated and they fell asleep.

The Jerusalemite practice of attending a banquet or signing a document only after ascertaining the identities of the other recliners or witnesses (as well as the link to Exod 23:1) is already attested in Mekh. Kaspa 2:

---

6. The text is cited according to Yerushalmi Demai. (See Sarason, *Demai*, 143, 357n 70.) Right before mentioning the shoulder clasp banquet practice, Yerushalmi Avodah Zarah enlists the uncommon phrase "טַעֲנַת חִנָּם," which also appears in the description of the very same banquet practice in Lamentations Rabbati. Since the two elements in the description of the shoulder clasp banquet practice in Lamentations Rabbati – the ritual transfer of the clasp and its social function, i.e., the prevention of a "טַעֲנַת חִנָּם" ("a wasted invitation") – also appear side by side in y. Avod. Zar. 1:3, 39c, it seems likely that the talmudic text served as a source of inspiration for Lamentations Rabbati. In other words, two distinct (and uncommon) literary elements in Yerushalmi Avodah Zarah – the shoulder clasp ritual and the phrase "טַעֲנַת חִנָּם" – were most likely combined in Lamentations Rabbati (where the latter was enlisted to explain the social function of the former). (For the notion that the integration or conflation of scattered literary elements is more likely than the dispersal of integrated elements, see Shamma Friedman, "A Good Story Deserves Retelling: The Unfolding of the Akiva Legend." *JSIJ* 3 [2004]: 87–88; Amram Tropper, *Like Clay in the Hands of the Potter: Sage Stories in Rabbinic Literature* [כחומר ביד היוצר: מעשי חכמים בספרות חז"ל], [Jerusalem: Zalman Shazar Center, 2011], 129–30; *Rewriting Ancient Jewish History*, 138, 173.)

"אל תשת ידך עם רשע" (שמות כג:א)... כך היו בקיי[7] הדעת שבירושלם
עושין, לא היה אחד מהם הולך לבית המשתה עד שיודע מי הולך עמו, ולא
היה חותם בגט עד שיודע מי חותם עמו.[8]

You shall not join hands with the guilty (to act as a malicious witness)
(Exod 23:1) ... The cautious-minded in Jerusalem behaved as follows:
None of them would go to a banquet-house until he knew who would
be going with him, nor sign a document until he knew who would
be signing with him.

The teaching, ascribed to Rabban Simeon ben Gamaliel, regarding
the Jerusalemite custom to hang a cloth over the entryway to the banquet
as well as the Jerusalemite custom to entrust the banquet to a cook
already appear side by side in t. Ber. 4:9–10:

אמ' רבן שמעון בן גמליאל: זה מנהג גדול היה בירושלם, פורסין מטפחת על
גבי הפתח. כל זמן שהמטפחת פרוסה אורחין נכנסין, נסתלקה מטפחת אין
רשות לאורחין ליכנס. ועוד מנהג אחר היה בירושלם מוסרין סעודה לטבח.
אם נתקלקל דבר בסעודה עונשין את הטבח, הכל לפי כבוד האורחין, והכל
לפי כבוד בעל הבית.

Rabban Simeon ben Gamaliel said: There was a fine custom in Jerusalem that they would hang a cloth over its (the banquet-hall's)
entryway; so long as the cloth was spread, guests would enter, but
once the cloth was removed, no guests had permission to enter. Another custom in Jerusalem was that they would entrust the banquet
to a cook. If anything spoiled at the banquet, they would punish the
cook, everything according to the honor of the guests and everything
according to the honor of the host.[9]

---

7. See Shamma Friedman, *Talmud Ha-Igud: Babylonian Talmud Gittin IX: Edition
with Commentary* (תלמוד האיגוד: המגרש, גיטין פרק תשיעי מן התלמוד הבבלי עם
פרשנות על דרך המחקר), (Jerusalem: The Society for the Interpretation of the
Talmud, 2020), 434, 443–44, 447–49.
8. Mekh. Kaspa 2 (*Mekhilta de-Rabbi Ishmael*, ed. H.S. Horovitz and I.A. Rabin,
[1931; Repr., Jerusalem: Shalem, 1997], 322) according to Oxford 151. See also b.
Sanh. 23a.
9. T. Ber. 4:9–10 according to Vienna Heb. 20. Cf. b. B. Qam. 93b. See also
Lieberman, *Tosefta Ki-Fshuṭa*, vol. 1, 63.

In sum, four of Lamentations Rabbati's Jerusalemite banquet customs already appear as Jerusalemite customs in earlier rabbinic sources, one appears as a royal practice, and one, so far as I can tell, has no precedent in rabbinic literature. The unprecedented custom – the custom to wait for a second invitation – provides the immediate literary context for the story of Bar Qamtza and the juxtaposition of this particular custom to our story is explored below. As a group (neatly framed by two invitation customs), the banquet customs collected here in Lamentations Rabbati form a new tradition about Second Temple times. By forging an assemblage of Jerusalemite banquet customs out of scattered literary materials, Lamentations Rabbati paints a colorful portrait of the refined and genteel banqueters of late Second Temple Jerusalem. In this assortment, a handful of unrelated "fine" customs of "the cautious-minded in Jerusalem" are transformed into a pattern said to characterize a community. The biblical phrase, "בני ציון היקרים," "the precious (yeqarim) children of Zion," is very similar to the rabbinic term "יקירי ירושלים," "the nobles (yaqirei) of Jerusalem," hence it seems likely that Lamentations Rabbati has equated the two, viewing "the precious children of Zion" as the Jerusalem nobles of late Second Temple times.[10] Identifying these noble Jerusalemites with Lamentations' "precious children of Zion," Lamentations Rabbati enrolls their decorous banquet customs as the cultural backdrop for the story of Bar Qamtza in which the noble Jerusalemites fail to live up to the high standards of their banquet etiquette.[11]

---

10. See m. Yoma 6:4; t. Arak. 2:2; b. Yoma 69a; b. Sukkah 37a. See also Samuel Klein, "Anshei yerushalayim, yaqirei yerushalayim, neqiyei-hadaat shebeyerushalayim, benei-tzion" ("אנשי ירושלים, יקירי ירושלים, נקיי-הדעת שבירושלים, בני-ציון"), Jewish Studies 1 (1926): 72–78; Friedman, Gittin, 434n6; cf. Gedaliahu Alon, Studies in Jewish History in the Times of the Second Temple, the Mishna and the Talmud (מחקרים בתולדות ישראל בימי בית שני ובתקופת המשנה והתלמוד), 2 vols. (Tel Aviv: Hakibutz Hameuchad, 1957–1958), vol. 2, 26n47.

11. See Saldarini, "Rabbinic Response," 454; David Noy, "The Sixth Hour is the Mealtime for Scholars: Jewish Meals in the Roman World," in Meals in a Social Context: Aspects of the Communal Meal in the Hellenistic and Roman World, ed. Inge Nielsen and Hanne Sigismund Nielsen (Langelandsgade: Aarhus University Press, 1998), 139; Isaiah M. Gafni, "Jerusalem in Rabbinic Literature" ("ירושלים בספרות חז"ל"), in The History of Jerusalem: The Roman and Byzantine Periods (70–638 CE), ed. Yoram Tsafrir and Shmuel Safrai (Jerusalem: Yad Ben-Zvi

Ancient Jewish Banquet Customs

While Lamentations Rabbati portrays the banquet practices of the noble Jerusalemites as exceptionally civil and unusually refined, these practices are closely related to ancient Jewish banquet customs more generally. Ancient Jewish banquet customs supply the social backdrop for the Jerusalemite banquet practices and the Jerusalemite banquet practices are best viewed as functional parallels, or perhaps even as enhancements or extensions, of rabbinic banquet regulations. For example, just before the Tosefta presents the Jerusalemite banquet practices regarding the cloth hanging over the banquet-hall entryway and the cook's responsibility for the meal, it regulates banquet procedures in t. Ber. 4:8:[12]

כיצד סדר סעודה? אורחין נכנסין ויושבין על ספסלים ועל גבי קתדראות
עד שיתכנסו; נתכנסו כולם נתנו להם לידים, כל אחד ואחד נוטל ידו אחת.
מזגו להם את הכוס, כל אחד ואחד מברך לעצמו. הביאו לפניהם פרפראות,
כל אחד ואחד מברך לעצמו. עלו והסבו ונתנו להם לידים, אע"פ שנטל ידו
אחת נוטל שתי ידיו. מזגו להם את הכוס, אע"פ שברך על הראשון מברך על
השיני. הביאו לפניהם פרפראות, אע"פ שברך על הראשונה מברך על השניה
ואחד מברך לכולן. הבא אחר שלש פרפראות אין לו רשות ליכנס.[13]

What is the order of a banquet? The guests enter and sit on benches or on chairs until (everyone has assembled), once everyone has entered, they give them water for (washing) their hands (and) each

---

1999), 44; Yael Levine Katz, "'Because of Qamtsa and Bar Qamtsa Jerusalem was Destroyed' – Studies in the Traditions of the Story" ("על קמצא ובר קמצא חרבה 'ירושלים' - עיונים במסורות הסיפור"), *Pathways through Aggadah* 3 (2000): 36. Cf. Yisraeli-Taran, *Legends of the Destruction*, 12, 17, who imagines that Lamentations Rabbati and simple Jews viewed the Jerusalemite banquet practices negatively, somewhat like Jesus's criticism of Pharisaic hierarchical banqueting customs and purity laws (see Luke 7:36–50, 11:37–54, 14:1–24, 15:1–2), but see also Ben Shahar's critique of her position (Ben Shahar, "Abolishment of the Sacrifice," 590–91).

12. See Dennis E. Smith, *From Symposium to Eucharist: The Banquet in the Early Christian World* (Minneapolis, MN: Fortress Press, 2003), 145–47; Seth Schwartz, "No Dialogue at the Symposium? Conviviality in Ben Sira and the Palestinian Talmud," in *The End of Dialogue in Antiquity*, ed. Simon Goldhill (Cambridge: Cambridge University Press, 2008), 208–9; Gil P. Klein, "Torah in Triclinia: The Rabbinic Banquet and the Significance of Architecture," *JQR* 102 (2012): 334–40; cf. Lieberman, *Tosefta Ki-Fshuṭa*, vol. 1, 62.

13. T. Ber. 4:8 according to Vienna Heb. 20. See also y. Ber. 6:6, 10d; b. Ber. 43a.

one washes one hand of his (for drinking wine and eating the first appetizers).[14] (When) they mix the cup (of wine) for them, each one recites the blessing for himself. (When) they bring appetizers before them, each one recites the blessing for himself. (When) they rise up (from the benches or chairs) and recline (on couches) and they give them water for (washing) their hands, even though each has already washed one hand, he washes both hands (to eat). (When) they mix the cup (of wine) for them, even though each has (already) recited the blessing over the first (cup), he recites a blessing over the second. (When) they bring appetizers for them, even though each has (already) recited a blessing over the first (appetizers), he recites a blessing over the second, and one person recites the blessing on behalf of everyone. One who arrives after three appetizers (have been served), is not allowed to enter.

The Jewish banquet regulated here, I suggest, is imagined as two parallel series of actions, one comprising the appetizer course and the other encompassing the main course and dessert. The arriving guests assemble, presumably in an anteroom, where they sit and wash one hand so that it may be used to grasp a cup of wine over which they recite a blessing. Then, presumably with the help of their clean hand, they help themselves to appetizers, over which they recite another blessing. Upon concluding the appetizer course, the guests recline on couches, apparently after having relocated to the dining room.[15] Having reclined, the guests wash both hands in preparation for the main course which follows. When wine is served once again the blessing over the wine is repeated, and when the banquet eventually concludes with appetizers for dessert, the blessing over the appetizers is repeated as well. In short, after the guests enter the anteroom where they sit, wash a hand, drink wine with a blessing and eat appetizers with a blessing, they enter the dining room where they recline, wash hands, drink wine with a blessing, and eat appetizers with a blessing. Furthermore, the two parallel series of actions are framed by two arrival practices: the halakhah opens with the expectation that a banquet will not start until all the banqueters have

14. See Lieberman, *Tosefta Ki-Fshuṭa*, vol. 1, 62.
15. See Smith, *From Symposium to Eucharist*, 145. See also Noy, "Jewish Meals," 137.

assembled, and concludes with an attempt to regulate the acceptable arrival time for banquet guests: "One who arrives after three appetizers (have been served), is not allowed to enter."

Fleshing out some of the grainy details of the rabbinic banquet, t. Ber. 5:5–6 regulates the hierarchy which determines the order in which guests recline, wash hands, and are served wine:

כיצד סדר הסב? בזמן שהן שתי מטות, גדול מסב בראשה של ראשונה, שני לו למטה ממנו. בזמן שהן שלש מטות, גדול מסב בראשה של אמצעית, שני לו למעלה ממנו, שלישי לו למטה ממנו. כך היו מסדירין והולכין.

סדר נטילת ידים כיצד? עד חמשה מתחילין מן הגדול, מחמשה ואילך מתחי׳ מן הקטן.

סדר מזיגת הכוס כיצד? בתוך המזון מתחילין מן הגדול, לאחר המזון מתחילין מן המברך. רצה לחלוק כבוד לרבו או למי שגדול ממנו, הרשות בידו.[16]

What is the order for reclining? When there are two couches, the greatest reclines at the head of the first (couch and) the second (in importance) to him reclines below him. When there are three couches, the greatest reclines at the head of the middle one, the second (in importance) to him above him (and) the third (in importance) to him below him. In this way they would go on and order (the recliners).

What is the order for washing hands? Up to 5 (people) they begin with the greatest, (but) from 5 and up they begin with the least important.

What is the order for mixing the (wine in the) cup (i.e., serving the wine)? During the meal they begin with the greatest, after the meal they begin with he who recites the blessing (of grace after meals). If he (the reciter of the blessing) wanted to honor his teacher or someone greater than him, he is allowed to do so.

These halakhot not only reveal that the guests in the banquet of t. Ber. 4:8 (cited above) are not all of a piece, they seek to establish or reinforce the key role that honor and prestige played in Jewish banquets. As far as the rabbis were concerned, the order in which Jewish banqueters

---

16. T. Ber. 5:5–6 according to Vienna Heb. 20. See also y. Ta'an. 4:2, 68a; y. Ber. 8:2, 12a; b. Ber. 46b.

reclined, washed hands, or were served wine was intricately entwined with the social structures, networks, and hierarchies in which the banqueters lived.[17]

From the point of view of Lamentations Rabbati, the rabbinic program to regulate Jewish banquets, a program which only makes sense within a rich ambient Jewish banquet tradition, serves as the baseline for the genteel customs of the noble Jerusalemites. While ancient Jews in general lived in a social world with vibrant banquet rituals that the rabbis hoped to imbue with rabbinic laws and values, the "children of Zion" (the nobles of Jerusalem), according to Lamentations Rabbati, cultivated a splendid banquet culture all of their own, head and shoulders above even rabbinic banquet practices.[18] All these banquet rituals, however, whether widespread Jewish banquet customs, rabbinic banquet regulations, or the exquisite banquet practices ascribed to the noble Jerusalemites of Second Temple times, were part and parcel of the wider phenomenon of Greek and Roman banqueting.

Some time ago scholars realized that the Passover Seder was actually a Jewish variation on the Greek festive meal called the symposium (συμπόσιον),[19] and on the heels of this insight followed the recognition

---

17. Cf. Katherine M.D. Dunbabin, *The Roman Banquet: Images of Conviviality* (Cambridge: Cambridge University Press, 2004), 39–40.

18. See Gafni, "Jerusalem," 43; Levine Katz, "Qamtsa," 36–37; Ben Shahar, "Abolishment of the Sacrifice," 590–91; cf. Yisraeli-Taran, *Legends of the Destruction*, 12, 17. See also Alan William Todd, "Feasts and the Social Order in Early Jewish Society (ca. Third Century BCE–Third Century CE)" (PhD diss., Duke University, 2014), 114–18.

19. See S. Stein, "The Influence of the Symposia Literature on the Literary Form of the Pesaḥ Haggadah," *JJS* 8 (1957): 13–44; Baruch M. Bokser, *The Origins of the Seder: The Passover Rite and Early Rabbinic Judaism* (Berkeley: University of California Press, 1984), 50–53, 61–62; Noy, "Jewish Meals," 140; Jonathan Brumberg-Kraus, "Meals as Midrash: A Survey of Ancient Meals in Jewish Studies Scholarship," in *Food and Judaism*, ed. Leonard J. Greenspoon, Ronald A. Simkins, and Gerald Shapiro (Omaha: University of Nebraska Press, 2005), 300–302; Joshua Kulp, "The Origins of the Seder and Haggadah," *CBR* 4 (2005): 117–18; Schwartz, "Conviviality," 208; David C. Kraemer, "Food, Eating, and Meals," in *The Oxford Handbook of Jewish Daily Life in Roman Palestine*, ed. Catherine Hezser (Oxford: Oxford University Press, 2010), 414; Jason König, *Saints and Symposiasts: The Literature of Food and the Symposium in Greco-Roman and Early*

that all Jewish banquets of late Second Temple and rabbinic times were indebted to the encircling banquet culture of contemporary Greeks and Romans.[20] Embedded in the surrounding Hellenistic and Roman banquet culture, the Jewish banquet tradition tailored and adapted widespread practices and ideals for the Jewish setting, adjusting them to the Jewish context and often interpreting them anew. Since the banquet cultures of the Greek and Roman worlds exerted a formative influence on Jewish banquet practices and ideals, I submit that Greek and Roman banquets form a crucial lens for interpreting both the banquet practices ascribed to the Second Temple Jerusalemites as well as to rabbinic banquet stories, such as the story of Bar Qamtza.

Christian Culture (Cambridge: Cambridge University Press, 2012), 134; Streett, *Lord's Supper*, 52–79; Todd, "Feasts," 110–13.

20. See, for example, Stein, "Symposia Literature," 16; Moshe Weinfeld, *The Organizational Patterns and the Penal Code of the Qumran Sect: A Comparison with the Guilds and Religious Associations of the Hellenistic Period* (Fribourg: Éditions Universitaires, 1986), 23–29; Smith, *From Symposium to Eucharist*, 1–2, 133–72; "The Greco-Roman Banquet as a Social Institution," in *Meals in the Early Christian World: Social Formation, Experimentation, and Conflict at the Table*, ed. Dennis E. Smith and Hal E. Taussig (New York, NY: Palgrave Macmillan, 2012), 32; "Next Steps: Placing this Study of Jewish Meals in the Larger Picture of Meals in the Ancient World, Early Judaism, and Early Christianity," in *Meals in Early Judaism: Social Formation at the Table*, ed. Susan Marks and Hal E. Taussig (New York, NY: Palgrave Macmillan, 2014), 174–81; Schwartz, "Conviviality," 193–200; John J. Collins, *Beyond the Qumran Community: The Sectarian Movement of the Dead Sea Scrolls* (Grand Rapids, MI: William B. Eerdmans, 2010), 79–85; Matthias Klinghardt, "A Typology of the Communal Meal," in *Meals in the Early Christian World: Social Formation, Experimentation, and Conflict at the Table*, ed. Dennis E. Smith and Hal E. Taussig (New York, NY: Palgrave Macmillan, 2012), 9; Jordan D. Rosenblum, *Food and Identity in Early Rabbinic Judaism* (Cambridge: Cambridge University Press, 2010), 32–33; Klein, "Torah in Triclinia," 326–27; Hal E. Taussig, "Introduction," in *Meals in the Early Christian World: Social Formation, Experimentation, and Conflict at the Table*, ed. Dennis E. Smith and Hal E. Taussig (New York, NY: Palgrave Macmillan, 2012), 1–2; Susan Marks, "Introduction," in *Meals in Early Judaism: Social Formation at the Table*, ed. Susan Marks and Hal E. Taussig (New York, NY: Palgrave Macmillan, 2014), 3–4; Jonathan Brumberg-Kraus, Susan Marks, and Jordan D. Rosenblum, "Ten Theses Concerning Meals and Early Judaism," in *Meals in Early Judaism: Social Formation at the Table*, ed. Susan Marks and Hal E. Taussig (New York, NY: Palgrave Macmillan, 2014), 18–28; Todd, "Feasts," 16–18, 76–80, 96–99.

Chapter 3

A Brief Overview of Greek and Roman Banquets[1]

G reek and Roman banquets formed one of the most meaningful social rituals in all classical and late antiquity. "Inextricably interwoven into the fabric of public and domestic life," banquets permeated the ancient Mediterranean world.[2] Ensconced within the social life and cultural practices of the Mediterranean landscape, Jewish banquets and rabbinic banquet discourse were heavily indebted to Greek and Roman banquets. In other words, Greek and Roman banquets exerted a profound influence on both the texture of Jewish banquets and their role in Jewish life and literature. For our purposes, the strong ties between the banquet practices and ideals of Jews and gentiles make Greek and Roman banquets a key interpretive lens for the banquet practices at the heart of Lamentations Rabbati's story of Bar Qamtza and its immediate literary context. Though Greek and Roman banquets share some features with modern banquets, they were quite unlike their modern counterparts in many respects. Hence, in order to appreciate their power as an interpretive lens, a brief overview of Greek and Roman banquets is in order.

---

1. On the term banquet, see Dunbabin, *Roman Banquet*, 4.
2. Dunbabin, *Roman Banquet*, 2. See also Klinghardt, "Typology," 18.

The Banquet as a Social Occasion

Whereas eating is a basic biological need, dining is a social occasion.[3] This fundamental distinction between biological consumption and a cultural event is already found in the words of a witty Roman who supposedly quipped after a solitary meal, "I have eaten, but not dined today" ("Βεβρωκέναι, μὴ δεδει πνηκέναι σήμερον").[4] Banquets, or the formal, festive, and communal meals of the Greeks and Romans, were a prominent way for ancient Greeks and Romans to consume a food surplus, but they were much more than mere economic activity in the service of biology. Banquets offered a relatively safe environment for communities to articulate their shared values via ritualized activity while also modeling social hierarchies.[5] Ancient groups formulated group identities at banquets, privileging the banqueting insider over the uninvited outsider while negotiating their members' positions within hierarchies of power.[6] Like their gentile contemporaries, the rabbis similarly divided the world into "those with whom one eats, and those with whom one does not eat."[7] Sources like t. Ber. 5:5–6 (cited above) reveal that the rabbis also shared the widespread belief that banquets should reflect social hierarchies of status and power.

3. See Keith Bradley, "The Roman Family at Dinner," in *Meals in a Social Context: Aspects of the Communal Meal in the Hellenistic and Roman World*, ed. Inge Nielsen and Hanne Sigismund Nielsen (Langelandsgade: Aarhus University Press, 1998), 36–38; Hal E. Taussig, *In the Beginning was the Meal: Social Experimentation and Early Christian Identity* (Minneapolis, MN: Fortress Press, 2009), 22; Richard S. Ascough, "Social and Political Characteristics of Greco-Roman Association Meals," in *Meals in the Early Christian World: Social Formation, Experimentation, and Conflict at the Table*, ed. Dennis E. Smith and Hal E. Taussig (New York, NY: Palgrave Macmillan, 2012), 61; Todd, "Feasts," 1–4.
4. Plutarch, *Quaest. conv.* 7.697C (Plutarch, *Moralia: Volume IX: Table-Talk, Books 7–9, Dialogue on Love*, trans. Edwin L. Minar, F.H. Sandbach, and W.C. Helmbold [LCL, Cambridge, MA: Harvard University Press and William Heinemann, 1961], ad loc.).
5. See Oswyn Murray, "Sympotic History," in *Sympotica: A Symposium on the Symposion*, ed. Oswyn Murray (Oxford: Clarendon Press, 1990), 3–13; Smith, *From Symposium to Eucharist*, 11–14.
6. See Dunbabin, *Roman Banquet*, 98; Taussig, *In the Beginning*, 21–22.
7. Rosenblum, *Food and Identity*, (2–6,) 101.

Banquets in Literature and Reality

Written and material remains refract the social reality of actual Greek and Roman banquets, and also reflect a culture intensely interested in these banquets. The vast quantity of both Greek and Roman banquet literature evinces, in fact, a fascination with banquets. The classical banquet literature explores in intricate detail voluptuous descriptions of banquet foods, fictional and historical banquet accounts, a wide range of banquet conversations, numerous forms of banquet entertainment, and strict codes of banquet conduct.[8] As a functioning social institution, the banquet must have largely followed standard protocols and accepted behaviors, likely making most banquets uneventful occasions. The banquet as a dynamic literary form, however, is another matter entirely. The arts transformed the banquet into a suspenseful and exciting event by playing with the audience's expectations, introducing twists and tensions, conflict and discord.[9] An audience's expectations stemmed not only from accepted banquet practices, but also from standard features of the banquet's literary tradition. Literary banquets featured stock characters, such as the host, the jester, the physician, the pair of lovers, and the uninvited guest, as well as stock motifs, such as a quarrel or contest.[10] Against the background of standard banquet practices, stock figures, and common motifs, literary banquets often highlighted the unusual, recruiting the joyful banquet setting as the ideal moment to strike down a protagonist at the height of his happiness.[11]

---

8. See Matthew B. Roller, *Dining Posture in Ancient Rome: Bodies, Values, and Status* (Princeton, NJ: Princeton University Press, 2006), 178–79; König, *Saints and Symposiasts*, 4, 11.

9. See William J. Slater, "Sympotic Ethics in the *Odyssey*," in *Sympotica: A Symposium on the Symposion*, ed. Oswyn Murray (Oxford: Clarendon Press, 1990), 215; George Paul, "Symposia and Deipna in Plutarch's *Lives* and in other Historical Writings," in *Dining in a Classical Context*, ed. William J. Slater (Ann Arbor: University of Michigan Press, 1991), 157–69.

10. See Joseph Martin, *Symposion: Die Geschichte einer literarischen Form* (Paderborn: Ferdinand Schöningh, 1931), 33–148; Smith, *From Symposium to Eucharist*, 6–7, 48–49; "Greco-Roman Banquet," 31–32.

11. See John H. D'Arms, "The Roman *Convivium* and the Idea of Equality," in *Sympotica: A Symposium on the Symposion*, ed. Oswyn Murray (Oxford: Clarendon Press, 1990), 314.

Banquet Structure

The final and main meal of the day in Greek and Roman times was eaten toward evening, though at times it might continue into the night. This dinner, the Greek δεῖπνον and Roman *cena*, ranged widely in size, duration, and formality, from simple, brief, and informal suppers to formal, extended, and elaborate banquets. In festive Greek banquets, the meal proper, the δεῖπνον (or συσσίτιον), was followed by a drinking party, the symposium (συμπόσιον), designed for drinking, conversation, and entertainment. The Roman communal meal opened with appetizers (as did the Greek dinner in Roman times), followed with the meal proper – *cena* (or courses, *fercula*), and concluded with desserts (*comissatio, convivium*, or *mensae secundae* ["second tables"]) which were accompanied by entertainment and conversation.[12]

The conversation at Greek and Roman banquets was meant to be pleasant and instructive.[13] In the rabbinic context, banquet conversation was sacralized, as were other features of Greek and Roman banquets such as hand-washing and wine-drinking. For the rabbis, Torah was the ideal banquet conversation topic.[14]

The entertainment at Greek and Roman banquets, provided by both guests and outside entertainers, might consist of music, lectures, debates, philosophical discussions, drama, pantomime, juggling, literary recitations, riddles, dexterity competitions, dancing, sex, drinking games, and other party games.[15] In tandem with a full belly and a wine-induced buzz, pleasing conversation and pleasurable entertainment were supposed to amplify the banquet's festive joy.[16]

Unlike Greeks, Romans drank alcohol throughout the meal while assigning food, rather than drink, the more prominent role in the literary *cena*.[17] Furthermore, unlike classical Greek banquets which were re-

---

12. See Smith, *From Symposium to Eucharist*, 21, 27; Dunbabin, *Roman Banquet*; Streett, *Lord's Supper*, 9–10. See also the structure of the rabbinic banquet in t. Ber. 4:8 cited above.

13. See Streett, *Lord's Supper*, 23.

14. See Rosenblum, *Food and Identity*, 19, 28.

15. See Bradley, "Roman Family at Dinner," 37–38; Klinghardt, "Typology," 13; König, *Saints and Symposiasts*, 6; Streett, *Lord's Supper*, 21–23.

16. See Smith, *From Symposium to Eucharist*, 12.

17. See Murray, "Sympotic History," 6; Emily Gowers, *The Loaded Table: Rep-*

served for (free) men alone, banquets in Roman times involved women as well.[18] As Beryl Rawson has noted:

> Unlike the Greek practice of the symposium, a drinking party that was exclusively male except for hired women, the Roman *conuiuium* could include women and sometimes children, and the emphasis was at least as much on food as on wine. Romans were sometimes keen to point out the difference etymologically. Whereas the Greek word *symposion* meant "a drinking together," and referred to a separate drinking session which followed a meal, the Latin *conuiuium*, suggesting "a living together," referred to a gathering of friends at a meal table for food, wine and conversation.[19]

Types of Banquets

Private individuals hosted banquets for all sorts of occasions and reasons, such as rites of passage, birthdays, weddings, funerals, anniversaries, companionship, hospitality, entertainment, intellectual discourse, and religious celebrations.[20] However, banquets were also sponsored by institutions, such as the imperial regime, municipalities, schools, and associations (that is, social organizations known as *collegia*), whether occupational, religious, funerary, or ethnic.[21] In all these cases, banquets solidified group or communal ties and helped form a strong sense of corporate identity.[22] Although the Roman state expected banqueters to

---

resentations of Food in Roman Literature* (Oxford: Clarendon Press, 1993), 29; Smith, *From Symposium to Eucharist*, 31; "Greco-Roman Banquet," 24–25; Dunbabin, *Roman Banquet*, 10–20, 157, 164; Roller, *Dining Posture*, 181–88; (cf. Klinghardt, "Typology," 10).

18. See Murray, "Sympotic History," 6; Dunbabin, *Roman Banquet*, 22; Streett, *Lord's Supper*, 15. See also Noy, "Jewish Meals," 138; Todd, "Feasts," 126–35.

19. Beryl Rawson, "Banquets in Ancient Rome: Participation, Presentation and Perception," in *Dining on Turtles: Food Feasts and Drinking in History*, ed. Diane Kirkby and Tanja Luckins (New York, NY: Palgrave Macmillan, 2007), 19. See Cicero, *Sen.* 13.45. See also Dunbabin, *Roman Banquet*, 13.

20. See Taussig, *In the Beginning*, 23; Ascough, "Greco-Roman Association Meals," 61–62; Streett, *Lord's Supper*, 25–30.

21. See Klinghardt, "Typology," 10; König, *Saints and Symposiasts*, 5; Streett, *Lord's Supper*, 42–47; Todd, "Feasts," 34–40. See also n. 48 below.

22. See König, *Saints and Symposiasts*, 25.

express support and loyalty to the empire, in practice banquets offered diverse opportunities for the development of local and anti-imperial cultures and ideologies.[23]

Banquet Settings

Because banquets varied in size, they varied in location as well. Large public banquets would have taken place in the open air – in the forum, streets, squares, gardens, porticoes, sanctuaries, theaters, and amphitheaters – while small private banquets would have been housed in more intimate settings, such as dining rooms like the Greek *andron* and Roman *triclinium*.[24] The late empire witnessed a tendency towards larger private feasts which, too big for *triclinia*, were housed in larger rooms. In tandem with this shift, the triclinium's classic pie-shaped couch constellation gave way to the semicircular couches known as *stibadium* or *sigma*.[25]

Reclining

A central and perhaps the quintessential feature of Greek and Roman banqueting was reclining.[26] In comfortable clothing and without shoes, banqueters would recline on couches around low banquet tables. Reclining on their left side, banqueters usually took food from a shared bowl with the fingers of the right hand (rather than a fork) and washed hands between courses.[27] Although reclining dates all the way back to the ancient Near East, it became the ultimate symbol for luxurious banquet feasting and dining leisure in Greece and Rome. To lie down while others served you was a sign of power, privilege, and prestige.[28] The Ro-

---

23. See Taussig, *In the Beginning*, 115–25; Streett, *Lord's Supper*, 1–3, 30–49.

24. See Dunbabin, *Roman Banquet*, 92; Todd, "Feasts," 23–28.

25. See Dunbabin, *Roman Banquet*, 6, 38–43, 146. See also Klein, "Torah in Triclinia," 342–52.

26. See Smith, *From Symposium to Eucharist*, 14–18; "Greco-Roman Banquet," 23–25; Dunbabin, *Roman Banquet*, 2, 108; Taussig, *In the Beginning*, 23; Ascough, "Greco-Roman Association Meals," 67.

27. See Bradley, "Roman Family at Dinner," 39. See also Shmuel Safrai, "Home and Family," in *Compendia Rerum Iudaicarum ad Novum Testamentum: The Jewish People in the First Century: Volume Two*, ed. Shmuel Safrai and Menahem Stern (Philadelphia, PA: Fortress Press, 1976), 743.

28. See Murray, "Sympotic History," 6; Dunbabin, *Roman Banquet*, 11.

mans associated reclining with leisure (*otium*), luxuries, and pleasures such as food, wine, companionship, conversation, and sex.[29] Eating at a banquet while sitting or standing was for those of lower social status.[30] Though initially a custom of the elites, the reclining banquet came to proliferate throughout the Roman world amongst peasants as well, all the while maintaining its connotations of privileged status and luxury.[31] Rabbinic literature also attests to the essential role of reclining at ancient Jewish banquets as it enlists the Hebrew word for reclining, "להסב," as a synonym for dining.[32]

The Banquet's Friendship Ethos and Roman Patronage

One striking feature of the banquet in Greek and Roman literature is its rich ideology. In the eyes of Greek and Roman authors, the banquet embodied core cultural values of the ancient world. As an ideal, the banquet was envisioned as a "temporary enclosed society" designed to cultivate festive joy through relaxation, entertainment, and pleasure.[33] The secluded banquet setting was supposed to be a safe, democratic, and welcoming environment that fostered fellowship and community, friendship, and equality.[34] In the words of Cato the Elder (according to

---

29. See Dunbabin, *Roman Banquet*, 108; Roller, *Dining Posture*, 15–19.

30. See Roller, *Dining Posture*, 85.

31. See Dunbabin, *Roman Banquet*, 13; Klinghardt, "Typology," 9; Ascough, "Greco-Roman Association Meals," 59; Streett, *Lord's Supper*, 11; Smith, "Next Steps," 177. See also Roller, *Dining Posture*, 36, 45.

32. See Noy, "Jewish Meals," 138; Brumberg-Kraus, Marks, and Rosenblum, "Ten Theses Concerning Meals"; Todd, "Feasts," 64. See also Safrai, "Home and Family," 736–38; David C. Kraemer, *Jewish Eating and Identity through the Ages* (London: Routledge, 2007), 80; Jordan D. Rosenblum, "Inclined to Decline Reclining? Women, Corporeality, and Dining Posture in Early Rabbinic Literature," in *Meals in the Early Christian World: Social Formation, Experimentation, and Conflict at the Table*, ed. Dennis E. Smith and Hal E. Taussig (New York, NY: Palgrave Macmillan, 2012), 267; Klein, "Torah in Triclinia," 334; Todd, "Feasts," 122. Cf. Dunbabin, *Roman Banquet*, 4.

33. Nicole Anne Hudson, "Food: A Suitable Subject for Roman Verse Satire" (PhD diss., University of Leicester, 1991), 200.

34. See Klinghardt, "Typology," 10–16; Streett, *Lord's Supper*, 24–25. (See also Brumberg-Kraus, Marks, and Rosenblum, "Ten Theses Concerning Meals," 29.)

Plutarch), the banquet table was the "very best promoter of friendship" ("ἐν τοῖς μάλιστα φιλοποιὸν"), and Plutarch's wise Chilon, just like the noble Jerusalemites, withheld his consent to attend a banquet until he had ascertained with whom he would dine:[35]

> ὅθεν ἄριστα Χίλων, καλούμενος ἐχθές, οὐ πρότερον ὡμολόγης εν ἦ πυθέσθαι τῶν κεκλημένων ἔκαστον. ἔφη γάρ ὅτι σύμπλουν ἀγνώμονα δεῖ φέρειν καὶ σύσκηνον οἷς πλεῖν ἀνάγκη καὶ στρατεύεσθαι· τὸ δὲ συμπόταις ἑαυτὸν ὡς ἔτυχε καταμιγνύειν οὐ νοῦν ἔχοντος ἀνδρός ἐστιν.

Wherefore Chilon showed excellent judgement when he received his invitation yesterday, in not agreeing to come until he had learned the name of every person invited. For he said that men must put up with an inconsiderate companion on shipboard or under the same tent, if necessity compels them to travel or to serve in the army, but that to trust to luck regarding the people one is to be associated with at table is not the mark of a man of sense.[36]

Banqueters bonded over shared food, drink, conversation, and pleasure, creating or enhancing a sense of group solidarity and common identity.[37] As an imagined ideal, the banquet was a harmonious social setting perfectly suited for the cultivation of strong ties between the members of a group, social class, association, or community.[38]

However, while the banquet ideal of friendship between equal peers

---

35. Plutarch, *Cat. Maj.* 25.3 (Plutarch, *Lives*, trans. Bernadotte Perrin, vol. 2 [LCL, Cambridge, MA: Harvard University Press and William Heinemann, 1914], ad. loc.). See also Plutarch, *Quaest. conv.* 1.612D, 1.614E–615D, 1.660A–B, 7.697C–E.
36. Plutarch, *Sept. sap. conv.* 148A (Plutarch. *Moralia, Volume II: How to Profit by One's Enemies. On Having Many Friends. Chance. Virtue and Vice. Letter of Condolence to Apollonius. Advice About Keeping Well. Advice to Bride and Groom. The Dinner of the Seven Wise Men. Superstition*, trans. Frank Cole Babbitt [LCL. Cambridge, MA: Harvard University Press and Willliam Heinemann, 1928], ad loc.). See also Plutarch, *Sept. sap. conv.* 147F–148B; *Quaest. conv.* 7.708A–D; Seneca, *Lucil.* 19, 10. See also Armand Kaminka, *Studies in Bible, Talmud and Rabbinic Literature: Book 2: Studies in Talmud* (מחקרים במקרא ובתלמוד ובספרות הרבנית: ספר שני: מחקרים בתלמוד), (Tel Aviv: Dvir, 1951), 64.
37. See Smith, *From Symposium to Eucharist*, 9–10, 54–55. (See also 1QS 6.2–6; 1QSa 2.17–20; Philo, *Prob.* 86; Josephus, *J.W.* 2.128–33; 1 Cor 10:17.)
38. See König, *Saints and Symposiasts*, 82; Streett, *Lord's Supper*, 15.

might have found fertile ground in "the relatively homogeneous social structure" of the classical Greek polis, even in the classical polis peers usually would not have been perfectly equal.[39] Moreover, the stark social divisions of the Roman world would have clashed even more strongly with any sort of equality ideal which sought to erase social status, even if only temporarily. Patronage, or the patron-client (*patronus-cliens*) relationship, was a fundamental and distinctive feature at the heart of Roman society. Wealthy and well-respected patrons would grant their social inferiors all sorts of goods, favors, and services, and, in return, clients and other dependents would honor their patrons and support their ambitions for public office. In a social order populated by patrons and clients and defined by hierarchical social structures, no one would have seriously imagined that banqueters would agree to shed their everyday social roles and status at the banquet hall entrance. Instead, it seems more likely that equality, for both Greeks and Romans, did not mean treating all banqueters alike, but rather treating each and every banqueter according to his or her social status.[40] Indeed, the Roman banquet was an excellent venue for a host to supply a congenial networking medium for his guests while he displayed his own wealth and social status.[41] Through banquets, Roman hosts translated financial assets into social capital. In short, when the hierarchical structure of Roman patronage with its emphasis on reciprocal relations was mapped onto the solidarity banquet ethos of friendship and community, tensions and cracks were bound to emerge. These fissures, which prompted regulations and inspired literary explorations, were found amongst Jews as well.[42] In short, while ancient banquets fostered group solidarity on the one hand, they delineated gradations of social status on the other.

---

39. Murray, "Sympotic History," 5.

40. See Smith, *From Symposium to Eucharist*, 11–12; Streett, *Lord's Supper*, 25. See also D'Arms, "Roman *Convivium*," 311–12, 317–18; Taussig, *In the Beginning*, 70; König, *Saints and Symposiasts*, 26; Jae Won Lee, *Paul and the Politics of Difference: A Contextual Study of the Jewish-Gentile Difference in Galatians and Romans* (Eugene, OR: Pickwick, 2014), 71–72, 92.

41. See Bradley, "Roman Family at Dinner," 50–52; Dunbabin, *Roman Banquet*, 13, 43, 141; Streett, *Lord's Supper*, 8–9. See also Todd, "Feasts," 4–6, 29–34, 39–40.

42. Cf. Schwartz, "Conviviality," 212–15.

Banquet Protocols and Regulations

Greek and Roman banquets were designed to stimulate the senses with food, the intellect with conversation, and the emotions with festive joy and camaraderie. Despite these amicable and nonbelligerent goals, however, banquets were also potential sites of conflict and strife. Due to the key role of social stratification in Roman life, banquet interactions could easily yet inadvertently impugn a banqueter's honor and the flow of wine would only have exacerbated the situation. Honor and shame were of tremendous importance in the ancient Mediterranean setting and banquets created countless ways in which a banqueter could be shamed and his or her honor diminished.[43] In order to maintain decorum and ensure that all banqueters enjoyed themselves, the Greeks and Romans developed an extensive banquet etiquette.[44] While modern Westerners view banquet etiquette as the stuff of mere table manners and social convention, ancient philosophers and moralists viewed it as a matter of grave ethical concern, as a series of moral protocols designed to minimize social frictions and temper drunken quarreling and abusive behavior.[45]

Banquet protocols of Greek and Roman antiquity aspired to govern every possible dimension of the banquet. For example, the protocols hoped to regulate guest selection, invitations, dress, hand- and feet-washing, table settings, seating arrangements, meal order, menu building, food distribution, libations, conversation topics, and behavior.[46] These

---

43. On honor and shame in the Mediterranean setting, see Peregrine Horden and Nicholas Purcell, *The Corrupting Sea: A Study of Mediterranean History* (Oxford: Blackwell, 2000), 485–523; Paola Sacchi and Pier Paolo Viazzo, "Honour, History, and the History of Mediterranean Anthropology," *JMS* 22 (2013): 275–91.

44. See Dunbabin, *Roman Banquet*, 174; Klinghardt, "Typology," 15–16.

45. See Smith, *From Symposium to Eucharist*, 10; Streett, *Lord's Supper*, 11–12.

46. See Lucian (trans. A. M Harmon [LCL, Cambridge, MA: Harvard University Press, 1913], [vol. 1]), *Symp.* 8–9; (trans. M.D. Macleod [LCL, Cambridge, MA: Harvard University Press and William Heinemann, 1969], [vol. 7]), *Dial. d.* 15 (13); Plutarch, *Sept. sap. conv.* 148F–149B; *Quaest. conv.* 1.615D–617A; Sir 12:12; Luke 14:7–11. See also Klinghardt, "Typology," 21n51. (Cf. t. Ber. 5:5 [cited above].) Age and social status were crucial factors in seating arrangements. See D'Arms, "Roman *Convivium*," 315; "Slaves at Roman Convivia," in *Dining in a Classical Context*, ed. William J. Slater (Ann Arbor: University of Michigan Press, 1991), 172; Smith, *From Symposium to Eucharist*, 33, 135; Katherine M.D. Dunbabin,

protocols appear as values and ideals in moralistic and religious writings, such as Plutarch's *Table Talk*, Lucian's *Salaried Posts in Great Houses*, and Clement of Alexandria's *Paedagogus*; however, they also appear as official regulations in the by-laws of ancient guilds and associations.[47]

Many ancient social groups, whether professional guilds, burial societies, religious groups, or political associations, included regulations for banquets in their by-laws. Since banquets were prominent events in the social calendar of these clubs and associations, rules were often formulated in order to regulate behavior and prevent potential discord between members. For example, the by-laws of the funerary society dedicated to the goddess Diana and the deified Antinous, the statutes of the Egyptian devotees of Zeus Hypsistos, the rules of the Iobakchoi (or Bacchic association) in Athens, the sacred laws of the association devoted to Hercules (*Heraklistai*) and the so-called *Apostolic Tradition* attributed to the Christian Hippolytus all sought to regulate banquet behavior and protocol.[48] These regulations hoped to contain all sorts of unruly, inappropriate, or disruptive conduct, such as verbal abuse,

---

"Triclinium and Stibadium," in *Dining in a Classical Context*, ed. William J. Slater (Ann Arbor: University of Michigan Press, 1991), 123; *Roman Banquet*, 39; Streett, *Lord's Supper*, 17. See also Amram Tropper, "The Economics of Jewish Childhood in Late Antiquity," *HUCA* 76 (2005): 211–16. Cf. Todd, "Feasts," 43n4. On food distribution, see, for example, Martial, *Epigr.* 3.60; Pliny the Younger, *Ep.* 2.6; 1 Cor 11:20–22; Lucian (vol. 1), *Symp.* 42–46. (Cf. Todd, "Feasts," 43n4.) On conversation topics, see, for example, Plutarch, *Quaest. conv.* 1.612D–615C, 1.621C, 2.629E–631C; Dio Chrysostom, *Compot.* 27.3–4. On protocols for behavior, see, for example, Josephus, *J.W.* 2.132. See also Smith, *From Symposium to Eucharist*, 13–46; Streett, *Lord's Supper*, 10–16. On invitations, see Chapter 5 below.

47. See Lucian (trans. A. M Harmon [LCL, Cambridge, MA: Harvard University Press, 1921], [vol. 3]), *Merc. cond.* 14; Clement of Alexandria, *Paed.* 2.1–4.

48. On the regulations of the first three groups mentioned here, see Smith, *From Symposium to Eucharist*, 87–131. See also Ascough, "Greco-Roman Association Meals," 59. On the association devoted to Hercules, see Philip A. Harland, "Banqueting Values in the Associations: Rhetoric and Reality," in *Meals in the Early Christian World: Social Formation, Experimentation, and Conflict at the Table*, ed. Dennis E. Smith and Hal E. Taussig (New York, NY: Palgrave Macmillan, 2012), 80–82. On the protocols of the *Apostolic Tradition*, see Hippolytus, *Trad. ap.* 26–30 (Hippolytus (Hippolyte de Rome), *La Tradition Apostolique*, ed. and trans. Bernard Botte, 2nd ed. (Paris: Les Éditions du Cerf, 1984), 102–10).

physical assault, and reclining on a couch reserved for another. Club regulations, such as the rules of the Iobakchoi, not only levied fines for disorderly conduct, but even authorized officials to ask a disturbing banqueter to leave or to have bouncers expel him if he refused to leave on his own accord:

εὔκοσμος δὲ κληρούσθω ἢ καθιστάσθω ὑπὸ τοῦ ἱερέως, ἐπιφέρων τῷ ἀκοσμοῦντι ἢ θορυβοῦντι τὸν θύρσον τοῦ θεοῦ. ᾧ δὲ ἂν παρατεθῇ ὁ θύρσος, ἐπικρείναντος τοῦ ἱερέως ἢ τοῦ ἀρχιβάκχου ἐξερχέσθω τοῦ ἑστιατορείου. ἐὰν δὲ ἀπειθῇ, αἱρέτωσαν αὐτὸν ἔξω τοῦ πυλῶνος οἱ κατασταθησόμενοι ὑπὸ τῶν ἱερέων ἵπποι, καὶ ἔστω ὑπεύθυνος τοῖς περὶ τῶν μαχομένων προστείμοις.

The officer in charge of order shall be chosen by lot or be appointed by the priest, bearing the thyrsus of the god for anyone who is disorderly or creates a disturbance. And if the thyrsus be laid on anyone – (and) the priest or the *archibakchos* approves – he shall leave the banquet hall. If he refuses, those who have been appointed by the priests as bouncers shall take him outside of the door. And he shall be liable to the punishment that applies to those who fight.[49]

In expelling Bar Qamtza from his banquet, Bar Qamtza's host enlisted the widespread practice of ousting an unwanted guest.

The Jewish Banquet

Since Jewish banquet practices and ideals of late Second Temple and rabbinic times developed within the enveloping setting of Greek and Roman banquet culture, the ancient Jewish banquet is best viewed as a variation on the widespread banquet culture of the time. Whether in respect to the banquet's structure and types, norms and rituals, ethos and ethic, locations and regulations, hierarchy and literary representations, the Jewish banquet was heavily indebted to its Greek and Roman counterparts. Like banquets throughout the Mediterranean basin, Jewish banquets were instrumental in defining the boundaries of a community. Therefore, in

49. John S. Kloppenborg and Richard S. Ascough, *Greco-Roman Associations: Texts, Translations, and Commentary: I: Attica, Central Greece, Macedonia, Thrace* (Berlin: Walter de Gruyter, 2011), 245, lines 136–46; 248.

conjuring up the banquet practices of the late Second Temple Jewish community, Lamentations Rabbati also implicitly revealed the fault-lines along which the community might have collapsed.[50] The ancient banquet was highly regulated, both morally and legally, because it was a potentially volatile and explosive setting when handled poorly.[51]

Against the cultural backdrop of Jewish banquets and the overarching Mediterranean banquet tradition, Lamentations Rabbati introduces the refined banquet practices of the noble Jerusalemites and, in their wake, the story of Bar Qamtza. The noble Jerusalemites' banquet practices, which address concerns about invitations, fastidious eaters, fellowship, late entry, and poor cooking, are all in the spirit of Greek and Roman banquets. Accordingly, these Jerusalemite customs point to the encircling Mediterranean banquet tradition as a useful lens through which to view the story of Bar Qamtza. In this vein, perhaps the fantastically extravagant banquets of the wealthy elite in late antiquity inspired the notion that Jerusalem (of earlier Roman times) fell because of an inconsiderate elite too focused on its own wealth and luxurious living.[52]

Furthermore, the frame of the Jerusalemite banquet practices in Lamentations Rabbati offers a narrower and more focused interpretive lens. The Jerusalemite banquet practices are framed by two customs related to the invitation process, opening with the folded shoulder clasp custom intended to preempt and prevent wasted invitations and closing

---

50. Cf. König, *Saints and Symposiasts*, 6.

51. Cf. Gafni, "Jerusalem," 44; Julia Watts Belser, *Rabbinic Tales of Destruction: Gender, Sex, and Disability in the Ruins of Jerusalem* (Oxford: Oxford University Press, 2018), 166, 179; Albert I. Baumgarten, "Sages Increase Peace in the World: Reconciliation and Power," in *The Faces of Torah: Studies in the Texts and Contexts of Ancient Judaism in Honor of Steven Fraade*, ed. Michal Bar-Asher Siegal, Tzvi Novick, and Christine Hayes (Göttingen: Vandenhoeck & Ruprecht, 2017), 234–36. (See also Albert I. Baumgarten, "Rabbinic Literature as a Source for the History of Jewish Sectarianism in the Second Temple Period," *DSD* 2 [1995]: 36–52; Ruhama Weiss, *Meal Tests: The Meal in the World of the Sages* [אוכלים לדעת: תפקידן התרבותי של הסעודות בספרות חז"ל][Tel Aviv: Hakibutz Hameuchad, 2010], 16.) For some explosive banquets, see Mark 6:14–29; Matt 14:1–12; Livy, *Ab urbe cond.* 39:43; Plutarch, *Sert.* 26.3–6. On the banquet regulations in 1QS, see Todd, "Feasts," 172–83.

52. On the extravagant banquets of late antiquity, see Dunbabin, *Roman Banquet*, 141.

with the custom to wait for a banquet invitation's confirmation. This invitation-oriented frame primes the reader for a story about a banquet invitation, and the story of Bar Qamtza is indeed one of an invitation gone terribly wrong.

Chapter 4

The Immediate Literary Context

As a group, the six Jerusalemite banquet practices establish both a literary context and a genteel banquet atmosphere as the backdrop for the story of Bar Qamtza. However, the sixth and final Jerusalemite banquet practice, the practice which immediately precedes the story of Bar Qamtza, warrants a closer look because it may have a more direct bearing on the story's opening scene.

1 ד"א: "בני ציון היקרים" (איכה ד:ב):

2 מה היתה יקרותן?

3 לא היה אחד מהם הולך לסעודה עד שהיה נקרא ונשנה.

1 Another teaching: *The precious children of Zion* (Lam 4:2):

2 What was their preciousness?

3 Not one of them would attend a banquet until he was invited and (then) invited again.

According to this take on Lamentations' "precious children of Zion," the noble Jerusalem banqueters would not attend a banquet until they had received a second invitation confirming the original one. This confirmation practice (as noted above) appears nowhere else in rabbinic literature and though Lamentations Rabbati does not explain the custom, three possible rationales come to mind. The second invitation may simply have functioned as a useful reminder and a Jewish expression of the widespread "Near Eastern custom of first inviting guests on principle and sending for them later when the meal is ready."[1] In a related vein, the confirmation custom may have been designed to help a guest ensure that he was truly desired at a banquet in the spirit of Ben Sira's advice: "When an influential person invites you, be reserved, and he will invite you more insistently" ("קרב נדיב היה רחוק, וכדי כן יגישך").[2] In forcing the host to invite him a second time, the guest makes sure that the host honestly and truly wants him at the banquet. Alternatively, the custom may have been intended to help a guest avoid giving the impression that he was overly eager to attend a banquet. Just as the rabbis taught that one should initially refuse the request to serve as a prayer leader because it was considered in bad taste to seek out the spotlight, the confirmation custom may have sought to rein in, or at least disguise, a guest's unseemly yearning to attend a banquet.[3]

Whatever the exact rationale of the confirmation custom, its location in Lamentations Rabbati raises the question of how to interpret the custom's relevance to the story. Does the custom merely enhance the portrait of the banquet environment conveyed by the five preceding banquet practices or does it play a role in the story of Bar Qamtza? A priori, there seem to be two ways to interpret the confirmation custom's relationship to the story of Bar Qamtza.

One way argues that beyond enriching the cultural backdrop for a Jerusalem story and priming us for a story about a banquet invitation, the confirmation custom has no bearing on the story's narrative arc. Since the story mentions nothing out of the ordinary when relating Bar Qamtza's reception of the banquet invitation, we may assume that nothing significant occurred at that time. It is possible that standard

---

1. Uwe-Karsten Plisch, *The Gospel of Thomas: Original Text with Commentary* (Stuttgart: Deutsche Bibelgesellschaft, 2008), 159. See Luke 14:17; Matt 22:3. See also Ulrich Luz, *Matthew 21–28: A Commentary* (Minneapolis, MN: Augsburg Fortress, 2005), 52.

2. Sir 9:13 (*Sefer Ben-Sira Ha-shalem*, ed. Moshe Zvi Segal [Jerusalem: Bialik Institute, 1972], ad loc. with translation by *The New Oxford Annotated Bible: New Revised Standard Version with the Apocrypha: An Ecumenical Study Bible*, ed. Michael D. Coogan [Oxford: Oxford University Press, 2018], ad loc.).

3. For the notion that one should initially refuse a request to serve as a prayer leader, see b. Ber. 34a.

Jerusalem protocols were observed and Bar Qamtza attended the banquet only after receiving the confirmation invitation.[4] Alternatively, it is possible that the confirmation custom is irrelevant because there simply was not sufficient time to receive a second invitation. A person could expect a second invitation for a banquet scheduled some time in advance, but since Bar Qamtza received his invitation on the very day of the banquet – the messenger "went and brought" him to the banquet – there was no time for Bar Qamtza to receive a confirmation as well. Moreover, since sage stories sometimes ignore ritual details and legal minutia, it is quite possible that the story of Bar Qamtza simply overlooks the confirmation custom of the noble Jerusalemites.[5] In any event, the bottom line of this interpretive approach is that so long as the story makes no mention of the confirmation custom, there is no reason to grant it a role in the story.

By contrast, the second way to interpret the confirmation custom's relevance maintains that its juxtaposition to the story of Bar Qamtza transforms our expectations by alerting us to the practice. In the immediate wake of the confirmation custom, readers expect to hear of the custom's implementation; hence, the absence of the second invitation in the story of Bar Qamtza is striking. According to this interpretive lens, the confirmation custom's no-show in the story of Bar Qamtza is a resounding silence which implies that Bar Qamtza did not wait to receive a second invitation.[6] In his eagerness to attend the banquet, Bar Qamtza overlooked the custom of the noble Jerusalemites and attended the banquet on the basis of a single unconfirmed invitation. Presumably, Bar Qamtza would not have received the confirmation invitation since the messenger's error would have been detected quickly and the host's household would have made sure not to send Bar Qamtza a second invitation.

---

4. Levine Katz, "Qamtsa," 37.

5. If the story of Bar Qamtza had been drawn from somewhere else before being embedded in Lamentations Rabbati, its original author might not have even been aware of the confirmation custom which appears here in Lamentations Rabbati for the very first time.

6. See Elimelekh E. Halevi, *Gates of the Aggadah* (שערי האגדה), (Tel Aviv: 1963), 205; Saldarini, "Rabbinic Response," 454; cf. Levine Katz, "Qamtsa," 37n16.

Bar Qamtza's haste according to the second way of interpreting the confirmation custom's relevance to the story by no means mitigates the awful behavior of the other characters. The heartless conduct of both the host and the onlookers is inexcusable regardless of whether Bar Qamtza received a confirmation or not. Bar Qamtza's neglect of the confirmation custom, accordingly, has no bearing on the moral weight of the story, but it does carry some literary weight. In a retrospective assessment of the narrative as a whole, Bar Qamtza's neglect becomes yet another error in the cascade of errors which ultimately crescendos to calamity. If Bar Qamtza had followed the confirmation custom, he would not have attended the banquet and hence would not have triggered the series of events leading to the destruction of the temple. Like the messenger's mix-up of invitees, Bar Qamtza's slight error only took on catastrophic proportions because of the deep ethical failings of Second Temple Jewish society.

In sum, the confirmation custom either foreshadows a story about a banquet invitation or modifies the story's plotline by inverting our expectations. Although there is no unequivocal argument in favor of either one of these readings, the story itself makes no mention of Bar Qamtza's failure to wait for a second invitation and, as a rule, it is best not to add unvoiced wrinkles to the plot of a rabbinic sage story. Sage stories are usually quite brief and sometimes we have no choice but to read between their lines, but since, in this case, we have a perfectly viable alternative which does not involve inserting unmentioned elements into the plot, it is best not to do so.

Chapter 5

The Mistaken Invitation (ACT I SCENE 1)

The literary context of Lamentations Rabbati sets the stage for a Jerusalem banquet story without telegraphing where the story is headed. Lamentations Rabbati's list of banquet customs, in other words, gives no whiff of the story's ultimate end. In the same vein, the story itself nowhere reveals where it is headed and as it unfolds from scene to scene the narrative tension gradually escalates until the shocking catastrophic climax appears in the story's final line. Encountering it for the very first time, the original audience or readers of the story would have been unaware of the story's conclusion, which is worth keeping in mind when we read the story. With no hint that anything is wrong in Jerusalem, the story opens in Act I scene 1 with a banquet invitation:

4 מעשה באדם אחד בירושלם שעשה סעודה.

5 אמר לשלוחו: לך והבא לי בן קמצא רחמי; אזל ואייתי ליה בר קמצא שנאיה.

4 A story of one man in Jerusalem who made a banquet.

5 He said to his messenger: Go and bring me Ben Qamtza my friend; he (the messenger) went and brought him Bar Qamtza his enemy.

The story opens in Hebrew but then quickly transitions to Aramaic, as rabbinic stories sometimes do.[1] Since Aramaic was widely spoken during

---

1. See Mandel, "Tales of the Destruction," 148n29. The Hebrew of the opening ends with the words "Go and bring me Ben Qamtza."

41

the Amoraic times (circa 220–500 CE) in which Lamentations Rabbati emerged, it is only natural that the bulk of the story was composed in Aramaic. In contrast, since Hebrew was no longer a spoken language in the Amoraic period, Hebrew openings are likely a formal or rhetorical feature of (certain) sage stories. In our particular case, perhaps the Hebrew opening helped evoke a sense of antiquity for a story that takes place centuries before the Amoraic era.

The first line of the story, line 4, presents the story's social setting: "A story of one man in Jerusalem who made a banquet." The prominent appearance of Jerusalem, the banquet's location, in the story's very first line anchors the story within its immediate literary context. The banquet customs of the noble Jerusalemites set the backdrop for a story about one particular Jerusalemite's banquet.

The "one man" of the opening line remains nameless throughout the rest of the story, and, in and of itself, a name's absence should not be interpreted in a negative or critical vein. The ruler, officer, and priest also remain nameless, and, in general, the names of the characters populating rabbinic sage stories often remain unmentioned since these short stories home in on the bare essentials only.

On the heels of line 4's banquet setting, line 5 describes how a banquet invitation was mistakenly delivered to Bar Qamtza. In antiquity, the extending of invitations was part and parcel of the preparations for a banquet. Thus, in order to better appreciate Bar Qamtza's banquet invitation, let us consider the nature and role of banquet invitations amongst Jews and gentiles in Greek and Roman antiquity.

Banquet Invitations

In the steps leading up to a banquet, hosts (or sponsors) sent invitations to their intended guests and the invitees accepted or declined the invitations. As a rule, normative guests only attended banquets when invited since, as Vitruvius notes, it was considered improper to enter the private areas of a home, such as a dining room or bedroom, "uninvited" ("nisi invitas").[2] For his or her part, a banquet's host carefully fashioned the guest list in order to orchestrate the constellation of guests, calibrate

---

2. See Vitruvius, *De arch.* 6.5.1 (Vitruvius, *On Architecture: Books 6–10*, trans.

the banquet's level of intimacy, and keep out undesirables.[3] In light of the banquet's ethos of friendship and fellowship (discussed above in Chapter 3), hosts and guests well understood that the banquet offered the host a singular opportunity to create his own temporary community of select friends. As Plutarch explains, the right combination of guests was a crucial ingredient in the repertoire of a successful banquet:

κοινωνία γάρ ἐστι καὶ σπουδῆς καὶ παιδιᾶς καὶ λόγων καὶ πράξεων τὸ συμπόσιον. ὅθεν οὐ τοὺς τυχόντας ἀλλὰ προσφιλεῖς εἶναι δεῖ καὶ συνήθεις ἀλλήλοις, ὡς ἡδέως συνεσομένους· ὄψα μὲν γὰρ οἱ μάγειροι σκευάζουσιν ἐκ χυμῶν διαφόρων, αὐστηρὰ καὶ λιπαρὰ καὶ γλυκέα καὶ δριμέα συγκεραννύντες, σύνδειπνον δὲ χρηστὸν οὐκ ἂν γένοιτο καὶ κεχαρισμένον ἀνθρώπων μὴ ὁμοφύλων μηδ᾽ ὁμοιοπαθῶν εἰς τὸ αὐτὸ συμφθαρέντων.

A dinner party is a sharing of earnest and jest, of words and deeds; so the diners must not be left to chance, but must be such as are friends and intimates of one another who will enjoy being together. Cooks make up their dishes of a variety of flavours, blending the sour, the oily, the sweet, and the pungent, but you could not get good and agreeable company at dinner by throwing together men who are different in their associations and sympathies.[4]

Written and oral invitations were extended in advance, often by a (slave) courier known as a *vocator, invitator,* or *monitor,* and both actual and literary invitations from antiquity have been preserved.[5] Consider,

---

Frank Granger [LCL, Cambridge, MA: Harvard University Press, 1931], ad loc.). (See also Rev 19:9; Plutarch, *Sept. sap. conv* 147E.) Cf. Noy, "Jewish Meals," 138.

3. See Hudson, "Food," 200; König, *Saints and Symposiasts,* 192. Cf. the welcoming attitude (from later Geonic times) expressed at the beginning of the *Haggadah* (Shmuel Safrai and Ze'ev Safrai, *Haggadah of the Sages: The Passover Haggadah* [Jerusalem: Carta, 1998], 205): "כל דכפין ייתי ויכל, כל, [הגדת חז"ל: הגדה של פסח], [הגדת חז"ל: דצריך ייתי ויפסח," "All who hunger may come and eat, all who need may come and celebrate the Passover."

4. Plutarch, *Quaest. conv.* 7.708D. See also Plutarch, *Sept. sap. conv.* 147F–148A.

5. For examples of invitations extended in advance, see Plato, *Symp.* 174a; Xenophon, *Symp.* 1.3–4. On the slave courier, see D'Arms, "Roman *Convivium,*" 318; "Slaves," 172; Luz, *Matthew,* 52. In addition to (writing and) delivering invitations, slaves greeted banqueters, (determined their seating location), attended their

for example, the following third-century banquet invitation found among the Oxyrhynchus papyri in Egypt (P. Oxy. 33 2678):[6]

ἐρωτᾷ σε Διοσκοροῦς δειπνῆσαι εἰς γάμους τοῦ υἱοῦ τῇ ιδ τοῦ Μεσορὴ ἐν τῷ Σαβαζείῳ ἀπὸ ὥρ(ας) θ. διευτύχει.

Dioscoros invites you to dine at the wedding of her son on the 14th of Mesore in the temple of Sabazius from the ninth hour, farewell.[7]

While recording the event, date, and time of the banquet, this written wedding invitation does not mention the name of the guest, perhaps in order to allow Dioscoros's messenger to read out one and the same invitation to multiple guests.[8] Moreover, ancient written invitations generally did not mention the name of the invitee or his or her address. Hence, the invitation itself had no corrective value when accidentally delivered to an unintended guest. In Bar Qamtza's case, the story does not specify whether he received a written or oral invitation or whether a written invitation was read out to him by the host's messenger. In any case, the messenger's confusion was enough to bungle the invitation's delivery, and even a written invitation would not have set right the messenger's error.

The invitation process was often fraught with anxiety for both hosts and potential guests. Uninvited friends of a host who thought they ought to have been invited to a banquet might become gravely insulted for having been left out. In Lucian's *Symposium*, for example, Hetoemocles is indignant when he is not invited to the banquet his neighbor Aristaenetus makes for his son's wedding, and, when feeling neglected by a friend, Martial resentfully writes: "What has happened, I ask you, what has suddenly happened after so many mutual pledges, so many years, that I, your old comrade, am passed over (and not invited to your birthday feasts)?"

---

needs, cleaned up after them and restrained them if they became unruly. See Noy, "Jewish Meals," 138–39; Streett, *Lord's Supper*, 16. For actual invitations, see Chan-Hie Kim, "The Papyrus Invitation." *JBL* 94 (1975): 391–402. See Petronius, *Satyr.* 46 for an example of a literary invitation. See also Gowers, *Loaded Table*, 222–23; Smith, *From Symposium to Eucharist*, 22–23.

6. Kim, "Papyrus Invitation," 399–401.

7. Translation by Smith, *From Symposium to Eucharist*, 24.

8. See Kim, "Papyrus Invitation," 397.

("quid factum est, rogo, quid repente factum est, post tot pignora nos-tra, post tot annos quod sum praeteritus vetus sodalis?")[9] Preempting the host's attempt to exonerate himself by blaming his courier, Martial cautions him not to say: "I will have my *vocator* flogged (for not deliv-ering my invitations)" ("vapulet vocator").[10] This sort of miffed rancor also appears in the following king parable from Lamentations Rabbati, in which the king laments not being invited to his servant's banquet:

א״ר יודן: לעבדו של מלך שעשה סעודה והזמין את כל בני כנאותיו ולא הזמין רבו. אמ' המלך: הלואי השוה אותי עבדי לבני כנסיותיו.

Rabbi Yudan said: (A parable) to the servant of a king who made a banquet and invited all the children of his friends but did not invite his master. The king said: If only my servant would treat me as he does his fellow members in the assembly.[11]

In like manner, the following story from Qohelet Rabbah also de-scribes a similar sense of rejection:

ר' שמעון בר' עשה סעודת משתה בנו. קרא ר' לכל רבנן ואינשי למקרי לבר קפרא. אזל וכתב על תרעא: אחר שמחתך אתה מת, ומה יתרון לשמחתך? אמ': מאן עבד לן הדא? אמרי, בר קפרא דאנשיתו למקרי ליה, וכדון למקרי ליה לגרמיה סניא הוא, אזל ועבד אריסטון אחרן וקרא לכל רבנן וקרא ליה לבר קפרא ...

Rabbi Simeon the son of Rabbi (Judah Hanasi) made a wedding banquet for his son. Rabbi (Judah Hanasi) invited all the sages but forgot to invite Bar Qappara.[12] He (Bar Qappara) went and wrote

---

9. For Hetoemocles's indignation, see Lucian (vol. 1), *Symp.* 22–27. (See also Eris's jealousy when she is not invited to the wedding banquet of Thetis and Peleus in Colluthus, *The Rape of Helen* 38–45.) For Martial's resentment, see Martial, *Epigr.* 7.86 (Martial, *Epigrams*, trans. D.R. Shackleton Bailey, vols. 1–2 [LCL, Cambridge, MA: Harvard University Press, 1993], ad loc.).

10. Martial, *Epigr.* 7.86 with Shackleton Bailey's translation slightly modified.

11. Lam. Rab. Petiḥta 10 (p. 9) according to Munich 229. See also Appendix II, n. 55 below.

12. In some other versions of the story, Rabbi Simeon is the host. See, for example, Lev. Rab. 28:2 (*Midrash Wayyikra Rabbah*, ed. M. Margulies [1953–1960. Repr., New York, NY: Maxwell Abbell Publication Fund and The Jewish Theological Seminary of America, 1993], pp. 653–55). See also Hirshman's commentary, ad

on his (Rabbi Judah Hanasi's) gate: "After your rejoicing you will die, what profit is there in your joy?" He (Rabbi Judah Hanasi) said: "Who did this to us?" They said: "Bar Qappara whom you forgot to invite." Since inviting Bar Qappara alone would have been unseemly, he went and made another banquet and invited all the sages and invited Bar Qappara (as well) . . . [13]

Like Hetoemocles, Martial, and the king, Bar Qappara is also outraged when he is not invited to a banquet to which he feels he should have been invited.

For hosts, sending out invitations might entail the risk of rejection and a social snub.[14] In line with such concerns, Lucian has Lycinus suggest that Aristaenetus did not invite Hetoemocles because he feared Hetoemocles would turn down the invitation.[15] In a related vein, early followers of Jesus told a king parable in which a king was infuriated when his invited guests decided not to attend his banquet:

Καὶ ἀποκριθεὶς ὁ Ἰησοῦς πάλιν εἶπεν ἐν παραβολαῖς αὐτοῖς λέγων, Ὡμοιώθη ἡ βασιλεία τῶν οὐρανῶν ἀνθρώπῳ βασιλεῖ, ὅστις ἐποίησεν γάμους τῷ υἱῷ αὐτοῦ. καὶ ἀπέστειλεν τοὺς δούλους αὐτοῦ καλέσαι τοὺς κεκλημένους εἰς τοὺς γάμους, καὶ οὐκ ἤθελον ἐλθεῖν. πάλιν ἀπέστειλεν ἄλλους δούλους λέγων, Εἴπατε τοῖς κεκλημένοις Ἰδοὺ τὸ ἄριστόν μου ἡτοίμακα, οἱ ταῦροί μου καὶ τὰ σιτιστὰ τεθυμένα, καὶ πάντα ἕτοιμα· δεῦτε εἰς τοὺς γάμους. οἱ δὲ ἀμελήσαντες ἀπῆλθον, ὃς μὲν εἰς τὸν ἴδιον ἀγρόν, ὃς δὲ ἐπὶ τὴν ἐμπορίαν αὐτοῦ· οἱ δὲ λοιποὶ κρατήσαντες τοὺς δούλους αὐτοῦ ὕβρισαν καὶ ἀπέκτειναν. ὁ δὲ βασιλεὺς ὠργίσθη, καὶ πέμψας τὰ

loc. (Qoh. Rab. 1:3 [*Midrash Kohelet Rabbah 1–6*, ed. Marc Hirshman (Jerusalem: The Midrash Project of the Schechter Institute of Jewish Studies, 2016), 31]).

13. Qoh. Rab. 1:3 (p. 30) according to Vatican 291. Cf. Qoh. Zuta 1:3 (Reuven Kiperwasser, "Addenda: Kohelet Zuta Synopsis," in "Midrashim on Kohelet: Studies in their Redaction and Formation" [PhD diss., Bar-Ilan University, 2005], 6); Lev. Rab. 28:2 (pp. 653–55). See also Saul Lieberman, "Notes on Chapter I of Midrash *Kohelet Rabbah*" ("הערות לפרק א' של קהלת רבה"), in *Studies in Mysticism and Religion*, ed. E.E. Urbach, R.J. Zwi Werblowsky, and Ch. Wirszubski (Jerusalem: Hebrew University Magnes Press, 1967), 171.

14. For two biblical examples of rejected banquet invitations, see 1 Sam 20:25–32; Esth 1:12.

15. See Lucian (vol. 1), *Symp.* 28.

στρατεύματα αὐτοῦ ἀπώλεσεν τοὺς φονεῖς ἐκείνους καὶ τὴν πόλιν αὐτῶν ἐνέπρησεν. τότε λέγει τοῖς δούλοις αὐτοῦ Ὁ μὲν γάμος ἕτοιμός ἐστιν, οἱ δὲ κεκλημένοι οὐκ ἦσαν ἄξιοι· πορεύεσθε οὖν ἐπὶ τὰς διεξόδους τῶν ὁδῶν, καὶ ὅσους ἐὰν εὕρητε καλέσατε εἰς τοὺς γάμους. καὶ ἐξελθόντες οἱ δοῦλοι ἐκεῖνοι εἰς τὰς ὁδοὺς συνήγαγον πάντας οὓς εὗρον, πονηρούς τε καὶ ἀγαθούς· καὶ ἐπλήσθη ὁ γάμος ἀνακειμένων.

Once more Jesus spoke to them in parables, saying: "The kingdom of heaven may be compared to a king who gave a wedding banquet for his son. He sent his slaves to call those who had been invited to the wedding banquet, but they would not come. Again, he sent other slaves, saying, 'Tell those who have been invited: Look, I have prepared my dinner, my oxen and my fat calves have been slaughtered, and everything is ready; come to the wedding banquet.' But they made light of it and went away, one to his farm, another to his business, while the rest seized his slaves, mistreated them, and killed them. The king was enraged. He sent his troops, destroyed those murderers, and burned their city. Then he said to his slaves, 'The wedding is ready, but those invited were not worthy. Go therefore into the main streets, and invite everyone you find to the wedding banquet.' Those slaves went out into the streets and gathered all whom they found, both good and bad; so the wedding hall was filled with guests."[16]

When the king dispatches messengers to remind his invited guests of the imminent wedding banquet (and confirm their attendance), the guests refuse to come. In response to the guests' refusal the king sends another messenger to plead with them, explaining that the banquet is fully prepared and the only missing ingredient is their presence, but the guests make light of the king's repeated invitations. Some elect to work rather than attend the banquet and others abuse and even kill the king's slaves. Snubbed by the invitees the king is enraged and his predicament, like that of Aristaenetus, illustrates how ancient hosts had reason to

---

16. Matt 22:1–10 (*The Greek New Testament*, ed. Kurt Aland, Matthew Black, Carlo M. Martini, Bruce M. Metzger, and Allen Wikgren [Stuttgart: United Bible Societies, 1966], ad loc.). Cf. Plisch, *Gospel of Thomas* 64. See also D'Arms, "Roman *Convivium*," 313.

dread rejected invitations and no-shows. Parenthetically, it bears noting that the invitees' city which the king destroys presumably represents Jerusalem. Hence, long before the emergence of the Amoraic story of Bar Qamtza, the destruction of Jerusalem was already interpreted, back in the first century CE, as punishment for the heartless behavior of Jerusalemites in a banquet context.[17]

In order to minimize the likelihood of an invitee's snub as well as enhance the friendly atmosphere at his banquet, a host normally invited friends only, or, in the words of Lucian's parasite named Simon:

Ὅτι οὐδεὶς ἐχθρὸν ἢ ἀγνῶτα ἄνθρωπον ἀλλ οὐδὲ συνήθη μετρίως ἐπὶ δεῖπνον καλεῖ, ἀλλὰ δεῖ πρότερον οἶμαι τοῦτον γενέσθαι φίλον, ἵνα κοινωνήσῃ σπονδῶν καὶ τραπέζης καὶ τῶν τῆς τέχνης ταύτης μυστηρίων. ἐγὼ γοῦν πολλάκις ἤκουσά τινων λεγόντων, "Ποταπὸς δὲ οὗτος φίλος ὅστις οὔτε βέβρωκεν οὔτε πέπωκεν μεθ᾽ ἡμῶν," δῆλον ὅτι τὸν συμπίνοντα καὶ συνεσθίοντα μόνον πιστὸν φίλον ἡγουμένων.

That nobody invites an enemy or an unknown person to dinner; not even a slight acquaintance. A man must first, I take it, become a friend in order to share another's bowl and board, and the mystic rites of this art. Anyhow, I have often heard people say: "How much of a friend is he, when he has neither eaten nor drunk with us?" That is of course because they think that only one who has shared their meat and drink is a trusty friend.[18]

In keeping with the notion that a banquet is reserved for friends alone, Ben Sira cautions: "Do not invite everyone into your home, for many are the tricks of the crafty" ("לא כל איש להביא אל בית ומה רבו פצעי רוכל").[19] Furthermore, in the event that a crafty enemy does attend a banquet, Ben Sira advises the host to keep him at arm's length in order to minimize the potential fallout of his presence:

---

17. For the notion that the city in the parable represents Jerusalem, see Luz, *Matthew*, 54.

18. Lucian (vol. 3), *Par.* 22.

19. Sir 11:29. See also Sira 11:34: "Receive strangers into your home and they will stir up trouble for you, and will make you a stranger to your own family," "משוכן זריו זהיר דרכיך וינכרך במחמדיך."

אל תעמידהו אצלך למה יהדפך ויעמד תחתיך. אל תושיבהו לימינך למה
יבקש מושבך. ולאחור תשיג אמרי ולאנחתי תתאנח.

Do not put him (your enemy) next to you, or he may overthrow you
and take your place. Do not let him sit at your right hand, or else he
may try to take your own seat, and at last you will realize the truth
of my words, and be stung by what I have said.[20]

Since hosts normally did not send banquet invitations to their enemies, a host's enemy would likely be surprised to receive such an invitation. As an invitee, an enemy like Bar Qamtza might well have presumed
that by extending him an invitation, the host hoped to re-establish
friendly relations and reconcile their differences.[21]

In light of the friendship ethos of ancient banquets and the corresponding habit to populate guest lists with friends, the host's dis-
inclination to invite his enemy Bar Qamtza is entirely expected and
unsurprising. The norm in Jewish, Greek, and Roman society was to
celebrate banquets with friends, not enemies, and in accordance with
this norm, Bar Qamtza's preference to invite a friend over an enemy is
perfectly reasonable. In the Gospels, Jesus contests this norm when he
encourages banqueting with sinners, tax collectors, and social inferiors
such as the poor, crippled, lame, and blind.[22] Jesus's subversive stance,
however, is the exception to the rule, while the story of Bar Qamtza,
like most ancient banquet literature, does not seek to undermine the
banquet's friendship ethos or associated invitation practices. The story
does not condemn the host for preferring a friend over an enemy and so,
unlike Jesus, the story makes no attempt to upend widespread banqueting norms. Instead, the story of Bar Qamtza condemns abusive behavior
within the rubric of accepted banqueting norms. One message which
emerges from the story of Bar Qamtza is that although one may choose
not to dine in the presence of one's enemies, one must nonetheless treat
them in a compassionate and considerate manner if they should unexpectedly appear at one's dinner table.

---

20. Sir 12:12. See also Smith, *From Symposium to Eucharist*, 135; Todd, "Feasts,"
53–54.

21. See Chapter 17, n. 11 below.

22. Mark 2:13–17; Luke 5:27–32, 14:12–14. See also Streett, *Lord's Supper*, 133–59.

Mistaken Identity

The trigger which launches the story of Bar Qamtza and sets the narrative on its course is a case of mistaken identity. The theme of mistaken identity was widely popular in ancient literature, and well-known examples already appear in the Hebrew Bible and *The Odyssey*. In Genesis 38, Judah mistakes his disguised daughter-in-law Tamar for a prostitute, and in *The Odyssey* the disguised Odysseus is mistaken for a beggar when he finally returns home after the Trojan War.[23] At times, an individual, like Tamar or Odysseus, is mistaken for someone else because his or her identity was intentionally hidden behind a disguise. At other times, however, an individual is accidentally mistaken for someone else as in the following story from Leviticus Rabbah:

מעשה בר' יניי שהיה מהלך בדרך פגע בו אדם אחד שהיה משופע ביותר.
אמ' לו: משגח ר' לאיתקבלא גבן? אמ' ליה: מה דהני לך. הכניסו לתוך ביתו
בדקו במקרא ולא מצאו, בדקו במשנה ולא מצאו, בתלמוד ולא מצאו, בהגדה
ולא מצאו. אמ' ליה: בריך. אמ' ליה: יברך יניי בבייתיה. אמ' ליה: אית בך
אמ' מה דאנא אמ' לך? אמ' ליה: אין. אמ' ליה: אמור אכל כלבא פסתיה
דיניי. קם צריה....

A story of Rabbi Yannai who, when walking on the road, saw a most distinguished man (whose attire led Rabbi Yannai to believe that the man was a learned sage). He (Rabbi Yannai) said to him: Would you, Rabbi, care to accept my hospitality? He said to him: Whatever pleases you. He (Rabbi Yannai) brought him into his house and (over the course of the meal), he (Rabbi Yannai) tested him (the guest) in (knowledge of) Bible and found none, he tested him in (knowledge of) Mishnah and found none, in Talmud and found none, in haggadah and found none. (At the end of the meal) he (Rabbi Yannai) said to him: Recite the Grace (after Meals). He (the guest) said: Let Yannai recite the Grace in his own home. He (Rabbi Yannai) said to him: Are you able to repeat whatever I say to you? He said to him: Yes. He (Rabbi Yannai) said to him: Say a dog has eaten of Yannai's bread. He (the guest) rose and grabbed him (Rabbi Yannai)....[24]

23. See Homer, *Od.* 13.397–403.
24. Lev. Rab. 9:3 (pp. 176–79). My translation is indebted to that of J. Israelstam and Judah H. Slotki, trans., *Midrash Rabbah: Leviticus* (London: Soncino, 1939),

Mistaking a well-dressed man for a rabbinic sage, Rabbi Yannai invites the man to dine in the hopes of conversing with him about matters of Torah. Over the course of the meal, however, Rabbi Yannai discovers that his guest lacks knowledge of Bible, Mishnah, Talmud and haggadah, and hence, in effect, is not a rabbinic sage. When the guest declines to lead the recitation of the Grace after Meals, Rabbi Yannai expresses his disappointment and rudely calls the guest a dog. The guest is taken aback by this insult and, in response, rises and grabs hold of Rabbi Yannai. In the story's continuation Rabbi Yannai manages to resolve the conflict with his guest, but it's the conflict that interests us here, not its resolution. The story of Rabbi Yannai and his unlearned guest, I believe, offers a fascinating structural parallel to the story of Bar Qamtza. In both stories, an accident of mistaken identity prompts a host to invite someone to a banquet, but when the guest's true identity is revealed, the host callously embarrasses him.

Although the theme of mistaken (or veiled) identity appears across varied literary genres, it was especially popular in ancient comedy.[25] Moreover, in addition to the usual factors prompting a mistaken identity such as disguise, deception, or uncanny physical resemblance, comedy developed another factor: shared names. In Plautus's *Bacchides*, for example, a young man's heart temporarily breaks when he mistakes one woman named Bacchis for another.[26] In the course of the play, Mnesilochus sends his friend Pistoclerus to locate his beloved, a prostitute named Bacchis, but when he hears that Pisctoclerus not only located Bacchis but also slept with her, he is heartbroken. Mnesilochus's

---

ad loc. See also Avigdor Shinan, "R. Yannai, the Peddler and the Well-Dressed Man: A Study of the Structure of Two Stories from Leviticus Rabbah" ("רבי ינ"יי, הרוכל והאדם המשופע: עיון בתשתיתם של שני סיפורים במדרש ויקרא רבה"), *Criticism and Interpretation* 30 (1994): 19–23; Klein, "Torah in Triclinia," 358–60.

25. See, for example, Ian C. Storey and Arlene Allan, *A Guide to Ancient Greek Drama* (Chichester: Wiley Blackwell, 2014), 137–44. On the importance of ancient comedy as a backdrop for the story of Bar Qamtza, see Yitzhak Baer, "Jerusalem in the Times of the Great Revolt (Based on the Source Criticism of Josephus and Talmudic-Midrashic Legends of the Temple's Destruction)" ("ירושלים בימי המרד הגדול (על יסוד ביקורת המקורות של יוספוס ואגדות החורבן)"), *Zion* 36 (1971): 170; Saldarini, "Rabbinic Response," 449.

26. Plautus, *Bacc.* 489–525.

heartache quickly heals, however, because Pistoclerus promptly clarifies that he did not sleep with Mnesilochus's Bacchis but with her sister, also named Bacchis.[27] The temporary confusion of the two sisters in *Bacchides* is akin to the temporary mix-up of names in the opening of the story of Bar Qamtza. However, while the theme of mistaken identity only serves to complicate *Bacchides*'s central plotline, it is the spark which ignites Bar Qamtza's plot.[28]

In contrast to *Bacchides*, the mistaken identity theme functions as an integral element in Plautus's play *Menaechmi* just as it does in the story of Bar Qamtza. In *Menaechmi* (a major source of inspiration for William Shakespeare's *The Comedy of Errors*), identical twins, both called Menaechmus, are separated in their youth, and, while one grows up in their hometown of Syracuse, the other is kidnapped and raised in Epidamus. Years later when Menaechmus of Syracuse, a bachelor, travels to Epidamus, he is mistaken time and again for his married twin. In a memorable scene of this comedy of errors, the mistress of Menaechmus of Epidamus invites Menaechmus of Syracuse to a banquet, mistaking him for his twin, and Menaechmus of Syracuse gladly attends the banquet intended for his brother.[29] Hence, like the story of Bar Qamtza, *Menaechmi* revolves around a case of mistaken identity triggered by a confusion of names and a banquet invitation therefore extended to the wrong man.

Although the similarities between the story of Bar Qamtza and Plautus's comedies seem too strong to be mere chance, they do not warrant the conclusion that the rabbis were familiar with these specific plays. Instead, the most we can safely say is that certain elements of the popular ambient culture seeped into the literary imagination behind the story of Bar Qamtza.[30] In particular, I propose that the name mix-up variation on the mistaken identity theme and its role in a botched banquet invitation were elements ultimately drawn from ancient comedy.

---

27. Plautus, *Bacc.* 539–640.
28. See Shirley Anne Murray, "Quis Ego Sum Saltem? An Investigation of Plautus' Captiui, Menaechmi and Amphitruo with Special Reference to Problems of Identity" (MA thesis, University of KwaZulu-Natal, 2007), 119–20.
29. See Plautus, *Men.* 355–477.
30. See Chapter 1, n. 3 above.

The Names of the Host's Friend and Enemy

In the case of the Bavli, the names of the host's friend and enemy are consistent across the textual witnesses: Qamtza is the name of the friend and intended guest while Bar Qamtza is the name of the enemy and actual guest. In Lamentations Rabbati, however, the textual evidence is less decisive.

In respect to the enemy's name, the textual evidence is largely in favor of Bar Qamtza. Whereas Cambridge 495 reads Ben Qamtza, T-S C 1.69 + T-S AS 78.27 reads Ben Kamtzora, and Parma 2393 reads Qamtza, the other direct textual witnesses – Munich 229, the *editio princeps*, Casanatense H 3112, Parma 2559, Oxford 102, and London 27089 – all read Bar Qamtza.[31] Since the majority of textual witnesses, including representatives of both branches, read Bar Qamtza, while each of the three dissenting manuscripts offers a unique and unparalleled reading, the evidence favors Bar Qamtza.

In respect to the friend's name, the textual evidence is less clear-cut.[32] Branch A (Munich 229, Cambridge 495, the *editio princeps*, and T-S C 1.69 + T-S AS 78.27) reads Bar Qamtza, Parma 2393 and Oxford 102 read Ben Qamtza and Casanatense H 3112, Parma 2559, and London 27089 read Qamtza.[33] The Qamtza reading attested in three manuscripts aligns too suspiciously with the Bavli, and since two of these manuscripts include some other obvious signs of talmudic influence, it seems likely that the Qamtza reading is also the result of talmudic influence.[34] Hence, only two readings remain: Bar Qamtza and Ben Qamtza, but these two readings, I maintain, are synonymous since both refer to the son of Qamtza: while Bar Qamtza is Aramaic for son of Qamtza, Ben Qamtza is Hebrew for son of Qamtza. Like the figures in Plautus's comedies, the intended and accidental guest share one and the same name. Moreover,

---

31. Casanatense H 3112 actually reads "Bar Qimtza," "בר קימצא."
32. In a similar vein, the names in the epilogue's saying vary amongst the textual witnesses and the names a manuscript cites in the epilogue rarely align with the names it cites in the story's opening.
33. Casanatense H 3112 actually reads "Qimtza," "קימצא."
34. For signs of talmudic influence, see, for example, the description of the slander and blemishes in Casanatense H 3112 and Parma 2559.

the transition from Hebrew to Aramaic in Oxford 102 suggests that the identical name was simply coordinated with the language of its respective sentence: the name of the intended guest is Ben Qamtza since he is mentioned in a Hebrew sentence while the name of the actual guest is Bar Qamtza since he is mentioned in an Aramaic sentence. I suspect that when copyists altered the original name – Ben/Bar Qamtza – to Qamtza or Ben Qamtzora, they were simply trying to create an easy way for the reader to distinguish between the host's friend and his foe. In truth, however, the story already included a straightforward distinction between the two figures: the host explicitly told the messenger to invite the son of Qamtza "my friend" ("רחמי"), but the messenger mistakenly invited the son of Qamtza "his enemy" ("שנאיה"). If the two men had not shared the same name, the host would not have had to specify that he meant to invite the son of Qamtza *his friend*.

Conclusion

The opening of Lamentations Rabbati's story of Bar Qamtza is deeply embedded in ancient banquet practices and literary themes. The host's messenger in ancient times delivered banquet invitations, and if a host were ever criticized for his guest list, the messenger was a convenient person to blame. In the spirit of the messenger's image in Roman culture, the central character of our story's first scene is a messenger who is at fault for the botched delivery of a banquet invitation.

The messenger's error is one of mistaken identity, a common theme in ancient Jewish and classical literature. Confusing two people with the same name is a comic variation on the age-old literary theme of mistaken identity. In mistaking Ben/Bar Qamtza, the host's enemy, for Ben/Bar Qamtza, the host's friend, our story follows the established contours of ancient comedy. In addition, ancient comedy also set the literary backdrop for the accidental extension of a banquet invitation due to a mix-up of names. In other words, central elements of the story's opening scene were apparently inspired by well-known features of ancient comedy. The appearance of comic elements in so tragic a story, however, is unexpected, and I shall return to this puzzling matter in a later chapter.

Chapter 6

The Banquet Affair
(ACT I SCENE 2)

In the wake of the banquet invitation delivered in Act I scene 1, Act I scene 2 jumps forward in time to the banquet itself:

6 עַל וישב בין האורחים; עאל ואשכחיה ביני ארסטטיה.

6 He (Bar Qamtza) **entered** and sat **among** the guests; he (the host) **entered** and found him (Bar Qamtza) **among** the banqueters.

The scene's perfectly balanced opening line sets the stage for the conflict between the banquet host and Bar Qamtza. After Bar Qamtza "entered" and sat "among" the guests, the host "entered" and discovered Bar Qamtza "among" the banqueters. While making his grand entrance before his waiting guests, the host is shocked to find Bar Qamtza sitting among them. Perhaps Bar Qamtza is sitting, rather than reclining, because the banquet has just begun and Jewish banqueters, according to t. Ber. 4:8 (cited above), started off sitting and only transitioned to the reclining position after the first appetizer course.[1] In addition, whereas Bar Qamtza sits among the "guests," "האורחים," the host finds Bar Qamtza among the "banqueters," "ארסטטיה," a Greek loanword stemming from

---

1. In contrast, line 15 – "מה אלין מסבין יתבין בשלותהון!," "How do they (dare) recline and sit at ease!" – does not seem to use the terms "sit" and "recline" to refer to distinct positions.

ἄριστης ("banqueter"), i.e., one who participates in a banquet or ἄριστον.[2] The Hebrew word for "guests," "אורחים," which appears in the first half of line 6, could have easily been repeated in the second half, making it possible that a Greek loanword for banqueters was introduced in order to evoke the atmosphere of Greek and Roman banquets.[3] By using the Greek term for "banqueters" instead of the Hebrew term for "guests," the story seems to conjure up images of elegant reclining, fine dining, fellowship, and entertainment, just those luxuries and pleasures which the host does not wish to bestow upon Bar Qamtza.

Appalled by his enemy's presence at his banquet, the host promptly sets out to expel Bar Qamtza:

7 אמר ליה: [את] שנאי ואת יתיב בגו ביתאי, קום ופוק לך מגו ביתאי!

8 אמר ליה: לא תבסרני ואנא יהיב לך טימי מגוסי.

9 אמר ליה: לית את מסובי הכא.

10 אמר ליה: לא תבסרני ואנא יהיב לך דלא אכיל ולא שתי.

11 אמר ליה: לית את מסובי הכא.

12 אמר ליה: אנא יהיב לך טימי הדה סעודתא.

13 אמר ליה: קום פוק ליך!

7 He said to him: [You] are my enemy and (yet) you sit within my home! Get up and get yourself out of my home!

8 He said to him: Do not shame me and I will pay you the cost of my meal.

---

2. See Nurit Shoval-Dudai, *A Glossary of Greek and Latin Loanwords in Post-Biblical Jewish Literature* (גלוסר המילים השאולות מן היוונית ומן הרומית במקורות היהודיים הבתר־מקראיים), (Israel: The Academy of the Hebrew Language, 2019), 60. See also Marcus Jastrow, *A Dictionary of the Targumim, the Talmud Babli and Yerushalmi, and the Midrashic Literature* (London: Luzac and G.P. Putnam, 1903), 120; Sokoloff, *Dictionary of Jewish Palestinian Aramaic*, 52; Henry George Liddell and Robert A. Scott, *A Greek-English Lexicon* (Oxford: Clarendon Press, 1966), 241; Daniel Sperber, *Greek in Talmudic Palestine* (Ramat Gan: Bar-Ilan University Press, 2012), 160n34. A second Greek loanword, "טימי," "cost," stemming from τιμή, appears (twice) later on in the scene and it too may have helped evoke a Hellenistic or Roman atmosphere.

3. Perhaps the transition from (mostly) Hebrew to Aramaic has something to do with the introduction of a Greek loanword.

9 He said to him: You are not reclining here.

10 He said to him: Do not shame me and I will pay you without eating or drinking.

11 He said to him: You are not reclining here.

12 He said to him: I will pay you the cost of the banquet.

13 He said to him: Get up and get yourself out!

The heated negotiation between the host and Bar Qamtza is framed by the host's repeated demand: "Get up and get yourself out!" The host will not suffer Bar Qamtza's presence at his banquet and he insists that Bar Qamtza exit the premises. In response to the host's initial demand, Bar Qamtza replies with a request: "Do not shame me and I will pay you the cost of my meal." Dreading the public humiliation of being thrown out of a banquet, Bar Qamtza offers the host a financial incentive to allow him to remain: Bar Qamtza will cover the expense of his meal. Unmoved by Bar Qamtza's offer, however, the host proclaims: "You are not reclining here," i.e., you will not transition from your sitting position (in the anteroom) to the reclining position (in the banquet hall) and remain for the main course of the banquet. In response to the host's refusal, Bar Qamtza ups the ante and offers not only to pay for his meal but also to refrain from eating or drinking. Bar Qamtza's two offers share the same literary format, "Do not shame me and I will pay you...", and their common structure highlights the gradual increase from offer to offer. The host, however, refuses the more generous offer as well, proclaiming a second time: "You are not reclining here." Reiterating his categorical rejection, the host refuses to budge. Desperate to remain at the banquet, Bar Qamtza volunteers to pay for the entire banquet, but, in response to this third offer, the host concludes the conversation by repeating his initial demand: "Get up and get yourself out!" By way of Bar Qamtza's ever more generous proposals and the host's repeated refusals, the tension escalates, gradually revealing Bar Qamtza's grave fear of humiliation and the host's blinding hatred.[4]

Reading scene 2 one might wonder about certain plot elements left unstated. Did Bar Qamtza attend the banquet after receiving a single

---

4. Cf. Levine Katz, "Qamtsa," 36.

invitation or did he wait for a second one?[5] Did Bar Qamtza realize an innocent mistake had been made or did he imagine that the host had intentionally set him up for a fall? Did the host figure out that his enemy's presence along with the absence of his friend of the same name was most likely the result of a name mix-up or, alternatively, did he suspect that Bar Qamtza intentionally set out to provoke him? Since the story does not indicate how to read between the lines and answer these questions, it seems that these lacunae are not essential to the plot.[6] Whether or not Bar Qamtza received one or two invitations, he probably assumed that the host had invited him for a reconciliation, although the host's hostile reaction to his presence would have quickly disabused him of this optimistic notion.[7] For his part, the host apparently never realized that Bar Qamtza had been invited to his banquet by accident. He also presumably believed that Bar Qamtza should have understood that, as his enemy, Bar Qamtza was unwelcome at his banquet regardless of any mitigating circumstances.

Widening our interpretive lens to include Greek and Roman banquet literature promises to shed new light on Act 1 scene 2, revealing how three features of the story resonate loudly against the literary backdrop of ancient banquet stories. The three resonating features are the abusive host, the uninvited guest, and the banquet conflict.

The Abusive Host

Across antiquity, the abusive and domineering host was a staple of banquet stories.[8] In the king parable of Matthew 22, the king has his attendants throw out a guest for not wearing a robe even though the king himself had filled the wedding hall with people randomly gathered off the street who did not have the time to return home and don special wedding garb:[9]

---

5. See Chapter 4 above.
6. See Levine Katz, "Qamtsa," 38; cf. Furstenberg, "Qamtza," 109. See also Chapter 4 above and Chapter 10, n. 2 below.
7. See D'Arms, "Roman *Convivium*," 313. See also Chapter 5, n. 21 above.
8. See L.R. Shero, "The Cena in Roman Satire," *Classical Philology* 18 (1923): 135; Gowers, *Loaded Table*, 26.
9. See Matt 22:8–10 (cited above in Chapter 5). See also Luz, *Matthew*, 46, 55–56.

εἰσελθὼν δὲ ὁ βασιλεὺς θεάσασθαι τοὺς ἀνακειμένους εἶδεν ἐκεῖ ἄνθρωπον οὐκ ἐνδεδυμένον ἔνδυμα γάμου, καὶ λέγει αὐτῷ Ἑταῖρε, πῶς εἰσῆλθες
ὧδε μὴ ἔχων ἔνδυμα γάμου; ὁ δὲ ἐφιμώθη. τότε ὁ βασιλεὺς εἶπεν τοῖς
διακόνοις, Δήσαντες αὐτοῦ πόδας καὶ χεῖρας ἐκβάλετε αὐτὸν εἰς τὸ
σκότος τὸ ἐξώτερον· ἐκεῖ ἔσται ὁ κλαυθμὸς καὶ ὁ βρυγμὸς τῶν ὀδόντων.
πολλοὶ γάρ εἰσιν κλητοί, ὀλίγοι δὲ ἐκλεκτοί.

But when the king came in to see the guests, he noticed a man there
who was not wearing a wedding robe, and he said to him, "Friend,
how did you get in here without a wedding robe?" And he was
speechless. Then the king said to his attendants, "Bind him hand
and foot, and throw him out into the outer darkness, where there
will be weeping and gnashing of teeth. For many are called, but few
are chosen."[10]

In a similar king parable from rabbinic literature, the king punishes
guests who did not bathe and dress up in preparation for his banquet
even though he had not announced when the banquet would take
place:

אמשל משל למה הדבר דומה. למלך שעשה סעודה והזמין הכל ולא קבע להם
זמן. אלו שהיו מקפידין על דבר המלך הלכו ורחצו וסכו וגיהצו את בגדיהם
והתקינו עצמן לסעודה. אילו שלא מקפידין על דבר המלך הלכו ונתעסקו
במלאכתן. כיון שהגיע זמן סעודה אמ' המלך: יבואו כולם בבת אחת. אילו
באו בכבודן ואילו באו בניוולן. אמ' המלך: אילו שהתקינו עצמן לסעודה יאכלו
בסעודתי ואילו שלא התקינו את עצמן לסעודתי לא יאכלו בסעודתי. יכול
יפטרו וילכו להן? אמ' המלך: לאו, אילו יהיו אוכלין ושותין ושמחין ואילו
עומדין על רגליהן ורואין ולוקין ומצטטערין שנ' "כה אמר ה' עבדי יאכלו
ואתם תערבו הנה עבדי ישתו ואתם תצמאו הנה עבדי ישמחו ואתם תבושו
הנה עבדי ירנו מטוב לב ואתם תצעקו מכאב לב ומשבר רוח תילילו" (ישעיה
סה:יג-יד). מי גרם להם? לפי שלא הקפידו על דבר המלך.

I will tell you a parable to what the matter may be compared. To a
king who made a banquet and invited everyone but did not set a time
for them (to come). Those who heeded the words of the king went
and washed (themselves) and anointed (themselves) and ironed
their clothes and prepared themselves for the banquet. Those who

---

10. Matt 22:11–14.

did not heed the words of the king went and occupied themselves with their work. When the time of the banquet arrived, the king said: Let everyone come at once. Those (who had prepared themselves) came in their dignified (attire) and those (who had not prepared themselves) came in their dirty (attire). The king said: Those who prepared themselves for the banquet will dine at my banquet and those who did not prepare themselves for my banquet will not dine at my banquet. Might they depart and go away? The king said: No, those (who prepared themselves) will dine, drink, and rejoice, and those (who did not) will stand on their feet, watch, be chastised and suffer as it is said: *Assuredly, thus said the Lord God: My servants shall eat, and you shall hunger; my servants shall drink, and you shall thirst; my servants shall rejoice, and you shall be shamed; my servants shall shout in gladness, and you shall cry out in anguish, howling in heartbreak* (Isa 65:13–14). What caused them (to suffer)? That they did not heed the word of the king.[11]

Infuriated by those who had not heeded his invitation immediately and therefore attended his party dirty and disheveled, the king forced them to stand by and watch as the clean and elegantly clad banqueters happily dined and drank.

The Roman satirist Juvenal critiques selfish and abusive hosts, like the host Virro, who mistreat poor guests of lower social status.[12] These hosts serve splendid and expensive dishes to themselves and their peers while only offering basic fare to guests of lower rank.[13] In addition, Juvenal

---

11. Midr. Mish. 16 (*Midrash Mishle*, ed. Burton L. Visotzky [New York, NY: The Jewish Theological Seminary of America, 2002], 131–32). Other versions of the parable appear in b. Shabb. 153a and Qoh. Rab. (in Midr. Rab.) 9:8. (According to Seneca the Elder, Cicero's son Marcus had a banquet guest flogged when he found out that the man had once insulted his father [*Suas.* 7.13]. See also Katherine M.D. Dunbabin, "Ut Graeco More Biberetur: Greeks and Romans on the Dining Couch," in *Meals in a Social Context: Aspects of the Communal Meal in the Hellenistic and Roman World*, ed. Inge Nielsen and Hanne Sigismund Nielsen [Langelandsgade: Aarhus University Press, 1998], 91.)

12. See Juvenal, *Sat.* 5.111–13. (The ideal host was expected to treat his guests fairly. See Hudson, "Food," 198.)

13. See Juvenal, *Sat.* 5.24–155.

warns that if, as a humble guest, you should dare present yourself as someone important, "you'll be dragged by the foot and dumped out of doors like Cacus when Hercules beat him up" ("Duceris planta velut ictus ab Hercule Cacuset ponere foris").[14] Like Juvenal's caricatured banquet host, Horace's earlier portrait of the self-centered and conceited host Nasiedienus and Petronius's depiction of the vulgar and boorish host Trimalchio critique what many Roman authors of the time perceived as the deterioration of Roman values – the moral decline from modesty and frugality to gluttony and luxury.[15] Nostalgically viewing the past as an idyllic era in which simple Romans maintained modest and unassuming lifestyles, these Roman satirists enlisted the boorish (nouveau-riche) and domineering banquet host in order to criticize the lavish excess and wealthy decadence of their own times.

Moreover, Juvenal added a further element to the satirists' critique when he enrolled the gluttonous banquet host in his indictment of the Roman system of patronage.[16] Roman patronage, as noted above, was a reciprocal relationship between patrons and clients entailing mutual services and benefits. Traditionally, social venues like banquets were used to enhance and negotiate patronage relationships by fostering friendships and mediating relationships. For Juvenal, however, the awful behavior of hosts like Virro revealed that the patronage system had gone awry. When wealthy Roman patrons did not hesitate to utterly humiliate their socially inferior clients, patronage's core value of reciprocity collapsed.

I propose that against the backdrop of the conceited and domineering

---

14. Juvenal, *Sat.* 5.125–27 (*Juvenal and Persius*, trans. Susanna Morton Braund [LCL, Cambridge, MA: Harvard University Press, 2004], ad loc.).

15. See, for example, Polybius, *Hist.* 6.57; Sallust, *Bell. Iug.* 4.5–9; Florus, *Epit.* 1.47; Lucan, *Phars.* 1.158–82; Livy, *Ab urbe cond.* 39:6; Tacitus, *Hist.* 2.38; Pliny, *Nat.* 14.28; Horace, *Sat.* 2.6. See also A.W. Lintott, "Imperial Expansion and Moral Decline in the Roman Republic," *Historia* 21 (1972): 626–38; Barbara Levick, "Morals, Politics, and the Fall of the Roman Republic," *Greece and Rome* 29 (1982): 53–62.; Deri Pode Miles, "Forbidden Pleasures: Sumptuary Laws and Ideology of Moral Decline in Ancient Rome" (PhD diss., University College London, 1987), 30–34, 330–33. On the portraits of Nasiedienus and Trimalchio, see Horace, *Sat.* 2.8; Petronius, *Satyr.* 26–79. See also Shero, "Cena," 135, 139; Hudson, "Food," 31–32.

16. Susanna Morton Braund, trans., *Juvenal and Persius*, 213.

hosts of ancient banquet literature, the abusive and uncaring host in the story of Bar Qamtza emerges as a stock character and grim caricature. In line with Matthew's king, Virro, and other abusive hosts in ancient banquet literature, our host is a volatile and disruptive force at his very own banquet.

Like the tales of the Roman satirists, the story of Bar Qamtza enlists the abusive host to convey a social critique (and moral lesson). However, this Jewish critique differs markedly from those in the parallel Roman satires. Whereas Roman satirists recruited the conceited or abusive host to condemn a gluttonous society or a failing patronage system, the story of Bar Qamtza does not address these matters.[17] Neither the story nor its immediate literary context indicate that late Second Temple Jerusalemites were ludicrously lavish, and it is highly unlikely that Bar Qamtza, the host's enemy, was the host's client as well. In other words, neither gluttony nor patronage is at issue. Rather, I submit that the host's behavior is unconscionable and inexcusable because ancient Jewish morals dictated that no Jew should ever treat a fellow Jew in so humiliating a fashion. The host's deep hatred and lack of empathy for Bar Qamtza disclose his own fractured sense of solidarity with a fellow Jew.[18]

All societies feature personal relationships anchored in reciprocal exchange and a sense of corporate solidarity based on shared ideals or myths, but the balance of these two forms of social relations differs from society to society. Roman society, which assigned a prominent role to patronage and euergetism (i.e., private benefactions donated in exchange for public honors), was largely defined by reciprocity, whereas Jewish society, which valued (unreciprocated) charity and promoted a broad sense of mutual responsibility, was largely defined by solidarity.[19] Hence,

---

17. See Ben Shahar, "Abolishment of the Sacrifice," 591. Cf. Yisraeli-Taran, *Legends of the Destruction*, 12–13; Levine Katz, "Qamtsa," 38.
18. Cf. Jonathan Wyn Schofer, *Confronting Vulnerability: The Body and the Divine in Rabbinic Ethics* (Chicago, IL: University of Chicago Press, 2010), 96–97, 107.
19. See Martin Goodman, *The Ruling Class of Judaea: The Origins of the Jewish Revolt Against Rome AD 66–70* (Cambridge: Cambridge University Press, 1987), 126–29, 247; "The Origins of the Great Revolt: A Conflict of Status Criteria," in *Greece and Rome in Eretz Israel: Collected Essays*, ed. A. Kasher, U. Rappaport,

while the host's inordinate hatred for his enemy did not violate Roman norms of reciprocity, his antipathy for a fellow Jew shows a flawed and weak sense of Jewish solidarity.

Viewing the host's immoral behavior as a key moment in the process which ultimately led to the fall of Jerusalem, commentators have linked our story to a well-known Tannaitic tradition. The period of the Tannaim (circa 60–220 CE) preceded that of the Amoraim, and the noted tradition appears, with some differences, in the Tosefta and both Talmuds:[20]

אמר ר' יוחנן בן תורתא: מפני מה חרבה שילו? מפני בזיון קדשים שבתוכה. ירושלים בניין הראשון מפני מה חרבה? מפני עבודה זרה וגילוי עריות ושפיכות דמים שהיה בתוכה. אבל באחרונה מכירין אנו בהן שהן עמילין בתורה וזהירין במעשרות, מפני מה גלו? מפני שאוהבין את הממון ושונאין איש את רעהו לפני המקום ושקלה הכתוב כנגד עבודה זרה וגלוי עריות ושפיכות דמים.[21]

Rabbi Yohanan ben Torta said: On account of what was Shiloh destroyed? On account of the desecration of sanctified objects which (took place) in it. On account of what was Jerusalem's first building destroyed? On account of idolatry, licentiousness, and bloodshed which was in it. But regarding the latter (building), we know of them (the people of that time) that they labored in Torah and were meticulous about tithes, on account of what were they exiled? On account of loving money and hating one's fellow before the Place

---

and G. Fuks (Jerusalem: Yad Ben Zvi and Israel Exploration Society, 1990), 49; *Rome and Jerusalem: The Clash of Ancient Civilizations* (London: Penguin, 2008), 235–36; Seth Schwartz, *Were the Jews a Mediterranean Society? Reciprocity and Solidarity in Ancient Judaism* (Princeton, NJ: Princeton University Press, 2010), 1–20; Tzvi Novick, "Charity and Reciprocity: Structures of Benevolence in Rabbinic Literature," *HTR* 105 (2012): 33–35, 52. See also Paul Veyne, *Bread and Circuses: Historical Sociology and Political Pluralism* (London: Allen Lane, 1990), 19–34, who compares Roman reciprocity to Christian solidarity.

20. See, for example, Maharsha in b. Git., ad loc. (s.vv. *uvaʿal devaveih bar qamtza*); b. Yoma 9b (s.vv. *aval miqdash bet*); Efron, "Bar-Kokhva," 210; Levine Katz, "Qamtsa," 50. Cf. David C. Kraemer, *Responses to Suffering in Classical Rabbinic Literature* (Oxford: Oxford University Press, 1995), 143.

21. T. Menaḥ. 13:22 according to Vienna Heb. 20 with abbreviations completed. See also y. Yoma 1:1, 38c; b. Yoma 9a–b.

(God) and Scripture considers it (hating one another[22]) equivalent to idolatry, licentiousness and bloodshed.

According to this tradition, attributed to Rabbi Yohanan ben Torta, the Jews of the late Second Temple period conscientiously studied the Torah and carefully tithed their produce. They did not desecrate the temple, as did the Israelites responsible for the destruction of the tabernacle at Shiloh, and were innocent of the three cardinal sins – licentiousness, idolatry and murder – which brought down the First Temple. In contrast to the sins of earlier generations, the fatal flaws of these late Second Temple Jews were common moral shortcomings: greed and hatred.[23]

If we read our story through the prism of the tradition attributed to Rabbi Yohanan ben Torta, we find that the host's vicious reception of Bar Qamtza is a perfect example of "hating one's fellow before God" (while the accompanying notion of "loving money" is akin to Roman complaints over the deterioration of traditional Roman frugality). Since the destruction of the Second Temple could have been ascribed to any of a slew of moral flaws or sins, the central role ascribed to hatred in both Rabbi Yohanan ben Torta's tradition and the story of Bar Qamtza is striking and strongly suggests that the earlier "hatred" tradition helped inspire our story.[24] In presenting the host's enmity for a fellow Jew as an ultimate cause of the destruction of the Second Temple, the story of Bar Qamtza, I suggest, echoed the Tannaitic tradition attributed to Rabbi Yohanan ben Torta while giving it narrative form, installing the early message in a new medium. For both sources, the Second Temple

---

22. See t. Menaḥ. 13:22 according to the *editio princeps* and Genizah Fragment T-S F2(2).76; cf. Genizah Fragment Paris Mosseri VIII 472.

23. In a similar (and perhaps inspirational) vein, Josephus argued that the fall of Jerusalem ultimately stemmed from (the Thucydidean notion of) civil strife. See, for example, Josephus, *J.W.* 1.10. See also Per Bilde, "The Causes of the Jewish War according to Josephus," *JSJ* 10 (1979): 198; Gottfried Mader, *Josephus and the Politics of Historiography: Apologetic and Impression Management in the Bellum Judaicum* (Leiden: Brill, 2000), 55–103; Jonathan Price, "Josephus' Reading of Thucydides: A Test Case in the *Bellum Iudaicum*," in *Thucydides – A Violent Teacher?: History and its Representations*, ed. Georg Rechenauer and Vassiliki Pothou (Göttingen: V & R Unipress, 2011), 79–98; Chapter 9 below.

24. The destruction of the temple not only *could have* been ascribed to other sins, it *was*. See, for example, the list on b. Shabb. 119b.

flourished only so long as the members of the Jewish community lived together in peaceful harmony. Once the social ties and sense of solidarity that bound the Jewish community together weakened enough to permit the emergence of cold-hearted hatred, the temple's end was just a matter of time. In pinpointing the absence of Jewish solidarity, rather than covenantal violations or cardinal crimes, as an ultimate cause of the temple's destruction, our story promotes an idea that has resonated powerfully throughout Jewish history.[25]

It bears noting that in lieu of the Tosefta's phrase – "ושונאין איש את רעהו לפני המקום," "and hating one's fellow before the Place (God)" – both Talmuds enlist the phrase "שנאת חינם," literally "free hatred."[26] The phrase "שנאת חינם" is usually translated as "groundless hatred" or "hatred without cause,"[27] and, in accordance with these translations, some commentators have argued that the host loathed Bar Qamtza for no reason at all.[28] However, since all animosity stems from some perceived

---

25. Goldenberg has argued that since the sages could think of no monumental crime that would have warranted the suffering incurred during the first century revolt against Rome, they resorted to the "moral generality" (Robert Goldenberg, "Early Rabbinic Explanations of the Destruction of Jerusalem," *JJS* 33 [1982]: 523) of Rabbi Yohanan ben Torta's tradition which, as nothing more than "homiletic moralizing," failed to relieve the people's despair (Robert Goldenberg, "The Destruction of the Jerusalem Temple: Its Meaning and Its Consequences," in *The Cambridge History of Judaism: Volume IV: The Late Roman-Byzantine Period*, ed. Steven T. Katz [Cambridge: Cambridge University Press, 2006], 197n17). I submit, however, that Goldenberg has overlooked the ideological core of the Tannaitic tradition (and of our story) which contends that the flourishing of the Jewish community is predicated on a strong sense of solidarity and mutual care.

26. I wonder if perhaps the juxtaposition of financial greed and hatred inspired the application of "free," another notion from the financial realm, to hatred. The introduction of the term "free hatred," which lent a financial dimension to hatred, perhaps facilitated the omission of greed from the Bavli's version of the tradition. See also Jonathan Klawans, "Josephus, the Rabbis, and Responses to Catastrophes Ancient and Modern," *JQR* 100 (2010): 294. (The term "שנאת חינם" also appears in Genizah Fragment T-S F2(2).76 of Tosefta Menahot but is probably not original there.)

27. See, for example, Leo Jung, trans. *The Babylonian Talmud: Yoma* (London: Soncino, 1939), ad loc.

28. See Maharsha in the Bavli, ad loc. (s.vv. *deshada bei muma beniv*); Moses Sofer, *Hidushei hatam sofer: Gittin* (חידושי חתם סופר: גיטין), (Jerusalem: s.n., 5730

wrong, slight, or prejudice, it is unlikely that anyone ever imagined that the Jews of the late Second Temple period hated randomly and without any cause.[29] Accordingly, "hatred for no *good* reason" better captures the true sense of the hyperbolic "שנאת חינם." Furthermore, while our story (as argued above) never reveals why the host hates Bar Qamtza, Bar Qamtza's drastic actions in the future suggest that some measure of disapproval or dislike may have been warranted. Hence, the host's moral flaw is not baseless hatred but irrational hatred, that is, excessive enmity disproportionate to the underlying cause. Barring grave criminal violations, nothing Bar Qamtza could have done would have justified the host's hateful behavior towards him.

The Uninvited Guest

I would like to suggest that Bar Qamtza is perceived as the ἄκλητος – the univited guest – who appears as a stock figure in the banquet literature of classical antiquity. Ancient sources make it clear that it was highly improper to enter a banquet uninvited;[30] yet despite this ideal, or perhaps because of it, the uninvited guest appears time and again in banquet stories, often as a disruptive force.[31] The uninvited guest complicated

---

[1969–1970]), ad loc. (52c, s.vv. *mai dekhtiv*); Beni Kalmanzon and Shimon Fogel, *Why the Land is in Ruins: Investigations into the Legends of the Destruction* (על מה אבדה הארץ: עיונים באגדות החורבן), (Otniel: Giluy, 5769 [2008–2009]), 21–22. Cf. Jonathan Duker, "Piety or Privilege? A Talmudic View of the Fall of the Second Commonwealth," *Milin Havivin* 5 (2010–2011): 42–43.

29. In fact, when Ben Sira enlists a similar phrase in the passage: "יש נכלם ומבטיח רעהו וקונהו שונא חנם," "There exists a person who promises to a friend a favor out of shame and made him an enemy to no purpose" (Sir 20:23 according to Genizah Fragment T-S 12.867 with translation by Benjamin G. Wright, "Wisdom of Iesous son of Sirach," in *A New English Translation of the Septuagint*, ed. Albert Pietersam and Benjamin G. Wright [New York, NY: Oxford University Press, 2007], 735), the cause for the hatred – unfulfilled promises – is made explicit. Shamed by his poverty, the pauper promises his friend riches he cannot deliver and thereby unwisely turns his friend into an enemy. (Cf. Ps 69:5.)

30. See Chapter 5, n. 2 above. See also Cynthia Damon, *The Mask of the Parasite: A Pathology of Roman Patronage* (Ann Arbor: University of Michigan Press, 1997), 59–60.

31. See Burkhard Fehr, "Entertainers at the *Symposion*: The *Akletoi* in the Archaic Period," in *Sympotica: A Symposium on the Symposion*, ed. Oswyn Murray

the banquet: he had not been assigned a seat, he was not taken into consideration when the food and drink were prepared, and he might taint the friendly atmosphere of the banquet calibrated by the careful choice of guests.

In the *Iliad*, Menelaus shows up uninvited to his brother Agamemnon's banquet presumably because he felt that his close relationship with his brother rendered an invitation unnecessary.[32] Similarly, in Plutarch's *Symposium of the Seven Sages*, Gorgus, the brother of Periander, the host, is welcomed by his brother to the banquet even though he was not invited.[33] In the *Odyssey*, Odysseus, disguised as a beggar, is graciously hosted by his swineherd Eumaeus even though he was not invited to Eumaeus's banquet.[34] Later on, when the disguised and uninvited Odysseus begs for scraps (in his own castle), the abusive Antinous throws a footstool at him.[35]

Archilochus describes how a certain Pericles shamelessly entered banquets uninvited as if he were the host's good friend. Drinking unmixed wine, rather than the traditional blend of wine and water, and neglecting to help fund the banquets, Pericles attended in order to satiate his hunger rather than cultivate friendships. In a similar vein, Asius tells of an old fat-licker who crashed a wedding because he desired broth.[36]

In Plato's *Symposium*, Socrates encourages Aristodemus to attend Agathon's banquet even though he was not invited, and Aristodemus agrees to attend – albeit as Socrates' guest. When Aristodemus enters

---

(Oxford: Clarendon Press, 1990), 185–95; Joel C. Relihan, "Rethinking the History of the Literary Symposium," *ICS* 17 (1992): 215–16; Matthias Klinghardt, *Gemeinschaftsmahl und Mahlgemeinschaft: Soziologie und Liturgie frühchristlicher Mahlfeiern* (Tübingen: A. Francke, 1996), 84–97; Taussig, *In the Beginning*, 26, 83; Sean Corner, "The Politics of the Parasite (Part One)," *Phoenix* 67 (2013): 45–50; Lee, *Paul*, 83; Louise A. Gosbell, *"The Poor, the Crippled, the Blind, and the Lame:" Physical and Sensory Disability in the Gospels of the New Testament* (Tübingen: Mohr Siebeck, 2018), 190–92.

32. See Homer, *Il.* 2.408–9.

33. See Plutarch, *Sept. sap. conv.* 160D. See also Relihan, "Literary Symposium," 225.

34. Homer, *Od.* 13.401–45.

35. Homer, *Od.* 17.445–62.

36. See Athenaeus, *Deipn.* 1.7F, 3.125D–E. See also Gosbell, *Disability in the Gospels*, 191.

the banquet hall without Socrates, who had fallen behind, Agathon warmly welcomes him, assigning him a place to recline and apologizing for having failed to find him the day before when he had searched him out to invite him.[37] Later on, the drunken Alcibiades enters the banquet uninvited and, like Aristodemus, he reclines only when Agathon invites him to do so. Unlike Aristodemus, however, Alcibiades disrupts the banquet by entering late and drunk, and by appointing himself head of the symposium.[38] In Xenophon's *Symposium*, Philip the comedian arrives uninvited to Callias's private banquet, and, when he asks to be admitted, Callias offers him a seat with the expectation that Philip would enhance the banquet with comic entertainment.[39] Towards the end of Plato's *Symposium*, a group of revelers sneak in to the drinking-party and without waiting for Agathon's invitation, they take over the banquet and ruin its order and decorum.[40]

In Plautus's *The Persian*, Dordalus the pimp appears at a banquet uninvited, and, though he is offered a place to recline, the banqueters proceed to mock and assault him.[41] In Petronius's *Satyricon*, the drunken Habinnas enters Trimalchio's banquet uninvited, functioning as a disruptive force akin to the drunken Alcibiades of Plato's *Symposium*.[42] In Plutarch's *Brutus*, Favonius enters Cassius's banquet uninvited, and, when assigned a modest place to recline, Favonius aggressively makes his way to the central couch.[43] Like Plutarch's Favonius, Lucian's Alcidamas also enters a banquet uninvited and also refuses the seat offered him. In addition, Alcidamas is a nuisance throughout Aristaenetus's banquet, knocking over the lamp and then setting out to rape the flute-girl in the sudden darkness at the banquet's end.[44] In Macrobius's *Saturnalia*, the banqueters frown when the uninvited (and abrasive) Evangelus interrupts

---

37. See Plato, *Symp.* 174A–175A.
38. See Plato, *Symp.* 212D–213A. See also Gosbell, *Disability in the Gospels*, 191.
39. See Xenophon, *Symp.* 1.11–16.
40. See Plato, *Symp.* 223B.
41. See Plautus, *Pers.* 777–858.
42. See Petronius, *Satyr.* 65–66.
43. See Plutarch, *Brut.* 34.4.
44. See Lucian (vol. 1), *Symp.* 12, 45–47.

their leisurely gathering. The kind-hearted host, Praetextatus, however, welcomes Evangelus along with his uninvited friend Dysarius.[45]

In short, at times the uninvited guest of classical banquet literature is simply a close friend or relative of the host who feels comfortable joining the banquet without a formal invitation, but at other times the uninvited guest is a gatecrasher or parasite.[46] Usually the uninvited guest does not recline until the host extends him an invitation and assigns him a place to do so, but in some cases the uninvited guest disregards the seat selected for him or does not even bother to wait for an impromptu invitation. As a parodic and stock figure, the uninvited guest is hungry and gluttonous, needy and dependent, mocked and abused, comical and entertaining. With his inappropriate behavior, he is disruptive and abrasive, willing to suffer insults and humiliation in order to fill his empty belly.[47]

Though not a late-comer to the banquet, Bar Qamtza is viewed by the host as a typical parasitic uninvited guest: an unwanted and intrusive guest who lacks a formal invitation. As the uninvited guest, Bar Qamtza's purportedly inappropriate behavior triggers a quarrel which ultimately leads to his embarrassing ejection from the banquet. However, the truth of the matter is that Bar Qamtza *was* invited to the banquet and his behavior demonstrates that he is not the typical uninvited guest or greedy parasite. Unlike the typical uninvited guest, Bar Qamtza is willing to abstain from eating and even to pay for the entire banquet.[48] He is neither greedy nor gluttonous, and unlike a parasite he is unwilling to suffer shame and humiliation. I propose that Bar Qamtza is not a parasitic uninvited guest, but is only mistaken for one, a mistake that transforms the story from a comedy into a tragedy. The various comic elements of Act I seem to set the stage for a comedy, but when the host treats Bar Qamtza as an uninvited guest, as an inferior ripe for

---

45. See Macrobius, *Saturn.* 1.7.1–2, 1.7.10. See also Relihan, "Literary Symposium," 239.

46. See W. Geoffrey Arnott, *Alexis: The Fragments: A Commentary* (Cambridge: Cambridge University Press, 1996), 611.

47. See Fehr, "Entertainers at the *Symposion*," 186–87.

48. In the continuation of the Bar Qappara story cited in Chapter 5, Bar Qappara similarly hopes to show that he does not pine for the banquet's culinary delights.

humiliation, he sets in motion the series of events which culminates in the tragic destruction of the temple.

The Banquet Conflict

Just like Act I scene 2's abusive host and uninvited guest, the scene's conflict is also a common feature of classical banquet stories.[49] For example, in *The Flatterers* of Eupolis, the slave Acestor is dragged out of a banquet for making a distasteful joke.[50] Throughout the final scene of Plautus's *The Persian*, Dordalus is physically assaulted and verbally abused by a group of banqueters.[51] When Fortunata rebukes her husband Trimalchio for kissing a waiter in the banquet of Petronius's *Satyricon*, Trimalchio throws a cup at her face and then upbraids her.[52] In Juvenal's depiction of Virro's banquet, a fight breaks out amongst the guests of humbler station when they are served bad wine.[53] In Lucian's account of Aristaenetus's banquet, the banquet disintegrates into a brawl when Zenothemis takes Hermon's portion of fowl for himself because it was plumper than his own serving.[54] In light of the numerous conflicts in ancient literary banquets, the altercation between the host and Bar Qamtza, which leads to Bar Qamtza's expulsion from the banquet, is in keeping with the conflict theme of ancient banquet literature. Just as the pretext for the conflict in the story of Bar Qamtza is a case of mistaken identity typical of ancient comedy, the conflict itself is a common theme in ancient banquet stories.

Although inappropriate, disruptive, and abusive behavior plagued literary banquets, it threatened actual banquets as well. Many ancient

---

49. See Chapter 3, n. 51 above. See also Henry A. Fischel, "Studies in Cynicism and the Ancient Near East: The Transformation of a *Chria*," in *Religions in Antiquity: Essays in Memory of Erwin Ramsdell Goodenough*, ed. Jacob Neusner (Leiden: Brill, 1968), 372–411.
50. See Athenaeus, *Deipn.* 6.236E–237A. See also John Wilkins, *The Boastful Chef: The Discourse of Food in Ancient Greek Comedy* (Oxford: Oxford University Press, 2000), 75.
51. See n. 41 above.
52. Petronius, *Satyricon* 74.
53. See Juvenal, *Sat.* 5.25–29. See also Shero, "Cena," 238–40.
54. See Lucian (vol. 1), *Symp.* 43–47.

social groups, as noted above, sought to regulate banquet behavior; the Iobakchoi even authorized officials to expel disruptive or disturbing banqueters.[55] Hence, the conflict theme of ancient banquet literature amplified a potential threat to actual banquets, transforming actual (but infrequent) conflict into a standard feature of the literary banquet. In addition, Greek and Roman banquet regulations suggest that the altercation in the story of Bar Qamtza not only embodied a common literary theme but also evoked the threat of conflict widely feared by actual ancient banqueters. However, whereas banquet by-laws were primarily designed to regulate the behavior of unruly guests, it is the banquet host who instigates the conflict in the story of Bar Qamtza. Bar Qamtza's mortifying expulsion, through no fault of his own, gave concrete expression to many a banqueter's worst nightmare – a cruel host who abuses his authority to utterly humiliate a guest.

Conclusion

The messenger's confusion of the two Bar (or Ben) Qamtzas in Act 1 scene 1 triggers an explosive clash between the host and Bar Qamtza in scene 2. The dramatic tension gradually escalates as Bar Qamtza's offers become ever more generous, while the host remains stubbornly unbending. Bar Qamtza's consecutive pleadings pointedly illustrate his great fear of humiliation. This intense dread of humiliation is in keeping with the significant role assigned to honor and shame in ancient rabbinic circles, as well as in the Roman Mediterranean and ancient Persia – cultures which assigned public dignity far more importance than do modern western societies.[56] For his part, the host's repeated refusals express his severe loathing of Bar Qamtza. Echoing the Tannaitic claim that the Second Temple was destroyed on account of hatred, the story of Bar Qamtza gives it narrative form.

The scene's various elements – the abusive host, the uninvited guest, and the banquet conflict – are, as outlined above, common features

---

55. See Chapter 3, n. 49 above.
56. See Jeffrey L. Rubenstein, *The Culture of the Babylonian Talmud* (Baltimore, MD: Johns Hopkins University Press, 2003), 67–79; Schwartz, *Reciprocity and Solidarity*, 140–65. See also Chapter 3, n. 43 above.

of Greek and Roman banquet stories. Intricately entwined within the banquet literary tradition, the story of Bar Qamtza enlists the tradition's stock characters and standard themes while adjusting and transforming them for the local Jewish context. The abusive Jerusalemite host is akin to the self-centered host of ancient banquet stories, but while the domineering Roman host is the epitome of decadence, moral decay, or the uncouth patron, our story's Jewish host is an example of irrational hatred and a deficient sense of solidarity. In the host's eyes, Bar Qamtza is the comical and parasitic uninvited guest familiar from ancient banquet literature, a social inferior to be ridiculed and humiliated. In his own eyes, however, Bar Qamtza is a proper guest, no different than any other. When these two views collide, they erupt in a heated conflict, as literary banquets often do, causing our story quickly to transition from comedy to tragedy.

Chapter 7

The Passive Bystanders
(ACT I SCENE 3)

On the heels of the conflict between the banquet host and Bar Qamtza, Act I scene 3 indicts the passive bystanders, that is, Bar Qamtza's fellow banqueters who witness his humiliation but fail to protest. The scene unfolds in two parallel lines, the first in Hebrew, which condemns the sage Zechariah ben Avqulas, and the second in Aramaic, which denounces the Jerusalemite banqueters:

14 והיה שם זכריה בן אבקולס והיה ספק בידו למחות ולא מיחה.

15 מאן דנפק ליה, אמר בנפשיה: מה אלין מסבין יתבין בשלותהון?!

14 Zechariah ben Avqulas was present and he had the opportunity to protest but did not protest.

15 When he (Bar Qamtza) went out he said to himself: How do they (dare) recline and sit at ease!

The appearance of a Hebrew line, line 14, in a mostly Aramaic story is striking, and two other factors further compound line 14's poor fit in the narrative. First, lines 14 and 15 both indict passive bystander(s), so when juxtaposed to line 15, line 14 is largely redundant. Second, whereas line 15 naturally refers to Bar Qamtza's fellow banqueters, presumably the afore-mentioned "precious children of Zion," line 14's Zechariah ben Avqulas appears nowhere else in the running narrative; Zechariah ben Avqulas shows up once again only in the second (late and supplementary) epilogue, line 32.[1] In sum, since line 14 stands out as a Hebrew line in a mostly Aramaic story – because it is repetitious and refers to a character otherwise unmentioned in the story – it seems likely, as Paul Mandel has suggested, that lines 14 and 32 were added to an earlier reading of the story which did not refer to Zechariah ben Avqulas.[2] Although no textual witness has preserved this earlier reading, the arguments in its favor are strong. I will therefore investigate the earlier line, line 15, first, before turning to line 14, the later addition.

Line 15

Expelled from the banquet at the start of line 15 – "When he went out" – Bar Qamtza silently broods over the seemingly oblivious behavior of his fellow banqueters. How, Bar Qamtza asks himself, could witnesses to the host's abusive behavior go on to "recline and sit at ease?" Furiously indignant, Bar Qamtza wonders how onlookers to the wrong done him could possibly sit idly by. Is there any justification for continuing to dine at a banquet from which a fellow banqueter was so ruthlessly ejected?

In contrast to scene 2's focus on the host's abusive behavior, scene 3 turns to the guests, to the passive banqueters who refuse to stand by Bar Qamtza. If scene 2, in line with the Tannaitic tradition attributed to Rabbi Yohanan ben Torta, identified hatred as an ultimate cause of the temple's destruction, scene 3 marks out apathy as a more proximate and immediate cause. Not hatred, but the callous indifference of the Jerusalemites, perhaps in tandem with greed (in the spirit of Rabbi Yohanan ben Torta's factor of "loving money"), infuriates Bar Qamtza. Unwilling to lift a finger to help a fellow guest and disrupt their dinner or endanger their relationship with the host, the guests turn a blind eye to Bar Qamtza's humiliation.[3]

While the guests' cold apathy does not echo the Tannaitic tradition which interprets the temple's fall as a punishment for hatred, it gives

---

1. While the appearance of one summarizing epilogue is entirely natural, the appearance of a second is surprising and seemingly redundant.
2. See Mandel, "Tales of the Destruction," 148–49.
3. Cf. Furstenberg, "Qamtza," 109.

narrative form to a theme found in Lamentations Rabbati (and else-where in rabbinic literature):[4]

אמר רב עמרם בריה דר' שמעון בר אבא א"ר שמעון בר אבא א"ר חנינא: לא
חרבה ירושלם אלא בשביל שלא הוכיחו זה את זה שנא' "היו שריה כאילים"
(איכה א:ו). מה איל זה ראשו של זה בצד זנבו של זה, אף ישראל שבאותו
הדור כבשו פניהם בקרקע ולא הוכיחו זה את זה.

Rav Amram son of Rabbi Simeon bar Abba said in Rabbi Simeon bar
Abba's name in Rabbi Hanina's name: Jerusalem was destroyed only
because they did not rebuke one another for it is said: *Their leaders
were like stags* (Lam 1:6). Just as with the stag, the head of one is at
the side of the other's tale, so Israel of that generation hid their faces
in the earth and did not rebuke one another.[5]

ר' סימון בשם ר' שמעון בר אבא ור' שמעון בן לקיש בשם ר' יהושע: מה
"אילים" (איכה א:ו) הללו בשעה שרב הופכין פניהם אלו מאלו, כך היו גדולי
ישראל רואין דבר עבירה והופכין פניהם ממנו. אמ' להם הב"ה: תבא שעה
ואני עושה לכם כן.

Rabbi Simon said in the name of Rabbi Simeon bar Abba and Rabbi
Simeon ben Lakish said in the name of Rabbi Joshua: As *stags* (Lam
1:6) turn their faces one beneath the other in the time of intense heat,
so the eminent of Israel would see a transgression and turn their faces
from it. The holy one, blessed be he, said to them: A time will come
and I will do the same to you.[6]

The theme set forth in these traditions is that Jerusalem fell because
the eminent of Israel turned their faces away from transgression, hiding
their faces in the earth rather than rebuking one another. When the
eminent of Israel failed to oppose iniquity, and cowardly overlooked
transgressions, when they worried more for their own comfort than for
the welfare of others, they undermined the legitimacy of their leadership.

---

4. See Yisraeli-Taran, *Legends of the Destruction*, 17.

5. Lam. Rab. 1:20 (p. 93) according to Munich 229 with translation by H. Freed-man, *Shabbath* (London: Soncino, 1972), ad loc., slightly revised. See also b. Shabb. 119b.

6. Lam. Rab. 1:6 (p. 70) according to Munich 229 with translation by Cohen, *Midrash Rabbah*, ad loc., slightly modified.

In Bar Qamtza's eyes, ignoring wrongful behavior and failing to reprove the wrongdoer is precisely the fault of his fellow banqueters. Instead of confronting the host and protesting his cruelty, they not only turned away their faces, they continued to joyfully participate in his banquet. While the messenger's unfortunate error followed by the host's excessive hatred set the stage, it is the banqueters' indifference to his plight which spurs Bar Qamtza to action.

The transition from the host's blind hatred in scene 2 to the guests' aloof indifference in scene 3 intensifies the story's critique of Jewish solidarity in two ways. First, scene 3 broadens the scope of the guilty party. Whereas scene 2 homes in on the moral flaw of a solitary individual, scene 3 reveals the moral shortcomings of a group, of the community of Jerusalemites who merrily sit by while one of their own is savagely disgraced. Unlike the abusive host who could be excused or explained away as a rare and atypical rotten apple, the passive bystanders reveal the moral bankruptcy of Jerusalemite society as a whole.

Second, scene 3 enhances the critique of the Jews' deficient solidarity by removing hatred from the equation. Hatred is such a powerful and overwhelming emotion that the behavior it triggers might be viewed as an anomaly, unrepresentative of the ambient society's values. In other words, it is theoretically possible that the host's community was imbued with a robust sense of solidarity but his inordinate hatred for Bar Qamtza blinded him to the social ties which bind them together. Scene 3, however, comes to belie this possibility and expose the defective fellowship of the ambient Jerusalem community. The casual neglect and cowardly indifference of the guests, unprompted by any overpowering emotion, exposes their fractured sense of solidarity. The fact that the Jerusalemites could behave so heartlessly in the absence of any strong emotions suggests that the ties of solidarity between them were so weak that they cared little for one another. In short, scene 3 confirms that the host's poor sense of solidarity was indeed representative of the underlying social setting.

We have seen how scenes 2 and 3 apparently give narrative form to two earlier rabbinic traditions concerning the fall of the Second Temple. Scene 2 echoes a tradition which attributed the temple's destruction to hatred, and scene 3 echoes a tradition which attributed the fall of Jerusalem to the eminent of Israel's failure to rebuke one another. With a plethora of options, it is unclear why our story entwined these two themes in particular or why it arranged them in this specific order, but perhaps the story took its cue from the following well-known biblical passage:

לא תשנא את אחיך בלבבך הוכח תוכיח את עמיתך ולא תשא עליו חטא (ויקרא יט:יז).

You shall not hate your brother in your heart. Reprove your kinsman but incur no guilt because of him (Lev 19:17). [7]

In diametric opposition to the first biblical exhortation, the banquet host hates his brother in his heart and then, in diametric opposition to the second exhortation, the banqueters fail to reprove their kinsman and consequently incur guilt because of him. In other words, perhaps this famous biblical passage established, or at least reflects, the hatred-rebuke complex which was adopted in scenes 2 and 3. Moreover, the next stage in our story is the counterpart to the very next clause in Leviticus: "לא תקם ולא תטר את בני עמך," "You shall not take vengeance or bear a grudge against your countrymen."[8] In diametric opposition to this third exhortation, Bar Qamtza takes vengeance and bears a grudge against his countrymen. The addition of this third exhortation creates the tripartite hatred-rebuke-revenge complex which perhaps established, or at least reflects, the hatred-rebuke-revenge complex adopted in the story of Bar Qamtza.

It also bears stressing that regardless of its sources of inspiration, a narrative, like the story of Bar Qamtza, cannot be reduced to its themes, messages, or morals.[9] With its unfurling plotline, fateful conversations, suspenseful tension, exciting crescendo, character development, memorable features, effective communication, persuasive force, emotional

---

7. I have slightly altered the *JPS* translation here, translating "אחיך" as "your brother" rather than as "your kinsman."

8. Lev 19:18.

9. See Roger C. Schank and Tamara R. Berman, "The Pervasive Role of Stories in Knowledge and Action," in *Narrative Impact: Social and Cognitive Foundations*, ed. Melanie C. Green, Jeffrey J. Strange, and Timothy C. Brock (Mahwah, NJ: Lawrence Erlbaum Associates, 2002), 287, 293–94; Schofer, *Confronting Vulnerability*, 77–78.

power, evocative language, didactic thrust, and purportedly historical account, the story of Bar Qamtza is much more than the sum of its individual parts. It transports the reader to an imagined world while offering an intense vicarious experience. Like many other good stories, the story of Bar Qamtza has the power "to move readers and provoke insights into self and society."[10]

Line 14

Line 14, the secondary and later layer of the scene, is made up of two clauses: "Zechariah ben Avqulas was present" ("והיה שם זכריה בן אבקולס") and "he had the opportunity to protest but did not protest" ("והיה ספק בידו למחות ולא מיחה"). The first clause notes the presence of the sage Zechariah ben Avqulas at the banquet and more on this clause below. The second clause describes Zechariah's failure to fulfill the obligation incumbent upon those with the opportunity to protest transgressive or immoral behavior. This latter clause was not invented for our story but rather is a set phrase that appears, with slight variations, multiple times in rabbinic literature.[11] Consider the use of the phrase in Yerushalmi Ketubbot:

... ללמדך שכל מי שהוא ספיקה בידו למחות ואינו ממחה קלקלה תלוייה בו.

... It comes to teach you that anyone who has an opportunity to protest (corruption) but does not protest, the corruption depends upon him.[12]

---

10. Timothy C. Brock, Jeffrey J. Strange, and Melanie C. Green, "Power Beyond Reckoning: An Introduction to Narrative Impact," in *Narrative Impact: Social and Cognitive Foundations*, ed. Melanie C. Green, Jeffrey J. Strange, and Timothy C. Brock (Mahwah, NJ: Lawrence Erlbaum Associates, 2002), 9. More generally, see Jonathan Culler, *Literary Theory: A Very Short Introduction* (Oxford: Oxford University Press, 1997), 91–93 and the collection of articles in Timothy C. Brock, Jeffrey J. Strange, and Melanie C. Green, eds., *Narrative Impact: Social and Cognitive Foundations* (Mahwah, NJ: Lawrence Erlbaum Associates, 2002).
11. See, for example, Sifre Deut 337 (*Sifre on Deuteronomy*, ed. Louis Finkelstein [1939; Repr., New York, NY: The Jewish Theological Seminary of America, 1993], 386–87); y. Peʾah 1:1, 16a; y. Shabb. 5:4, 7c; y. Soṭah 9:10, 24a; b. Sanh. 103a; b. Avod. Zar. 18a.
12. Y. Ketub. 13:1, 35c.

This talmudic passage explicitly states that one who neglects the opportunity to protest corruption is implicated in that very corruption. Similarly, the following interpretation of Deuteronomy 27:26 in Leviticus Rabbah claims that, given the opportunity, one who fails to protest a Torah violation is cursed:

ר' אחא בש' ר' תנחום בר' חייה: למד אדם ולימד ושימר ועשה והיתה ספק בידו למחות ולא מיחה, להחזיק ולא החזיק, הרי זה בכלל ארור, הה"ד "אשר לא יקים" (דברים כז:כו).

Rabbi Aha (said) in the same of Rabbi Tanhum son of Rabbi Hiyya: (Regarding) a man (who) learned and taught and observed (the commandments) and performed them, if he had an opportunity to protest (wrongdoing) but did not protest, to maintain (sages) but did not maintain, lo he is among the *cursed* as it is written: (*Cursed be he*) *who will not uphold* (Deut 27:26).[13]

In short, these sources illustrate that the rabbis enlisted the phrase "he had the opportunity to protest but did not protest" to assert that a passive onlooker was held accountable, at least in part, for the wrongdoings he had failed to protest. This specific phrase was apparently selected for our story in order to indicate that in silently watching the host's unconscionable behavior, Zechariah ben Avqulas was implicated in his sin. The second epilogue (line 32), which holds Zechariah ben Avqulas accountable for the temple's destruction, corroborates Zechariah's role as the culpable sage.

Although lines 14 and 15 both concern a passive onlooker(s), the thrust of each line is distinct. While line 15 extends the story's plot, unveiling the trigger for Bar Qamtza's drastic measures in Act II, line 14 interpolates a theological aside which implicates a rabbinic sage in the banquet host's egregious sin. From Bar Qamtza's perspective, Zechariah ben Avqulas is just another callous guest, but, from the storyteller's theological point of view, Zechariah ben Avqulas's presence makes a rabbinic sage accountable for failing to protest the host's abusive behavior.

Let us return now to line 14's first clause: "Zechariah ben Avqulas was present." Zechariah ben Avqulas – called "**Rabbi** Zechariah ben

---

13. Lev. Rab. 25:1 (p. 569). Cf. y. Sotah 7:4, 21d.

Avqulas" in line 32 (according to most textual witnesses[14] and the Bavli as well) – was apparently a minor rabbinic sage, attested by his single appearance in all Tannaitic literature.[15] Zechariah ben Avqulas's name is somewhat similar to the name of a leading Jewish rebel mentioned by Josephus in *The Jewish War*, a priest named "Zacharias son of Amphicalleus," "Ζαχαρίας δέ τις υἱὸς Ἀμφικάλλει," who was imprisoned in the temple (in 67 CE) because of his leading role in the Jewish revolt against Rome.[16] In light of the rough similarity between the names of these two Zechariahs, scholars have long viewed Zechariah ben Avqulas as a rabbinic variation on Zacharias son of Amphicalleus.[17] If there is any merit to this suggestion, perhaps the account of Zacharias son of Amphicalleus's role in the first Jewish revolt against Rome inspired the rabbis to similarly implicate Zechariah ben Avqulas in the very same revolt. In any event, the name "Avqulas" likely refracts the Greek word

---

14. Casanatense H 3112 and Parma 2559 do not include the word "Rabbi."
15. See t. Shabb. 16:7 (cited below in Chapter 9). See also Mandel, "Tales of the Destruction," 144. Cf. Kalmanzon and Fogel, *Legends of the Destruction*, 25.
16. Josephus, *J.W.* 4.225–28 (Josephus, *Flavii Iosephi Opera*, ed. Benedictus Niese [Berlin: Weidmann, 1955], vol. 4, 377).
17. See I.M. Jost, *Geschichte der Israeliten seit der Zeit der Maccabaer bis auf unsre Tage*, vol. 2 (Berlin: Schlesingerschen Buch- und Musikhandlung, 1821), *98–*99 n14; H. Graetz, *Geschichte der Juden von den ältesten Zeiten bis auf die Gegenwart*, vol. 3 (Leipzig: Oskar Leiner, 1906), 820–22n29; Joseph Derenbourg, *Essai sur l'histoire et la géographie de la Palestine* (Paris: l'imprimerie impériale, 1867), 267; Baer, "Jerusalem," 170; Menahem Stern, "Aspects of Jewish Society: The Priesthood and Other Classes," in *Compendia Rerum Iudaicarum ad Novum Testamentum: The Jewish People in the First Century: Volume Two*, ed. Shmuel Safrai and Menahem Stern (Philadelphia, PA: Fortress Press, 1976), 578–79; Shaye J.D. Cohen, "Parallel Historical Tradition in Josephus and Rabbinic Literature," in *Proceedings of the Ninth World Congress of Jewish Studies*, vol. B (Jerusalem: World Union of Jewish Studies, 1986), 11–12; Rokéaḥ, "Zechariah," 54; "Word-Play Nonetheless: A Rejoinder" ("תגובה: תגובה מלים מלים מלים אחק משחק זאת ובכל"), *Zion* 53 (1988): 317–22; Schwartz, "Zechariah," 313–16; Israel Ben-Shalom, *The School of Shammai and the Zealots' Struggle Against Rome* (רומי נגד הקנאים ומאבק שמאי בית), (Jerusalem: Yad Ben-Zvi and Ben-Gurion University of the Negev Press, 1993), 239–40; Rubenstein, *Talmudic Stories*, 348n28; Furstenberg, "Qamtza," 101. See also Goldenberg, "Rabbinic Explanations," 521n21; Saldarini, "Rabbinic Response," 451n28; Efron, "Bar-Kokhva," 91n210; Mandel, "Tales of the Destruction," 142–43; Ben Shahar, "Abolishment of the Sacrifice," 574–75.

"εὔκολος," meaning "contented" or "good-natured," and perhaps reflects Zechariah's unwillingness to confront the host, a trait characterized as meekness in the second epilogue: "The meekness of Rabbi Zechariah ben Avqulas burnt down the sanctuary."[18]

In addition to his presence in the two versions of the story of Bar Qamtza, Zechariah ben Avqulas appears in only one more tradition in all classical rabbinic literature, t. Shabb. 16:7 (which is partially paralleled in b. Shabb. 143a):[19]

בית הלל אומ': מגביהין מעל השלחן עצמות וקלפין; בית שמיי אומ': מסלק את הטבלה כולה ומנערה. זכריה בן אבקילס לא היה נוהג לא כדברי בית שמיי ולא כדברי בית הלל אלא נוטל ומשליך לאחר המטה. אמ' ר' יוסה: ענותנותו של ר' זכריה בן אבקילס היא שרפה את ההיכל.[20]

Beit Hillel said: One may raise (with his hand) from the table bones and nutshells (on the Sabbath); Beit Shammai said: One must remove the entire board and shake it (rather than lift the bones and nutshells by hand since they may not be handled on the Sabbath). Zechariah ben Avqilas followed neither the words of Beit Shammai nor the words of Beit Hillel but rather took (the bones and nutshells) and threw (them) behind the couch. Rabbi Yose said: The meekness of Rabbi Zechariah ben Avqilas burnt down the sanctuary.

Despite the slight differences in name, Zechariah ben *Avqulas* of the story of Bar Qamtza and the Tosefta's Zechariah ben *Avqilas* are one and the same person. The absence of the title "Rabbi" in the

---

18. See Efron, "Bar-Kokhva," 91n210; Yisraeli-Taran, *Legends of the Destruction*, 14–15; Mandel, "Tales of the Destruction," 143; Kalmin, *Jewish Babylonia*, 45; Ben Shahar, "Abolishment of the Sacrifice," 574; cf. Rokéaḥ, "Zechariah," 54; Rubenstein, *Talmudic Stories*, 348n28; Furstenberg, "Qamtza," 107n14. On the definition of the Greek word "εὔκολος," see Liddell and Scott, *Lexicon*, 718.

19. M. Shabb. 21:3, according to some textual witnesses, has the positions of Beit Hillel and Beit Shammai reversed, but the original configuration of the dispute, which is debated by scholars, is immaterial for our purposes. See Jacob Nahum Epstein, *Introduction to the Mishnaic Text* (מבוא לנוסח המשנה), (Jerusalem: Hebrew University Magnes Press and Dvir, 2000), 357–58; Lieberman, *Tosefta Ki-Fshuṭa*, vol. 3, 267–69. In Bavli Shabbat, the saying regarding Zechariah ben Avqulas's meekness does not appear.

20. T. Shabb. 16:7 according to Vienna Heb. 20.

anonymous portion of the Tosefta's tradition is unsurprising, since the rabbinic practice was to refer to Second Temple sages simply by name. In accordance with this practice, our scene in Lamentations Rabbati also refers to Zechariah by name only. When the Tosefta's Rabbi Yose and the epilogue of the story in Lamentations Rabbati (as well as the Babylonian version of the story) refer to Zechariah as Rabbi Zechariah, they are retrojecting the title "Rabbi" onto a late Second Temple figure.[21] In a similar vein, variations on the spelling of "ben Avqilas/ben Avqulas" across the textual witnesses are also unsurprising given that "Avqilas/Avqulas" is an unusual Jewish name. In short, there is no good reason to doubt the identification of the Tosefta's Zechariah ben Avqilas with the Zechariah ben Avqulas of our story.

According to t. Shabbat 16:7, whereas Beit Shammai and Beit Hillel argued over the proper way to remove bones and nutshells from the Sabbath table, Zechariah ben Avqulas refrained from even placing bones or nutshells on his Sabbath table in the first place, pitching them behind the couch instead. One might imagine that Zechariah's extreme behavior stemmed from his favoring a more stringent ruling than the rulings proposed by Beit Shammai and Beit Hillel, but, according to Rabbi Yose, it was Zechariah's paralyzing meekness ("ענותנות") which inhibited him from staking out a legal stance.[22] In keeping with the sense of his name "εὔκολος," i.e., "contented" or "good-natured," Rabbi Zechariah's timidity induced him to take great pains so as to avoid the situation debated by Beit Shammai and Beit Hillel.[23] With acerbic hyperbole, Rabbi Yose

---

21. See Furstenberg, "Qamtza," 103n3.

22. Although "ענותנות" is usually understood as meekness, humility, or timidity, it is possible that it also indicated cleverness or trickery (see Edward Yechezkel Kutscher, "Addenda to the Lexicographical Section" ["נוספות למדור המילוני"], ANDRL 1 [1972]: 103). Hence perhaps the Tosefta's Rabbi Yose condemned Zechariah for his excessively clever legal maneuvering. In any event, Lamentations Rabbati did not understand Rabbi Yose in this manner though perhaps the Bavli did. See Chapter 21, n. 4 below. (For the notion that Zechariah favored a more stringent ruling, see Rokéah, "Zechariah," 55.)

23. See Lieberman, Tosefta Ki-Fshuṭa, vol. 3, 269. See also Furstenberg, "Qamtza," 106; Mandel, "Tales of the Destruction," 144.

declares that Zechariah's meekness, which generated a superfluous stringency, was responsible for the burning of the sanctuary.[24]

Rabbi Yose's condemnation of Zechariah ben Avqulas's meekness in the Tosefta is identical to his condemnation of Zechariah ben Avqulas in the second epilogue (and highly similar to Rabbi Yohanan's condemnation in the Bavli explored in Chapter 21 below):[25]

T. SHABB. 16:7:	LAM. RAB. 4:2 (LINE 32):
אמ' ר' יוסה: ענותנותו של ר' זכריה בן אבקילס היא שרפה את ההיכל.	א"ר יוסי: ענותנותו של ר' זכריה בן אבקולס שרפה את ההיכל.
Rabbi Yose said: The meekness of Rabbi Zechariah ben Avqilas is what burnt down the sanctuary.	Rabbi Yose said: The meekness of Rabbi Zechariah ben Avqulas burnt down the sanctuary.

Since these two practically identical traditions share the very same content and language, it stands to reason that they are closely connected. Some scholars argue that the fact that Zechariah ben Avqulas was condemned for the same flaw on more than one occasion suggests that meekness was a consistent characteristic and a recurring problem with his leadership.[26] Others maintain that Rabbi Yose's condemnation of Zechariah in the Tosefta stems from Lamentations Rabbati's version of the Bar Qamtza story (or some similar unattested source[27]) since Zechariah's behavior in the Tosefta is entirely unrelated to the burning of the sanctuary.[28] In contrast, Yitzhak Baer argues that the story

---

24. See Schofer, *Confronting Vulnerability*, 82.

25. The Genizah fragment, T-S C 1.69 + T-S AS 78.27, identifies Rabbi Yose as the Amora Rabbi Yose bar Rabbi Abun, but the parallel statement in the Tosefta reveals that Rabbi Yose bar Halafta was intended. See Rubenstein, *Talmudic Stories*, 358n92; Mandel, "Tales of the Destruction," 147n27; Ben Shahar "Abolishment of the Sacrifice," 583n72; cf. Yisraeli-Taran, *Legends of the Destruction*, 105n19; Kalmin, *Jewish Babylonia*, 207n48 and Appendix II below.

26. See, for example, Lieberman, *Tosefta Ki-Fshuṭa*, vol. 3, 269.

27. See, for example, Furstenberg, "Qamtza," 101–2; Kalmin, *Jewish Babylonia*, 45.

28. See, for example, Halevi, *Gates of the Aggadah*, 204; Efron, "Bar-Kokhva," 91n211; Ben-Shalom, *School of Shammai*, 241–42; Yisraeli-Taran, *Legends of the Destruction*, 16, 105n19; Levine Katz, "Qamtsa," 44; Binyamin Lau, *Sages – Volume 1: The Second Temple Period* (חכמים - כרך ראשון: ימי בית שני), (Jerusalem: The Jewish Agency for Israel – Eliner Library and Beit Morasha, 2006), 265; Shmuel

of Bar Qamtza, the later source, enlisted Tosefta Shabbat, the earlier source, but inserted Zechariah into the story of Bar Qamtza because of a misunderstanding: Rabbi Yose's moral teaching about the dangers of meekness in the legal realm was misread as an actual description of the events leading up to the destruction of the temple.[29] While Baer's claim that the later (Amoraic) source was dependent on the earlier (Tannaitic) one is the simplest and most direct explanation of the extant material, I side with scholars who view the later instantiation of the saying as a creative expansion and interpretation of the earlier one, not the result of a misunderstanding. Rabbi Yose's hyperbolic Tannaitic statement in the Tosefta was unexpectedly and excessively severe *in later Amoraic eyes*, which read the early hyperbolic statement literally. Thus, in an attempt to explain the grounds for the grave condemnation, Zechariah was introduced into the story of Bar Qamtza.[30] The insertion of both

---

Safrai and Zeʾev Safrai, *Mishnat Eretz Israel: Tractate Shabbat* (משנת ארץ ישראל: מסכת שבת), vol. 2 (Jerusalem: E.M. Liphshitz, 2008), 507. Some of these scholars also argue that while the saying regarding Zechariah's meekness originated in the context of the Lamentations Rabbati's Bar Qamtza story, it fits poorly in the Babylonian parallel. See Efron, "Bar-Kokhva," 91; Yisraeli-Taran, *Legends of the Destruction*, 19–21; Levine Katz, "Qamtsa," 45. (Kalmin's suggestion [*Jewish Babylonia*, 48–49] that the story of Bar Qamtza and the Zechariah tradition were integrated independently on two separate occasions, once in Lamentations Rabbati and once in the Bavli, is highly unlikely, as Ben Shahar has noted ["Abolishment of the Sacrifice," 595n124]. However, Kalmin's problematic reasoning is the principle underlying the "operating instructions" argument which has recently been enlisted by Ben Shahar and others. See, for example, Meir Ben Shahar, "The High Priest and Alexander the Great" ["הכוהן הגדול ואלכסנדר מוקדון"], in *Josephus and the Rabbis*, ed. Tal Ilan and Vered Noam [Jerusalem: Yad Ben-Zvi, 2017], 135; Vered Noam, "Introduction," ["מבוא"], in *Josephus and the Rabbis*, ed. Tal Ilan and Vered Noam [Jerusalem: Yad Ben-Zvi, 2017], 12–13.)

Others argue that in both the Tosefta and the Babylonian version of the Bar Qamtza story, the term "ענוותנותו" is employed ironically and that Zechariah ben Avqulas (or Amphicalleus) is actually being impugned for his zealous extremism. See, for example, Rokéaḥ, "Zechariah," 56; Furstenberg, "Qamtza," 107–8; Mandel, "Tales of the Destruction," 154–55.

29. See Baer, "Jerusalem," 170–71.

30. See, for example, Saldarini, "Rabbinic Response," 450–51; Rubenstein, *Talmudic Stories*, 164, 358–59n92; Furstenberg, "Qamtza," 107n13, 108n21; Mandel, "Tales of the Destruction," 144–45.

Zechariah ben Avqulas and Rabbi Yose's censorious statement into the story of Bar Qamtza is a creative recasting of the earlier tradition, not a product of its misinterpretation. In order to explain how Zechariah ben Avqulas was responsible for the burning of the sanctuary, he was inserted into the story of Bar Qamtza and transformed into an important guest who had failed to protest the host's abusive treatment of Bar Qamtza.

Conclusion

The two layers of Act 1 scene 3, lines 14 and 15, both relate to the passive banqueters witnessing Bar Qamtza's humiliation, but each layer ascribes a different role to these unresponsive bystanders. Line 15, the scene's original line, reveals that Bar Qamtza opted to take unparalleled measures only after the "precious children of Zion" failed to intervene and put an end to his humiliation. Following line 15, Jerusalem was not destroyed because of hatred, but rather because the Jerusalemites of late Second Temple times "did not rebuke one another." Although scenes 2 and 3 each give narrative form to a different cause for the temple's destruction – hatred and apathy – both enlist causes which highlight the lack of solidarity amongst Jews in late Second Temple times.

Line 14 introduces a rabbinic sage into a story which otherwise did not refer to any rabbis or rabbinic institutions. While the original reading of the story held the "precious children of Zion" responsible for the fall of Jerusalem and the destruction of the temple, the added layer of line 14 holds a rabbinic sage, and by association the rabbinic movement, accountable. Zechariah was apparently interpolated into the story in order to justify the Tosefta's hyperbolic condemnation: "The meekness of Rabbi Zechariah ben Avqulas burnt down the sanctuary." Finding it hard to imagine how Zechariah's legal timidity could have possibly warranted so severe a result, the story illustrates how his passive demeanor could have triggered the chain of events which ultimately led to the destruction. In addition, Zechariah's insertion into the story initiated a process of rabbinization, transforming the story into a narrative starring a rabbi, a process which intensified in the Bavli's later version of the story.[31]

Act I, as a whole, is a banquet story heavily indebted to Greek and Roman banquets as well as to the classical banquet literary tradition. Distinct elements of the setting and plot, such as the banquet practices and invitation protocols of the Jerusalemites, the culpable messenger, the confusion of names, the abusive host, the uninvited guest and the banquet conflict, are all variations on practices or literary themes familiar from the ambient Greek or Roman setting. In a similar vein, the structure of the plot – the innocent error which triggers a chain of further errors or miscalculations – is highly reminiscent of the ancient comedy of errors. The messenger's innocent mistake followed by the host's unrelenting cruelty and the banqueters' thoughtless indifference prompts Bar Qamtza's furious overreaction which plays out in Act II.

Furthermore, like the satires and comedies of ancient times, the story of Bar Qamtza enlists the banquet to critique Jewish society as a whole. The ancient banquet served as an excellent foil for social and moral critique because it was viewed as a mirror of local culture.[32] With the help of this foil, Act I condemned the dearth of solidarity amongst the noble Jerusalemites of late Second Temple times. Focusing on hatred for one's fellow and the failure to protest abuse, Act I suggests that these timeless moral shortcomings were the ultimate causes underlying the fall of Jerusalem and the destruction of its temple.

---

31. See Chapter 18 below.

32. See Murray, "Sympotic History," 3–13; Mary Douglas, "Deciphering a Meal," *Daedalus* 101 (1972): 61; Geoffrey Herman, "Table Etiquette and Persian Culture in the Babylonian Talmud" ("פרסאי בצרכי סעודה בקיאי מינייכו': נימוסי שולחן ותרבות פרס בתלמוד הבבלי"), *Zion* 77 (2012): 152, 170–71.

Chapter 8

The Name Bar Qamtza

In the wake of Act I, the name of the character at the heart of the act, Bar Qamtza, bears consideration. The name Bar Qamtza, like the name Qamtza, appears nowhere in all classical rabbinic literature except in our story (and its parallel version in the Bavli), and was thus apparently not a common name. Indeed, perhaps the rarity of the name Bar Qamtza enhanced the likelihood of a mix-up (even if only fictional) since the more unusual or unfamiliar a name, the more likely two people with such a name might be confused. In any event, scholars reason that Bar Qamtza's unusual name is most probably meant to convey a meaning, but they differ on what that meaning may be. Some suggest that since "Qamtza" is Aramaic for locust, Bar Qamtza's name likens him to a plague of locusts which swarm the land, causing destruction, famine, and death.[1] Others focus on Qamtza's verbal root in Hebrew, ק.מ.צ, suggesting either that Bar Qamtza was (ironically) called a stingy "miser," "קמצן," or that the destruction of Jerusalem was prompted by a minor and insignificant failing – a mere "handful" or "קומץ."[2] Though all these interpretations

---

1. See Saldarini, "Rabbinic Response," 449; Rokéaḥ, "Zechariah," 53n1; Sokoloff, *Dictionary of Jewish Palestinian Aramaic*, 567; Rubenstein, *Talmudic Stories*, 148.
2. On the "miser" definition, see Rokéaḥ, "Zechariah," 53n1; Rubenstein, *Talmudic Stories*, 347n23; Israel J. Yuval, *Two Nations in Your Womb: Perceptions of Jews and Christians in Late Antiquity and the Middle Ages*, trans. Barbara Harshav and Jonathan Chipman (Berkeley: University of California Press, 2006), 51. On the "handful" definition, see Israel J. Yuval, "'The Lord will take Vengeance, Vengeance for his Temple' – historia sine ira et studio" ("נקמת ה' היא נקמת היכלו': היסטוריה

87

are suggestive, it is hard to know which meaning, if any, was originally intended or how ancient audiences would have interpreted the name Bar Qamtza.

Compsus Son of Compsus

While the unusual name Bar Qamtza appears nowhere in ancient Jewish sources outside (the parallel versions of) our story, scholars have linked the name to that of a pro-Roman Jewish figure mentioned by the first-century Jewish historian Josephus.[3] According to his *Life*, when Josephus arrived in Tiberias during the early days of the Jewish revolt, one of the three factions in the city was made up of refined men who opposed the insurrection and supported the Jewish king and the Romans.[4]

Στάσεις τρεῖς ἦσαν κατὰ τὴν πόλιν, μία μὲν ἀνδρῶν εὐσχημόνων, ἦρχε δ' αὐτῆς Ἰούλιος Κάπελλος. οὗτος δὴ καὶ οἱ σὺν αὐτῷ πάντες, Ἡρώδης ὁ Μιαροῦ καὶ Ἡρώδης ὁ τοῦ Γαμάλου καὶ Κομψὸς ὁ τοῦ Κομψοῦ... πάντες οὖν οἱ προειρημένοι κατὰ τὸν καιρὸν ἐκεῖνον ἐμμένειν συνεβούλευον τῇ πρὸς τοὺς Ῥωμαίους καὶ τὸν βασιλέα πίστει.

Three factions were in the city: one of refined men, and it was headed by Iulius Capellus. This man certainly, and all those with him – Herod son of Miarus, Herod son of Gamalus, and Compsus son of Compsus... at that time all of those mentioned counseled (the people) to stand firm in loyalty to the Romans and to the king.[5]

לֹלֹא חֲרוֹן וְלֹלֹא מַשּׂוֹא פָּנִים ("), *Zion* 59 (1994): 356; *Two Nations*, 50. More generally, see Furstenberg, "Qamtza," 110n23; Schofer, *Confronting Vulnerability*, 96–97. Cf. Yisraeli-Taran, *Legends of the Destruction*, 13, who suggests that since the temple priests performed "קמיצה" (or the handful ritual), the name "קמצא" might have been associated with the priesthood.

3. On the female name "קמצו" ("Qamtzu"), see Tal Ilan, *Lexicon of Jewish Names in Late Antiquity: Part IV: The Eastern Diaspora 330 BCE – 650 CE* (Tübingen: Mohr Siebeck, 2011), 423. See also Tal Ilan, *Lexicon of Jewish Names in Late Antiquity: Part I: Palestine 330 BCE – 200 CE* (Tübingen: Mohr Siebeck, 2002), 408.

4. Cf. Josephus, *J.W.* 2.568–76, where Josephus does not mention these Tiberian factions. See Steven Mason, *Flavius Josephus: Translation and Commentary: Volume 9: Life of Josephus* (Leiden: Brill, 2001), 39n196.

5. Josephus, *Life* 32–34 (ed. Niese, vol. 4, 326–27) with translation by Mason, *Life*, 39–41.

Since Compsus son of Compsus favored the Romans over the rebel Jews, and because the name "Compsus" (Κομψός) is quite similar to the name Qamtza, scholars have suggested that Compsus, or at least his name, ultimately inspired the use of the name Qamtza in our story. In other words, Compsus son of Compsus's pro-Roman stance presumably facilitated the transformation of his persona (as "son of Compsus" or "Bar Qamtza") into an enemy of the Jewish temple. In the Bavli, his name was split between the host's friend Qamtza and the host's enemy Bar, or son of, Qamtza.[6]

Although the link between Bar Qamtza and Compsus son of Compsus has a suggestive flare, some scholars question this supposed connection due to salient differences between the two figures. On the linguistic plane, the name Compsus must undergo a few vowel and consonant changes in order to become Qamtza. On the geographical plane, Josephus situates Compsus in Tiberias while rabbinic legend locates Bar Qamtza in Jerusalem. On the literary plane, Josephus embeds Compsus in a context nothing like the story of Bar Qamtza, and even though Compsus belongs to the faction opposed to Josephus, Josephus portrays him far more positively than the Bar Qamtza of rabbinic legend.[7] Josephus describes Compsus as one of the "refined men" of Tiberias and his name, which means "nice, refined, gentlemanly, pleasant, smart, ingenious," is the "perfect name for the leader of the pro-Roman faction secretly (in the narrative) favored by Josephus."[8] On the historical plane, there is no evidence that the rabbis were otherwise familiar with the figure of Compsus. In my opinion, while these varied differences on their own do not form

---

6. See Derenbourg, *Essai*, 267; Baer, "Jerusalem," 169; Rubenstein, *Talmudic Stories*, 347n23; Furstenburg, "Qamtza," 101; Kalmin, *Jewish Babylonia*, 49; cf. Yisraeli-Ṭaran, *Legends of the Destruction*, 13–14. Arguing that our story was most probably inspired by a popular saying of the time which was creatively misunderstood, Paul Mandel imagines that the original saying attributed the temple's destruction to pro-Roman leaders like Compsus son of Compsus. See Mandel, "Tales of the Destruction," 147–48. (Scholars have also suggested that perhaps the original saying featured Compsus son of Compsus and his brother Crispus, who is mentioned in Josephus, *Life* 33. See Furstenberg, "Qamtza," 110n23.)

7. See Ben Shahar, "Abolishment of the Sacrifice," 575, 581, 592. See also Shaye J.D. Cohen, *Josephus in Galilee and Rome: His Vita and Development as a Historian* (Leiden: Brill, 1979), 256n36.

8. Mason, *Life*, 40n201.

an insurmountable obstacle to the notion that Bar Qamtza's character or name was ultimately inspired by Josephus's Compsus son of Compsus, they establish a benchmark for us, revealing the criteria needed to identify a closer match and more likely source of inspiration.

Ben Qamtzar

Following the benchmark set by Compsus son of Compsus, it is worth considering another figure from late Second Temple times whose name bears an uncanny and even closer resemblance to Bar Qamtza, namely Ben, or son of, Qamtzar. After m. Yoma 3:10 lists some individuals whose contributions to the Jerusalem temple ensured that they would be favorably remembered, m. Yoma 3:11 disparages a number of temple officials (or, more precisely, private suppliers to the temple[9]) who refused to divulge their families' secret professional lore, including a man by the name of Ben Qamtzar:

ואילו לגניי: בית גרמו לא רצו ללמד על מעשה לחם הפנים. בית אבטינס לא רצו ללמד על מעשה הקטרת. הוגדס בן לוי היה יודע פרק בשיר ולא רצה ללמד. בן קמצר לא רצה ללמד על מעשה הכתב. על הראשונים נאמר "זכר צדיק לברכה" (משלי י:ז) ועל אלו נא' "שם רשעים ירקב" (משלי י:ז).

But (the memory) of these (was kept) in dishonor: They of the House of Garmu did not want to teach (any other) how to prepare the Shewbread. They of the House of Abtinas did not want to teach (any other) how to prepare the incense. Hugdas[10] ben Levi knew a (special) chapter in song but he did not want to teach it (to any other). Ben Qamtzar did not want to teach (any other) in (his special) writing craft. Of the former group it is said, *The name of the righteous is invoked in blessing* (Prov 10:7), and of the latter it is said *but the fame of the wicked rots* (Prov 10:7).[11]

---

9. See Shmuel Safrai and Zeʾev Safrai, *Mishnat Eretz Israel: Tractate Yoma* (משנת ארץ ישראל: מסכת יומא), (Jerusalem: E.M. Liphshitz, 2010), 136.

10. "Hugdas" is spelled in various ways across the textual witnesses. See Yehoshua Rosenberg, "Mishna 'Kippurim' (Yoma): A Critical Edition with Introduction" ("משנה 'כיפורים': מהדורה ביקורתית, בצרוף מבוא"), 2 vols. (PhD diss., Hebrew University, 1995), vol. 2, 34.

11. M. Yoma 3:1 according to MS Parma with Herbert Danby's translation (*The Mishnah* [Oxford: Oxford University Press, 1933] 166), slightly modified.

The Mishnah states that since Ben Qamtzar did not reveal his secret writing craft (which involved penning four letters at one time according to the Bavli[12]), he was included in the list of temple officials whose reputations were ruined because they obstinately kept their family lore a secret. The memory of these disgraced officials, according to the Mishnah, was held in shame, and regarding people like them Proverbs ominously taught: "the fame of the wicked rots."

In line with the Mishnah's harsh view of these temple officials, the Tosefta explains why these secretive temple officials were so deplorable:

הם בקשו להרבות כבודן ולמעט כבוד שמים לפיכך כבודן נתמעט וכבוד שמים נתרבה, ולא נמצא להם שם טוב וזכר טוב לעולם.

They sought to increase their honor and diminish the honor of heaven therefore their honor was diminished and the honor of heaven was increased, and they never attained a good reputation and good memorial.[13]

Since these temple officials hoped to enhance their own glory and reputation at God's expense, their glory and memorial were forever diminished in a measure for measure comeuppance.

In contrast to the Mishnah, however, the Tosefta singles out Ben Qamtzar as especially wicked. In the Tosefta, all the officials offer a justification for keeping their lore a secret save for Ben Qamtzar. Whereas the House of Abtinas, the House of Garmu, and Hugdas[14] ben Levi

---

12. See b. Yoma 38b.

13. T. Kipp. 2:8 according to Vienna Heb. 20 with translation indebted to Jacob Neusner, trans. *The Tosefta: Moed* (New York, NY: Ktav, 1981), 196. See also Song Rab. 3:8 (*Song of Songs Rabbah*, ed. Shimshon Donsky [Jerusalem: Dvir, 1980], 89), where the House of Qamtzar replaces Ben Qamtzar, the Tosefta's explanation is applied to the House of Qamtzar alone, and it is stated that the House of Qamtzar will not merit a grandchild or great-grandchild.

14. Although the textual witnesses of the Tosefta vary in the spelling of this name, all agree that it begins with an aleph, as in "אגדיס" "Agdis." See *The Tosefta According to Codex Vienna, with Variants from Codex Erfurt, Genizah Mss. and Editio Princeps (Venice 1521), Zera'im – Nezikin*, ed. Saul Lieberman (New York, NY: The Jewish Theological Seminary of America, 1955–1988), vol. 2, 234. See also n. 10 above.

all explain that their families preserved their lore in secret so as to ensure that it would not be enlisted in the idolatrous practices of the pagans responsible for the temple's future destruction (which they had foreseen), Ben Qamtzar does not:

בן קמצר היה יודע את הכתב ולא רצה ללמד. אמרו לו: מה ראית שלא ללמד? דמם.[15] אלו מצאו תשובה לדבריהם, בן קמצר לא מצא תשובה לדבריו.

Ben Qamtzar knew (the special craft of) writing and did not want to teach it (to any other). They said to him: Why did you see (fit) not to teach (anyone else)? He was silent. The others found an answer for their position, Ben Qamtzar did not find an answer for his position.[16]

Unlike the Mishnah, which portrays Ben Qamtzar as no better or worse than the officials listed by his side, the Tosefta indicates that Ben Qamtzar was the sole official with no excuse for keeping his family traditions a secret.[17]

In the Tosefta's wake, the Yerushalmi intensifies the critique of Ben Qamtzar by claiming that Ben Qamtzar alone was excluded from the list of temple officials cited in Mishnah Sheqalim:

וכולהן מצאו מתלא לדבריהן חוץ מבן קמצר, כיי דתנינן תמן: אילו הן הממונין שהיו במקדש (משנה שקלים ה:א-ב).

And all of them found an excuse for their position save for Ben Qamtzar, as we learned there: "And these are the officers who served in the temple..." (m. Sheqal. 5:1–2).[18]

M. Sheqal. 5:1–2 presents a long list of temple officials and, as noted by the Yerushalmi, it includes all the secretive officials mentioned in Mishnah Yoma save for Ben Qamtzar:

---

15. See Edward Yechezkel Kutscher, "Some Problems of the Lexicography of Mishnaic Hebrew and its Comparison to Biblical Hebrew" ("מבעיות המילונות של לשון חז"ל"), *ANDRL* 1 (1972): 77–78.

16. T. Kipp. 2:8 as in n. 13 above.

17. See also the comment attributed to Rabbi Akiva in t. Kipp. 2:7.

18. Y. Yoma 3:9, 41a–41b.

ואילו הן הממונים שהיו במקדש...הוגרס בן לוי על השיר, בית גרמו על
מעשה לחם הפנים, בית אבטינס על מעשה הקטרת.

And these are the officers who served in the temple ... Hugras ben
Levi was over the song, the House of Garmu was over the preparation
of the showbread, and the House of Abtinas was over the preparation
of the incense.[19]

Since all the officials supplied a good excuse for keeping their tradi-
tions a secret save for Ben Qamtzar, the Yerushalmi concludes that Ben
Qamtzar's unjustified secretive behavior prompted his omission from
Mishnah Sheqalim's list of temple officials.[20]

The inclination of both the Tosefta and the Yerushalmi to amplify
Ben Qamtzar's wickedness while exculpating the other secretive officials
becomes even more explicit and pronounced in the Bavli's version of
the Ben Qamtzar tradition:

תנו רבנן: בן קמצר לא רצה ללמד את הכתב. אמרו לו: מה ראיתה שלא
ללמד? דמם. כולן מצאו תשובה לדבריהן בן קמצר לא מצא תשובה לדבריו.
על הראשונים נאמר "זכר צדיק לברכה" (משלי י:ז) ועל בן קמצר וחביריו
נאמר "ושם רשעים ירקב" (משלי י:ז).

---

19. M. Sheqal. 5:1–2 according to MS Kaufmann with Danby's translation (*Mishnah*, 157).

20. The Yerushalmi also intimates that once the secretive families revealed the
underlying reason for their refusal to teach their professional lore, they recovered
their good names, whereas Ben Qamtzar, the sole official who offered no such
reason, remained in a state of disgrace. The Yerushalmi creates this impression
by juxtaposing the statement attributed to Rabbi Akiva, "מעתה אין אנו צריכים
להזכירן לגנאי," "from now on we must not keep their memory in dishonor," to
the claim (cited above) that all of the families found an excuse for their secretive
behavior save for Ben Qamtzar. Unlike the Tosefta, which brings the statement
attributed to Rabbi Akiva elsewhere (see n. 17 above), the Yerushalmi situates
it right before the statement differentiating Ben Qamtzar from all the other
secretive families, and, by doing so, it implies that while the other families
were no longer held in disgrace (and accordingly merited a positive mention in
Mishnah Sheqalim), Ben Qamtzar remained in a state of dishonor and shame. The
impression created in the Yerushalmi by means of juxtaposition is made explicit
in the Bavli as explained below. (See Lieberman, *Tosefta Ki-Fshuṭa*, vol. 4, 765;
Safrai and Safrai, *Yoma*, 139–49.)

Our rabbis taught: Ben Qamtzar would not teach (any other his special craft of) writing. They said to him: Why did you see (fit) not to teach? He was silent. All of them found an answer for their position, Ben Qamtzar did not find an answer for his position. Of the former it is said, *The name of the righteous is invoked in blessing* (Prov 10:7), and of Ben Qamtzar and his like it is said, *but the fame of the wicked rots* (Prov 10:7).[21]

In this account of the Ben Qamtzar tradition, the condemning phrase, "the fame of the wicked rots," focuses on Ben Qamtzar and his ilk while the laudatory phrase, "the name of the righteous is invoked in blessing," denotes all the temple officials who adduced a good excuse for their secretive behavior. In other words, the Bavli contends that while all the other secretive officials rehabilitated their good name when they offered a reasonable explanation for keeping their lore a family secret, Ben Qamtzar alone remained disgraced and dishonored because only he supplied no reason at all for refusing to divulge his secret writing technique.

In sum, Ben Qamtzar is portrayed quite negatively throughout rabbinic literature. The Mishnah includes Ben Qamtzar in a list of temple officials condemned for keeping secret their professional lore. The Tosefta reveals that Ben Qamtzar was the only temple official with no excuse for his secretive behavior. The Yerushalmi claims that Ben Qamtzar alone was intentionally omitted from Mishnah Sheqalim's list of temple officials because he was the sole official without a good reason for keeping his lore a secret. And the Bavli states that, in the end, Ben Qamtzar remained the solitary disgraced temple official since all the other secretive officials successfully rehabilitated their reputations by revealing the reason for keeping their lore a family secret.

One striking feature of the Ben Qamtzar tradition in all its forms is the severity of the rabbinic response to Ben Qamtzar's secret. Ben Qamtzar did not break any laws or commit any sins; he neither injured other people nor disrespected the divine. Moreover, in light of modern patent and copyright law, Ben Qamtzar's unwillingness to share trade

---

21. B. Yoma 38b according to MS Munich 6.

secrets emerges as a sensible economic decision designed to prevent him from aiding competitors who might use his own techniques to steal his business.[22] Yet despite these mitigating factors, the rabbis castigate and disparage Ben Qamtzar in extreme tones. According to rabbinic tradition, since Ben Qamtzar was a selfish man who sought to increase his own glory at God's expense, he would never attain "a good reputation and good memorial." Due to his wickedness Ben Qamtzar was omitted from the Mishnah's list of temple officials, and Proverbs exclaimed about people like him "but the fame of the wicked rots." Considering that Ben Qamtzar's trade secrets, which hurt no one, were most likely supposed to protect his own financial interests, was the rabbinic reaction not excessive?

The rabbinic reaction in this case is a fine example of rabbinic hyperbole. The rabbis often amplified and overstated their case in order to transmit a message loudly and clearly or to convey their pleasure or displeasure in no uncertain terms. Perhaps the excessive reaction also stemmed from frustration with figures like Ben Qamtzar, who placed their personal or familial welfare over the best interests of the community. In any event, hyperbole and exaggerated declarations sometimes posed a challenge for later sages, who often took them at face value. In this particular case I would like to suggest that, in the absence of any grave crime or weighty flaw, some later rabbis were perplexed by the severity of the rabbinic reaction to Ben Qamtzar's trade secrets and in an attempt to explain what sort of deed truly warranted the censure directed at Ben Qamtzar, Bar Qamtza was born. In other words, I submit that Ben Qamtzar served as a central source of inspiration in the literary formation of Bar Qamtza.

From a linguistic perspective, the "bar" (or "son of") in Bar Qamtza is simply the Aramaic equivalent for the Hebrew "ben" of Ben Qamtzar, and the names Qamtza (קמצא) and Qamtzar (קמצר) are practically identical.[23] The sole difference between the two names is that Qamtzar

---

22. See Tropper, "Economics," 221–22.

23. Some manuscripts employ the Hebrew term "ben" rather than the Aramaic equivalent "bar," thereby modeling the easy transition between "ben" and "bar" (and perhaps preserving an echo of the underlying "ben"). See the popular saying

ends with an unusual final *resh* (ר)[24] while Qamtza ends with a common final *aleph* (א), a popular suffix for Aramaic names. Since cases of Aramaicization in which the Aramaic suffix *aleph* replaces the final letter or syllables of a name are well attested in late antiquity – for example, Alexandros (Ἀλέξανδρος) becoming Alexa (אלכסא), Yohanan (יוחנן) becoming Yohana (יוחנא) and Matitya (מתתיה) becoming Matya (מתיא)[25] – Bar Qamtza may well be an Aramaic or truncated version of Ben Qamtzar (or perhaps an alternative form of pronunciation).

In addition, since the pool of personal names used at the time was limited, nicknames were popular. Therefore, when a man is referred to as the son of "X" and "X" is a rare (and possibly derogatory) name, "X" was most probably not the man's father's name but the man's nickname.[26] Hence, it is quite likely that the rare (and likely unique) nickname Ben Qamtzar evolved into the equally rare nickname Bar Qamtza.

Insofar as etymology is concerned, the origin of the name Qamtzar is disputed. The name has been linked to a similar Persian name, but it has also been derived from the Hebrew verbal root ק.מ.צ. either with the meaning "קמצן," "miser," reflecting here Ben Qamtzar's refusal to share his trade secrets, or, the meaning "to compress, close the hand, grasp," referencing Ben Qamstar's scribal profession which involved grasping a writing utensil.[27] Moreover, Qamtzar has also been viewed as an alternative form of the Aramaic word Qamtza (קמצא) or locust.[28] The Aramaic word "כמצורא," "Kamtzora" (and pay no mind to the opening letter *kaf* [כ] since the letters *kaf* and *qof* [ק] were often interchangeable[29]) also

---

in MS Munich 229, MS Cambridge 495 and the *editio princeps*. See also MS Parma 2393 and MS Oxford 102 which refer to the host's friend as Ben Qamtza.

24. See Ilan, *Lexicon Part I*, 351, 414.

25. See Ilan, *Lexicon Part I*, 25.

26. See Ilan, *Lexicon Part I*, 46. Cf. Furstenberg, "Qamtza," 108n19.

27. On the Persian name similar to Qamtzar, see Ilan, *Lexicon Part I*, 351; Ferdinand Justi, *Iranisches Namenbuch* (Marburg: N.G. Elwert'sche, 1895), 154–55. For the "miser" definition, see Samuel Klein, "Leheqer hashemot vehakinuyim" ("לחקר השמות והכינויים"), *Lĕšonénu* 1 (1929): 343, and for "close the hand," see Jastrow, *Dictionary*, 1386–387.

28. See Ilan, *Lexicon Part I*, 351.

29. See Epstein, *Introduction*, 1227; Zvi Meir Rabinovitz, *Ginzé Midrash: The Oldest Forms of Rabbinic Midrashim according to Geniza Manuscripts* (גנזי מדרש:

means locust,[30] and one textual witness of Lamentations Rabbati even calls the mistakenly invited guest "Bar Kamtzora."[31] In short, Qamtza and Qamtzar may have well been variations on one and the same word, and, even if not, it is easy to see how the typical change of a single consonant could have transformed Qamtzar into the Aramaic Qamtza. Needless to say, Qamtzar is linguistically much closer to Qamtza than to Compsus.

Unlike Compsus son of Compsus whom Josephus situates in Tiberias, Ben Qamtzar, like Bar Qamtza, is found in Jerusalem. Furthermore, just as rabbinic tradition links Ben Qamtzar to the temple, viewing him as a temple official, rabbinic tradition links Bar Qamtza to the temple as well, in the presumption that he had some familiarity with temple practice.

Josephus's *Life* preserves the only ancient record of Compsus son of Compsus, and it is distinctly possible that the rabbis never heard of him. They certainly never mention him by name in rabbinic literature. By contrast, Ben Qamtzar appears multiple times in rabbinic literature and was undoubtedly well known in rabbinic circles.

Whereas the literary connection between Compsus and Bar Qamtza is weak, especially since the only extant record of Compsus portrays him in a positive light, the story of Bar Qamtza is easily viewed as an expansion of the Ben Qamtzar tradition. In light of the rabbis' hyperbolic vilification of Ben Qamtzar, the story of Bar Qamtza emerges as an attempt to clarify the rabbis' harsh appraisal of Ben Qamtzar by

---

לצורתם הקדומה של מדרשי חז"ל לפי כתבי יד מן הגניזה), (Tel Aviv: The Chaim Rosenberg School for Jewish Studies, Tel Aviv University, 1976), 146.

30. See Michael Sokoloff, *A Dictionary of Jewish Babylonian Aramaic of the Talmudic and Geonic Periods* (Ramat-Gan: Bar Ilan University Press and Johns Hopkins University Press, 2002), 586.

31. See T-S C 1.69 + T-S AS 78.27. In the wake of Paul Mandel, scholars today tend to view this Geniza fragment as the earliest extant reading of our tradition, and, if so, "Kamtzora" may have preserved an echo of the underlying "Qamtzar." I tend to doubt, however, that "Kamtzora" reflects the earliest reading of the text and believe, rather, that it is best viewed simply as evidence for the ease of the transition between "Qamtza" and "Qamtzar." (For two places where Qamtzar was mistakenly transformed into Qamtzah or Qamtza, see m. Yoma 3:11 according to MS Paris 330.1 [Rosenberg, "Kippurim," vol. 2, 35]; b. Yoma 38b according to MS Wien – Oesterreichische Nationalbibliothek Hebr. Frag. A 38.)

supplying us with the untold story underlying his shameful disgrace. In other words, since preserving a professional secret does not seem to warrant so vitriolic a response, our story was designed, at least in part, to reveal the opprobrious deed which called for the rabbis' caustic response. Indeed, the only other named figure in the story of Bar Qamtza, Zechariah ben Avqulas, was also apparently introduced into the story in order to explain a similarly puzzling and hyperbolic condemnation in early rabbinic literature.[32]

Conclusion

In our search for the underlying source of inspiration for the name Bar Qamtza, Ben Qamtzar has emerged as a much stronger candidate than Compsus son of Compsus. Unlike Compsus, Ben Qamtzar was unquestionably known to the rabbis, and of the two names, Ben Qamtzar is much closer to Bar Qamtza and could have also been easily viewed as an alternative form of the name. Whereas Compsus lived in Tiberias, Ben Qamtzar, like Bar Qamtza, was linked to the Jerusalem temple. Most importantly perhaps, the rabbis' truculent and belligerent attitude towards Ben Qamtzar would have set the stage for later sages to creatively flesh out the truly pernicious behavior which purportedly prompted the rabbinic call for Ben Qamtzar's eternal condemnation. In light of all these considerations, it seems most likely to me that the well-known Ben Qamtzar tradition influenced the literary formation of

---

32. In a similar vein, the Amoraic depiction of Dama ben Netinah stems from earlier Tannaitic traditions about a similarly named cow. See Shamma Friedman, "'History and Aggadah': The Enigma of Dama Ben Netina" ("דמא בן נתינה - לדמותו ההיסטורית: פרק בחקר האגדה התלמודית"), in *Hiyagon L'Yona: New Aspects in the Study of Midrash, Aggadah and Piyut in Honor of Professor Yona Fraenkel*, ed. Joshua Levinson, Jacob Elbaum, and Galit Hasan-Rokem (Jerusalem: Hebrew University Magnes Press, 2006), 106–8, 120–21, and the Amoraic narrative adduced in b. B. Bat. 21a to explain why Joshua ben Gamla is remembered for good, seeks to improve upon the earlier Tannaitic explanation given in m. Yoma 3:9 by replacing Joshua ben Gamla's temple donation (as per the mishnah) with an educational reform.

our story (and epilogue[33]), triggering the emergence of Bar Qamtza as a late manifestation of Ben Qamtzar and priming ancient audiences to expect very little from Bar Qamtza.

---

33. See Chapter 12 below.

Chapter 9

Bar Qamtza's Revenge
(ACT II SCENE 1)

The Slander

In Act II scene 1, Bar Qamtza's revenge unfolds. The humiliation Bar Qamtza endured at the banquet compounded by his fellow banqueters' apparently callous indifference whip him up to concoct an evil scheme with catastrophic consequences not only for the elite banqueters of Jerusalem, but also for the Jewish people the world over. The scene opens with the first stage in his wicked plot, a pernicious and slanderous lie:

16 מה עשה?

17 הלך לו אצל השילטון,

18 אמר: אלין קורבניא דאת משלח אינון אכלין יתהון ומקרבין אחרנין בחילופין.

16 What did he do?

17 He went to the ruler

18 (and) said: Those offerings that you send, they eat them and offer up others in their stead.

In the act's very first line, the narrator asks how Bar Qamtza carried out his revenge: "What did he **do**?" "מה עשה?" The Hebrew verb used in this line, ע.ש.ה., echoes the Hebrew verb used in very first line of Act I (line 4): "A story of one man in Jerusalem who **made** – שעשה – a banquet."[1] In addition, the verb reappears later on in Act II scene 1 (line

---

1. Branch A enlists the Aramaic equivalent: ע.ב.ד.

23) when Bar Qamtza follows through with his plan and blemishes the animals: "He (Bar Qamtza) got up in the night and [secretly] **made them – ועשאן –** (the animals) blemished." The use of the same verb in the opening lines of both acts naturally draws attention to their parallel placement and roles; just as Act I opened with the host's initiative, his exclusive banquet, Act II opens with Bar Qamtza's corresponding initiative – his revenge for having been expelled from the banquet. As we will see below, Act II scene 1 echoes Act I scene 1 in various other ways as well.

In response to the question, what did Bar Qamtza do? – the narrative states: "he went to the ruler," "הלך לו אצל השילטון." The Hebrew word "שילטון" ("ruler") in rabbinic literature often denotes a local authority, such as the local Roman governor. Because a Judaean provincial who wished to report subversive behavior would have naturally turned to Rome's local representative, it seems that the "ruler" referred to here is the local Roman governor.[2] Later on in the story (in lines 29–30), the ruler reappears to receive the follow-up report and destroy the temple, but there he is called "מלכא," the Aramaic term for "chief" or "king." Although the term "king" (in both Aramaic and Hebrew) is often enlisted in rabbinic literature to denote the emperor, it is also used to denote other officials, such as governors.[3] Since the "ruler" of line 17 most likely refers to the local governor, the "king" (of line 29) apparently refers to this governor as well.[4]

At his audience with the governor, Bar Qamtza reports that rather than sacrificing the animals which the Romans send to Jerusalem as offerings, the Jews eat them and offer up others, presumably inferior ones, instead. If the governor's offerings were mere private affairs, the magnitude of his eventual reaction – enrolling the Roman army to

2. See Jastrow, *Dictionary*, 1581–582; Sokoloff, *Dictionary of Jewish Palestinian Aramaic*, 637.

3. See Jastrow, *Dictionary*, 791; Ignaz Ziegler, *Die Königsleichnisse des Midrasch beleuchtet durch die römische Kaiserzeit* (Breslau: Schlesische Verlags-Anstalt v. S. Schottlaender, 1903), xxvi-xxxii; Sokoloff, *Dictionary of Jewish Palestinian Aramaic*, 339–40.

4. See Halevi, *Gates of the Aggadah*, 203–4nn3–4. (Cf. T-S C 1.69 + T-S AS 78.27 ad loc. and see Chapter 1, n. 7 above.)

destroy the Jerusalem temple – would be difficult to explain. Hence, it seems that the governor's offerings were affairs of state. The notion that the Roman authorities sponsored offerings in the temple of Jerusalem is also corroborated by other ancient sources.

According to the first-century Jewish philosopher Philo, the emperor Augustus instituted the practice of funding daily sacrifices in the Jerusalem temple. As the emperor's tribute to the Jewish deity, two lambs and a bull were sacrificed daily up to Philo's own time.[5] According to Josephus, on the other hand, the Jewish community, at its own expense, offered up sacrifices twice a day "for Caesar and the Roman people," "περὶ μὲν Καίσαρος καὶ τοῦ δήμου τῶν Ῥωμαίων."[6] In respect to the funding of the emperor's daily sacrifices, some historians prefer Josephus's position, some prefer Philo's, and yet others seek to harmonize the conflicting accounts, viewing them as two representations of the very same source of funding, i.e., Jewish taxes paid to Rome.[7] In any event, most scholars believe that these daily sacrifices functioned as public symbols of Jewish allegiance to Rome in lieu of the imperial cult, and as signs of the imperial recognition of the Jewish deity.[8] Hence, by claiming that the Jews refused to sacrifice the daily Roman offerings, Bar Qamtza was implying that the Jews had repudiated their allegiance to Rome[9] (or, at

---

5. See Philo, *Legat.* 147, 291, 317, 355–57.

6. Josephus, *J.W.* 2.197 (ed. Niese, vol. 4, 192) with translation by Steven Mason, *Flavius Josephus: Translation and Commentary: Volume 1B: Judean War 2* (Leiden: Brill, 2008), 164. See also Josephus, *Ag. Ap.* 2.77.

7. Daniel R. Schwartz, *Agrippa I: The Last King of Judaea* (Tübingen: Mohr Siebeck, 1990), 200–1, for example, prefers Josephus's position (see also n. 14 below); John M. G. Barclay, *Flavius Josephus: Translation and Commentary: Against Apion* (Leiden: Brill, 2007), 210n268, prefers Philo's position; and the following scholars harmonize the two accounts: E. Mary Smallwood, *The Jews under Roman Rule: From Pompey to Diocletian* (Leiden: Brill, 1976), 148n20; Emile Schürer, Geza Vermes, Fergus Millar, and Matthew Black, *The History of the Jewish People in the Age of Jesus Christ (175 BC–AD 135)*, (Edinburgh: T.&T. Clark, 1979), 312; Mason, *Judean War*, 164n1240; Ben Shahar, "Abolishment of the Sacrifice," 572.

8. See Mason, *Judean War*, 164n1240, 314–15n2575; cf. Minika Bernett, *Der Kaiserkult in Judäa unter den Herodiern und Römern* (Tübingen: Mohr Siebeck, 2007).

9. See Halevi, *Gates of the Aggadah*, 204n5. (See also T-S C 1.69 + T-S AS 78.27 ad loc.; Casanatense H 3112 ad loc.; Parma 2559 ad loc.)

the very least, that they were humiliating Rome and taking advantage of Roman largesse).[10]

In light of the weighty symbolism carried by the emperor's daily sacrifices, perhaps it is no surprise that, according to Josephus's *The Jewish War*, the cessation of these sacrifices (in the summer of 66 CE) laid a foundation for the Jewish revolt against Rome:[11]

ἅμα δὲ καὶ κατὰ τὸ ἱερὸν Ἐλεάζαρος υἱὸς Ἀνανία τοῦ ἀρχιερέως, νεανίας θρασύτατος, στρατηγῶν τότε τοὺς κατὰ τὴν λατρείαν λειτουργοῦντας ἀναπείθει μηδενὸς ἀλλοτρίου δῶρον ἢ θυσίαν προσδέχεσθαι. τοῦτο δ' ἦν τοῦ πρὸς Ῥωμαίους πολέμου καταβολή· τὴν γὰρ ὑπὲρ τούτων θυσίαν καὶ[12] Καίσαρος ἀπέρριψαν.

Meanwhile, in the temple, Eleazar son of the high priest Ananias, a very bold young man serving as commandant at the time, induced those performing the services of worship to accept no gift or sacrifice from any outsider. This was a foundation of war against the Romans, for they cast aside the sacrifice on behalf of these (the Romans) and Caesar.[13]

Although chief priests, notable Pharisees, and other leaders sought to convince the rebels to reverse course and accept the sacrifices and gifts of the gentiles, they refused to do so and thereby established a "foundation of the war."[14]

---

10. See Saldarini, "Rabbinic Response," 454.

11. For other pivotal moments in the eruption of the revolt according to Josephus, see Josephus, *J.W.* 2.260; 2.284; 4.318. See also Bilde, "Causes of the Jewish War," 184–85, 198; Mason, *Judean War*, 314n2573; Ben Shahar, "Abolishment of the Sacrifice," 576–77. Josephus portrayed a conflict between Jews and gentiles in Caesarea along with Florus's gross misconduct in both Caesarea and Jerusalem and the hotheaded reactions of Jewish youth as the series of events which culminated in the cessation of the sacrifices on behalf of the emperor. See Josephus, *J.W.* 2.277–409.

12. Following Henry St. J. Thackeray, trans., in Josephus, *The Jewish War* (LCL, Cambridge, MA: William Heinemann and Harvard University Press, 1927–1928), vol. 1, 282n2, I have included the word "καὶ" here. Cf. Josephus, *J.W.*, ed. Niese, vol. 4, 230.

13. Josephus, *J.W.* 2.409 (ed. Niese, vol. 4, 230) with translation by Mason, *Judean War*, 313–14. The notion that this was a foundation of the war with Rome is reiterated later on in Josephus, *J.W.* 2.417.

14. See Josephus, *J.W.* 2.410–17 with translation by Mason, *Judean War*, 318.

Like our story of Bar Qamtza, Josephus, already back in the first century, entwined the Jewish revolt against Rome with the Jewish refusal to offer up sacrifices on the Romans' behalf.[15] For both Josephus and the story of Bar Qamtza, the rejection of the Roman offerings was a central trigger or "foundation" of the Jewish war. The shared intimate tie between the rejection and the revolt is so striking and uncanny that it is highly unlikely that it was devised on two separate and independent occasions. Rather, it seems most probable that the rabbinic story ultimately drew the interlocked elements, i.e., the refusal to sacrifice on behalf of Rome and the revolt against Rome, from a Josephus-like tradition.[16] In other words, the rabbis inherited the interlocked elements from a tradition much like the one found in Josephus's *The Jewish War*.[17]

In line with the literary freedom typical of rabbinic creativity, the author of the Bar Qamtza story viewed the refusal-revolt matrix as a literary kernel, as raw material to be molded into a narrative. Although the parallel in *The Jewish War* teaches *us* that the refusal-revolt matrix might have been a historical kernel, the rabbinic author treated it no differently than the other literary materials from which he drew inspiration. Most strikingly, he transformed an intentional and provocative act of insurrection into a hesitant and reluctant decision.[18] Unlike Josephus's rebels who refuse to accept gentile offerings with fierce conviction, the

---

See also Daniel R. Schwartz, *Studies in the Jewish Background of Christianity* (Tübingen: Mohr Siebeck, 1992), 102–16; cf. Barclay, *Against Apion*, 210n268; Ben Shahar, "Abolishment of the Sacrifice," 570–73, 586–90 (n. 101). (See also Steven Mason, *A History of the Jewish War AD 66–74* [Cambridge: Cambridge University Press, 2016], 276, who contends that the rejection of foreign sacrifices was primarily directed against local enemies of the Jews and not the Romans.)

15. For some discussions of this matter, see Halevi, *Gates of the Aggadah*, 204; Baer, "Jerusalem," 170–71; Saldarini, "Rabbinic Response," 451n29; Furstenberg, "Qamtza," 112; Mandel, "Tales of the Destruction," 142–43; Kalmin, *Jewish Babylonia*, 207n49; Ben Shahar, "Abolishment of the Sacrifice," 570; Watts Belser, *Rabbinic Tales of Destruction*, 183.

16. See Tropper, *Rewriting Ancient Jewish History*, 111.

17. If it was Josephus who devised (or popularized) the notion that the refusal to sacrifice Roman offerings served as a foundation for the revolt, then it is likely that the role of the Roman offerings in the story of Bar Qamtza ultimately stemmed from Josephus himself. Cf. Ben Shahar, "Abolishment of the Sacrifice," 592.

18. See Mira Balberg, "Imperial Gifts between Romans and Rabbis," *Jews and Empires: Frankel Institute Annual* (2015): 40.

temple authorities refuse to offer up the Romans' blemished calf in Act II scene 2 only after Bar Qamtza forces them into a corner. In our story, the rebellious refusal to offer up the Roman sacrifices only appears in Bar Qamtza's deceptive slander and the Romans' consequent misreading of the situation in Jerusalem.

By turning to the governor, Bar Qamtza raises the stakes of the feud from a domestic dispute to a political conflict,[19] with the Jerusalemite banqueters along with Zechariah ben Avqulas serving as the mediating element which facilitated the transition from the domestic plane to the political one. Hell-bent on punishing the Jerusalem nobles for their inaction, Bar Qamtza seeks to eradicate the primary locus of their authority and the ultimate source of their wealth. Though it would have been obvious to Bar Qamtza that the fallout of his plot would extend far beyond the Jerusalem elite, perhaps his boiling rage blinded him to the pain and suffering he would be causing multitudes of innocent people. Perhaps his vengeful plot, which was out of all proportion to the wrong done him, reflects a morally flawed character and helps us understand why the host wanted nothing to do with him in the first place. Alternatively, perhaps Bar Qamtza, like the divine hand guiding his disproportionate response, held the Jewish people collectively responsible for his humiliating experience since the banqueters represented, and perhaps embodied, the Jewish nation as a whole (or its leading elite). With banquets in the Roman world delineating insiders from outsiders and friend from foe, Bar Qamtza may have viewed his unprotested ejection from the Jerusalem banquet as a sign that he was an outsider, even a foe, and his excessive response was accordingly that of a onetime intimate who had been mercilessly spurned.

The Slander's Reception

After Bar Qamtza delivers his fabricated slander to the governor, his evil scheme encounters a minor obstacle which he quickly manipulates to his own advantage:

---

19. See Saldarini, "Rabbinic Response," 450; Ruth Calderon, *A Talmudic Alfa Beta: Private Collection* (אלפא ביתא תלמודי: אוסף פרטי), (Tel Aviv: Miskal – Yedioth Ahronoth and Chemed, 2014), 189; Haim Weiss, "'From that Hour the Doom Was Sealed': On Class Reversals in the 'Legends of Destruction'" ("'יעל אותה שעה נחתם גזר הדין': על היפוכים מעמדיים וחורבן הבית"), *JSJF* 31 (2018): 4–5.

19 נזף ביה; עאל לגביה תוב,

20 אמר ליה: כל אלין קורבניא דאת משלח אינון אכלין להון ומקרבין אחרנין בחלופיהון

21 ואין לית את מהימן לי, שלח עמי חד אפרכוס וקורבניא עמיה ואת ידע.

19 He reprimanded him. (Nonetheless,) he (Bar Qamtza) came to him (the ruler) again.

20 He said to him: All those offerings that you send, they eat them and offer up others in their stead

21 and if you do not believe me, send with me an officer and offerings with him and you will know.

The governor's immediate response to Bar Qamtza's slanderous report is to sharply rebuke Bar Qamtza, dismissing his report as implausible and unbelievable. We may presume that the governor viewed the Jews as loyal subjects; after all, he had no reason to question the amicable stance of the Jerusalem leadership, and the Jews had been sacrificing daily offerings on behalf of Rome for generations. In point of fact, the governor's rebuke is well warranted; Bar Qamtza's report was false and the Jews of Jerusalem had no intention to rebel or otherwise provoke the wrath of Rome. Moreover, the governor's refusal to believe Bar Qamtza paints him in a highly positive light. By depicting the governor as a fair and benevolent leader, not party to Bar Qamtza's evil machinations, the story stakes out a distinctive political ideology.

There exists a broad spectrum of possible Jewish attitudes to gentile authorities. At one end lies sweeping assimilation and full cooperation, while at the other lies total rejection and violent confrontation. "Between these two extremes exists a wide range involving varying degrees of accommodation, integration, withdrawal, segregation, and resistance."[20] The Book of Esther is the classic Jewish expression of a largely accommodating stance towards an imperial regime.[21] In Esther, the Jews are

20. Matthew S. Rindge, "Jewish Identity under Foreign Rule: Daniel 2 as a Reconfiguration of Genesis 41," *JBL* 129 (2010): 95. See Natalie B. Dohrmann, "Law and Imperial Idioms: Rabbinic Legalism in a Roman World," in *Jews, Christians, and the Roman Empire: The Poetics of Power in Late Antiquity*, ed. Annette Yoshiko Reed and Natalie B. Dohrmann (Philadelphia: University of Pennsylvania Press, 2012), 72; Tropper, *Simeon the Righteous*, 153–54; Secunda, *Iranian Talmud*, 82–84.
21. See W. Lee Humphreys, "A Life-Style for Diaspora: A Study of the Tales of

loyal subjects who pose no threat to the regime and, as a result, the benevolent monarch bears the Jews no ill will. This idyllic status quo is disrupted, however, when an evil counselor, Haman, convinces the king that the Jews pose a threat to the peace of his realm. In a similar vein, the story of Bar Qamtza, as I read it, describes a world in which there is no inherent conflict between the Jews and the gentile authorities, and conflicts only arise when an evil counselor hatches a plot. Bar Qamtza functions as Haman's counterpart but, unlike Haman, Bar Qamtza is Jewish. Hence, it seems that, as in Esther, the story of Bar Qamtza expresses a strongly accommodating stance towards the gentile regime, typical of a colonized (or diasporic) Jewish community accustomed to negotiating life under a gentile imperial regime. Unlike Esther, however, the story of Bar Qamtza's accommodating stance is so appeasing that even the evil advisor is Jewish.

The notion that Jews were ultimately to blame for the temple's destruction or desecration was not a rabbinic innovation. Some Second Temple sources lay the blame for the ultimate desecration of the temple during Hasmonaean times on Jews like Menelaus or the Tobiads, and Josephus underscored the role of intra-Jewish conflict in the revolt against Rome which culminated in the temple's destruction.[22] Implicating Jews in such tragedies absolved the gentile authorities from wrong-

---

Esther and Daniel," *JBL* 92 (1973): 211–23; Arndt Meinhold, "Die Gattung der Josephsgeschichte und des Esterbuches: Diasporanovelle I," *ZAW* 87 (1975): 306–24; "Die Gattung der Josephsgeschichte und des Esterbuches: Diasporanovelle II," *ZAW* 88 (1976): 72–93; Susan Niditch, *Underdogs and Tricksters: A Prelude to Biblical Folklore* (San Francisco, CA: Harper & Row, 1987), 126–45. On the calibration or rejection of Esther's political ideology in Second Temple times, see, for example, Daniel R. Schwartz, "From the Maccabees to Masada: On Diasporan Historiography of the Second Temple Period," in *Jüdische Geschichte in hellenistisch-römischer Zeit*, ed. Aharon Oppenheimer and Elisabeth Müller Luckner (Munich: Oldenbourg, 1999), 29–40; *2 Maccabees* (Berlin: Walter de Gruyter, 2008), 45–56; *Judeans and Jews: Four Faces of Dichotomy in Ancient Jewish History* (Toronto: University of Toronto Press, 2014), 14; Noah Hacham, "3 Maccabees and Esther: Parallels, Intertextuality, and Diaspora Identity," *JBL* 126 (2007): 765–85; "*Bigthan and Teresh* and the Reason Gentiles Hate Jews," *VT* 62 (2012): 348–52; Aaron J. Koller, *Esther in Ancient Jewish Thought* (Cambridge: Cambridge University Press, 2014), 136–51. (See also Chapter 11, n. 15.)

22. See 2 Macc 4:47, 13: 4; Josephus, *J.W.* 1.10, 1.31–35; *Ant.* 12.384.

doing, thereby buttressing an accommodating stance towards the foreign rulers. From a theological perspective, the implication of corrupt Jews could be enlisted to justify the temple's desecration or destruction as divine punishment.[23]

Although the governor rejects the slanderous report out of hand, Bar Qamtza refuses to quit. Fueled by his burning anger, Bar Qamtza's determination does not waver, and a minor setback, the governor's reprimand, only encourages him to try harder.[24] Returning to the governor, Bar Qamtza first repeats his lie practically word for word: "All those offerings that you send, they eat them and offer up others in their stead." However, having learned from experience that his slander will not be granted a welcome reception, this time Bar Qamtza tacks on some practical advice: "if you do not believe me, send with me an officer and offerings and you will know." The underlying logic of this advice is that the governor has nothing to lose by checking Bar Qamtza's report of subversive Jewish activity and much to gain if the report should prove to be accurate.[25]

The combination of an intelligence report with practical advice is familiar from other stories about advisers to gentile rulers in antiquity. For example, when Joseph interprets Pharaoh's dreams, he also spells out how Pharaoh might take advantage of the years of plenty in preparation for the subsequent years of famine.[26] Similarly, when Haman slanders the Jews before Ahasuerus, telling him that the Jews are a scattered and dispersed people "whose laws are different from those of any other people and who do not obey the king's laws,"[27] he also recommends promulgating an edict calling for the destruction of this subversive

---

23. See 2 Macc 4:7–17, 5:15–20, (13:3–8). See also Bruce William Jones, "Antiochus Epiphanes and the Persecution of the Jews," in *Scripture in Context: Essays on the Comparative Method*, ed. Carl D. Evans, William W. Hallo, and John B. White (Eugene, OR: Pickwick, 1980), 272.

24. Perhaps Bar Qamtza's second audience with the governor echoes the Jerusalemite practice to extend a second (confirmation) invitation to a banquet.

25. Cf. a similar Roman response to an alleged Jewish revolt in Josephus, *J.W.* 2.333–35.

26. See Gen 41:25–36.

27. Esth 3:8.

people.[28] Like these earlier advisers, Bar Qamtza also attaches practical advice to his report, although his goal differs. Joseph and Haman's practical advice revolves around translating an intelligence report (or dream interpretation) into action, while Bar Qamtza's advice is designed to sway the ruler to confirm an intelligence report he does not believe.

In hopes of persuading the governor to corroborate his report, Bar Qamtza advises the governor as follows: "שלח עמי חד אפרכוס וקורבניא עמיה ואת ידע," "send with me an officer and offerings and you will know." By sending an objective officer and the tribute back to Jerusalem with Bar Qamtza, the governor can easily verify whether the Jews in fact do not sacrifice the daily offerings on behalf of Rome.

On the linguistic plane, Bar Qamtza's advice echoes the parallel scene in Act I in various ways. The officer sent in Act II scene 1, "חד אפרכוס," literally "one officer" (line 21), parallels the "אדם אחד," "one man" (line 4), who threw the banquet in Act I scene 1. The verbal root ש.ל.ח., meaning "to send," which originally appeared in Act I scene 1 – "לשלוחו," literally "to the one he sent" (line 5), appeared once again in Bar Qamtza's report "אלין קורבניא דאת משלח," "those offerings that you send" (lines 18 and 20), and appears a third time in Bar Qamtza's advice: "שלח עמי חד אפרכוס," "send with me an officer" (line 21). By repeating the word "send," the sending of the Roman offerings and officer in Act II echo the sending of the banquet invitations in Act I. Similarly, the use of the Greek loanword "אפרכוס," "officer" ("ἔπαρχος"[29]) (line 21) in Act II, recalls the use of another Greek loanword, "ארסטטיה," "banqueters" (line 6) in Act I.[30] The first Greek loanword highlights the intersection of Greek and Jewish culture in Jerusalem banquets and the second underscores the Roman rule over Judaea. Together the loanwords remind us of the pervasive presence of Greek culture and Roman authority in both the private and public spheres. Whereas Act I enlists the asymmetrical relationship between host and guest in banquets of the Greek and Roman world, Act II presumes the asymmetrical relationship between Rome and Judaea.

28. See Esth 3:8–9.
29. See Sokoloff, *Dictionary of Jewish Palestinian Aramaic*, 27.
30. See Chapter 6, nn. 2–3 above.

The Deception

Bar Qamtza's second audience with the governor succeeds where the first failed, and the governor sends an officer and animals along with Bar Qamtza in order to confirm or discredit Bar Qamtza's report. With the officer and animals en route to Jerusalem, Bar Qamtza finds a way to ensure that the priests of Jerusalem will reject the governor's tribute:

22 כי אתי בשבילא עד דאפרכוס דמיך,

23 קם בליליא ועשאן בעלי מומין [בסתר].[31]

22 While they were traveling on the path, the officer fell asleep.

23 He (Bar Qamtza) got up in the night and [secretly] made them (the animals) blemished.

On the road to Jerusalem, Bar Qamtza waits for the officer to fall asleep and in the dead of night he ("secretly") blemishes the animals.[32] The Bible prohibits the sacrifice of blemished animals on various occasions, and, due to the biblical prohibition, Bar Qamtza was quite certain that the priests would be unwilling to sacrifice the Romans' blemished animals.[33] Having been forced to "stand up," "קום," and get out of the banquet (lines 7 and 13), Bar Qamtza took revenge when he "got up," "קם," or literally "stood up," and blemished the Romans' intended sacrificial animals.

The fact that Bar Qamtza blemishes the animals in secret, while the accompanying Roman officer is fast asleep, reveals two features of the officer's role in the story. First, Bar Qamtza must hide his blemishing activity because the officer obviously knows that blemished animals may not be sacrificed. Since the Romans had been sending offerings to Jerusalem for generations and, in any event, since Greek and Roman tradition similarly demanded that sacrificial animals be unblemished,

---

31. The phrase "בדוקין שבעין," "on the white of the eye," was apparently interpolated into Oxford 102 and Parma 2393 due to the influence of the Bavli. London 27089 reads here "בסתר," "secretly."

32. See Ben Shahar, "Abolishment of the Sacrifice," 590. (Cf. Friedman, "Dama Ben Netina," 124–25 and the sources cited there.)

33. See Lev 22:17–25; Deut 15:21, 17:1.

the officer responsible for the Roman tribute would have understood the practical ramifications of Bar Qamtza's underhanded activity.[34]

Second, as a fair and honest representative of Rome, the officer is not party to Bar Qamtza's devilish scheme. Were the officer to discover Bar Qamtza's deception, he would certainly have revealed it to the governor. Therefore, in order to properly execute the deception, Bar Qamtza must pull the wool over the officer's eyes. Bar Qamtza's efforts to fool the officer reinforce the story's political ideology of accommodation already expressed in the governor's reprimand. Just like the governor, the officer bears the Jews no ill will; both are honest and decent administrators led astray by an angry and vindictive Jewish advisor.

Echoes of Act I

In addition to the linguistic echoes of Act I scene 1 noted above, Act II opens with some striking thematic parallels to Act I. Both Acts involve banquets and invitations: the domestic banquet of Act I parallels the divine banquet – the temple offerings, of Act II – [35] and the banquet invitation of Act I parallels the invitation to send offerings in Act II. Both Acts spotlight the banquet's unwelcome guest(s): Bar Qamtza is the unwelcome banqueter in Act I, and the blemished animals are the unwelcome tribute in Act II. Just as the host condemns Bar Qamtza for some damning flaw in Act I, Jewish law condemns the Romans' flawed offerings in Act II. Both Acts revolve around a misunderstanding: Bar Qamtza thinks the host invited him to his banquet (due to the messenger's accidental error) and the governor comes to believe that the Roman offerings are unwelcome (due to Bar Qamtza's intentional deception). Just as Act I scene 1 sets the stage for the ejection of Bar Qamtza in

---

34. See Gunnel Ekroth, "Animal Sacrifice in Antiquity," in *The Oxford Handbook of Ancient Animals in Classical Thought and Life*, ed. Gordon Lindsay Campbell (Oxford: Oxford University Press, 2014), 332–33. Cf. Balberg, "Imperial Gifts," 41. Balberg's claim that "the rabbinic account…serves to make the point that at the end of the day, Jews and Romans do not speak the same essential sacrificial language," is only appropriate for the Bavli's version of the story, as we shall see below in Part II.
35. Cf. Levine Katz, "Qamtsa," 40; Mandel, "Tales of the Destruction," 150.

Act I scene 2, Act II scene 1 sets the stage for the rejection of the Roman offerings in Act II scene 2. In sum, by reverberating themes from Act I, Act II transitions from a domestic to a political plane, completing the transformation of a situational comedy into a national tragedy.

Chapter 10

Rejecting the Roman Offerings
(ACT II SCENE 2)

After Bar Qamtza plants the seed of suspicion in the Roman governor's heart and then secretly blemishes the Roman authorities' sacrificial animals in Act II scene 1, the Roman delegation arrives in the Jerusalem temple in Act II scene 2:

24 כיון שראה הכהן אותן הקריב אחרים תחתיהן.

25 אמ׳ ליה: למחר אנא קריב להון.

26 אתא יומא אחרינא, אמר ליה: לית את מקריב להון.

27 אמר ליה: למחר.

28 אתא יומא תליתאה ולא קריבהון.

24 When the priest saw them, he offered up others in their place.

25 He (the priest) said to him (the officer): Tomorrow I will offer them up.

26 The next day came and he (the officer) said to him (the priest): You are not offering them up.

27 He said to him: Tomorrow.

28 The third day came and he did not offer them up.

Upon arrival, the Romans naturally hand over the animals intended for sacrifice to the temple authorities, but the priest in charge does not offer them up. "When the priest saw them," i.e., when the priest saw the animals' blemishes, he understood that biblical law prohibited their sacrifice so he "offered up others in their place." Whereas the priest replaces the dedicated blemished animals with other unblemished animals in order to uphold biblical law, from the Roman officer's perspective the priest behaves exactly as Bar Qamtza predicted. Indeed, even the language used to describe the priest's action, "he offered up others in their place" ("הקריב אחרים תחתיהם"), recalls the language of Bar Qamtza's claim from scene 2, "they offer up others in their stead," ("ומקרבין אחרנין בחלופיהון" [lines 18 and 20]). Seeing the Roman officer's displeasure (or surprise), the priest assures him: "Tomorrow I will offer them up." While the priest has no reason to imagine that the Roman officer is beginning to suspect his motives, he can well see that the officer expects the tribute to be sacrificed.

On the next day, the officer notices that the sacrificial animals he delivered were still not offered up, and admonishes the priest: "לית את מקריב להון," "You are not offering them up."[1] The opening phrase of his rebuke, "לית את," "**You are not**," echoes the opening phrase of the host's declarations in Act 1 scene 2: "לית את מסובי הכא," "**You are not** reclining here" (lines 9 and 11). In both cases, the phrase depicts rejection and exclusion – the host rejects Bar Qamtza as a guest, and the priest rejects the Roman animals as sacrificial offerings. The parallel rejections with their shared opening phrase, as we shall see below, are not the only links between the two scenes.

In response to the officer's complaint, the priest repeats the delay tactic he employed the day before. "Tomorrow," the priest assures the officer, the Roman animals will be offered up. In pushing off the Roman officer for two consecutive days, the priest seeks to buy time, apparently hoping that the officer will lose interest or will be called away to handle more pressing matters. The officer, however, returns on the third day and, despite the priest's promises to the contrary, he does not offer up the offerings. The priest, however, does not try to push off the officer a third time because, after failing twice to keep his word, he recognizes that he has forfeited his credibility. As the scene closes, we conclude that the

---

1. Alternatively, the sentence could be read as a question: "You are not offering them up?"

officer not only recognizes that the priest has no intention of offering up the Roman tribute, but that the officer also views the series of delays as confirmation of Bar Qamtza's claim that the Jews refuse to sacrifice the Roman tribute and offer up other animals instead.

The Three-Day Delay

The three-day delay would have provided the temple authorities with plenty of time to weigh in on the matter, hence we may presume that the priest is not acting as a radical lone wolf but rather as a representative of the temple leadership. The delay reveals that the temple authorities had ample opportunity to change their minds, rethink their position, and sacrifice the Romans' blemished animals. Since humiliating the Roman authorities by rejecting their tribute was a highly precarious affair, the potential danger involved should have justified a temporary abrogation of the biblical law of blemishes. The priesthood, however, does not opt for this pragmatic and judicious solution, presumably because it simply cannot imagine defiling the temple with blemished animals.

The three-day delay also offers the priest ample opportunity to explain to the officer that the biblical law of blemishes prevents him from sacrificing the Romans' animals. Despite having the opportunity to pursue this avenue, the priest elects not to do so, presumably because he knows that doing so would be doomed to failure.[2] The priest can well see from the Roman officer's daily visits that the officer expects the

---

2. Furstenberg argues that the priest's failure to communicate the blemish issue to the Roman officer exacerbated the inherent tension between Jews and Romans, transforming it into mutual suspicion. Hence, for Furstenberg, a major crux of the story, the communication failure which led to the Roman attack, must be read between the lines. (See Furstenberg, "Qamtza," 109.) In my opinion, however, the plot of a rabbinic sage story should not rest so heavily on matters left unsaid (see Chapter 6, n. 6 above) and, furthermore, the Roman-Jewish tension Furstenberg reads into the scene doesn't fit with the accommodating Jewish stance developed in the previous scene. The officer suspects the priest's intentions because of Bar Qamtza's slander, not because of any inherent tension between Romans and Jews. Similarly, the priest refrains from discussing the blemish issue because he apparently realizes it will make no difference. The heart of the scene is not a communication failure but the priest's tragic obduracy.

animals to be sacrificed and, in truth, since the Roman officer is entirely unaware of Bar Qamtza's intervention, he honestly believes that he has delivered perfect and unblemished specimens. Regardless of whether the priest suspects Bar Qamtza (or the Romans) of foul play, or whether he concludes that the animals were blemished by accident or after delivery, the officer's behavior conveys his presumption that the Roman delegation followed standard protocols and delivered unblemished animals.[3] Under these conditions, the priest recognizes that if he were to claim that the Roman animals were blemished, the officer would surmise that the priest had fabricated a feeble excuse so as to cover up his tragic and stubborn refusal to sacrifice the Roman offerings.

Insofar as the Romans are concerned, the three-day delay underscores their friendly attitude towards the Jews. Like the governor, the officer is not wont to suspect the Jews of subversive or antagonistic conduct. Only when the Roman animals are rejected again and again, only when the evidence is too great to ignore, is he forced to render his judgment.

After Act II scene 2's introductory line (line 24), the scene unfolds in an ABAB format. The A lines, lines 25 and 27, transmit the priest's commitment to offer up the animals "tomorrow," and the B lines, lines 26 and 28, describe how when the following day arrives – "the next day came," "the third day came," – the priest "did not offer them up." This repetitive literary format magnifies the dramatic tension of the scene as the priest, in his desperation, pushes off the officer twice with his assurances regarding "tomorrow," and, for his part, the officer's patience gradually wears thin.[4]

Furthermore, the repetitive literary format and growing tension of the scene echoes the similarly repetitive literary format and escalating

---

3. It seems unlikely that the priest would have suspected the Romans themselves of blemishing the animals since the Roman authorities, as imagined in the story, had harmonious relations with the Jews and harbored no wish to antagonize them.
4. On (incremental) repetition as a means to intensify the emotional weight of a passage, see Albert B. Friedman, Edward Doughtie, and T.V.F. Brogan, "Incremental Repetition," in *The New Princeton Encyclopedia of Poetry and Poetics*, ed. Alex Preminger and T.V.F. Brogan (Princeton, NJ: Princeton University Press, 1993) 581–82.

tension of the previous act's parallel scene, Act I scene 2.[5] The officer's extended negotiations with the priest in Act II scene 2 parallel Bar Qamtza's extended negotiations with the host in Act I scene 2. The three consecutive days during which the priest consistently refuses to offer up the Roman offerings echo the rejection of Bar Qamtza's three ever-more-desperate pleas to remain at the banquet. In short, the Roman attempts to find a place in the Jerusalem temple's divine banquet mirrors Bar Qamtza's attempts to find a place in a Jerusalemite's domestic banquet, and the priest's consistent rejections of the Roman tribute echoes the host's insistent rejections of Bar Qamtza himself.

The Parallel Rejections

The parallel rejections at the center of each act beg a comparison, and one possible comparative lens enlists the former – the host's rejection of Bar Qamtza – in the interpretation of the latter – the priest's rejection of the Roman sacrificial animals. The host's ruthless removal of Bar Qamtza stems from an intense enmity that, as noted above, betrays a severe dearth of Jewish solidarity. In a similar manner, the rejection of the Romans' blemished animals also betrays a deficient sense of Jewish solidarity. The temple leadership endangers the temple and countless Jewish lives when it arouses the wrath of an empire by rejecting its sacrificial animals.

I believe, however, that an alternative comparative lens or, more precisely, a contrasting lens, offers an even more incisive reading that focuses on salient differences brought to the fore by a comparison of the parallel rejections. In Act II, the Jerusalem priesthood is exacting and uncompromising in its performance of the temple cult, and, despite the potential fallout of their decision, the dedicated priesthood refuses to violate cultic law. In Act I, by contrast, the host's rejection of Bar Qamtza, along with the apparent acquiescence of the unresponsive onlookers, depicts a Jerusalem community whose members do not care for one another. Failing to look out for Bar Qamtza, the Jerusalemites exhibit their deficient sense of Jewish solidarity and flawed moral compass.

---

5. See Mandel, "Tales of the Destruction," 149–50.

Consequently, the comparison of the two parallel rejections brings into sharp relief the gaping chasm between the Jerusalem elite's attitudes to cultic law, on the one hand, and moral law, on the other. Whereas the "precious children of Jerusalem" conscientiously perform the cultic law in all its minutiae, they neglect to fulfill basic moral laws. While they are fastidious and exacting when it comes to ritual, they are defective and weak when it comes to solidarity. In short, comparing the two parallel rejections teaches that without fostering the moral virtues, the temple cult by itself is of no value.

For the author and early audiences of the story of Bar Qamtza, the temple cult was a thing of the past: the sacrificial cult was not revived after the destruction of the temple in 70 CE. Long after the cessation of the temple service, however, the temple cult remained the ultimate symbol of ritual law, that is, of the many precepts between man and God. Hence, in order to translate the moral thrust of the story for a world lacking the temple service, perhaps ancient Jews would have viewed sacrificial worship as a proxy for ritual law more generally. Perhaps they would have interpreted the tension between Act II and Act I as the jarring juxtaposition of intense ritual piety and severe moral shortcomings.

Chapter 11

The Roman Response
(ACT II SCENE 3)

The third scene of Act II, which is also the story's final scene, presents the Roman response to the Jewish refusal to offer up the Roman delegation's sacrificial animals. The brief account of the Roman response unfolds in two steps: the officer's report to the governor and the governor's course of action.

29 שלח ואמר למלכא: ההיא מילתא דיהדייא קושטא הוא!

30 מיד סלק וחרב בי מקדשא.

29 He (the officer) sent (a message) to the king saying: The statement of the Jew is true!

30 Immediately he rose up and destroyed the temple.

The scene opens with the Roman officer's dispatch to the governor who authorized his mission, i.e., to the "king."[1] The officer "sent (a message)," "שלח," to the governor, and the reappearance of the verbal root ש.ל.ח., meaning to send, neatly corresponds to its earlier appearances in Act II.[2] Just as the governor "sent" the officer along with sacrificial animals in order to check Bar Qamtza's slanderous claims, the officer "sent" his report on the matter back to the governor.

---

1. See Chapter 9, n. 4 above.
2. On the earlier appearances of this verbal root, see Chapter 9 above.

After the priest attempted to replace the Roman sacrificial animals with other animals and then refused to offer up the Roman animals for three days in a row, the officer concludes that Bar Qamtza's intelligence report is accurate and accordingly informs his superior: "The statement of the Jew is true." The officer did not actually see the Jews eat the Roman animals as Bar Qamtza had claimed they would, but it would have been natural for him to surmise that if the Jews did not offer up the animals to God, they kept them for themselves. In any event, the significance of Bar Qamtza's report from the Roman perspective is the symbolic ramification of the humiliating refusal, i.e., the rejection of Roman authority; hence the officer did not need to actually see the Jews eating the Roman animals in order to confirm the gist of Bar Qamtza's claim. Despite the Roman authorities' initial hesitation and disbelief, the officer's experience seemed to prove Bar Qamtza right.

In response to the officer's report, the governor reacts quickly and decisively: "Immediately he rose up and destroyed the temple." The humiliating rejection of the Romans' sacrificial animals and the repudiation of Roman authority warrant a harsh and unequivocal response. The Romans, who otherwise tolerated the Jewish religion, destroyed the temple in which the local elite dared to defy their rule.

The phrase "חרב בי מקדשא," "destroyed the temple," also appears in line 31, in the first epilogue's pronouncement that: בין קמצא לבין "קמצא חריב בי מקדשא," "Between Qamtza and Qamtza the temple was destroyed." Some form of this saying may have preceded the formation of the story (as noted in Chapter 12 below), and, if so, the phrase "destroyed the temple" in our scene was probably drawn from the epilogue. In any case, the phrase focuses on the temple, the locus of the subversive Jewish behavior, and, unlike Josephus's long history, it does not consider the tremendous cost of the Jewish war against the Romans. This short phrase gives no sense of the loss of life, the suffering, and the enslavement of Judaeans during the war since it does not intend to offer a historical account of the war. Instead, it focuses on the war's central calamity from a religious perspective. Many Jews viewed the Jerusalem temple as the central medium of their communion with God and the primary conduit for absolution. Its destruction was perceived as a catastrophic blow to the Jewish people's relationship with the divine.

Like the first two scenes of Act II, the third scene also correlates to its parallel scene in Act I. Just as Act I scene 3 depicts Bar Qamtza's furious reaction to his humiliating ejection from the banquet, Act II scene 3 describes the Romans' furious response to the humiliating rejection of their sacrificial animals. Bar Qamtza was spurred to action by his indignation over the Jerusalemites who ate at the banquet from which he was ejected as the Roman officer is similarly prompted into action by his "realization" that the Jerusalem priests eat the Roman animals intended for sacrifice. For his part, Bar Qamtza translates his fury into the vengeful plot of Act II and, for their part, the Romans translate their fury into the destruction of the temple.

While Act II follows Act I causally and chronologically – Bar Qamtza's humiliation in Act I prompts his revenge in Act II – the second Act correlates to the first from start to finish.[3] Unaware of the messenger's accidental error, Bar Qamtza mistakenly expects to be welcomed at a domestic banquet; unaware of the blemishes Bar Qamtza intentionally inflicted, the Romans mistakenly expect their tribute to be welcomed at a divine banquet. Bar Qamtza's extended negotiations with the host, which illustrate the severe moral shortcomings of the Jerusalem elite, contrast sharply with the extended negotiations between the officer and priest, which illustrate the Jerusalem elite's deep commitment to cultic law. Finally, Bar Qamtza's revenge prefigures the Romans' revenge. In fact, the Romans' revenge, i.e., the destruction of the temple, is the ultimate realization of Bar Qamtza's own revenge.

---

3. In my opinion, sensitivity to the chronological and causal relationship between Acts I and II (see Mandel, "Tales of the Destruction," 149–50) only enhances our appreciation for the structural ties between the two acts (cf. Ben Shahar, "Abolishment of the Sacrifice," 590).

Chapter 12

The Coda

After Act II culminates with the destruction of the temple, the story as a whole concludes with a brief coda constituted of two epilogues:

31 הדא היא דבריתא אמרין: בין קמצא לבין קמצא חריב בי מקדשא.

32 א"ר יוסי: ענותנותו של ר' זכריה בן אבקולס שרפה את ההיכל.

31 Hence people say: Between Qamtza and Qamtza the temple was destroyed.

32 Rabbi Yose said: The meekness of Rabbi Zechariah ben Avqulas burnt down the sanctuary.

The first epilogue (line 31) adduces a purportedly popular saying – "Hence people say" – regarding the destruction of the temple, and the second epilogue (line 32) cites a rabbinic teaching about the temple's destruction attributed to Rabbi Yose. The second epilogue (as discussed above in Chapter 7) is a late and secondary layer of the story. It reproduces an early hyperbolic statement attributed to Rabbi Yose and, in tandem with line 14 – "Zechariah ben Avqulas was present and he had the opportunity to protest but did not protest" – transforms our story from one unrelated to the rabbis into one starring a rabbinic sage. Since the second epilogue was explored above at length, let us consider here the story's original epilogue: "Between Qamtza and Qamtza the temple was destroyed."

"Between Qamtza and Qamtza"

From a text critical perspective, the epilogue's dictum is highly unstable. Some textual witnesses (in line with the Bavli), read between "Qamtza" and "Bar Qamtza;"[1] others read between "Qamtza" and "Ben Qamtza;"[2] the Genizah fragment reads between "Kamtza" and "Kamtzora;" Casanatense H 3112 reads between "Bar Qamtza" and "Bar Qamtza;" and our preferred manuscript, Oxford 102, reads between "Qamtza" and "Qamtza." Amongst this variety it is very hard to recover the original text with any confidence. With that being said, Oxford 102's reading, "Qamtza and Qamtza," and Casanatense H 3112's reading, "Bar Qamtza and Bar Qamtza," have the advantage of referring to two individuals with the very same name and, as argued above, it seems likely that in the original reading of the text, the messenger confused two people with the same name in typical comic fashion. Just as Oxford 102 has the messenger mistake one "son of Qamtza" for another "son of Qamtza" in Act I scene 1, Oxford 102's epilogue refers to the tragic mix-up of the two identically named men, enlisting "Qamtza" as an abbreviated form of "son of Qamtza" ("Ben/Bar Qamtza"). Over time, I imagine, copyists sought to ease the reading experience by distinguishing between the two characters with the same name and thus transformed the messenger's original error into a mix-up between similar, but not identical, names.

The first epilogue, "Between Qamtza and Qamtza the temple was destroyed," is presented as a popular folk saying. While the saying may have drawn inspiration from our story, encapsulating the story's plot within a pithy witticism, it is also possible that some form of the saying preceded the story and was modified to fit the local context.[3] If some form of the saying preceded the story, this form probably linked the infamous Ben Qamtzar of Tannaitic tradition to the destruction of the temple, a connection our story subsequently fleshed out in narrative form. In other words, just as the second epilogue stems from a hyperbolic Tannaitic statement regarding Zechariah ben Avqulas, the first epilogue

---

1. See Parma 2393, London 27089 and Parma 2559.
2. See Munich 229, Cambridge 495 and the *editio princeps*.
3. See Yisraeli-Taran, *Legends of the Destruction*, 14; Mandel, "Tales of the Destruction," 147–48; Furstenberg, "Qamtza," 109.

may well stem from a hyperbolic Tannaitic statement regarding Ben Qamtzar.

Regardless of the saying's origins, the epilogue links the saying to our story when it is introduced with the clause: "Hence people say." Read through the lens of this clause, the saying – "Between Qamtza and Qamtza the temple was destroyed" – telescopes our story, referring to the two Qamtzas (or sons of Qamtza) from the story's opening scene and to the destruction of the temple from its closing scene. Bringing the temple's destruction and its ultimate trigger into sharp relief, the saying supplies a brief, witty, and memorable recapitulation.

The Meek Zechariah ben Avqulas

At some point after the original formation of the story, the second epilogue in line 32 – "The meekness of Rabbi Zechariah ben Avqulas burnt down the sanctuary" – was added along with its corresponding line, line 14, in Act I scene 3. These two additions not only initiated the rabbinization of the story which the Bavli later on intensified, they also supplemented, with explicit statements, the condemnation implied by the narrative. The epilogue explains that Zechariah was meek, i.e., timid and cowardly, and line 14 similarly explains, with the help of standard talmudic terminology, that Zechariah should have protested. Although the use of explicit statements rather than narrative in lines 14 and 31 is another sign that these were added to the original story, they are nonetheless in keeping with the story's critique of the passive bystanders. Zechariah ben Avqulas's cowardice stems from a defective sense of solidarity. His fear to stand up to the host and risk his own comfort in order to protect a fellow Jew reveals that he cares too much for himself and too little for his community. Like the other Jerusalemite banqueters, Zechariah cannot rouse himself to defend a powerless guest. When the eminent of Israel abandon their fellow Jews, God abandons Israel and the temple is destroyed.

Chapter 13

Part I's Conclusion

A misunderstanding at a private banquet ultimately leads to the destruction of the temple in Jerusalem. That is the arc of the story of Bar Qamtza in Lamentations Rabbati, and it is succinctly captured in the story's first epilogue: "Between Qamtza and Qamtza the temple was destroyed." In two consecutive yet parallel acts, the story traces this arc from beginning to end. After briefly reviewing highlights of my analysis of the story, I will conclude Part I with some thoughts on the relationship between the two acts.

A Brief Summary

At the very start of our journey, we selected a representative of the conservative branch of Lamentations Rabbati's manuscripts, Oxford 102, as the preferred (extant) reading of Lamentation Rabbati's text of our story. With text in hand, we turned to the story's literary context: the genteel and dignified banquet practices of the "precious children of Jerusalem." Save for the custom of sending a second invitation, these banquet practices already appear scattered throughout earlier rabbinic literature, causing their collection into an assemblage of Jerusalemite customs to create a pattern which characterizes the refined and elegant Jerusalem banqueters of late Second Temple times. Against the backdrop of the decorous banquet customs in Second Temple Jerusalem, the story of Bar Qamtza illustrates how the noble Jerusalemites failed to heed their own banquet etiquette. In addition, the first and last customs, which frame the collection of Jerusalem banquet practices, seek to regulate banquet invitations and fittingly set the stage for a story about an invitation gone horribly wrong.

The dignified banquet tradition of Second Temple Jerusalemites is best viewed as a set of functional parallels, enhancements, or extensions of rabbinic banquet regulations, and all Jewish banquet rituals in Roman Palestine – rabbinic, popular, and Jerusalemite – were embedded within the social, cultural and culinary realm of Greek and Roman banqueting. Banquets among the Greeks and Romans were important social events, rife with rituals that expressed shared values, reinforced social hierarchies, and demarcated insiders from outsiders. Banquets were highly structured dinners with regulated protocols celebrated on all sorts of occasions and in various locales. While leisurely relaxing in a reclining position, banqueters ate, drank, and were entertained in an atmosphere designed to foster friendships and invoke a sense of fellowship and community. Not only were actual banquets widespread across the Mediterranean basin, but banquets also emerged at the heart of a rich literary tradition. Banquet stories appear throughout Greek and Latin literature where they are populated by a host of stock characters and feature a set of typical themes. Since the banquet culture and literary tradition of the Greeks and Romans influenced and informed Jewish banquet practices and ideals, they served as a key interpretive lens in my analysis of the banquet story of Bar Qamtza.

Act I scene 1 opens the story with a banquet invitation mistakenly delivered to the wrong Bar (or Ben) Qamtza. Instead of inviting the host's friend, the host's messenger mistakenly invites the host's enemy of the very same name. The messenger's mistake begins the story on a humorous note, and the central role of the banquet invitation in this opening scene neatly aligns with the prominence of banquet invitations in the adjacent Jerusalemite banquet tradition.

From the perspective of Greek and Roman banquet culture, Act I scene 1's depiction of the banquet invitation is perfectly natural. Because it was considered improper to enter the private realm of a person's home uninvited and a host had the right to select his guests as he saw fit, the extension and reception of invitations were crucial elements in the preparation of a banquet in classical antiquity. For his part, the host was often anxious lest his invitees might decline his invitation, and, for their part, the host's friends might worry about not receiving an invitation. If a host were ever criticized for his guest list, he could handily blame his messenger for bungling the invitation process. In this vein, the messenger in our scene is faulted for inviting the wrong Bar Qamtza. Our messenger's error, confusing two people with the same name, is a comic variation on the ancient theme of mistaken identity, and the entertaining union of this error with a botched banquet invitation appears in ancient comedy as well. In other words, just as our messenger's responsibility for the invitation process is in keeping with the depiction of messengers in classical antiquity, our messenger's error is in keeping with the playful spirit of ancient comedy. From his perspective, Bar Qamtza most probably viewed the invitation he received in error as a reconciliatory gesture since banquet hosts, as a rule, did not invite their enemies.

After Act I scene 1 sets the stage, the conflict between the banquet host and Bar Qamtza erupts in Act I scene 2. When the host finds Bar Qamtza sitting in his home ensconced amongst his guests, he explodes and calls for Bar Qamtza to depart. In the hopes of preventing his humiliating expulsion from the party, Bar Qamtza negotiates with the host, making three ever more generous offers, each of which the host rejects. In line with the importance of honor and shame in Roman antiquity, Bar Qamtza was prepared to do almost anything to avoid humiliation. As he desperately raises the ante and the host consistently rejects his proposals, the dramatic tension of the scene escalates until the host adamantly repeats his original call for Bar Qamtza to exit the premises.

Three features of the scene, the abusive host, the uninvited guest, and the banquet conflict, loudly resonate against the literary backdrop of Greek and Roman banquet stories. The abusive and domineering host is a stock figure in Greek and Roman banquet stories, a volatile force enlisted, at times, to satirize a purportedly decadent society or a supposedly failing patronage system. In our story, the abusive host is enrolled to critique a Jewish community in which a Jew could so despise a fellow Jew. Giving narrative form to the Tannaitic saying attributed to Rabbi Yohanan ben Torta, which identified "hating one's fellow before God" as the ultimate cause of the temple's destruction, the abusive host signifies the dearth of empathy and solidarity which, in rabbinic eyes, plagued late Second Temple Jerusalem.

Like the abusive host, the uninvited guest or ἄκλητος is also a stock figure in the banquet literature of classical antiquity. Since it was unacceptable to enter a banquet without an invitation, the uninvited guest is usually a disruptive force, an unanticipated and often unwelcome interloper who lacks an assigned seat. The uninvited banqueter is often depicted as a gluttonous parasite, happy to entertain and be mocked so long as he is allowed to partake in the banquet. In the eyes of the host, Bar Qamtza is an unwelcome and intrusive bootlicker, an uninvited guest who may be humiliated at will. In truth, however, Bar Qamtza *was* invited to the host's banquet, and his willingness to abstain from eating and even cover the banquet's costs reveal that he is not a greedy parasite. Bar Qamtza is not an uninvited guest, he is only mistaken for one, and this mistake, on the heels of the messenger's error, ultimately leads to the disastrous fall of the temple.

Ancient banquet stories commonly feature brawls and verbal abuse, and these literary conflicts apparently amplified the fights which sometimes broke out at actual banquets. The host's cruel and reprehensible treatment of Bar Qamtza echoes the standard conflict theme of ancient banquet stories while also reflecting the fear shared by many ancient banqueters of a vicious and tyrannical host. When the host's view of Bar Qamtza as an uninvited, lowly, and hated parasite clashes with Bar Qamtza's view of himself as a properly invited respectable guest, the story erupts in tragic conflict.

Scene 3 concludes Act 1 with a dual indictment of the passive onlookers to Bar Qamtza's humiliating expulsion. The indictment unfurls over two textual layers, one early and original and the other late and secondary. The original layer impugns the Jerusalemite banqueters who go on to recline and savor the banquet even as the host embarrasses Bar Qamtza and mercilessly kicks him out of the feast. Focusing on the Jerusalemites' unwillingness to fulfill their communal responsibility, the original layer gives narrative form to a theme cited elsewhere in Lamentations Rabbati (and other Amoraic literature): "Jerusalem was destroyed only because they did not rebuke one another." Unlike scene 2, which focused on one Jerusalemite's acute hatred for another, scene 3 highlights the lack of solidarity across the Jerusalemite community. In turning a blind eye to Bar Qamtza's plight, the unresponsive bystanders infuriate Bar Qamtza to no end, planting in him a desire for revenge and the seeds for the destruction of the temple.

The second and later layer of scene 3, which implicates Zechariah ben Avqulas in Bar Qamtza's humiliation, was added to the story along with the second epilogue, which also mentions Zechariah ben Avqulas. In describing Zechariah's offense, the text enlists the standard rabbinic phrase "he had the opportunity to protest but did not protest." This portrait of Zechariah's passivity buttresses the scene's original theme – the failure of the noble Second Temple Jerusalemites' to fulfill their communal responsibilities – but transfers the brunt of the moral burden to a rabbinic sage. As we shall see in Part II, the process of rabbinization initiated in this late layer of Lamentations Rabbati is magnified later on in the Babylonian version of the story.

The interpolation of Zechariah ben Avqulas into Act I scene 3 is intricately intertwined with the addition of the second epilogue, "Rabbi Yose said: The meekness of Rabbi Zechariah ben Avqulas burnt down the sanctuary," an authentic Tannaitic tradition independently preserved already in the Tosefta. According to this Tannaitic tradition, the sanctuary burnt down because Zechariah adopted a meek approach to a legal dispute between Beit Hillel and Beit Shammai, and, in the hopes of offering a more believable rationale for this hyperbolic Tannaitic statement, someone inserted Zechariah ben Avqulas into our story.

In a similar vein, a hyperbolic and exaggerated Tannaitic statement most likely supplied a central literary kernel of our story. A well-known Tannaitic tradition castigates a late Second Temple official named Ben Qamtzar merely for preserving a trade secret. Puzzled by the extremely harsh rabbinic reaction to Ben Qamtzar's decision to keep his intellectual property a secret, a later author apparently invented the story of Bar Qamtza, the Aramaic equivalent of the name Ben Qamtzar, in order to explain what could have warranted such severe condemnation. With the advent of the story of Bar Qamtza, Ben Qamtzar was disparaged not simply for refusing to divulge trade secrets, but for plotting the destruction of the temple in Jerusalem.

Act II opens in scene 1 with a resentful and indignant Bar Qamtza enacting a diabolical plan against the Jerusalem elite who spurned him in Act I. At first, Bar Qamtza slanders the Jerusalem elite, informing the local Roman governor that the Jerusalemites eat the animals which the Roman authorities send as offerings to Jerusalem, sacrificing other animals in their stead. The offerings at issue are apparently the daily sacrifices made in honor of Rome, mentioned by Philo and Josephus, and the Romans would have viewed the Jewish refusal to sacrifice these offerings as rebellious defiance. Furthermore, in linking the refusal to offer up the Roman tribute to the destruction of the temple, our story echoes the refusal-revolt matrix already attested in Josephus's *The Jewish War*. In our story, a foundation of the Jewish war against Rome according to Josephus is transformed into Bar Qamtza's slanderous lie.

The Roman governor, however, does not believe Bar Qamtza and admonishes him. The governor sees no reason to accept Bar Qamtza's outlandish claim, and, as a good man and responsible official, he sides with the Jews. This highly positive depiction of the Roman governor, and the Roman officer in his wake, embodies the story's ideology of political accommodation. In the world of our story, Jews and Romans live together in peaceful harmony, and tensions only arise when evil counselors plant mistrust and misunderstanding in the hearts of the Roman authorities. From a theological perspective, when Roman responsibility is minimized and Jewish culpability is maximized, the temple's destruction is more easily interpreted as divine punishment.

In response to the governor's disbelief, Bar Qamtza invites him to send offerings with him to Jerusalem along with an officer to verify his claim. The governor accepts the invitation, and, on the way to Jerusalem, Bar Qamtza secretly blemishes the Roman animals under the cover of night because he knows that blemished animals are unwelcome in the temple and that the Roman officer would understand the ramifications of the blemishes. Furthermore, Bar Qamtza must keep his nefarious act hidden from the officer because the officer, just like the governor, bears the Jews no ill will. In short, the Romans expect their offerings to be welcomed in the temple just as Bar Qamtza, in Act I, expected to be welcomed at the banquet. Due to the messenger's error and Bar Qamtza's plot, however, both expectations stem from mistaken beliefs.

Act II scene 2 transitions to the temple where Bar Qamtza's plan unfolds as planned: when the priest charged with sacrificing the Roman animals sees they are blemished, he refuses to sacrifice them. The rejection of the Roman tribute, which is never officially acknowledged, prompts the Roman officer to negotiate with the Jewish priest. This drawn out negotiation parallels the drawn out negotiation between Bar Qamtza and the host in Act I scene 2, as the priest's ongoing refusal to sacrifice the Roman animals three days in a row echoes the host's persistent rejection of Bar Qamtza's three pleas to remain at the banquet. The unwelcome guest at the domestic banquet and the unwelcome tribute at the divine banquet are both repulsed by the Jerusalem elite, who are too much concerned with the temple cult and too little concerned with the welfare of their neighbors.

The three-day delay makes it clear that the priest had plenty of time to consult the temple authorities regarding this tricky affair. Hence, the ongoing rejection of the Roman offerings was not the shenanigan of an isolated maverick, but rather the decision of the temple authorities. For the Roman officer's part, his patient waiting over the course of three days indicates that he truly bore the Jews no ill will. Only after the Roman animals are rejected day after day after day does the officer conclude that Bar Qamtza's intelligence report was well founded.

The final scene, Act II scene 3, brings the story to its tragic denouement. The Roman officer reports back to the governor that Bar Qamtza's claim is true, and, as a result, the governor sets out with the Roman army and sacks the temple. The governor's harsh reaction is immediate and severe because the Jewish offense, the humiliation of the Roman authorities and the repudiation of Roman rule, was so grave. Just as Act I concluded in scene 3 with Bar Qamtza's fuming reaction to his humiliating expulsion, Act II concludes in scene 3 with the Romans' fuming reaction to their humiliating rejection.

In the story's coda, the first epilogue (which may have been inspired by the Tannaitic tradition about Ben Qamtzar) telescopes the story into a brief saying focused on the first and last scenes of the story: "Between Qamtza and Qamtza the temple was destroyed." Underlining the ultimate cause of the temple's destruction, i.e., the mistaken invitation, the first epilogue briefly recapitulates the story. Furthermore, by bringing the mistaken invitation into sharp relief, the first epilogue highlights that our story is a tragedy of errors, a plot generated by misunderstandings. Due to the messenger's accidental error in Act I, Bar Qamtza thinks he is a welcome guest whereas the host views him as uninvited, and due to Bar Qamtza's deception in Act II, the Romans misunderstand the Jewish refusal to sacrifice their tribute. At the heart of Act I is a comic misunderstanding typical of situational comedy, and at the heart of Act II is a tragic misunderstanding, deceitfully orchestrated to catastrophic ends.

The second and later epilogue cites the Tannaitic saying about "the meekness of Zechariah ben Avqulas." By mentioning "meekness," the second epilogue brings into sharp relief the moral cowardice of unresponsive bystanders like Zechariah, and by referring to Zechariah, a rabbinic sage, by name, it implicates the rabbinic leadership in the destruction of the temple.

In sum, the story of Bar Qamtza unwinds in two parallel acts with a brief coda tacked on. In both acts, a mistaken expectation arises in scene 1: Bar Qamtza expects to be welcomed at a domestic banquet because of the messenger's error and the governor expects his animals to be welcomed at a divine banquet because he is ignorant of Bar Qamtza's secret machinations. In a series of humiliating attempts to realize the mistaken expectation created in scene 1, scene 2 depicts an extended negotiation which fails miserably. Until the end, the host stubbornly refuses to allow Bar Qamtza, the unwelcome banqueter, to dine, and the priest adamantly refuses to sacrifice the Roman animals. Scene 3 then concludes each act with the injured party's furious reaction to his humiliating experience and his burning desire for retaliation.

The parallel structure of our story, i.e., the tripartite misunderstanding-negotiation-reaction complex shared by the story's two acts, reveals how the acts were carefully integrated into a single narrative and neatly arranged in a balanced whole. The repetitive nature of the balanced structure eases the narrative flow as the structure of Act II reiterates that of Act I. It would be a mistake, however, to gloss over the fundamental differences between the two acts simply because the narrative flows so well. While Act I portrays a domestic banquet, Act II culminates in a national catastrophe;[1] while Act I launches with comedy, Act II

1. See Rubenstein, *Talmudic Stories*, 148.

terminates in tragedy; while Act I highlights moral flaws, Act II focuses on cultic piety. These salient differences naturally raise the question of how precisely the two acts hang together. In order to shed some light on how to bridge the gap between banquet and temple, comedy and tragedy, morality and cultic piety, the story will now be interpreted through two interpretive lenses: the spirit of satire and Isaiah 1.

The Spirit of Satire

For the ancient Romans, satire was a literary genre, a critical and polemical outlook expressed in verse. The *spirit* of satire, however, infused other ancient literary genres as well, such as Old Comedy and Menippean satire (which mixed verse and prose). This satiric mode of discourse, the entertaining critique of vices and social injustices with the help of ridicule and laughter, is what interests us here.[2] This satiric, moralizing, and didactic modality, which critically engages with society, animated ancient comedy, Roman satire, and some rabbinic stories, like that of Bar Qamtza.[3] By mobilizing comic elements to critique Jewish society, the story of Bar Qamtza was composed in the spirit of satire.

The characters in ancient satire and comedy, often stock figures and even caricatures, served as useful vehicles for social commentary. The spirit of satire was not interested in the particular but in the general, not in the plight or faults of individuals but in social trends and widespread moral shortcomings. However, the satirist exposed the general behavior of a group or targeted a common moral failing with the help of the particular, in the guise of specific characters and singular events.[4] The

---

2. See Hudson, "Food," 6–7; Gowers, *Loaded Table*, 111, 120; Kirk Freudenberg, "Introduction: Roman Satire," in *The Cambridge Companion to Roman Satire*, ed. Kirk Freudenberg (Cambridge: Cambridge University Press, 2005), 17, 21; Daniel M. Hooley, *Roman Satire* (Oxford: Blackwell, 2007), 1–7, 141–43, 152; Jennifer L. Ferriss Hill, *Roman Satire and the Old Comic Tradition* (New York, NY: Cambridge University Press, 2015), 44.

3. Cf. Daniel Boyarin, *Socrates and the Fat Rabbis* (Chicago, IL: University of Chicago Press, 2009), 191.

4. See Hudson, "Food," 8, 14; Frances Muecke, "Rome's First Satirists: Themes and Genres in Ennius and Lucilius," in *The Cambridge Companion to Roman Satire*, ed. Kirk Freudenberg (Cambridge: Cambridge University Press, 2005), 34.

boorish hosts Virro, Nasiedienus, and Trimalchio, for example, were not designed as nuanced and realistic portraits of complex individuals but rather as embodiments of the gluttonous decadence which, according to the moralists of the time, plagued Roman society.

Ancient satires and comedies made extensive use of banquets, implanting social critique and moral instruction within the banquet setting far more than do their modern counterparts.[5] Banquets were an exemplary setting for satire because they were microcosms of society or, at least, carefully constructed visions of an ideal society. The controlled banquet environment, where communities expressed their ethos of friendship and equality while modeling social hierarchies, was the perfect context for the satirist's biting critique. Where better to mock a community's failure to live by its own high standards than the banquet hall – the ancient institution tailored to embody, if only temporarily, the ideal social corporation. As an expression of a community's ideal view of itself, the banquet was the perfect venue for unveiling the gap between an ancient community's lofty values and the social reality on the ground.[6] In the words of Nicola Anne Hudson, satirists "prefer to focus on the workings and failings of the system, where the individuals involved exercise their power-relations face-to-face, at dinner. The satirists' basic premise is that hosts and guests show their moral character in the way they behave, and are treated, at dinner."[7]

One common moral critique of ancient Roman society highlighted a supposed decline in morals which occurred when Rome grew fat from imperial expansion. As Rome imported foreign luxuries and purportedly immoral alien behaviors, the simple, modest frugality and rustic self-restraint of the originally agrarian Romans supposedly degenerated into the extravagant and ostentatious sloth of a decadent world power.[8] In the words of Velleius Paterculus, "The state passed from

---

5. See Shero, "Cena," 126–27; Hudson, "Food," 33; Gowers, *Loaded Table*, 111; Muecke, "Rome's First Satirists," 47; Hooley, *Roman Satire*, 4; Rawson, "Banquets in Ancient Rome," 15, 30; Gosbell, *Disability in the Gospels*, 188.

6. See Hudson, "Food," 16–33; 190, 200, 202; Gowers, *Loaded Table*, 28, 111; König, *Saints and Symposiasts*, 14, 200.

7. Hudson, "Food," 30.

8. See Chapter 6, n. 15 above.

vigilance to slumber, from the pursuit of arms to the pursuit of pleasure, from activity to idleness" ("in somnum a vigiliis, ab armis ad voluptates, a negotiis in otium conversa civitas").[9] For Roman satirists, banquets, with their focus on material pleasures, supplied the ideal setting for the condemnation of leisured gluttony and moral decay.[10] In addition, since Romans believed that the political order (and the patronage system) rested on the virtues of its citizens in the private sphere, moral decay was thought to instigate political chaos.[11] Hesitant to find systemic flaws in Roman social institutions, the Romans attributed political decline to the perversion of traditional Roman values.[12] In short, viewing banquets as reflections of society, satiric works enlisted banquets in order to depict a decadent community whose moral failings threatened to cripple the political order.

Reading the story of Bar Qamtza through the satiric lens reveals why the story enrolls a private banquet in order to critique an entire community and explain a national calamity. Because the private banquet Bar Qamtza attends, with its detailed protocols and rich ideology, represents Jewish society, or an ideal vision of Jewish society, the banqueters' moral deficiencies signify a far-reaching moral decay across the Jewish community. Furthermore, in typical satiric fashion, Bar Qamtza, the host, and the passive bystanders are not mere literary characters but representative figures who personify the elite of Jerusalem and the mainstays of Jewish society. In light of the work's satiric spirit, the flaws of the story's protagonists are understood to be the flaws of the Jewish community en masse, a community that could not safeguard its temple because it abided hatred and apathy. Due to its abuse of power, poor

---

9. Velleius Paterculus, *Hist. Rom.* 2.1.1–2 (Velleius Paterculus. *Compendium of Roman History*, trans. Frederick W. Shipley [LCL, Cambridge, MA: Harvard University Press, 1924], ad loc.).

10. See Hudson, "Food," 112–19; Gowers, *Loaded Table*, 29; Patrick Porter, "Unlawful Passions: Sumptuary Law and the Roman Revolution," *MHJ* 28 (2000): 6; Smith, *From Symposium to Eucharist*, 36–37, 63; Rawson, "Banquets in Ancient Rome," 24–26.

11. See Porter, "Unlawful Passions," 1–6. See also Halevi, *Gates of the Aggadah*, 236.

12. See Levick, "Fall of the Roman Republic," 61; T.N. Mitchell, "Cicero on the Moral Crisis of the Late Republic," *Hermathena* 136 (1984): 22–23.

hospitality, and heartless conduct, the Jewish community no longer merited a temple.[13]

Unlike the Roman satirists who enlist the banquet to critique gluttonous decadence, the story of Bar Qamtza uses the banquet to critique a dearth of Jewish solidarity. By focusing on Bar Qamtza's public humiliation and the violation of the banquet's ethos of friendship and equality rather than on lavish extravagance, the story embeds the satiric banquet in a Jewish context. Giving narrative form to rabbinic traditions which ascribed the destruction of the temple to "hating one's fellow" and failing to "rebuke one another," the story forms a Jewish variation on the satiric banquet.

Furthermore, the moral shortcoming shared by the host and bystanders, i.e., their faulty sense of solidarity, is a timeless flaw. From time immemorial, the biblical exhortations to "love your fellow as yourself" (Lev 19:18), to "not hate your brother in your heart" and to "reprove your kinsman," (Lev 19:17) (and also to "not take vengeance" [Lev 19:18]) have been repeated by Jewish educators and moralists the world over. By satirizing common moral flaws which plague each and every generation, the story of Bar Qamtza directed a didactic message to its late antique audience. While the story explicitly locates the ultimate cause for the fall of Jerusalem within the context of late Second Temple Jerusalemite banquet practices, the story's late antique audience would have felt at home in the story's banquet context. Since banquets remained popular throughout late antiquity, the story's readers might have wondered whether Bar Qamtza would have fared any better in the banquets of their own time.

The satiric spirit of our story not only eases the transition from the private realm to the public one, but also illuminates the story's curious blend of comedy and tragedy. Scholars have long wondered why the

---

13. In modern times, hospitality has emerged at the very center of Jacques Derrida's ethical philosophy (which developed in conversation with the philosophy of Emmanuel Levinas). See, for example, Jacques Derrida, *Of Hospitality: Anne Dufourmantelle invites Jacques Derrida to Respond*, trans. Rachel Bowlby (Stanford, CA: Stanford University Press, 1999); *Adieu to Emmanuel Levinas*, trans. Pascale-Anne Brault and Michael Naas (Stanford, CA: Stanford University Press, 2000).

story fuses frivolous mistaken identities and misunderstandings typical of comedy with a grave and harrowing destruction.[14] The fact that authors in late antiquity felt comfortable mixing genres sets the backdrop for our story's combination of distinct genres, but it does not explain why the story did so.[15] If we think of the story primarily as an attempt to pinpoint or imagine the grounds for the destruction of the temple, then the comedy-tragedy complex is confounding; the comic elements seem trivial and puerile in relation to the temple's tragic fate. From this point of view, the story's comic and tragic tones merge in a cacophonous dissonance. However, if we view the story through the satiric lens, if we think of the story first and foremost as a lesson or social critique, then the comedy-tragedy complex falls into place. The story's comic elements serve the satiric spirit of the story by lampooning ancient Jewish society and laying bare its putrid moral underbelly, while the story's tragic elements spell out the heavy price of Jewish society's pervasive callousness. When the story's comic elements are seen through the lens of satire, the transition to tragedy is natural.

Isaiah 1

In looking back at the past, "Roman writers usually saw their own history in moral terms, as a departure from an earlier golden age of virtue and simplicity. The supposed moral decline was often seen in terms of physical indulgence – too much money, too many grand houses, too many extravagant feasts, too many fine clothes, and, often associated with

---

14. See Baer, "Jerusalem," 170; Saldarini, "Rabbinic Response," 449; "Good from Evil: The Rabbinic Response," in *The First Jewish Revolt: Archaeology, History, and Ideology*, ed. Andrea M. Berlin and J. Andrew Overman (London: Routledge, 2002), 230.

15. See Scott Fitzgerald Johnson, "Introduction," in *Greek Literature in Late Antiquity: Dynamism, Didacticism, Classicism*, ed. Scott Fitzgerald Johnson (Burlington, VT: Ashgate, 2006), 8; Geoffrey Greatrex, "Introduction," in *Shifting Genres in Late Antiquity*, ed. Geoffrey Greatrex and Hugh Elton with the assistance of Lucas McMahon (Burlington, VT: Ashgate, 2015), 1–7. (On the mixed genre of tragicomedy, see Gesine Manuwald, "Tragedy, Paratragedy, and Roman Comedy," in *The Oxford Handbook of Greek and Roman Comedy*, ed. Michael Fontane and Adele C. Scafuro [Oxford: Oxford University Press, 2014], 583–86.)

all of these, too much irresponsible sexual pleasure."[16] In Roman eyes, moral rot naturally led to political disorder and decline. The story of Bar Qamtza, if viewed through this Roman lens, would become a narrative of moral degeneration naturally leading to a national calamity.

In a similar vein, some modern scholars, like David Kraemer, have argued that story of Bar Qamtza is entirely naturalistic, attributing the temple's destruction "solely to human causes," to the "the mechanical result of human frailties and failures," and to "natural political laws."[17] Since neither sin nor God are explicitly mentioned in the story, Kraemer maintains that none of the characters' actions should be viewed as sinful, nor should these actions' eventual consequences be interpreted as divine punishment. Although Kraemer does not adopt the Roman lens of moral decay, his naturalistic interpretation aligns with it neatly.

I suspect, however, that most ancient Jewish readers would not have viewed the story of Bar Qamtza in a purely naturalistic light. The rabbinic traditions that are given narrative form in the story of Bar Qamtza, i.e., the traditions about "hating one's fellow" and failing to "rebuke one another," certainly viewed the destruction of the Second Temple as a divine punishment for Jewish transgressions. The earliest interpretation of the story of Bar Qamtza, which appears in the Bavli and is explored below in Chapter 17, explicitly states that God helped Bar Qamtza avenge his humiliation. More generally, most Jewish traditions regarded the destruction of both temples – from prophetic writings through post-biblical works like Josephus's *The Jewish War* and down to rabbinic literature – as a divine punishment for Israel's transgressions. Hence, unlike the naturalistic lens often enlisted in the interpretation of Roman history, most ancient Jews would have read the story of Bar Qamtza through the lens of divine retribution. In the story of Bar Qamtza, moral decline does not simply lead to political disaster as it

---

16. Rawson, "Banquets in Ancient Rome," 26. See also nn. 8–12 above. Cf. the Greek theory of the natural cycle of constitutions. See, for example, Plato, *Resp.* 8.545A ff.; Polybius, *Hist.* 6.7–9.

17. Kraemer, *Suffering*, 143, 182. For a naturalistic interpretation of the story of Bar Qamtza which highlights the contingency of the historical process, see Halevi, *Gates of the Aggadah*, 205, 208; Saldarini, "Rabbinic Response," 450; Levine Katz, "Qamtsa," 49. Cf. Yisraeli-Taran, *Legends of the Destruction*, 20–21.

does in the Roman context, rather it undermines the Jewish *right* to a temple. In keeping with the standard practice of rabbinic sage stories, God is not explicitly mentioned in the story. But, the way the story harps on moral flaws implies the presence of God's invisible hand. In rabbinic eyes, nothing about the natural order dictates that the host's humiliation of Bar Qamtza would ultimately wreak havoc in Jerusalem. When the temple is destroyed as a result of immoral behavior, the destruction is best viewed as a punishment.

Reading the story of Bar Qamtza in its entirety, the strident moral tone of Act I raises the question of how the two acts hang together – how the cruel and immoral behavior of Act I interplays with the excessive cultic piety of Act II. In Chapter 10 above, I offered two ways to bridge the gap between the two acts. The first interpreted the priests' rejection of the Roman sacrificial animals and callous endangerment of Jewish lives in Act II as a further expression of the defective sense of Jewish solidarity already illustrated in Act I, while the second contrasted the Jewish elite's conscientious dedication to the cultic law in Act II with their moral bankruptcy in Act I. With the help of Isaiah 1, I would like to bolster the second reading and underline the contrast it asserts between moral degeneracy and cultic piety.

The first chapter of Isaiah famously opens the prophecies of Isaiah ben Amoz "concerning Judah and Jerusalem" (1:1). First off, Isaiah condemns the Israelites for spurning and forsaking God (1:2–6), and then points out that as a result of Israel's rebellion, "your land is a waste, your cities burnt down… Fair Zion is left like a booth in a vineyard, like a hut in a cucumber field, like a city beleaguered" (1:7–8). Following this description of a desolate Jerusalem, Isaiah explains the nature of the Israelites' iniquities:

שמעו דבר יהוה קציני סדם האזינו תורת אלהינו עם עמרה. למה לי רב זבחיכם יאמר יהוה שבעתי עלות אילים וחלב מריאים ודם פרים וכבשים ועתודים לא חפצתי. כי תבאו לראות פני מי בקש זאת מידכם רמס חצרי. לא תוסיפו הביא מנחת שוא קטרת תועבה היא לי חדש ושבת קרא מקרא לא אוכל און ועצרה. חדשיכם ומועדיכם שנאה נפשי היו עלי לטרח נלאיתי נשא. ובפרשכם כפיכם אעלים עיני מכם גם כי תרבו תפלה אינני שמע ידיכם דמים מלאו. רחצו הזכו הסירו רע מעלליכם מנגד עיני חדלו הרע. למדו היטב דרשו משפט אשרו

חמוץ שפטו יתום ריבו אלמנה. לכו נא ונוכחה יאמר יהוה אם יהיו חטאיכם
כשנים כשלג ילבינו אם יאדימו כתולע כצמר יהיו. אם תאבו ושמעתם טוב
הארץ תאכלו. ואם תמאנו ומריתם חרב תאכלו כי פי יהוה דבר. איכה היתה
לזונה קריה נאמנה מלאתי משפט צדק ילין בה ועתה מרצחים. כספך היה
לסיגים סבאך מהול במים, שריך סוררים וחברי גנבים כלו אהב שחד ורדף
שלמנים יתום לא ישפטו וריב אלמנה לא יבוא אליהם.

Hear the word of the Lord, you chieftains of Sodom; give ear to
our God's instruction, you folk of Gomorrah! What need have I of
all your sacrifices? Says the Lord. I am sated with burnt offerings of
rams, and suet of fatlings, and blood of bulls, and I have no delight in
lambs and he-goats. That you come to appear before me – who asked
that of you? Trample my courts no more; bringing oblations is futile,
incense is offensive to me. New moon and Sabbath, proclaiming of
solemnities, assemblies with iniquity, I cannot abide. And when
you lift up your hands, I will turn my eyes away from you; though
you pray at length, I will not listen. Your hands are tainted with
crime – Wash yourselves clean; Put your evil doings away from my
sight, cease to do evil; Learn to do good. Devote yourselves to justice;
aid the wronged. Uphold the rights of the orphan; defend the cause
of the widow. Come, let us reach an understanding, says the Lord.
Be your sins like crimson, they can turn snow-white; be they red as
dyed wool, they can become like fleece. If, then, you agree and give
heed, you will eat the good things of the earth. But if you refuse and
disobey, you will be devoured (by) the sword – for it was the Lord
who spoke. Alas, she has become a harlot, the faithful city that was
filled with justice, where righteousness dwelt, but now murderers.
Your silver has turned to dross, your wine is cut with water. Your
rulers are rogues and cronies of thieves, everyone avid for presents
and greedy for gifts; they do not judge the case of orphans and the
widow's cause never reaches them (Isa 1:10–23).

In a word, Isaiah explains that Zion suffers affliction because, even
though its people worship God, they neglect to do good. Although the
Israelites offer up sacrifices and oblations, they neglect the orphan and
widow; although they bring incense and pray, they are selfish and unjust.[18]

---

18. See also Hos 6:6; Mic 6:6–8.

Isaiah 1's central teaching, the notion that sacrifices are unwanted in the absence of solidarity, manifests a principle also reflected in the structure of the story of Bar Qamtza. By contrasting the cruelty and apathy of the Jerusalem banqueters in Act I with the zealous cultic piety of the Jerusalem priests in Act II, the story of Bar Qamtza, just like Isaiah, contrasts piety to morality and ritual to righteousness.[19] The Jews' defective sense of solidarity sets in motion the chain of events leading to the temple's destruction. When the priests' cultic piety propels the chain forward, the audience is reminded of Isaiah's words: "What need have I of all your sacrifices? Says the Lord." Without solidarity, cultic piety not only cannot save the temple, it contributes to its ruin.

---

19. Cf. Goldenberg's assessment of our story discussed above in Chapter 6, n. 25.

Part II

Bar Qamtza in the Babylonian Talmud

So Pooh pushed and pushed and pushed his way through the hole, and at last he got in.

"You were quite right," said Rabbit, looking at him all over. "It is you. Glad to see you."

"Who did you think it was?"

"Well, I wasn't sure. You know how it is in the Forest. One can't have *anybody* coming into one's house. One has to be *careful*."

A. Milne, *Winnie-the-Pooh*, 22–23.

Let us say yes *to who or what turns up*, before any determination, before any anticipation, before any *identification*, whether or not it has to do with a foreigner, an immigrant, an invited guest, or an unexpected visitor, whether or not the new arrival is the citizen of another country, a human, animal, or divine creature, a living or dead thing, male or female.

Jacques Derrida, *Of Hospitality*, 77.

Chapter 14

The Text

Having investigated Lamentations Rabbati's story of Bar Qamtza, Part II now turns to the parallel story in the Bavli. Unlike Lamentations Rabbati, which was edited in Byzantine Palestine, the Bavli was edited in sixth- or seventh-century CE Babylonia. Whereas the local Jewish community in Palestine and the Greek and Roman cultures of the Roman Empire were natural interpretive lenses for Lamentations Rabbati's version of our story, the rabbinic landscape of the Babylonian sages and the Bavli's ambient Persian setting are natural interpretive lenses for the parallel Babylonian version.[1]

Furthermore, in contrast to the many and substantial variations among the textual witnesses of the Palestinian version, variations among the Bavli's textual witnesses are mostly slight and insignificant. Hence, identifying a preferred textual witness of the Babylonian story is not nearly as consequential as our selection of branch **B** for Lamentations Rabbati's parallel. Although the Babylonian text is cited below (mostly) according to Vatican 130, one would hardly feel the difference were it replaced with almost any other textual witness.[2]

---

1. See *The Talmud in its Iranian Context*, ed. Carol Bakhos and M. Rahim Shayegan (Tübingen: Mohr Siebeck, 2010); Secunda, *Iranian Talmud*. On the Syriac Christian context for the Bavli, see Michal Bar-Asher Siegal, *Early Monastic Literature and the Babylonian Talmud* (Cambridge: Cambridge University Press, 2013).

2. The text of b. Git. 55b–57a is cited below according to Vatican 130 with slight

The Babylonian story of Bar Qamtza opens the "legends of destruction," a collection of stories about the fall of three Judaean cities, Jerusalem, Tur Malka, and Bethar.[3] This collection is found on b. Gittin
55b–58a within the talmudic commentary to m. Gittin 5:6. M. Gittin 5:6
discusses stages in the evolution of the law of the *siqriqon*, a law which
relates to the purchase of Jewish property confiscated by the Romans
during wartime, and also refers in passing to Jews of Judaea slain in
battle.[4] In the wake of the mishnah's reference to the Jewish fatalities

corrections on the basis of other textual witnesses and with all abbreviations
completed. Comparison of the textual witnesses – St. Petersburg – RNL Evr. I
187, Arras 889, Soncino Print (1488), Munich 95, Vatican 140, Munich 153, T-S NS
329.428, and St. Petersburg – RNL Evr. II A 389/4 – reveals only minor variations
among them. (The Yemenite compilations – New York-JTS Rab. 1718.93–100 and
New York-JTS Rab. 1729.64–67 – include some further variations but these are
usually best viewed as late revisions (in line with Saul Lieberman's assessment
of the textual fluidity of these compilations. See Saul Lieberman, *Yemenite
Midrashim: A Lecture on the Yemenite Midrashim, their Character and Value* [מדרשי
תימן: הרצאה על מדרשי תימן על מהותם וערכם], [Jerusalem: Shalem, 1962], 3, 39). On
the textual witnesses of Bavli Gittin, see Hillel Porush, *The Babylonian Talmud
with Variant Readings: Gittin* (מסכת גיטין עם שינויי נוסחאות), (Jerusalem: Yad
Harav Herzog and The Institute for the Complete Israeli Talmud, 1999–2013),
vol. 1, 15–69, vol. 3, 84–87, 108–15; Menashe Pniel, "The Text of Tractate Gittin
Chapter VIII in the Babylonian Talmud" ("נוסח פרק 'הזורק גט' בבבלי: על-פי כתבי-
יד, קטעי גניזה, קטעי כריכה ודפוס ראשון, בצירוף מבוא ודיון בעניייני נוסח") (MA thesis,
Bar-Ilan University, 2014), 1–107; Shamma Friedman, "Untangling Branches of
Transmissions of the Babylonian Talmud" ("אחת דבר אלהים שתים זו שמעתי': בירור
מנגנון הפילוג לענפים בנוסח התלמוד הבבלי על פי פרק תשיעי במסכת גיטין"), in *Professor
Meir Benayahu Memorial Volume*, ed. Moshe Bar Asher, Yehudah Liebes, Moshe
Assis, and Yosef Kaplan, vol. 1 (Jerusalem: Yad Harav Nissim, 2019), 103–73. (On
debates regarding Yemenite manuscripts more generally, see the discussions
and references in Tropper, *Rewriting Ancient Jewish History*, 20–30; Jason Sion
Mokhtarian, "Clusters of Iranian Loanwords in Talmudic Folkore: The Chapter
of the Pious (b. Ta'anit 18b–26a) in Its Sasanian Context," in *The Aggada of the
Bavli and Its Cultural World*, ed. Geoffrey Herman and Jeffrey L. Rubenstein
(Providence, RI: Brown Judaic Studies, 2018), 128n13.)

3. See Weiss, *Studies*, 262–63. On the scope of the Bavli's "legends of destruction," see Weiss, "Class Reversals," 3–4n3. See also Jeffrey L. Rubenstein, "The
Story-Cycles of the Bavli: Part 1," in *Studies in Rabbinic Narrative: Volume One*,
ed. Jeffrey L. Rubenstein (Providence, RI: Brown Judaic Studies, 2021), 229, 266.

4. Scholars debate whether the law of the *siqriqon* dates all the way back to the

of a military conflict with Rome and to Judaean properties confiscated at that time, the Bavli digresses to sketch a narrative of Roman-Jewish conflicts, presenting, via the "legends of destruction," an overview of the disastrous confrontations between Rome and Judaea during the first two centuries CE.[5] In context, the "legends of destruction" supply a literary account of the historical backdrop to the law of the *siqriqon*,

---

first century Jewish revolt against Rome or only to the Bar Kokhba revolt of the second century. (See Lieberman, *Tosefta Ki-Fshuṭa*, vol. 8, 841–42; Shmuel Safrai, *In the Times of Temple and Mishnah: Studies in Jewish History* [בימי הבית ובימי המשנה: מחקרים בתולדות ישראל], vol. 1 [Jerusalem: Hebrew University Magnes Press, 1994], 63–64; David Rokéah, "Comments on the Revolt of Bar Kokhba" ["הערות כוזביות"], *Tarbiz* 35 [1966]: 125–27; Moshe Benovitz, "'It was taught bish'at herum': The First Act of the Emperor Pertinax (193 CE) and its Impact on Tannaitic Halakha" ["(193) בשעת חירום שנו': המעשה הראשון של הקיסר פרטינקס (לספירה) ועקבותיו בהלכה התנאית"], *Sidra* 19 [2004]: 18–19n40; Schwartz, *Reciprocity and Solidarity*, 115, 121; Ben Shahar, "Abolishment of the Sacrifice," 578–79 [n. 50].) In any event, the mishnah's discussion of the *siqriqon* and its reference to Jews slain by the Romans in battle apparently inspired the Bavli ad loc. to survey the military conflicts in Judaea during the first *and* second centuries, portraying them as a series of Judaean cities falling to Rome.

5. Since other mishnayot also refer to military conflicts with Rome (see, for example, m. Taʾan. 4:6 and m. Soṭah 9:12, 9:14), some scholars have sought further links between the "legends of destruction" and the local literary context in Gittin. For example, scholars have suggested that the similarity between the word "*siqriqon*" and the name "Abba Siqra," which appears later on in the "legends of destruction," triggered an associative link between m. Giṭ. 5:6 and the "legends of destruction" (see Efron, "Bar-Kokhva," 89nn197, 198; Rubenstein, *Talmudic Stories*, 162; Levine Katz, "Qamtsa," 34). Others have suggested links between the local context and the story of Bar Qamtza, alighting upon the similarity between the phrase "for the sake of peace with the kingdom" ("משום שלום מלכות") from the story of Bar Qamtza and the phrases "for the amendment of the world" ("מפני תקון העולם") from m. Giṭ. 5:1 and "in the interests of peace" ("מפני דרכי שלום") from m. Giṭ. 5:8–9; or between the sages' desire to bring a blemished offering in the story of Bar Qamtza and the phrase "for the amendment of the altar" ("מפני תקון המזבח") from m. Giṭ. 5:5. Transforming the literary context into an interpretative aid for our story, Rubenstein has suggested that the sages' unwillingness to sacrifice a blemished animal and thereby modify the law "for the amendment of the world" or "in the interests of peace" compares very unfavorably with the various adjustments to the law cited in the mishnayot in chapter five of Gittin. (See Rubenstein, *Talmudic Stories*, 160–65; Furstenberg, "Qamtza," 103n2; Ben Shahar, "Abolishment of the Sacrifice," 579 [n. 51]; Willem F. Smelik, *Rabbis,*

proposing a narrative for the ultimate causes underlying the harsh social and economic realities refracted through the mishnah.[6]

The Bavli not only opens its "legends of destruction" with the story of Bar Qamtza, it also explicitly presents the story as the first in a trilogy.[7] The second and third stories of the trilogy do not immediately build upon the story of Bar Qamtza, but are, rather, interspersed among the "legends of destruction." However, since the trilogy is explicitly delineated as an organic literary unit, I cite it here without the intervening legends:

1 אמר ר' יוחנן: מאי דכתיב "אשרי אדם מפחד תמיד ומקשה לבו יפול ברעה" (משלי כח:יד)?

2 אקמצא ובר קמצא[8] חרוב ירושלם,

3 אתרנגול ותרנגולתא חרוב טור מלכא,

4 אשקא דדייספק חרוב ביתר.[9]

5 אקמצא ובר קמצא חרוב ירושלם:

6 דההוא גברא, דרחמיה קמצא ובעיל דבביה[10] בר קמצא, עבד סעודתא.

Language and Translation in Late Antiquity [Cambridge: Cambridge University Press. 2013], 467–69.)

6. See Weiss, *Studies*, 262.

7. See Efron, "Bar-Kokhva," 77–78, 85; Yisraeli-Taran, *Legends of the Destruction*, 17; Rubenstein, *Talmudic Stories*, 140; Mandel, "Tales of the Destruction," 142.

8. In most textual witnesses, the name Qamtza appears with an opening *qof* (ק) and final *aleph* (א): "קמצא." Munich 153, however, reads "קמצה" with a final *he* (ה), the Yemenite compilations read "כמצא" with an opening *kaf* (כ), and St. Petersburg MS. Evr. II A 389/4 reads "כמצא" with a *kaf* (כ) in the introduction but "קמצא" with a *qof* (ק) in the body of the story. See Chapter 3, n. 29 below.

9. St. Petersburg – RNL Evr. I 187 reads "ביתתר" with two *tavs* (תת) and the Yemenite compilations read "בית תור," "Beit Tur."

10. The possessive suffix of "בעיל דבביה" ("his enemy") is missing from Vatican 130 and has been inserted here on the basis of other textual witnesses. (It bears noting that unlike all the Bavli's other textual witnesses which enlist the term "בעיל דבביה" for "his enemy," the Yemenite compilations consistently enlist the term "סנאה," like Lamentations Rabbati's "שנאיה." In addition, whereas the Bavli only deploys the terms "friend" and "enemy" in the story's introduction and Lamentations Rabbati only deploys them in the body of the story, the Yemenite compilations deploy the terms in both the introduction and the body. This repetition and apparent conflation of the Babylonian and Palestinian versions is likely a sign of late, secondary editing.)

7 אמר ליה לשמעיה:[11] זיל אייתי לי[12] קמצא, אזל אייתי ליה בר קמצא.[13]

8 אתא אשכחיה דהוה קא יתיב,

9 אמר ליה: מכדי ההוא גברא בעיל דבבא דהההוא גברא,[14] מאי בעית הכא?[15]
קום![16]

10 אמר ליה: הואיל[17] ואתאי[18] שיבקן וייהבנא לך דמי מאי דקאכילנא
ושתינא. אמר ליה: לא.

11 ייהבנא לך דמי פלגא דסעודתא.[19] אמר ליה: לא.

12 ייהבנא לך דמי כולה סעודתיך. אמר ליה: לא.[20]

13 נקט ליה בידיה ואפקיה.[21]

14 אמר: הואיל והוו יתבי רבנן ולא מחו ביה[22] איזיל ואיכול בהו קורצא בי
מלכא.

---

11. T-S NS 329.428 and the Yemenite compilations read "לשלוחיה," like Lamentations Rabbati, and not "לשמעיה" like the other textual witnesses of the Bavli.
(Cf. Arras 889 which includes both "לשלוחו" and "לשמעי'.")

12. The word "לי" ("to me"), which is missing from Vatican 130, has been inserted
on the basis of other textual witnesses.

13. In lieu of the word "אייתי" ("bring"), the Yemenite compilations read "קרייה"
("call").

14. The Yemenite compilations simplified this clause, omitting the two references
to "that/this man" ("ההוא גברא").

15. The Yemenite compilations inserted the word "את" ("you") immediately prior
to this phrase. Perhaps this addition was inspired by the (double) appearance of
the word "את" in the parallel phrase in Lamentations Rabbati.

16. The Soncino Print (1488), Arras 889, and Munich 153 include the word "פוק"
here, and, in a similar manner, Lamentations Rabbati reads here: קום ופוק לך
מגו ביתאי," "Stand and get yourself out of my home."

17. The word "הואיל" ("since"), which appears in all the other textual witnesses,
was inserted above the line in Vatican 130.

18. The Yemenite compilations include the word "לי" here.

19. While the word "דסעודתא" ("of the meal") appears with slight variations
in most textual witnesses, it is entirely absent from the Yemenite compilations.

20. This line – ".יהיבנא לך דמי כולה סעודתיך. אמר ליה: לא" ("I will give you money
for the cost of the whole banquet. He said to him: No.") – appears in all the textual
witnesses save for Vatican 130 and was most likely accidentally omitted through
a homoioteleuton. It has been inserted here according to Soncino Print (1488).

21. The rest of the textual witnesses read "נקטיה" and not "נקט ליה." Soncino Print
(1488) and Arras 889 include "ואוקמיה" ("and stood him up") before "ואפקיה"
("and threw him out").

22. Vatican 130 is the only textual witness which reads "בידי'" instead of "ביה."

15 אזל אמר ליה לקיסר: מרדו בך יהודאי.

16 אמר ליה: מי יימר?

17 אמר ליה: שדר להו קורבנא[23] וחזי אי[24] מקרבו ליה.

18 אזל שדר להו בידיה[25] עיגלא תילתא.

19 בהדי דקאתי שדא ביה מומא בניב שפתים, ואמרי לה בדוקין[26] שבעין,

20 דוכתא דלדידן מומא לדידהו לאו מומא.

21 סבור רבנן למיקרבה משום שלום מלכות.

22 אמר להו ר'[27] זכריה בן אבקולס: יאמרו בעלי מומין קריבין לגבי[28] מזבח!

23 סבור למיקטליה דלא ליזיל ולימא.[29]

24 אמר להו ר' זכריה בן אבקולס: יאמרו מטיל מום בקדשים יהרג!

25 א"ר יוחנן: ענוותנותו של ר' זכר' בן אבקולס

26 החריבה את ביתינו ושרפה את היכלנו והגלתנו[30] מארצנו ...

Since the word "בידי'" also appears in the previous line, it may well have been accidentally repeated here, though Vatican 130 may have also preferred the Palestinian rendering of the term "to protest" which includes the word "יד," "hand." (It also bears noting that the Soncino Print and the Yemenite compilations interpolated an explanatory gloss here. After the gloss, the Yemenite compilations omitted the phrase "איזיל ואיכול בהו קורצא בי מלכא" apparently due to a homoioteletuon [between "איזיל" and "אזל"].)

23. Vatican 140 adds here "השתא," "now."

24. T-S NS 329.428 and St. Petersburg – RNL Evr. II A 389/4 read "מי" instead of "וחזי אי." The Yemenite compilations read "מקרבי ליה ניהלך" instead of "אי מקרבו ליה."

25. The Yemenite compilations read "בהדיה" ("with him") instead of "בידיה" ("in his hand").

26. St. Petersburg – RNL Evr. II A 389/4 and the Yemenite compilations read "בחריץ" instead of "בדוקין."

27. Some textual witnesses omit the title "רבי" ("Rabbi") here but none omit it below. See T-S NS 329.428, Vatican 140 and Munich 153.

28. T-S NS 329.428 reads "על גבי" ("on top of") instead of "לגבי" ("by/on").

29. The Yemenite compilations read "דלא נזיל ניגלי" ("lest he go and reveal") rather than "דלא ליזיל ולימא" ("lest he go and say"). Since the emperor is not explicitly mentioned here, perhaps this reading seeks to clarify that the rabbis' concern was that Bar Qamtza would reveal the damaging information to the Roman authorities.

30. I have corrected Vatican 130's grammatically incorrect reading – "והגלנו" – to the grammatically correct – "והגלתנו," which also appears in the other textual witnesses.

27 תניא: א"ר אלעזר:[31] בוא וראה כמה גדול כח של בושה

28 שהרי סייע הקב"ה את בר קמצא והחריב את ביתו ושרף את היכלו.

29 אתרנגול ותרנגולתא חרוב טור מלכא:

30 דהוו נהיגי כי הוה חתנא וכלתא הוו מפקי קמייהו תרנגול ותרנגולתא

31 כלומר פרו ורבו כתרנגולין.

32 יומא חד הוה חליף גונדא דרומאי שקלינהו מינייהו.[32]

33 נפלי עלייהו מחונהו.

34 אתאו אמרו ליה לקיסר: מרדו בך יהודאי!

35 אתא עלייהו ...

36 אשקא דדייספק חרוב ביתר:

37 דהוו נהיגי כי איתיליד להו ינוקא שתלי ארזא[33] ינוקתא שתלי תורניתא

38 וכד הוו מינסבי קייצי להו ועביד להו גנאנא.

39 יומא חד הוה חלפה ברתיה דקיסר שקא דדייספק איתבר קצו ארזא ועיילו לה

40 נפול עלייהו ומחונהו.

41 אתו אמרו ליה לקיסר: מרדו בך יהודאי!

42 אתא עלייהו.

1 Rabbi Yohanan said: What is meant by the verse: *Happy is the man who is anxious always, but he who hardens his heart falls into misfortune?* (Prov 28:14)

2 On account of Qamtza and Bar Qamtza Jerusalem was destroyed,

3 on account of a cock and a hen Tur Malka (the King's Mountain) was destroyed,

4 on account of a shaft of a litter Bethar was destroyed.

5 On account of Qamtza and Bar Qamtza Jerusalem was destroyed:

6 certain man, whose friend was (called) Qamtza and enemy was (called) Bar Qamtza, made a banquet.

---

31. Munich 95 reads "אליעזר," ("Eliezer") while Vatican 140, New York – JTS Rab. 1718.93–100, and Graz. Fragm. A 1.4, Ink. A 59.38 all read "שמעון בן אלעזר," ("Simeon ben Eleazar").

32. Vatican 140 adds here "וקטלונהו" ("and they killed them"), making explicit what was otherwise implied.

33. The words "ינוקא שתלי ארזא" ("a boy, they would plant a cedar") were accidentally repeated here in Vatican 130.

7 He said to his servant: Go, bring me Qamtza. He went and brought him Bar Qamtza.

8 He (the host) came and found (Bar Qamtza) sitting

9 (and) said to him: Since that certain man (you) is an enemy of this certain man (me), what do you want here? Get up!

10 He said to him: Since I have come, let me be and I will pay you the cost of whatever I eat and drink. He said to him: No.

11 I will give you money for the cost of half the banquet. He said to him: No.

12 I will give you money for the cost of the whole banquet. He said to him: No.

13 He took him with his hand and threw him out.

14 He (Bar Qamtza) said: Since the sages were sitting there and did not protest to him, I will go and inform the king's palace against them.

15 He went (and) said to the emperor: The Jews are rebelling against you.

16 He said to him: Says who?

17 He said to him: Send an offering and see if they offer it.

18 He (the emperor) went and sent in his (Bar Qamtza's) hand a three- year-old calf.

19 While on the way, he inflicted a blemish on its upper lip, and some say on the white of its eye,[34]

20 place where it is a blemish for us (Jews but) for them (gentiles) it is not a blemish.

21 The sages thought to offer it for the sake of peace with the kingdom.

22 Rabbi Zechariah ben Avqulas said to them: They will say that blemished animals may be offered on the altar!

23 They thought to kill him (Bar Qamtza) lest he go and say (to the emperor that his calf was not offered).

---

34. The precise meaning of the phrase "בדוקין שבעין," translated here as "on the white of its eye," is unclear. Cf. Jastrow, *Dictionary*, 287, 318.

24 Rabbi Zechariah ben Avqulas said to them: They will say that one who inflicts a blemish on a consecrated animal is to be put to death!

25 Rabbi Yohanan said: The meekness of Rabbi Zechariah ben Avqulas

26 destroyed our temple, burnt our sanctuary and exiled us from our land...

27 It was taught: Rabbi Eleazar said: Come and see how great is the power of shame,

28 for God assisted Bar Qamtza and destroyed his temple and burnt his sanctuary.

29 On account of a cock and a hen Tur Malka (the King's Mountain) was destroyed:

30 It was the custom that when there was a bride and groom, they would put out before them a cock and a hen,

31 as if to say: be fruitful and multiply like chickens.

32 One day a troop of Roman soldiers passed by (who) took (the chickens) from them.

33 They (the Jews) fell upon them and beat them.

34 They (the Roman soldiers) came and said to the emperor: The Jews have rebelled against you!

35 He (the emperor) came (in battle) upon them (the Jews)...

36 On account of a shaft of a litter Bethar was destroyed:

37 It was the custom that when a boy was born to them they would plant a cedar; a girl, they would plant an acacia,

38 and when they married they would cut them down and make from them a bridal canopy.

39 One day the emperor's daughter passed by (when) the shaft of her litter broke, so they cut down a cedar tree and brought it to her.

40 They (the Jews) fell upon them and beat them.

41 They (the Romans) came and said to the emperor: The Jews have rebelled against you!

42 He (the emperor) came (in battle) upon them (the Jews).

Despite the many and fascinating differences between the Palestinian and Babylonian versions of the story of Bar Qamtza, both follow the same basic literary structure: both versions comprise two parallel acts – the banquet act and the revenge act – with three scenes apiece: the invitation scene, the negotiation scene, and the response scene. In both versions, Act I opens in scene 1 with a mistaken banquet invitation. In scene 2, Act I continues with an extended negotiation that culminates in Bar Qamtza's expulsion from the banquet, and scene 3 concludes Act I with Bar Qamtza's reaction to his fellow banqueters' apparent acquiescence to his shameful treatment at the hands of the host. In parallel fashion, Act II opens in scene 1 with an underhanded invitation: Bar Qamtza invites the emperor to send tribute to the temple in Jerusalem and then blemishes the emperor's tribute in order to ensure its rejection by the Jewish authorities. Scene 2 follows with an extended negotiation which culminates in the rejection of the blemished tribute and scene 3 concludes Act II with the enraged Romans demolishing the Jerusalem temple.

One readily apparent difference between the Babylonian and Palestinian versions of our story is the literary context. Whereas Lamentations Rabbati situates the story within its exposition of Lamentations 4:2, the Bavli opens the "legends of destruction" with the story of Bar Qamtza, presenting the tragic story as the first in a series of disastrous historical events.[35] This literary context, that is, the overarching trilogy, is the perfect starting point for our analysis of the Babylonian story of Bar Qamtza.

---

35. Lamentations Rabbati brings two other stories in its exposition of Lam 4:2 but the three stories do not form a trilogy like the stories of Bar Qamtza, Tur Malka, and Bethar in the Bavli. See Yisraeli-Taran, *Legends of the Destruction*, 17. Cf. Levine Katz, "Qamtsa" 35.

Chapter 15

The Preface

The trilogy of destruction stories which opens with the story of Bar Qamtza is preceded by a preface:

1 אמר ר' יוחנן: מאי דכתיב "אשרי אדם מפחד תמיד ומקשה לבו יפול ברעה" (משלי כח:יד)?

2 אקמצא ובר קמצא חרוב ירושלם,

3 אתרנגול ותרנגולתא חרוב טור מלכא,

4 אשקא דדייספק חרוב ביתר.

5 אקמצא ובר קמצא חרוב ירושלם.

1 Rabbi Yohanan said: What is meant by the verse: *Happy is the man who is anxious always, but he who hardens his heart falls into misfortune?* (Prov 28:14)

2 On account of Qamtza and Bar Qamtza Jerusalem was destroyed,

3 on account of a cock and a hen Tur Malka (the King's Mountain) was destroyed,

4 on account of a shaft of a litter Bethar was destroyed.

5 On account of Qamtza and Bar Qamtza Jerusalem was destroyed.

The preface to the trilogy commences with a question in line 1 attributed to Rabbi Yohanan, "What is meant by the verse: *Happy is the man who is anxious always, but he who hardens his heart falls into misfortune?*" (Prov 28:14); and follows in lines 2–4 with an answer, also presumably

attributed to Rabbi Yohanan:[1] "On account of Qamtza and Bar Qamtza
Jerusalem was destroyed, on account of a cock and a hen Tur Malka was
destroyed, on account of a shaft of a litter Bethar was destroyed."

Prov 28:14

The preface's question draws our attention to Proverbs 28:14 as it asks to
clarify or illustrate the verse's meaning. The first leg in the verse's proverb,
"Happy is the man who is anxious always," recommends constant anxiety,
perpetual fear, and, at first glance, this sentiment seems to conflict with
other passages in Proverbs which indicate that the righteous are "supposed to be confident and unafraid."[2] For example, Proverbs 1:33 states,
"But he who listens to me will dwell in safety, untroubled by the terror
of misfortune," ("וְשֹׁמֵעַ לִי יִשְׁכָּן בֶּטַח, וְשַׁאֲנַן מִפַּחַד רָעָה") and Proverbs
3:23–26 assures us:

אָז תֵּלֵךְ לָבֶטַח דַּרְכֶּךָ וְרַגְלְךָ לֹא תִגּוֹף. אִם תִּשְׁכַּב לֹא־תִפְחָד וְשָׁכַבְתָּ וְעָרְבָה
שְׁנָתֶךָ. אַל־תִּירָא מִפַּחַד פִּתְאֹם וּמִשֹּׁאַת רְשָׁעִים כִּי תָבֹא. כִּי־יְהוָה יִהְיֶה בְכִסְלֶךָ
וְשָׁמַר רַגְלְךָ מִלָּכֶד.

Then you will go your way safely and not injure your feet. When you
lie down you will be unafraid; you will lie down and your sleep will
be sweet. You will not fear sudden terror or the disaster that comes
upon the wicked. For the Lord will be your trust; he will keep your
feet from being caught.[3]

If, then, the person who trusts in God is unafraid, what type of fear is
laudable and good? What sort of anxiety does our proverb recommend?

---

1. Rhetorical questions of the type "מאי דכתיב," "What is meant by the verse," are
usually followed by relatively brief answers (in Hebrew) purportedly articulated
by the questioner himself. In our case, the relatively brief answer of the preface
(in Aramaic) was presumably understood as Rabbi Yohanan's response to his own
rhetorical question. Furthermore, the trilogy itself, which unpacks the preface,
was probably viewed, like other stories about earlier times, as a Tannaitic tradition.
(See Levine Katz, "Qamtsa" 45; cf. Yisraeli-Taran, *Legends of the Destruction*, 21–22.
See also the discussion below at the end of the chapter.)
2. Michael V. Fox, *Proverbs 10–31* (New Haven, CT: The Anchor Yale Bible,
2009), 826.
3. See also Prov 28:1 (and the perilous fear of 29:25).

A hint to the proverb's meaning may perhaps be elicited from the first leg of a similar proverb found in Proverbs 14:16:

חכם ירא וסר מרע וכסיל מתעבר ובוטח.

A wise man is diffident and shuns misfortune, but a dullard rushes in confidently.[4]

Healthy fear is the prudent anticipation of the consequences of one's actions; it is, in rabbinic parlance, the wisdom to discern "what is about to come to pass" ("הרואה את הנולד").[5] Hence, the happy person shuns misfortune, cautiously avoiding deeds (or sins) with potentially bitter repercussions.[6]

The second leg of our proverb, "but he who hardens his heart falls into misfortune," forms an antithetic parallelism (in a chiastic structure[7]) with the first leg. The second leg, in other words, underscores the misfortune which befalls the person who does not wisely foresee the potentially harmful fallout of his or her actions. Whereas Proverbs 14:16 contrasts the thoughtful prudence of the wise with the impulsiveness of the fool who rushes blindly into trouble, our proverb contrasts cautious foresight with the obstinate inflexibility of a hardened heart. Whereas Proverbs 14:16 contrasts foresight to impetuosity, our proverb takes a different path, recognizing that foresight is only of value to a person who is willing to revise his or her behavior in light of its likely consequences. A stubborn and intransigent person with a hardened heart will suffer the misfortune of the impulsive fool, not due to a lack of foresight, but to an inability or unwillingness to change. In short, Proverbs 28:14 not only commends judicious prudence but also warns of the heavy penalty

---

4. See also Prov 22:3. I have altered the *JPS* translation here in order to bring it in line with the translation of Prov 28:14, so that in both cases "רע" is translated as "misfortune."

5. B. Tamid 32a (with translation by Maurice Simon, trans. *The Babylonian Talmud: Tamid* [London: Soncino, 1948], ad loc.).

6. See Fox, *Proverbs*, 826; Victor Avigdor Hurovitz, *Proverbs: Introduction and Commentary* (משלי עם מבוא ופירוש), vol. 2, *Mikra Leyisra'el* (Tel Aviv: Am Oved and Hebrew University Magnes Press, 2012), 537.

7. See Hurovitz, *Proverbs*, 537.

incurred by those who recognize the potentially disastrous cost of their actions but nonetheless refuse to change their ways.[8]

With its positive appraisal of cautious foresight and negative assessment of unyielding intractability, the question in the trilogy's preface offers us an interpretive lens and frame of reference for what follows.[9] Priming the reader to be attentive to expressions of insufficient foresight and obdurate behavior, this lens naturally picks out certain features of the subsequent stories over others. In other words, the preface's question suggests that we read what follows through the prism of Proverbs 28:14; that is, with the expectation that the stories will illustrate the unfortunate consequences of insufficient foresight and unbending obstinacy.[10]

The Three Revolts

The preface's answer, which refers to the three stories by their opening lines,[11] supplies a historical frame for the trilogy.[12] The story of Bar

---

8. Cf. Julia Watts Belser, who recently defined the hardening of the heart as a "refusal to accede to God's will" (*Rabbinic Tales of Destruction*, 142) and accordingly argued that Titus was guilty of this character flaw while the sages in the story of Bar Qamtza were not (140–43). Watts Belser's definition, however, is not in tune with the use of the term in Proverbs, and Titus does not actually appear in the trilogy introduced by the preface. In addition, Watts Belser claims that the rabbis deploy Prov 28:14 to indict Roman hubris and to prophetically envision Rome's fall, but these themes are not developed in the subsequent trilogy.

9. See b. Git. 55b, Tosafot ad loc. (s.vv. *ashrei adam mefahed tamid*); cf. Maharsha ad loc. (s.vv. *amar rabi yohanan*).

10. See Rubenstein, *Talmudic Stories*, 151. Cf. Saldarini, "Rabbinic Response," 448, who questioned the utility of this interpretive lens.

11. See Ch. N. Bialik and Y. Ch. Ravnitzky, *Sefer Ha'aggada* (ספר האגדה), ed. with a new commentary by Avidgor Shinan (Jerusalem: Avi Chai, Kinneret, Zmora-Bitan, and Dvir, 2015), 218. Since our story nowhere blames Qamtza, some commentators have been puzzled by the story's apparently incriminating preface: "on account of Qamtza and Bar Qamtza Jerusalem was destroyed." However, once we recognize that the preface is merely using the phrase "Qamtza and Bar Qamtza" as a shorthand way to refer to our story, it becomes clear that the preface is not condemning Qamtza. (See Chaim Yosef David Azulai, *Sefer Petah Einayim* [ספר פתח עינים], [Livorno: bedefus Eliezer Saʾadon, 1789–1790], ad loc. [238b]; cf. Judah ben Bezalel Loew, *Sefer Hidushei Agadot Maharal Miprag* [ספר חידושי אגדות מהר"ל מפראג], vol. 2 [London: Honig and Sons, 1960], 99.) Similarly, since

Qamtza serves as the first in this series of three stories and each narrates the events which ultimately caused the fall of a Judaean city (or region[13]). While Jerusalem fell in 70 CE during the first Jewish revolt against Rome, and Bethar, as well as (the region identified here as the city) Tur Malka, fell some 65 years later during the Bar Kokhba revolt, the Talmud presents their stories as a trilogy – as a long yet unified narrative.[14] With no attempt to date the three revolts which led to the destruction of these three Judaean cities, or to establish the time which elapsed between them, the Talmud presents the revolts in chronological order. Just as Tannaitic sources present a series of three Jewish wars against Rome – the war of Vespasian, the war of Quietus, and the last war – the Bavli similarly envisions three Jewish revolts against Rome which led to the destruction of three Jewish cities: Jerusalem, Tur Malka, and Bethar.[15]

Telegraphing the Conclusion

Immediately following the trilogy's preface in lines 1 to 4, the Talmud repeats the preface's declaration: "on account of Qamtza and Bar Qamtza Jerusalem was destroyed." The repeated declaration in line 5 functions as

---

the preface is simply referring to each story by its opening line, it may not be highlighting the insignificant or trivial nature of the cause for the destruction. Cf. Joseph Hayyim ben Elijah, *Sefer ben Yehoyada: Gittin* (ספר בן יהוידע: גיטין), (Jerusalem: Hatzvi, 1997), ad loc. (61, s.v. *aqamtza*); Yisraeli-Taran, *Legends of the Destruction*, 18. See also Chapter 22 below.

12. See Eli Yassif, *The Hebrew Folktale: History, Genre, Meaning*, trans. Jacqueline S. Teitelbaum (Bloomington: Indiana University Press, 1999), 211, 242–43; Ben Shahar, "Abolishment of the Sacrifice," 593–96.

13. See Yuval Shahar, "Har Hamelekh – A New Solution to an Old Puzzle" ("הר המלך - לפתרונה של חידה"). *Zion* 65 (2002): 295.

14. On Tur Malka, see Shahar, "Har hamelekh," 294–95; Ze'ev Safrai, "Har hamelekh adayin hidah" ("הר המלך עדיין חידה"), *JSRS* 19 (2010): 77–79.

15. See m. Soṭah 9:14 (according to MS Kaufmann); t. Soṭah 15:8 (see Tosefta, ed. Lieberman, vol. 3, 242n79). The war of Vespasian refers to the first Jewish revolt against Rome usually dated 66–73 (or 74) CE; the war of Quietus refers to the diaspora revolt usually dated 115 (or 116)–117 CE; and the last war refers to the Bar Kokhba revolt usually dated 132–136 (or 135) CE. (See also Amram Tropper, "On Children, Cypresses, Chickens and Catastrophe" ["על ילדים, ארזים, תרנגולים וחורבן"], *JSJF* 24–25 [2006–2007]: 82.)

a preface to the story of Bar Qamtza, and later on, the trilogy's other two declarations – "on account of a cock and a hen Tur Malka was destroyed, on account of a shaft of a litter Bethar was destroyed" – reappear as prefaces to their respective stories. In each case, the preface signals the beginning of a new story, thereby easing the literary transition. In addition, each preface flash-forwards to the end of its story, reciting the story's tragic conclusion at the outset. In the case of Lamentations Rabbati, since the audience only discovers the tragic consequences of the banquet in the story's final line, the dramatic tension continues until the very end. By contrast, the Babylonian version forfeits dramatic tension before the story even gets started, when the preface telegraphs the story's end. In giving away the story's end, the Babylonian version shifts the narrative tension "from *what* will happen (since this is known) to *how* and *why* it happened."[16] Sacrificing dramatic suspense for an overarching historical frame, the Babylonian trilogy seeks to teach how and why Jerusalem, Tur Malka, and Bethar fell. As a group, the prefaces to the three individual stories echo the trilogy's earlier preface, reminding us of the interpretive lens and historical frame presented there.

Dating the Trilogy

Introduced by prefaces which lack the standard introductory formulae for the citation of Tannaitic materials, it is possible that the trilogy's implied author was Rabbi Yohanan, a first generation Amora, or some late, anonymous editor. However, since the Bavli tends to view stories about Tannaitic times as (non-mishnaic) Tannaitic traditions (or baraitot) even when they were formed in later periods, it is likely that the trilogy was viewed as a Tannaitic tradition.[17] With no whiff of the story

---

16. Rubenstein, *Talmudic Stories*, 147. See also Shlomith Rimmon-Kenan, *Narrative Fiction: Contemporary Poetics* (London: Routledge, 1983), 48.

17. See, for example, Tropper, *Sage Stories*, 113; *Rewriting Ancient Jewish History*, 168–69; "'Teach Me the Whole Torah while I Stand on One Foot': On the Formation of a Story" ("'על מנת שתלמדני כל התורה כולה כשאני עומד על רגל אחת': להתהוותו של סיפור"), in *Between Babylonia and the Land of Israel: Studies in Honor of Isaiah M. Gafni*, ed. Geoffrey Herman, Meir Ben Shahar, and Aharon Oppenheimer (Jerusalem: Zalman Shazar Center, 2016), 270.

of Bar Qamtza in Tannaitic literature, and no reference to the latter two
stories in *any* prior literature, the trilogy most likely emerged only during
Amoraic times; but, as noted, since the trilogy relates to the Tannaitic
period, the Talmud likely viewed it as a Tannaitic tradition.[18]

---

18. See Tropper, "Chickens and Catastrophe," 80. The baraita on b. Git. 57a which
refers to Bar Qamtza is most probably inauthentic, as noted below in Chapter 17.

Chapter 16

The Banquet Invitation
(ACT I SCENE 1)

Act I of the Babylonian story of Bar Qamtza, the banquet act, begins inauspiciously, just like Lamentations Rabbati's parallel version, with a banquet invitation gone wrong:

6 דההוא גברא, דרחמיה קמצא ובעיל דבביה בר קמצא, עבד סעודתא.
7 אמר ליה לשמעיה: זיל אייתי לי קמצא, אזל אייתי ליה בר קמצא.

6 A certain man, whose friend was (called) Qamtza and enemy was (called) Bar Qamtza, made a banquet.

7 He said to his servant: Go, bring me Qamtza. He went and brought him Bar Qamtza.

"A Certain Man"

Scene 1 begins in line 6 with the Aramaic words "דההוא גברא," ("A certain man"), a standard opening phrase for rabbinic stories.[1] The familiar opening alerts us that the story has commenced and focuses our attention on one "certain man." This "certain man" remains nameless, just like the parallel "one man" in Lamentations Rabbati, and, again, just like in Lamentations Rabbati, the absence of a name, in and of itself, is unsurprising and implies no criticism.[2]

---

1. In contrast, Lamentations Rabbati's first line is formulated in Hebrew. See Chapter 5 above.
2. Cf. Duker, "Piety or Privilege," 43.

The story's opening phrase is followed by a relative clause – "whose friend was (called) Qamtza and enemy was (called) Bar Qamtza" – a clause pregnant with ramifications for all that follows. Unlike the "certain man" whose name is never mentioned, the names of his friend and enemy, Qamtza and Bar Qamtza, are of utmost importance to the story's plotline and therefore are introduced from the very start. In Lamentations Rabbati, the friend and foe share the very same name – "son of Qamtza," but the Bavli assigns them different names, "Qamtza" and "son of Qamtza," presumably in order to more easily differentiate between them.[3] In line 7, the confusion of these two highly similar names will launch the series of events which ultimately culminates in the cataclysmic destruction of Jerusalem.

The relative clause – "whose friend was (called) Qamtza and enemy was (called) Bar Qamtza" – is a parenthetical gloss which clarifies up front the nature of the host's ties to Qamtza and Bar Qamtza. In Lamentations Rabbati, by contrast, the nature of these ties are only noted as the story unfolds – "Go and bring me Ben Qamtza my friend; he went and brought him Bar Qamtza his enemy," – rather than in a parenthetical aside. Since the only distinguishing feature between the two men in Lamentations Rabbati is the nature of their relationships with the host, the host in Lamentations Rabbati commands the messenger to invite the son of Qamtza *his friend* so that the messenger does not invite the son of Qamtza *his enemy*. However, since the Babylonian version assigns each man a different name, the host has no need to specify that he means his friend. Thus, for the sake of clarity the nature of the men's relationships with the host is stated up front.

Although we are told that the "certain man" considered Qamtza his friend and Bar Qamtza his enemy, we are not told why. What shared history linked this man to his beloved Qamtza and why did he so detest Bar Qamtza? These issues remain unexplored, but one should not conclude from this that the "certain man" developed friendships and made enemies with no rhyme or reason.[4] Rather, it bears stressing, once again, that rabbinic stories reveal information only on a need to know basis.

---

3. See Chapter 5 above.
4. Cf. Sofer, *Hidushei hatam sofer*, ad loc. (52c, s.vv. *mai dekhtiv*); Kalmanzon and Fogel, *Legends of the Destruction*, 21–22. See also Chapter 6, nn. 28–29 above.

The prior history of the man's relationships with Qamtza and Bar Qamtza is apparently irrelevant to the course of the story.[5]

Nonetheless, it could be that one particular term does hint at the underlying cause for the host's animosity towards Bar Qamtza. The term for enemy enlisted here, "בעיל דבבא," is made up of two Akkadian loanwords which translate as enemy, foe, or *legal adversary*.[6] Although simpler Aramaic terms for enemy were at hand, and one such word, "סנאה" ("שנאה"), was used in Lamentations Rabbati's earlier version, the Babylonian editor opted for an Akkadian term instead.[7] Perhaps the Babylonian editor preferred this particular term over Lamentations Rabbati's simpler option because it filled in a literary lacuna in the earlier version of the story. Whereas Lamentations Rabbati never explained the cause of the host's enmity for Bar Qamtza, the term "בעיל דבבא," when understood as a legal adversary, suggests that the host and Bar Qamtza were bitter legal opponents. In addition, since intense hatred between Jews was considered improper, perhaps the Babylonian editor hoped to tone down the host's enmity for Bar Qamtza by replacing the standard Aramaic word for enemy used in Lamentations Rabbati, which stems from the verbal root meaning to hate (ש.נ.א.), with an Akkadian term that can denote a mere legal adversary.

"Made a Banquet"

Line 6, the very first sentence of the story proper, concludes with the predicate: "made a banquet." The "certain man," defined so far by the nature of his relationships with Qamtza and Bar Qamtza, decides to host a private banquet, presumably in Jerusalem.[8] Although the original

---

5. See Furstenberg, "Qamtza," 105.

6. See Sokoloff, *Dictionary of Jewish Babylonian Aramaic*, 227. Cf. Jastrow, *Dictionary*, 276.

7. See Jastrow, *Dictionary*, 1004; Sokoloff, *Dictionary of Jewish Babylonian Aramaic*, 821. See also Chapter 1, n. 10 above.

8. Whereas Lamentations Rabbati mentions Jerusalem in the story's very first line, "A story of one man in Jerusalem who made a banquet," the Bavli does not need to mention Jerusalem in its corresponding line because its preface – "On account of Qamtza and Bar Qamtza Jerusalem was destroyed" – already linked the story to Jerusalem.

story of this banquet emerged in a province of the Roman Empire, the banquet context would have been familiar to Babylonian Jews in Persia as well. Just as in the Roman world, banquets in ancient Persia were social events designed to foster a sense of community and brotherly love but, in practice, they were fraught with the potential for explosive conflict and deep humiliation.[9] Consequently, even though Babylonian Jews might not have been fully conversant with Greek and Roman banquet culture, they would have agreed that the banquet supplied a perfect setting for the eruption of a heated conflict between host and guest and for the transformation of a personal feud into a public humiliation.

Furthermore, in stating that the host "made a banquet," we can rest assured that he set in motion all the requisite protocols and preparations. Line 7 reveals, however, that the standard banquet preparatory routine was disrupted by an irregular and unexpected development. In preparation for his banquet, the host sends his servant to invite his friend Qamtza but the servant mistakenly invites Bar Qamtza instead. The language of the host's command "זיל אייתי לי קמצא", "Go, bring me Qamtza," is practically identical to the description of its fulfillment "אזל אייתי ליה בר קמצא," "He went and brought him Bar Qamtza." The shared language highlights the single significant difference between the command and its fulfillment: rather than inviting the host's friend as ordered, the servant invites the host's foe.

It would be a mistake to imagine that the servant intentionally invites the host's foe, whether out of malice or in the hopes of orchestrating a reconciliation, since in that case there would have been no need to mention the two men's similar names. As noted above, characters in rabbinic stories are usually not named without cause, and Qamtza and Bar Qamtza would have remained nameless, just like the host and his servant, if their names had no bearing on the story's plotline. Accordingly, the conspicuous presentation of Qamtza and Bar Qamtza's names indicates that the servant's error stemmed from his confusing these names. We can only wonder if the servant could have known he was inviting the host's enemy; because the story does not divulge this information, it is apparently irrelevant to the unfolding drama.

---

9. See Watts Belser, *Rabbinic Tales of Destruction*, 179–80.

Chapter 17

The Banquet Conflict (ACT I SCENE 2)

A ct I scene 2 transitions to the banquet itself. In line 8 the host arrives at his banquet only to find his enemy, Bar Qamtza, seated there:

8 אתא אשכחיה דהוה קא יתיב.

8 He (the host) came and found (Bar Qamtza) sitting.

Shocked by Bar Qamtza's presence at his private banquet, the host protests in line 9:

9 אמר ליה: מכדי ההוא גברא בעיל דבבא דההוא גברא, מאי בעית הכא? קום!

9 He said to him: Since that certain man (you) is an enemy of this certain man (me), what do you want here? Get up!

The term which opened the story, "a certain man," appears here twice, once in reference to the host and once in reference to Bar Qamtza. Whereas the host could have simply said "Since you are my enemy" in a straightforward manner, he apparently opted for these "circumlocutions to avoid negative direct speech."[1] In other words, while the host is willing to publicly acknowledge his enmity for Bar Qamtza, he does so only in coded language. Perhaps the host's need to encode his feelings reflects a gap between reality and propriety, between his hate-

---

1. Kalmin, *Jewish Babylonia*, 205n19. Cf. Duker, "Piety or Privilege," 43.

ful emotions and the moral code which disapproves of hatred between compatriots.[2] In any event, the host fails to understand why Bar Qamtza decided to crash his party – "what do you want here?" – and orders him to leave. Infuriated to find Bar Qamtza "sitting" at his banquet, the host directs Bar Qamtza to "Get up!" (or "Stand up!") and exit the premises immediately.

In its first few lines, our story not only mentions a few binary opposites – friend/enemy, master/servant, host/guest, sit/stand – it also inverts them.[3] The enemy is mistaken for a friend, the servant undermines his master, the host is anything but hospitable, and the sitting guest is asked to stand and leave. The inversion of these opposites invests the story with a topsy-turvy feeling which bodes ill for things to come.

The Negotiation

Hearing the host demand that he quit the banquet, Bar Qamtza responds in line 10:

10 אמר ליה: הואיל ואתאי שיבקן ויהיבנא לך דמי מאי דקאכילנא ושתינא.
אמר ליה: לא.

10 He said to him: Since I have come, let me be and I will pay you the cost of whatever I eat and drink. He said to him: No.

With the phrase "since I have come," "הואיל ואתאי," (which seems to carry the sense "since I am already here" or "since, as it has turned out, I have come"[4]), Bar Qamtza backs away from any attempt to defend his presence at the banquet, apparently acknowledging that he does not truly belong there.[5] But why not defend himself? Why not assert that he

2. See the previous chapter's discussion of the Akkadian loanword for enemy.
3. On the notion of binary opposites in myth, see Claude Lévi Strauss, *The Naked Man*, in *Introduction to a Science of Mythology*, vol. 4 (New York, NY: Harper & Row, 1981), 559; *The Story of Lynx* (Chicago, IL: University of Chicago Press, 1995), 185.
4. This seems to be the meaning of the phrase on b. Qidd. 70b and within the longer term "since it has come to our hand/attention," "הואיל ואתא לידן" (see b. Shabb. 81b; b. B. Qam. 89a; b. B. Metz. 16b; b. Shevu. 48a). Cf. b. Taʿan. 23b; b. Yevam. 92a.
5. See Furstenberg, "Qamtza," 105.

came at the behest of the host's very own servant? When Rav Nahman doubts that Rav Judah was summoned to his court on b. Qiddushin 70b, Rav Judah proves him wrong:

א״ל: מאי שיאטיה דמר הכא? אמר ליה: טסקא[6] דהזמנותא שדר מר אבתראי. אמר ליה: השתא שותא דמר לא גמירנא טסקא דהזמנותא משדרנא למר? אפיק דיסקא דהזמנותא מבי חדיה ואחזי[7] ליה. אמר ליה: הא גברא והא דסקא![8]

He (Rav Nahman) said to him (Rav Judah): What is the reason for the master (you) traveling here?[9] He (Rav Judah) said to him: The master (you) sent a subpoena document[10] after me. He said to him: Now that (it is apparent that) I have not (even) learned the master's (your) speech, would I send the master (you) a subpoena document? He (Rav Judah) drew out the subpoena document from his chest and showed (it) to him. He said: Here is the man and here is the document!

This quotation (extracted from the middle of a story) begins with Rav Nahman asking Rav Judah why he came to his court. When Rav Judah explains that he came in response to Rav Nahman's summons, Rav Nahman doubts Rav Judah, saying: "would I send the master a subpoena document?" In response to Rav Nahman's doubt, Rav Judah proffers the subpoena document itself, proving that he was, in fact, summoned to Rav Nahman's court. In light of Rav Judah's natural and reasonable response to Rav Nahman's doubt, we might wonder why Bar Qamtza does not offer a similar response to the host's question: "what do you want here?"

Unlike Rav Judah's official subpoena document, perhaps Bar Qamtza

---

6. Cf. MS Munich 95 where the word "דיסקא" appears in lieu of the word "טסקא" in both of its appearances. On these two occasions neither word appears in MS Oxford Opp. 248 (367) or MS Vatican 111.

7. See MS Munich 95, MS Oxford Opp. 248 (367) and MS Vatican 111 for the alternative reading "אחוי" or "ואחוי."

8. B. Qidd. 70b according to the Vilna edition. The manuscripts supply shorter (and probably earlier) readings of the story, but all readings agree that Rav Judah showed Rav Nahman the subpoena in order to prove that he had been summoned. (Cf. b. Sanh. 109b.)

9. See Sokoloff, *Dictionary of Jewish Babylonian Aramaic*, 1134.

10. See Sokoloff, *Dictionary of Jewish Babylonian Aramaic*, 330.

lacked written documentation of his invitation, and, without compelling written proof, Bar Qamtza's case would have rested on shaky ground. While Bar Qamtza could have argued that the host's servant actually brought him to the banquet, this argument would have lacked the force of written documentation, and in the wake of the host's anger, the servant, even if consulted, might not have fessed up to inviting him.

However, one can imagine other explanations for Bar Qamtza's behavior that are not predicated on the fear that his account of the invitation would not have been believed or corroborated. Perhaps Bar Qamtza saw no point in mentioning the mistaken invitation once he realized that, as a persona non grata, the accidental invitation was an irrelevant curiosity that would not sway the host. While Bar Qamtza may have initially underestimated the host's antipathy for him or interpreted the invitation as the first step in the host's attempt to reach out and reconcile their differences, perhaps the host's harsh reaction to his presence made it clear to Bar Qamtza that he was an unwanted guest who would remain so regardless of the mistaken invitation.[11] Perhaps Bar Qamtza considered it bad manners to confront or otherwise embarrass the host at his own banquet and accordingly sought a less adversarial solution to his predicament. Or, perhaps Bar Qamtza suspected that he had been intentionally set up for a fall, like Haman at Esther's second banquet (Esth 7:1–10), and therefore surmised that the host would not relent until Bar Qamtza groveled before him. However we read between the lines here, the fact of the matter is that Bar Qamtza does not adduce his invitation as a justification for his presence at the banquet.

Rather than defending himself, Bar Qamtza tries to mollify the host in lines 10–12 by offering him money:

10 ... שיבקן ויהיבנא לך דמי מאי דקאכילנא ושתינא. אמר ליה: לא.

11 יהיבנא לך דמי פלגא דסעודתא. אמר ליה: לא.

12 יהיבנא לך דמי כולה סעודתיך. אמר ליה: לא.

---

11. For the notion that Bar Qamtza underestimated the host's hatred, see Kalmanzon and Fogel, *Legends of the Destruction,* 21. For the interpretation that he thought the host was reaching out to reconcile with him, see Maharsha in the Bavli, ad loc. (s.vv. *veʾamar deʾazal aytei leih bar qamtza*); Mandel, "Tales of the Destruction," 149n32. See also D'Arms, "Roman *Convivium,*" 313.

10 He said to him: Since I have come, let me be and **I will pay you the cost of** whatever I eat and drink. **He said to him: No.**

11 **I will give you money for the cost of** half **the banquet. He said to him: No.**

12 **I will give you money for the cost of the** whole **banquet. He said to him: No.**

Fearing the humiliation of eviction from the banquet, Bar Qamtza initially offers to cover the expense of his own meal in the hopes that the host will reconsider and allow him to stay if he does not have to lay out any money for him. The host responds, however, with a categorical "No."

Figuring that his initial offer was too low, Bar Qamtza then proposes to pay for half of the banquet, suggesting, in essence, that he become the host's partner insofar as financing the banquet is concerned. Bar Qamtza apparently reasoned that if he were to help defray the cost of the banquet, even a host who did not like him would tolerate his presence there. The host responds once again, however, with an emphatic "No."

Finally, the desperate Bar Qamtza offers to cover the full costs of the banquet, proposing, in essence, to take the host's place as the banquet's financial patron. Were Bar Qamtza to pay for the banquet, the host would be able to make a second banquet with these funds and would lose absolutely nothing by permitting Bar Qamtza to stay: the host could enjoy his first banquet free of cost albeit with Bar Qamtza's presence; then he could make a second banquet without him.

In response to Bar Qamtza's third and ridiculously generous offer, the host not only repeats his unequivocal "No" in line 12, but also ejects Bar Qamtza from the banquet in line 13:

13 נקט ליה בידיה ואפקיה.

13 He took him with his hand and threw him out.

The host's hatred for Bar Qamtza is so powerful that even a lucrative financial incentive cannot convince him to put up with his presence at the banquet. With no attempt to understand what brought Bar Qamtza to his banquet and no interest in receiving Bar Qamtza's money, the host simply kicks Bar Qamtza out.[12]

---

12. See Levine Katz, "Qamtsa" 36.

In Lamentations Rabbati, Bar Qamtza's expulsion from the banquet is implied but never described. By contrast, the Bavli explicitly depicts the expulsion as a violent assault: the banquet host grabs Bar Qamtza and throws him out. Fleshing out details left unstated in Lamentations Rabbati, the Bavli clarifies the plotline, giving the host's cruelty physical expression and thereby magnifying Bar Qamtza's humiliation.

Over the course of Bar Qamtza's three proposals in scene 2, the dramatic tension of the story gradually escalates. The sums offered increase from proposal to proposal in line with Bar Qamtza's growing desperation.[13] From a literary perspective, the unchanging format of the proposals – "I will give you the cost of… He said to him: No" – underscores the increasing sums; the only element which changes from proposal to proposal is the amount offered. Furthermore, the thrice repeated phrase – "I will give you" – captures the pleading tone of Bar Qamtza's desperate bargaining which is consistently rebuffed by the host's uncompromising stance. Despite his frantic offers and solicitous tone, Bar Qamtza fails to move the host.[14]

A comparison of Bar Qamtza's three offers to the parallel offers in Lamentations Rabbati reveals that while the Bavli preserved the substance of the first and third offers, it altered the second one. In both versions, Bar Qamtza initially offers to pay for his own meal and in the end proposes to pay for the entire banquet, but his middle offer changes from version to version: in Lamentations Rabbati he proposes not to eat the meal he had already offered to fund, and in the Bavli he offers to bankroll half the banquet. The large gap between Bar Qamtza's second and third offers in Lamentations Rabbati, between not eating and paying for the whole banquet, perhaps provoked the Babylonian editor to bridge this gap by changing the second offer into a proposal to cover half the banquet. Furthermore, it is striking that the reference to eating and drinking in Bar Qamtza's *first* proposal in the Bavli, "I will pay you the cost of whatever I **eat** and **drink**" ("ויהיבנא לך דמי מאי דקאכילנא ושתינא"), enlists language found in his *second* proposal in Lamentations Rabbati, "I will pay you without **eating** or **drinking**" ("ואנא יהיב לך

---

13. See Levine Katz, "Qamtsa" 36; Furstenberg, "Qamtza," 105; Watts Belser, *Rabbinic Tales of Destruction*, 181–82.
14. See Chapter 10, n. 4 above.

שתי ולא אכיל דלא"). It appears that when the Babylonian editor opted to preserve only one proposal which related to Bar Qamtza's personal meal, he conflated the gist of Lamentations Rabbati's first proposal, i.e., Bar Qamtza's offer to pay for his own meal, with the words "eating" and "drinking" from its second proposal.

With the preface's biblical citation – "Happy is the man who is anxious always, but he who hardens his heart falls into misfortune" (Prov 28:14) – echoing in our minds, the host's repeated rejections of Bar Qamtza's overtures emerge as a perfect illustration of stubborn and foolish intractability. Like Pharoah's refusals of the Israelites' demands, the host is granted multiple opportunities to back down from his chosen course of action but fails to do so because of his hardened heart. As the story continues to unfold, it will become clear how the host's obdurate behavior sets in motion a cascade of events which ultimately brings about the destruction of Jerusalem. In refusing to budge from his position, the host's obstinacy and lack of foresight lead to grave misfortune.

The Moral Dimension

Although the preface primes us to be mindful of the host's inflexibility, it should not blind us to the story's moral dimension. The host's uncompromising behavior is not merely foolishly stubborn and pragmatically unwise, it is also callously humiliating and morally bankrupt. The trigger for all the misfortune that eventually follows is not morally neutral conduct but rather uncaring and coldhearted behavior. The host's continuous refusal to back down from ruthlessly humiliating another person magnifies his merciless character and moral shortcomings, ultimately leading to the destruction of Jerusalem and the temple. Following Lamentations Rabbati's lead, the host's behavior gives narrative form to the Tannaitic tradition which ascribed the destruction of the Second Temple to "hating one's fellow before God."

When the Talmud returns to our trilogy in lines 27–28 (after an extended detour exploring the temple's destruction), its resumptive repetition focuses on the story's moral and theological dimensions:

27 תניא: א"ר אלעזר: בוא וראה כמה גדול כח של בושה

28 שהרי סייע הקב"ה את בר קמצא והחריב את ביתו ושרף את היכלו.

27 It was taught: Rabbi Eleazar said: Come and see how great is the power of shame,

28 for God assisted Bar Qamtza and destroyed his temple and burnt his sanctuary.

The resumptive repetition opens with an introductory formula reserved for baraitot, i.e., non-mishnaic Tannaitic traditions (along with an attribution to a Tanna). However, since it has no parallel in rabbinic literature and also echoes the final line (or line 26) of our story – "The meekness of Rabbi Zechariah ben Avqulas **destroyed our temple, burnt our sanctuary**" – it is likely a late invention. [15] As noted above, the Bavli often presents traditions about early figures with the introductory formulae reserved for baraitot. In any event, this (supposed) baraita sums up our story by articulating its essential core: Bar Qamtza's humiliation was so powerful a force that God helped Bar Qamtza seek revenge. From God's perspective, a society that facilitated or condoned the host's humiliating behavior was no place for his temple.[16]

---

15. See Chapter 15, n. 17 above. Cf. Halevi, *Gates of the Aggadah*, 204; Rubenstein, *Talmudic Stories*, 347n24; Levine Katz, "Qamtsa" 48n45; Mandel, "Tales of the Destruction," 149n31. See also Yisraeli-Taran, *Legends of the Destruction*, 22 and Furstenberg, "Qamtza," 104 who attribute this baraita to an Amora. On the origins of the saying about Zechariah ben Avqulas, see Chapter 7 above.

16. See Goldenberg, "Rabbinic Explanations," 522; Weiss, "Class Reversals," 4; cf. Kraemer, *Suffering*, 181–82. Unlike Kraemer, Watts Belser acknowledges that "God's presence *is* significant in Bavli Gittin's account" (*Rabbinic Tales of Destruction*, 140), but she agrees with Kraemer (see Chapter 13 above) that our story has nothing to do with sin and punishment. For Watts Belser, when "God responds to the injustice of Bar Qamtza's public humiliation" (204–5), he is not chastising the Jewish people but rather expressing self-sacrificial empathy with Bar Qamtza's shame (xiv, 205). However, it is difficult to see how the loss of thousands of lives and the abrogation of Israel's traditional conduit for communication with the divine could have been viewed as an expression of God's empathizing self-sacrifice; by contrast such tragic events were perfectly aligned with the ancient covenantal view of collective or national punishment.

Chapter 18

Bar Qamtza's Indignation
(ACT I SCENE 3)

After the host manhandles Bar Qamtza and throws him out of the banquet, Bar Qamtza, in line 14, digests his humiliating experience and reacts. The public turmoil at the banquet in scene 2 gives way here, in scene 3, to the private turmoil churning in Bar Qamtza's soul:

14 אמר: הואיל והוו יתבי רבנן ולא מחו ביה איזיל ואיכול בהו קורצא בי
מלכא.

14 He (Bar Qamtza) said: Since the sages were sitting there and did not protest to him, I will go and inform the king's palace against them.

In response to the sordid events at the banquet, Bar Qamtza privately expresses his outraged reaction. This reaction opens with the word "Since," "הואיל," the very word which opened his earlier plea to the host (in line 10): "Since (הואיל) I have come, let me be and I will pay you the cost of whatever I eat and drink." In echoing the earlier use of "Since," the story underlines how much has changed since that first use. Whereas Bar Qamtza's first "Since" statement wistfully envisioned a harmonious resolution to an embarrassing and socially fraught situation, his second comes on the heels of a disastrous and shameful denouement.

"The Sages Were Sitting There"

Bar Qamtza's reaction to his humiliating expulsion from the banquet commences with an infuriating observation: "the sages were sitting there and did not protest to him." Just as the host begrudged Bar Qamtza *sitting* and enjoying himself at the banquet, Bar Qamtza is enraged that the rabbinic sages *were sitting* complacently at the banquet as spectators to his humiliation, not deigning to lift even a finger on his behalf.[1] Whether the sages presumed that the host was in the right or whether they were selfishly looking out for their own interests, they should never have let the host so humiliate Bar Qamtza.[2] Bar Qamtza's expectation that the sages protest the host's egregious behavior is in keeping with the regard for the sages as moral authorities which pervades rabbinic literature. Moreover, many rabbinic sources explicitly call upon the sages to protest illicit behavior. The term for protest used here, "מחו ביה," is a technical term for protesting forbidden activity, usually of a legal nature, enlisted here to reference immoral behavior.[3]

Surprisingly, the object of Bar Qamtza's seething rage is not the

---

1. In Vatican 130 (see Chapter 14, n. 22 above), the reading "ולא מחו בידי'," "and they did not prevent his *hand*," suggests that the sages did not attempt to forestall the very *hand* which threw Bar Qamtza out in the previous line: "נקט ליה בידיה ואפקיה," "He took him with his *hand* and threw him out."

2. For the notion that the sages presumed the host was in the right, see Sofer, *Hidushei hatam sofer*, ad loc. (52c, s.vv. *mai dekhtiv*). (See also the statement cited on b, Pesaḥ. 86b according to most manuscripts [cf. Pirk. B. Azz. 4:1 (*The Treatises Derek Erez: Masseket Derek Erez, Pirke Ben Azzai, Tosefta Derek Erez*, ed. and trans. Michael Higger [New York, NY: "Debe Rabanan," 1935], 193)]: "Whatever a host tells you, do" ["כל מה שיאמר לך בעל הבית עשה"]). For a creative link between the added phrase "except depart" ("חוץ מצא") found in certain textual witnesses and the story of Bar Qamtza, see Yehudah Aryeh Leib Alter, *Sefat Emet: Pesahim* (שפת אמת: פסחים), (New York, NY: Mordecai Judah Lubert and Mendel Eiger, 1954–1955), ad loc. (95). For the claim that the sages were looking out for themselves, see Rubenstein, *Talmudic Stories*, 148. It is difficult to interpret, like Joseph Hayyim ben Elijah, *Sefer ben Yehoyada*, ad loc. (61, s.vv. *amar hoʾil*), that the sages were unaware of Bar Qamtza's humiliation, since both Bar Qamtza and the divine will (through Bar Qamtza) held them accountable.

3. See, for example, m. Pesaḥ. 4:8; m. Ketub. 1:5; m. Menaḥ. 10:8; t. Pesaḥ. 3:19; t. Ketub. 1:1; y. Ber. 2:2, 4c; y. Eruv. 10:1, 27a; y. Sukkah 2:1, 52d; b. Avod. Zar. 18a; b. Shabb. 54b–55b. See also Rubenstein, *Talmudic Stories*, 348n27; Levine Katz,

host, who callously rejected his pleas and threw him out of the banquet, but rather the sages, the rabbinic leaders who neglected to intervene and rescue him from a mortifying situation. Bar Qamtza's anger at the sages surprises us not because it is unreasonable – which it is not – but because until now we did not even know that the sages were present at the banquet. Neither scene 1 nor scene 2 refers anywhere to the sages, and the first we learn of their presence at the banquet is here, in scene 3's presentation of the banquet's aftermath.[4] Why not disclose the sages' presence during the banquet's actual depiction in scenes 1 or 2? From a literary point of view one might argue that delaying mention of the sages intensifies the story's critique of their behavior, or, in the words of Jeffrey Rubenstein, "the sages might as well not have been present, since they took no action."[5] In a similar vein, by having Bar Qamtza disclose the sages' presence, the shock value of his revelation might enhance his grievance, making it even more compelling. However, although these interpretations are reasonable attempts to make literary sense of the story, the late appearance of the sages is literarily disruptive, and I suspect that it is a by-product of the localized way in which the Bavli recast our story.

A comparison of Bar Qamtza's condemnation of the banqueting sages in the Bavli to the parallel scene in Lamentations Rabbati indicates that the Babylonian version subtly reworked the Palestinian original. Like the Bar Qamtza of the early layer of Lamentations Rabbati (line 15) who cried to himself – "How do *they* (dare) recline and sit at ease!" – the Bar Qamtza of the Bavli also condemns passive banqueters (in the plural), and like the late layer of Lamentations Rabbati (line 14) which finds fault with a rabbinic sage, Zechariah ben Avqulas, because "he did not protest" ("ולא מיחה"), Bar Qamtza of the Bavli finds fault with the rabbinic sages because "they did not protest" ("ולא מחו"). The best explanation for the nature of these similarities to two distinct layers of Lamentations Rabbati is that the Bavli conflated the unprotesting banqueters (in plural)

"Qamtsa" 46n41; and the discussion of the term "he had the opportunity to protest but did not protest" ("והיה ספק בידו למחות ולא מיחה") in Chapter 7 above.

4. See Rubenstein, *Talmudic Stories*, 148.

5. Rubenstein, *Talmudic Stories*, 148. See also Duker, "Piety or Privilege," 43–44.

from Lamentations Rabbati's early version (line 15) with the rabbinic focus of its later layer (line 14), identifying some (or all) of the passive banqueters as rabbis! By creating a new version of the story which blamed the rabbis as a group, the Bavli intensified the rabbinization of the story, transforming the fault of a single rabbinic sage into the fault of the rabbinic leadership as a whole.[6] However, enhancing the profile of the rabbis in scene 3 came at the price of introducing the rabbis into the story at a relatively late stage. In short, just as Lamentations Rabbati introduced the Jerusalemite banqueters back in scene 1 in order to set the backdrop for their role in scene 3, one would expect the Bavli to have introduced the sages back in scene 1 in order to set the stage for Bar Qamtza condemning them in scene 3. The Babylonian editor did not do so probably because the inspirational trigger for the sages' insertion into the story was Zechariah ben Avqulas's parallel presence in Lamentations Rabbati, where he appears (within an unanticipated secondary addition) only in scene 3.

With the surprising and belated mention of the sages, scene 3 presents a new interpretive lens through which to reread scene 2. When initially reading scene 2, Bar Qamtza's multiple pleas impressed upon us the gravity of his desperation and the severity of the host's cruel intractability. In the wake of scene 3, however, Bar Qamtza's pleas take on a new light: the sages are given multiple opportunities to put an end to the banquet travesty but they flub them all and neglect their responsibilities. Rather than exercising their moral authority and challenging the host, the sages are cowardly or selfish at best and indifferent or apathetic at worst.[7] They ignore Bar Qamtza's plight, thereby implicitly condoning the host's heartless behavior. In the footsteps of Lamentations Rabbati's scene 3, the Bavli's scene 3 also gives narrative form to the rabbinic tradition which ascribed the destruction of Jerusalem to the failure of the eminent of Israel to oppose iniquity and rebuke one another. The Babylonian version, however, equates the eminent of Israel with the rabbinic sages rather than the nobles of Jerusalem. At its core, the sages' paralysis, just like the host's hatred, stems from a lack of solidarity with their Jewish

---

6. See Levine Katz, "Qamtsa" 41; Mandel, "Tales of the Destruction," 152; Ben Shahar, "Abolishment of the Sacrifice," 575–76.

7. See Rokéaḥ, "Zechariah," 55n11.

compatriots. Neither empathizing with Bar Qamtza nor identifying with his pain, the sages' permit his shameful degradation.

Informing the Emperor

Furious with the sages for not intervening, Bar Qamtza decides to take revenge by going to the "king's palace," that is, to the Roman emperor, where he plans to inform against the sages by means of a slanderous accusation.[8] Since the sages sat quietly on the sidelines while the host utterly humiliated him, Bar Qamtza resolves to punish them equally pitilessly. The term used here for informing the gentile authorities, "איכול קורצא," comprises two Akkadian loanwords (just like the term enlisted above for "enemy" ["בעיל דבבא"]) whose literal meaning is unclear.[9] Nonetheless, this originally Akkadian term is the standard way the Bavli refers to the act of informing on one's fellow Jew(s), which makes its presence in our story perfectly natural.[10]

While Lamentations Rabbati naturally imagines that Bar Qamtza would have cast aspersions on the Jews before the *local governor*, Bar Qamtza of the Bavli vilifies the Jewish leadership before the *Roman emperor*.[11] From the distant perspective of the Babylonian editor, the emperor, a far more familiar Roman figurehead than the local governor,

---

8. For a comparison between Bar Qamtza and Judas Iscariot, see Yuval, *Two Nations*, 51; cf. Yisraeli-Taran, *Legends of the Destruction*, 105–6n23.

9. See Sokoloff, *Dictionary of Jewish Babylonian Aramaic*, 1003. Cf. Jastrow, *Dictionary*, 1425. See also Dan 3: 8, 6:25.

10. With that being said, Lamentations Rabbati's earlier version of the story did not include a comparable technical term; it simply stated that Bar Qamtza went to the governor and spoke to him. Hence, perhaps the term "איכול קורצא" was introduced into the Babylonian version of the story in order to perform double (or triple) duty: not only does it explain why Bar Qamtza went to the authorities, its evocative words might have resonated in other ways as well. Were the Akkadian word "איכול" read as a Hebrew or Aramaic word it would mean "I will eat," and so, perhaps Bar Qamtza's statement could also be read as a play on words which intimates that since he was not permitted to *eat* at the host's banquet, he would *eat* (i.e., inform) instead at the emperor's palace. In mobilizing the word "*qurtza*," "קורצא," which can be read as a play on the similar word "Qamtza," "קמצא," the story might be aligning Bar Qamtza with the destructive forces he is about to unleash.

11. See Yisraeli-Taran, *Legends of the Destruction*, 17. (Cf. Friedman, "Dama Ben Netina," 91–92.)

was the natural choice to insert in the story. Furthermore, in line with the tendency of the Bavli to portray the Sasanian monarch as the ultimate symbol of Persian imperial authority, our Babylonian story views the Roman emperor, rather than the local governor, as the ultimate symbol of Roman imperial authority.[12]

Rabbinizing the Story

By approaching the emperor, Bar Qamtza raises the stakes of the conflict from a domestic dispute to a political struggle wherein the rabbinic sages, not the Jerusalem elite as per Lamentations Rabbati, were the mediating element which enabled this transition.[13] In Bar Qamtza's eyes, the guilty rabbinic sages represented, and perhaps even embodied, the Jewish nation as a whole (or at its best) and were hence instrumental in the amplification of a private altercation into a national calamity. Although the preface's verse "Happy is the man who is anxious always, but he who hardens his heart falls into misfortune" primes us to search for injudicious shortsightedness, any pragmatic shortcomings of the sages' inaction pale in comparison to the sages' moral cowardice and indifference.

The Babylonian story of Bar Qamtza could have easily implicated others in the fall of Jerusalem and the destruction of the temple, but it primarily holds the sages accountable. Rather than blaming the Romans, Christians, Samaritans, heretics, or other Jewish groups (such as the Jerusalem elite), the rabbis exclaim, perhaps surprisingly, *nostra culpa*.[14] In a similar vein, when accounting for other disastrous historical events (in rabbinic eyes), such as the birth of Christianity, the rabbis also blamed their rabbinic predecessors.[15] Nonetheless, the rabbis were

---

12. See Jason Sion Mokhtarian, *Rabbis, Sorcerers, Kings, and Priests: The Culture of the Talmud in Ancient Iran* (Oakland: University of California Press, 2015), 74–93.
13. Had the Bavli wished to critique the mores of the Judaean elite in late Second Temple Jerusalem, it would not have replaced them with rabbinic sages.
14. See Richard I. Rubenstein, *The Religious Imagination: A Study in Psychoanalysis and Jewish Theology* (Lanham, MD: University Press of America, 1968), 35; Jonathan Klawans, *Purity, Sacrifice, and the Temple: Symbolism and Supersessionism in the Study of Ancient Judaism* (Oxford: Oxford University Press, 2005), 185.
15. See Tropper, *Simeon the Righteous*, 190–95; Calderon, *Alfa Beta*, 189. Cf. Cohen,

almost certainly not responsible for the destruction of the temple or the birth of Christianity. Jewish society of late Second Temple times was overseen by a complex configuration of leaders and, while the Pharisees, and perhaps a few sages, played some leadership role, they were by no means the chief rulers of the people.[16] Hence, rabbinic claims of responsibility are predicated on the prior rabbinization of late Second Temple history. In other words, I propose that self-blame and rabbinization are flipsides of one and the same coin: only when rabbinic sages are retrojected into the leadership of the late Second Temple period can they be held responsible for the events of that time, both good and bad.

Conclusion

Let us conclude our discussion of Act 1 with a brief overview of its narrative arc. The act begins in scene 1 with a case of mistaken identity: instead of inviting the host's friend, Qamtza, to a private banquet, a servant accidentally invites the host's enemy, Bar Qamtza. Bar Qamtza

---

"Parallel Historical Tradition," 11–12; Rubenstein, *Talmudic Stories*, 167–69; Mandel, "Tales of the Destruction," 153n39; Furstenberg, "Qamtza," 104; Kalmin, *Jewish Babylonia*, 43–48; Ben Shahar, "Abolishment of the Sacrifice," 586; Watts Belser, *Rabbinic Tales of Destruction*, 182.

16. In addition, most scholars today maintain that the rabbis were not the official leaders of the Jewish people for some (or many) centuries following the destruction of the temple, though the measure of the rabbis' popularity and influence is still disputed. See Seth Schwartz, *Imperialism and Jewish Society 200 BCE to 640 CE* (Princeton, NJ: Princeton University Press, 2001), 110–28; Tropper, *Rewriting Ancient Jewish History*, 127; Robert Brody, "'Rabbinic' and 'Nonrabbinic' Jews in Mishnah and Tosefta," in *The Faces of Torah: Studies in the Texts and Contexts of Ancient Judaism in Honor of Steven Fraade*, ed. Michal Bar-Asher Siegal, Tzvi Novick, and Christine Hayes (Göttingen: Vandenhoeck & Ruprecht, 2017), 275–91; Lee I. Levine, "Jews and Judaism in Palestine (70–640 CE): A New Historical Paradigm," in *The Faces of Torah: Studies in the Texts and Contexts of Ancient Judaism in Honor of Steven Fraade*, ed. Michal Bar-Asher Siegal, Tzvi Novick, and Christine Hayes (Göttingen: Vandenhoeck & Ruprecht, 2017), 395–412; Stuart S. Miller, "The Study of Talmudic Israel and/or Roman Palestine: Where Matters Stand," in *The Faces of Torah: Studies in the Texts and Contexts of Ancient Judaism in Honor of Steven Fraade*, ed. Michal Bar-Asher Siegal, Tzvi Novick, and Christine Hayes (Göttingen: Vandenhoeck & Ruprecht, 2017), 433–54.

then attends the banquet, apparently assuming that the host wished to reconcile, but the host's atrocious behavior at the banquet quickly disabuses him of that notion. In scene 2 the host ruthlessly ejects the unwelcome Bar Qamtza despite his desperate pleas to remain. Rather than justifying his presence at the banquet, Bar Qamtza makes the host three ever more lucrative offers, but the host's hatred for his fellow Jew is so great that he rejects them all. In scene 3 the audience learns that the leading rabbinic sages of the late Second Temple period implicitly condoned the host's awful behavior by silently watching his confrontation with Bar Qamtza without intervening. The sages' apparent indifference to his plight so infuriates Bar Qamtza that he decides to avenge his humiliation by slandering the Jews before the emperor. In short, a mistaken identity triggers a terrible expression of hatred which the rabbinic sages overlook, and the neglect of their moral responsibility plants in Bar Qamtza a fierce desire for revenge. Insofar as the moral failings of the characters are concerned, the host's intense hatred, the sages' apathy, and Bar Qamtza's overblown thirst for revenge all reflect the absence of fellowship and solidarity.

Chapter 19

The Sacrifice Slander (ACT II SCENE 1)

Bar Qamtza's evil plan unfolds in Act II, on the heels of his declaration to avenge his shameful expulsion from the banquet. Act II scene 1 opens with Bar Qamtza at the emperor's palace, far away from the site of his humiliation, where he carefully lays the groundwork for the revenge he so craves. The story does not reveal how Bar Qamtza managed to arrange an audience with the emperor or how long it took him to do so, but his yearning for revenge apparently emboldened him to overcome any obstacles along the way:

15 אזל אמר ליה לקיסר: מרדו בך יהודאי.

16 אמר ליה: מי יימר?

17 אמר ליה: שדר להו קורבנא וחזי אי מקרבו ליה.

18 אזל שדר להו בידיה עיגלא תילתא.

19 בהדי דקאתי שדא ביה מומא בניב שפתים, ואמרי לה בדוקין שבעין,

20 דוכתא דלדידן מומא לדידהו לאו מומא.

15 He went (and) said to the emperor: The Jews are rebelling against you.

16 He said to him: Says who?

17 He said to him: Send an offering and see if they offer it.

18 He (the emperor) went and sent in his (Bar Qamtza's) hand a three-year-old calf.

19 While on the way, he inflicted a blemish on its upper lip, and some say on the white of its eye,

20 a place where it is a blemish for us (Jews but) for them (gentiles) it is not a blemish.

The Slander and its Reception

In the first line of the scene, line 15, Bar Qamtza travels to the emperor and informs him: "The Jews are rebelling against you!" In Lamentations Rabbati, by contrast, Bar Qamtza ascribes subversive activity to the Jews without explicitly noting that they are rebelling. Lamentations Rabbati's Bar Qamtza tells the Roman authorities that the Jews replace the Roman animals sent for sacrifice with animals of their own, thereby implying that the Jews had broken with Rome (or, at the very least, were humiliating Rome). Hence, what Lamentations Rabbati only implies, the Bavli states explicitly and unequivocally.[1] Bar Qamtza's report of rebellion, however, is an audacious and slanderous lie. The Jews are not rebelling and Rome has no particular reason to suspect that a Jewish insurrection is underway. Bar Qamtza understands, however, that he will be heard out since the emperor cannot afford to ignore any report of a possible uprising. In addition, Bar Qamtza's Jewish origins would have lent credence to his claim that he was privy to an insurgency in the making.

The phrase "מרדו בך יהודאי," "The Jews are rebelling against you," appears in all three stories of our trilogy and serves as a refrain that binds the trilogy together.[2] The emperor hears of a Jewish revolt in each story, and, in the final two stories – regarding Bethar and Tur Malka – the emperor's immediate response to the alarming news is to engage the Jews in battle and suppress their rebellion. In the story of Bar Qamtza, by contrast, the emperor cautiously hesitates. Rather than swiftly marching off to war, the emperor first questions Bar Qamtza – "Says who?" – and then he patiently investigates the matter until he finds clear evidence of a rebellion.

What explains the emperor's differing responses to the report of

---

1. See Ben Shahar, "Abolishment of the Sacrifice," 593.
2. See Mandel, "Tales of the Destruction," 152–53, 156. See also y. Sukkah 5:1, 55b (and parallels); b. Yoma 69a (and parallels).

a Jewish revolt? Since the emperor at the time of Bar Qamtza was Vespasian – not Hadrian as at the time of the latter two stories – should we imagine that the different responses stem from the distinct and unique personalities of the two emperors? I fear that this is a poor answer. The emperor appears as a nameless stock figure in all three stories, and if the traits of specific emperors were at play, the emperors would not have been presented in so generic and stereotypical a fashion. Instead, perhaps Bar Qamtza's report is especially suspect because it is the first ever of a Jewish revolt against Rome, or because it, unlike the Roman reports of the latter stories, stems from an unknown entity, that is, from a Judaean provincial. I believe, however, that there is a far simpler explanation for the different Roman responses, namely, the weight of evidence in each case. In the final two stories, the claim that the Jews are rebelling relies on the report of an actual Jewish attack against Romans, but no such evidence accompanies Bar Qamtza's claim. When Bar Qamtza informs the emperor about the Jewish revolt, he provides no evidence. The emperor, therefore, as a responsible leader who thinks favorably of the Jews, does not rashly rush off to war. Instead, he waits until Bar Qamtza adduces compelling evidence for the Jews' disloyal intentions, and only then does he set off to punish them.[3]

In response to the emperor's skeptical response, Bar Qamtza (in line 17) advises the emperor how to corroborate his report and determine whether the Jews are, in fact, rebelling: "Send an offering and see if they offer it" ("שדר להו קורבנא וחזי אי מקרבו ליה"). Bar Qamtza's advice is short, pithy, and well-balanced, with the verbal root ק.ר.ב. appearing twice – once in the word "קורבנא," "offering," in the first half of his brief statement and once in the word "מקרבו," "they offer," in the second half. The implication of Bar Qamtza's advice is that the emperor's offering will not fulfill its destiny; the Jews will not offer it up to God in their sanctuary. Refusing to accept the emperor's offering is obviously a grave political statement. As the leader of the Roman Empire, any rejection of his offering signifies a repudiation of Roman rule and a confirmation of Bar Qamtza's report. Once Bar Qamtza's initial report of a Jewish rebellion planted the seed of suspicion in the emperor's heart and incited

---

3. Cf. Ben Shahar, "Abolishment of the Sacrifice," 594n118.

him to test the loyalty of his Jewish subjects, Bar Qamtza offered him the perfect test: a show of loyalty through sacrifice.

The One-Off Sacrifice

Like the "קורבנא" – the "offering" or "gift"[4] – sent by the emperor to the temple in Jerusalem, other offerings or gifts were sent by a gentile to a Jew (or vice versa[5]) in stories of the Bavli, such as the following story from Bavli Zevaḥim:

> כי הא דאיפרא הורמיז אימיה דשבור מלכא שדרה עגלא תולתא לקמיה דרבא.
> אמרת ליה: קרביה ניהליה לשם שמים. אמר להו (לרב אחא ו[6])לרב ספרא ולרב
> אחא בר הונא: זילו ודברו תרי עולמי גילאי וחזו היכא דמסקא ימא סירטון
> ואייתו ציבי חדתי ואפקון נורא ממגאנא[7] חדתא וקרבא ניהלא לשם שמים.[8]

As in the case of Ifra Hormiz, mother of King Shapur, (who) sent a three- year-old calf to Rava. She said to him: Sacrifice it for the sake of heaven. (Rava) said to (Rav Aha,) Rav Safra, and Rav Aha bar Huna: Go and get two (gentile) youths of the same age and see where the sea has raised up alluvium and bring new twigs and make a fire with a new flint and sacrifice it for the sake of heaven.

In this story, Ifra Hormiz, the mother of the king of Persia, sends an offering to the Babylonian sage Rava, asking him to sacrifice it on her behalf. Since Jews are only permitted to sacrifice animals within the temple precincts in Jerusalem and the story takes place in Babylonia over two hundred years after the temple's destruction, Rava ensures

---

4. See Jastrow, *Dictionary*, 1411; Sokoloff, *Dictionary of Jewish Babylonian Aramaic*, 1002. (See also b. Ḥul. 8a.)

5. See b. Avod. Zar. 64b–65a; b. Sanh. 108b according to Oxford Heb. c 17/63–64. It bears noting that other stories tell of Ifra Hormiz sending charitable donations to rabbinic sages. See b. B. Bat. 8a–b, 10b–11a (cited below in Chapter 20).

6. "Rav Aha" is absent from all the other textual witnesses and the appearance of Rav Aha bar Huna after Rav Safra in every textual witness makes it likely that Rav Aha was accidentally inserted into Vatican 121.

7. The meaning of this word is unclear. See Sokoloff, *Dictionary of Jewish Babylonian Aramaic*, 640.

8. B. Zevaḥ. 116b according to Vatican 121 (with the name "Rabbah" changed to "Rava" in light of New York-Columbia X 893 T 141 and the printed editions).

that non-Jews properly sacrifice Ifra Hormiz's offering to God, that is, to the God of the Jewish people. For our purposes, this story helpfully illustrates how an offering sent by a non-Jewish leader was viewed in Babylonia as a gentile's one-off request that the Jews offer up to God a sacrifice on his or her behalf. Just as Ifra Hormiz sends an animal to Rava to be sacrificed for the sake of heaven, Bar Qamtza suggests that the Roman emperor send an animal to Jerusalem to be sacrificed for the sake of heaven.

Whereas the Bavli's story of Bar Qamtza relates to a one-off sacrifice, Lamentations Rabbati and Josephus refer to the daily sacrifices offered on the emperor's behalf. Noting this discrepancy, some scholars have argued that the Babylonian editor of our story was unfamiliar with the emperor's perpetual sacrifices and mistakenly transformed the daily practice into a one-off occasion.[9] However, the one-off imperial offering of the Bavli's Bar Qamtza story is perfectly in line with the Persian practice (according to the Bavli) of sending a one-off gift or offering; it is the very sort of royal offering that Ifra Hormiz sends Rava in Bavli Zevaḥim. Hence, I suspect that the Babylonian editor of our story transformed the emperor's perpetual sacrifices into a solitary offering not out of ignorance, but in order to reflect the one-off royal offering familiar to him from the local cultural setting in Persia.[10] In other words, the Babylonian editor inherited Lamentations Rabbati's refusal-revolt matrix (which ultimately stems from a Josephus-like tradition) and then modified it in line with a familiar Persian practice. Furthermore, once the Babylonian story changed Lamentations Rabbati's daily sacrifice into a one-time offering (with no previous history), Bar Qamtza's claim in Lamentations Rabbati regarding the replacement of Roman animals with Jewish ones was no longer relevant and hence was omitted.[11]

---

9. See Mandel, "Tales of the Destruction," 153n38; Ben Shahar, "Abolishment of the Sacrifice," 576, 596.

10. In addition, since the Babylonian editor of our story apparently relied on Lamentations Rabbati's version (or something quite like it [see Appendix 1 below]), it seems unlikely that he would have mistaken the multiple sacrifices mentioned there for a one-off sacrifice.

11. Cf. Schwartz, "Zechariah," 313n3.

The Calf

Acquiescing to Bar Qamtza's suggestion, the emperor in line 18 "went and sent in his (Bar Qamtza's) hand a three-year-old calf." The verb "אזל," "went," which opens line 18, echoes the "אזל," "went," which opens the scene at the start of line 15, underscoring how Bar Qamtza prompted the emperor to take action.[12] Similarly, the emperor in line 18 "שדר," "sent" the animal as per Bar Qamtza's suggestion in line 17 to "שדר," "send" the animal. In addition, not only does the emperor dispatch an animal as recommended, he even entrusts it to Bar Qamtza, sending it "בידיה," "in his hand." In a measure for measure comeuppance, Bar Qamtza's "hand" avenges the injustice done to him back in line 13 when he was thrown out of the banquet by the host's "hand" – "נקט ליה בידיה ואפקיה," "He took him with his hand and threw him out."

The animal selected by the emperor for the offering is an "עיגלא תילתא," "a three-year-old calf," which was considered a prime and exceptional animal since biblical times (and perhaps also evoked associations with the Israelite's sinful Golden Calf).[13] Along with the emperor's patient investigation, his choice of a fine animal reveals the careful and thoughtful behavior of a leader positively inclined towards the Jews. Rather than depicting "imperial power and arrogance" or "the violence, hubris, and ignorance of colonial dominance,"[14] the story seems to portray the emperor as a respectful and patient monarch.

In addition, the Aramaic term "עיגלא תילתא," "a three-year-old calf," which is found about a dozen times in the Bavli but nowhere in early Palestinian literature,[15] strikingly appears in the story of Ifra Hormiz

---

12. The word "אזל," "went," does not appear in various manuscripts such as T-S NS 329.428, Arras 889, Vatican 140, and St. Petersburg – RNL Evr. II A 389/4.
13. See Sokoloff, *Dictionary of Jewish Babylonian Aramaic*, 1198.
14. Watts Belser, *Rabbinic Tales of Destruction*, 137. Cf. Saldarini, "Rabbinic Response," 255; Amos Funkenstein, *Perceptions of Jewish History* (Berkeley: University of California Press, 1993), 203–4n101; Yisraeli-Taran, *Legends of the Destruction*, 22; Klawans, "Josephus," 294–95.
15. So far as I know, the term appears in Palestinian literature only once, in the Lamentations Rabbati version of our story according to two manuscripts: Casanatense H 3112 and Parma 2559. However, no other textual witness of Lamentations Rabbati cites the term and since the term is also absent from Palestinian literature more generally, it most likely migrated in medieval times

cited above.[16] In that Babylonian account of a royal personage sending an offering to the Jews, Ifra Hormiz sends a three-year-old calf to Rava. In other words, in the only two stories in the Bavli (so far as I know) in which a gentile leader sends an animal to the Jews to be sacrificed for the sake of heaven, the animal in both cases is an "עיגלא תילתא," "a three-year-old calf."[17] Since this term does not appear in Lamentations Rabbati's earlier version of the Bar Qamtza story, it is likely that the term migrated to the story of Bar Qamtza from the similar scenario depicted in the story of Ifra Hormiz and Rava.[18] While it is possible that the only two Babylonian stories about a one-off offering sent by the gentile authorities independently identified the offering as "a three-year-old calf," I find it more probable that the Babylonian story of Bar Qamtza borrowed the two entwined elements – the "three-year-old calf" and the one-off royal offering – from the story of Ifra Hormiz.

The Blemish

With the calf in hand, Bar Qamtza sets off to Jerusalem in line 19. On his way, Bar Qamtza takes the next crucial step in his evil plan: he inflicts a blemish on the emperor's calf, thereby rendering it unfit for

---

from the Bavli's version of our story to the Lamentations Rabbati version preserved in Casanatense H 3112 and Parma 2559. See also Shamma Friedman, "Now You See It, Now You Don't: Can Source-Criticism Perform Magic on Talmudic Passages about Sorcery?" in *Rabbinic Traditions between Palestine and Babylonia*, ed. Ronit Nikolsky and Tal Ilan (Leiden: Brill, 2014), 65n102.

16. See Vatican 121 (cited above); Munich 95; New York – Columbia X 893 T 141; Paris – AIU H147A. (Interestingly, the printed editions replace the term "three-year-old calf" with "offering" ["קורבנא"].)

17. Neusner stated that "the gift of an animal sacrifice to Rava has its parallel in the gift by an Arab of an animal sacrifice to Rav Judah in the preceding generation" (*A History of the Jews in Babylonia IV. The Age of Shapur II* [Leiden: Brill, 1969], 37). I suspect, however, that he mistakenly conflated two sources which he himself juxtaposed on Jacob Neusner, *A History of the Jews in Babylonia III: From Shapur I to Shapur II* (Leiden: Brill, 1968), 30, the very page to which he refers in *Jews in Babylonia IV*, 37n1. In the first source – b. Arak. 6b, an Arab named Sha'azreq sends Rav Judah a menorah, and in the second source – b. Avod. Zar. 64b–65a, Rav Judah sends a "קורבנא" to a gentile. It seems that Neusner accidentally replaced Sha'azreq's menorah with Rav Judah's "קורבנא."

18. See n. 15 above.

sacrifice in the Jerusalem temple. The Aramaic word for "inflict" enlisted here – "שדא," echoes the similar sounding words "שדר," "send," of line 17 and "שדר," "he sent," of line 18. By interlocking these three lines with similar sounding words, the story maps out the gradual unfolding of Bar Qamtza's sinister plot. Having convinced the emperor to test the Jews' loyalty by sending them an animal for sacrifice, Bar Qamtza ensures that the Jews will be unwilling to sacrifice the emperor's calf. Foreseeing that the Jewish authorities will refuse to offer up a blemished calf, Bar Qamtza expects their refusal to confirm his claim that the Jews are rebelling.

Bar Qamtza carefully blemishes the calf's upper lip though the Talmud also notes that some claim that the blemish was placed on the white of the calf's eye. Whether on the upper lip or white of the eye, the location of the blemish is significant because, as the Talmud clarifies in line 20's explanatory gloss, the blemish was intentionally situated in "a place where it is a blemish for us (Jews but) for them (gentiles) it is not a blemish." Since a blemish on the upper lip or white of the eye did not disqualify a calf for sacrifice in gentile eyes, there was no cause, in Roman eyes, for the Jews to reject the emperor's perfectly unblemished calf.

The notion that Jews and gentiles differed over the question whether a blemish on the white of the eye rendered cattle unsuitable for sacrifice never appears in Palestinian sources, but does appear on two other occasions in the Bavli:

אנן דשכיחי מומין דפסלי אפילו בדוקין שבעין בעינן תלתין יומין, אינהו דמחוסר אבר אית להו בתלתא יומי סגי.

We (Jews), for whom blemishes (disqualifying a sacrifice) abound, since we disqualify (an offering) even because of a blemish on the white of the eye, require thirty days (to prepare an animal for sacrifice), (but for) the pagans, since they only take note of a missing limb, three days suffice.[19]

הוי בה רבא: במאי? אילימא בדוקין שבעין השתא לבני נח חזיא לגבוה בבמה דידהו לעבודת כוכבים מיבעיא? אלא במחוסר אבר וכדרבי אלעזר, דאמר ר'

---

19. B. Avod. Zar. 5b with translation by A. Mishcon and A. Cohen, trans. *The Babylonian Talmud: 'Abodah Zarah* (London: Soncino, 1935), ad loc., slightly revised.

אלעזר: מנין למחוסר אבר שהוא אסור לבני נח? שנאמר "ומכל החי מכל בשר
שנים מכל" (בראשית ו:יט), אמרה תורה הבא בהמה שחיין ראשי אברין שלה.

Rava objected: What (sort of blemish did Rabbi Abbahu have in
mind when he stated in the name of Rabbi Yohanan that he who
sacrifices a blemished animal to an idol is free of liability)? Shall
I say (a blemish) on the white of the eye? Since, (however,) such
an animal was qualified to be offered by the sons of Noah to God
upon their altars, how much more so (was it qualified) for idolatry!
Rather (he must be thinking of a blemish like) a missing limb and in
accordance with Rabbi Eleazar for Rabbi Eleazar said: Whence is it
that (an animal) missing a limb is prohibited (as an offering) to the
sons of Noah? As it is stated: *And of all that lives, of all flesh, you shall
take two of each* (Gen. 6:19), the Torah declares (by stating *all that
lives* and *all flesh*), bring an animal which has all its limbs living.[20]

According to these Babylonian texts, nothing less than the absence of
a limb disqualified an animal for a gentile sacrifice, whereas a blemish on
the white of the eye was enough to render cattle ineligible for a Jewish
sacrifice. Since the contrasting attitudes of Jews and gentiles towards
blemished eyes are never mentioned in Palestinian literature and appear
for the very first time in the Bavli, it is most likely that a Babylonian
editor incorporated this Babylonian conception into the story.[21] The
Babylonian provenance of this idea is strengthened by the fact that
the term "white of its eye," "דוקין שבעין," which appears on multiple
occasions in the Bavli, is never found in Palestinian literature,[22] and the

---

20. B. Avod. Zar. 51a with translation by Mishcon and Cohen, ʿAbodah Zarah,
ad loc. somewhat revised. See also Levine Katz, "Qamtsa," 39n18; Duker, "Piety
or Privilege," 45 (52n15).

21. The contrasting attitudes of Jews and gentiles towards blemished lips and
eyes appear in Lamentations Rabbati's version of our story according to two
manuscripts only: Casanatense H 3112 and Parma 2559. Like "עגלא תלתא" (see
n. 15 above) the presence of the contrasting attitudes in these two manuscripts
is most probably the result of a late interpolation which stems from the Bavli's
parallel version of the story. See also Jeffrey L. Rubenstein, "Criteria of Stammaitic
Intervention in Aggada," in *Creation and Composition: The Contribution of the
Bavli Redactors (Stammaim) to the Aggada*, ed. Jeffrey L. Rubenstein (Tübingen:
Mohr Siebeck, 2005), 428.

22. The term "דוקין שבעין," "white of the eye," not only appears within the

term "upper lip," "נִיב שְׂפָתִים," which is drawn from Isaiah 57:19, assumes no legal function in any Palestinian work.[23] In short, both the placement of the blemish and its legal significance were apparently Babylonian contributions to our story.

In all classical rabbinic literature, the upper lip plays a legal role in only one other text: b. Ḥullin 128b. The Talmud there contends, in the name of Rav Papa, that if an upper lip is severed from a living animal or creeping thing, the lip imparts impurity (as a limb severed from the living) according to Rabbi Yose Hagelili but does not impart impurity according to Rabbi Akiva. Since the upper lip contains no bones, the legal stance attributed to Rabbi Akiva does not consider it a full-fledged limb. In a similar vein, the Bavli indicates that a blemish on the white of the eye was viewed as a relatively minor blemish.[24] A blemish on the white of the eye does not render fowl impure and, according to Rabbi Akiva, if an animal with a blemish on the white of the eye was accidentally placed on the altar, it is sacrificed.[25] As a group, these legal texts give the impression that in a dire emergency, upper lip and white of the eye blemishes would have been viewed as minor and marginal blemishes and therefore rather easy to overlook.[26] The fact that in Act II scene 2 the rabbis refuse to sacrifice an animal with such a slight blemish only serves to compound their myopic and obtuse piety.

Beyond their legal ramifications, it is also worth noting a possible symbolic dimension to the calf's blemishes. Bar Qamtza inflicts a blemish on the calf's eyes or mouth, two parts of the body heavily implicated in the banquet fiasco of Act I. The eyes of the sages failed to see Bar Qamtza's terrible humiliation, and their mouths failed to speak out in protest.[27] In other words, the calf's physically defective eyes and mouth

---

interpolation in Lamentations Rabbati's Casanatense H 3112 and Parma 2559 (see the previous note), but was also interpolated into Parma 2393 and Oxford 102. Otherwise, it appears nowhere in Palestinian literature.

23. See Rubenstein, "Stammaitic Intervention," 429; Levine Katz, "Qamtsa" 40.
24. See, for example, b. Beṣah 27a; b. Bek. 28a.
25. See b. Pesaḥ. 73a; b. Zevaḥ. 35b, 77b, 85b; b. Menaḥ. 79a; b. Bek. 16a. See also Levine Katz, "Qamtsa" 39n18.
26. See Rubenstein, *Talmudic Stories*, 149, 349n31.
27. See Abraham Samuel Benjamin Wolf Sofer, *Hidushei ketav sofer hashalem al*

are ultimately a tragic consequence of the sages' morally defective eyes and mouths.

Unlike Lamentations Rabbati, the Bavli does not explicitly mention the Roman official sent along with Bar Qamtza, focusing Act II, just like Act I, on Bar Qamtza. In Lamentations Rabbati, the Roman officer is entrusted with the Roman animals in Act II scene 1; he negotiates with the priest in scene 2; and he reports back to his superior in scene 3. In the Bavli, by contrast, Bar Qamtza is entrusted with the Roman animal in our scene, scene 1.[28] Scene 2 depicts a rabbinic debate which also involves Bar Qamtza, and scene 3 cuts to the chase, skipping over the Roman report straight to the destruction of the temple itself. With the emperor as the sole gentile character explicitly mentioned in the Babylonian story, it seems that the Babylonian editor was more interested in exploring internal Jewish conflicts and less interested in describing the interplay between the Roman figures involved.[29] However, the presence of a Roman official (or Roman officials) is implied since Bar Qamtza's need to shield the blemish from Roman eyes presupposes Roman oversight.

In Lamentations Rabbati, Bar Qamtza "secretly" blemishes the animals in the dead of night. Wondering how it would help to covertly inflict blemishes in the cover of night when the Romans would easily see the blemishes the following morning, the Babylonian editor apparently transferred the object of secrecy from the activity to the blemish itself, making the blemish one that would be invisible to the Romans even in broad daylight. Alternatively, perhaps the Babylonian editor felt that since Lamentations Rabbati already mentioned that Bar Qamtza acted at night, it was redundant to tell us that Bar Qamtza also worked in secret and therefore he interpreted "secretly" in reference to the nature of the blemish rather than the act of blemishing. Hence, in explaining how Bar Qamtza hid the blemish from Roman eyes, the Babylonian editor enlisted a Babylonian distinction between Jewish and gentile attitudes towards minor blemishes.

---

hashas: Gittin (חידושי כתב סופר השלם על הש"ס: גיטין), (Jerusalem: Mehon Daʻat Sofer, 2006–2007), 564. See also Lau, *Sages*, 266.

28. See Efron, "Bar-Kokhva," 91.

29. Cf. Mandel, "Tales of the Destruction," 152, 154.

From Palestine to Babylonia

Over the course of this chapter we have seen time and again how the Babylonian editor of the story of Bar Qamtza introduced Babylonian elements into the story. The one-off royal offering, the Aramaic term for "a three-year-old calf," the distinction between Jewish and gentile attitudes towards minor blemishes, and the white of the eye and upper lip blemish locations all appear elsewhere in the Bavli but nowhere in Palestinian Jewish literature. Since it is far more likely that a Babylonian editor inserted Babylonian elements culled from his local cultural context than that a Palestinian editor elected to identify a story's Babylonian elements and then delete them, the presence of Babylonian elements in the Babylonian version, but not in the Palestinian parallel, reveals that a Babylonian editor recast the earlier and pre-existing Palestinian tradition (or some tradition quite like it). In the process of clarifying and fleshing out the originally Palestinian story, the Babylonian editor naturally reworked the story in light of the Babylonian cultural setting (with the one-off offering of Persian royalty), Babylonian legal discourse (with the Bavli's distinction between Jewish and gentile attitudes towards blemishes) and Babylonian literary elements (with the Bavli's three-year-old calf and blemish locations).

Chapter 20

To Sacrifice or Not to Sacrifice? (ACT II SCENE 2)

After Act II scene 1 concludes with Bar Qamtza inflicting a blemish on the emperor's calf while en route to Jerusalem, Act II scene 2 jumps forward in time to the moment just after the delivery of the blemished calf to the temple authorities. With the arrival of the emperor's calf, the Jewish authorities face a quandary: should they sacrifice the blemished animal or not? The debate which ensues is presented in Act II scene 2.

21 סבור רבנן למיקרבה משום שלום מלכות.

22 אמר להו ר' זכריה בן אבקולס: יאמרו בעלי מומין קריבין לגבי מזבח!

23 סבור למיקטליה דלא ליזיל ולימא.

24 אמר להו ר' זכריה בן אבקולס: יאמרו מטיל מום בקדשים יהרג!

21 **The** sages **thought to** offer it for the sake of peace with the kingdom.

22 **Rabbi Zechariah ben Avqulas said to them: They will say that blemished** animals may be offered on the altar!

23 **They thought to** kill him (Bar Qamtza) lest he go and say (to the emperor that his calf was not offered).

24 **Rabbi Zechariah ben Avqulas said to them: They will say that** one who inflicts a **blemish** on a consecrated animal is to be put to death!

With Bar Qamtza and the emperor now offstage, the sages and Zechariah ben Avqulas feature in scene 2's debate over the sacrifice. Whereas Zechariah is new to the story, the sages are not. The sages already appeared in line 14, when Bar Qamtza condemned them for not protesting his humiliating removal from the host's banquet. Now, the sages must decide whether they will embrace Bar Qamtza and sacrifice the offering he has brought on the emperor's behalf, or if, like the banquet host in Act I, they too will reject him. The sages, who did not protest at the banquet, are now confronted with the fallout of their inconsiderate inaction, and their second encounter with Bar Qamtza grants them the opportunity to redeem their earlier blunder. As the audience, we hope that the sages will change their ways but, mindful of the story's preface, we suspect that they will not.

Further Rabbinizing the Story

In reality, just as the sages, as depicted in Act I, were not the actual leaders of late Second Temple times, they also were not the temple authorities as portrayed here in Act II.[1] When Lamentations Rabbati ascribed the rejection of the Roman animals to a Jewish priest, it offered a realistic portrait of the temple administration. By contrast, the Babylonian story rabbinizes Second Temple history in both acts, consistently placing the rabbis at the helm of Jewish society.[2] Rather than describing the back and forth between the Roman officer and the Jewish priest as did Lamentations Rabbati, the Babylonian story introduces a legal discussion more at home in the study houses of Babylonia than in the temple of Jerusalem.[3] In fact, the academic dispute between Zechariah and

---

1. See Yisraeli-Taran, *Legends of the Destruction*, 18; Rubenstein, *Talmudic Stories*, 172; Mandel, "Tales of the Destruction," 153n39; Kalmin, *Jewish Babylonia*, 47. Since there is a tendency in rabbinic literature to portray the leading Pharisees of Second Temple times as rabbinic sages, it is possible that the role of the sages in our story is a late recasting of the role of the Pharisees as portrayed by Josephus (cf. Ben Shahar, "Abolishment of the Sacrifice," 595), but even according to Josephus, the Pharisees were not the ruling faction within the temple administration.
2. See Chapter 18 above. See also Saldarini, "Rabbinic Response," 451; Yisraeli-Taran, *Legends of the Destruction*, 17.
3. See Efron, "Bar-Kokhva," 91.

the sages is in keeping with the scholastic culture refracted throughout the Bavli. In comparison to the populist rabbis of Palestinian rabbinic sources, the rabbis of the Bavli were a more elitist and insular group who highly prized abstruse dialectical argumentation in the relative seclusion of their study houses.[4] Moreover, if, as some maintain, the rabbis of Sasanian Persia, unlike their Palestinian counterparts, enjoyed a high measure of judicial authority,[5] perhaps it was only natural for the Babylonian story to view the past in its own image, projecting the (relatively) robust rabbinic judicial authority of Sasanian times onto the sages of late Second Temple Jerusalem.

In Lamentations Rabbati Zechariah ben Avqulas is a passive by-stander to Bar Qamtza's humiliation in Act I, but, in the Bavli, Zecha-riah is relocated to Act II. In Act I, the Bavli finds fault with the sages as a group for failing Bar Qamtza, not with Zechariah ben Avqulas, and Zechariah appears for the first time in the Babylonian story only here in Act II scene 2.

As a member of the rabbinic community Zechariah ben Avqulas would not have been a dominating force in the temple bureaucracy. Yet, in line with the Babylonian story's rabbinizing drift, his voice none-theless determines temple policy. Furthermore, though Zechariah ben Avqulas was apparently only a minor rabbinic sage, attested by

---

4. See Rubenstein, *The Culture of the Babylonian Talmud*, 1–53, 123–62. Cf. Se-cunda, *Iranian Talmud*, 141–42.

5. See Mokhtarian, "Iranian Loanwords," 106–9. On the role of rabbinic jurists in Sasanian Persia more generally, see Jacob Neusner, *A History of the Jews in Babylonia: Part 2: The Early Sasanian Period* (Leiden: Brill, 1966), 30–35; Isaiah M. Gafni, *Babylonian Jewry and its Institutions in the Period of the Talmud* (יהדות בבל ומוסדותיה בתקופת התלמוד), (Jerusalem: Zalman Shazar Center, 1986), 18; *The Jews of Babylonia in the Talmudic Era: A Social and Cultural History* (יהודי בבל בתקופת התלמוד: חיי החברה והרוח), (Jerusalem: Zalman Shazar Center, 1990), 101–4, 226–32; Richard Kalmin, *The Sage in Jewish Society of Late Antiquity* (New York, NY: Routledge, 1999), 12; Richard Hidary, *Dispute for the Sake of Heaven: Legal Pluralism in the Talmud* (Providence, RI: Brown University Press, 2010), 158–60; Maria Macuch, "Jewish Jurisdiction within the Framework of the Sasanian Legal System," in *Encounters by the Rivers of Babylon: Scholarly Conversations between Jews, Iranians and Babylonians in Antiquity*, ed. Uri Gabbay and Shai Secunda (Tübingen: Mohr Siebeck, 2014), 147–60; Secunda, *Iranian Talmud*, 90–93; Mokhtarian, *Culture of the Talmud*, 81–82, 94–123.

his single appearance in all Tannaitic literature, he functions here as a leading rabbi.[6] Zechariah's central role in Act II, therefore, does not stem from his having been a powerful temple official or a famous rabbinic sage, since he was neither. Rather, the Bavli has creatively reworked Zechariah's role in Lamentations Rabbati which, in turn, was inspired by Zechariah's solitary appearance in Tannaitic literature. On the heels of the Palestinian story of Bar Qamtza, which introduced Zechariah into our story in order to give narrative form to the saying "The meekness of Rabbi Zechariah ben Avqilas burnt down the sanctuary," the Bavli gives narrative form to the same saying, but in a very different way. Hoping to offer what he considered a more compelling reason for Zechariah's condemnation in Tannaitic tradition, the Babylonian editor assigned Zechariah a central role within a more familiar context, the legal debate typical of Babylonian study houses.[7]

"For the Sake of Peace with the Kingdom"

Faced with the question of what to do about the emperor's blemished calf, the sages do not try to convince the Romans that the calf is blemished according to Jewish law and hence invalid for sacrifice. As Bar Qamtza imagined, the Roman view of blemishes apparently rendered moot this line of argument. Instead, the sages, in line 21, think "to **offer** it for the sake of peace with the **kingdom**," "למיקרבה משום שלום מלכות." Echoing Bar Qamtza's language from line 17 – "שדר להו **קורבנא** וחזי אי **מקרבו ליה**," "Send an **offering** and see if they **offer** it," and line 14 – "איזיל **ואיכול בהו קורצא בי מלכא**," "I will go and inform the **king**'s palace against them," the sages embrace a stance which could potentially undermine Bar Qamtza's plans. Because the welfare of the Jewish people, according to the sages, far outweighs the sin of sacrificing a blemished animal, the emperor's blemished calf should certainly be sacrificed. Expressing a strong sense of solidarity with the Jewish people, the sages reveal, at least momentarily, that Bar Qamtza might have underestimated them.

The Hebrew phrase "שלום מלכות," "peace with the kingdom," appears

---

6. See t. Shabb. 16:7 (cited below in Chapter 9). See also Mandel, "Tales of the Destruction," 144. Cf. Kalmanzon and Fogel, *Legends of the Destruction*, 25.

7. See Yisraeli-Taran, *Legends of the Destruction*, 18–19.

in three other sugyot in the Bavli, two in Gittin and one in Bava Batra, but nowhere else in classical rabbinic literature.[8] The phrase's appearance only in the Bavli suggests that it is a *Babylonian legal term* and, therefore, another distinctly Babylonian contribution to our story. Moreover, the Bava Batra story in which the phrase appears bears a striking resemblance to our own story:

איפרהורמיז אימיה דשבור מלכא שדרה ארבע מאה ארנקי דדינרי לקמיה דר'
אמי לא קבלינהו. שדרינהו לקמיה דרבא וקבלינהו. שמע ר' אמי ואיקפד,
אמ': לית ליה "ביבוש קצירה תשברנה נשים באות מאירות אותה" (ישעיהו
כז:יא)? ורבא משום שלום מלכות הוא דעבד. איבעי ליה למתבינהו לעניי
אומות העולם! רבא נמי לעניי אמות העול' יהבינהו ור' אמי דאיקפד סיומי
הוא דלא סימוה קמיה.[9]

Ifra Hormiz the mother of King Shapur sent a purse with four hundred dinars to Rabbi Ammi (for charity) and he did not accept it. She (then) sent them to Rava and he accepted them. (When) Rabbi Ammi heard (that Rava had accepted the money), he was angry and said: Does he (Rava) not have (the verse) *When its crown is withered, they break; women come and make fires with them* (Isa 27:11) (that is, when the nations of the world's merits dry up they wither away and burn up easily, so why help them attain merit by accepting their charity)? Rava did so (i.e., accepted the money) for the sake of peace with the kingdom. (Rabbi Ammi was angry) because he (Rava) should have distributed (the money) to the gentile poor. But Rava did give (the money) to the gentile poor! Rabbi Ammi was angry because he had not heard the complete account.

---

8. See b. Git. 80a, 86a; b. B. Bat. 10b–11a. In Bava Batra, Escorial G-I-3 and Oxford Opp. 249 (369) use the Aramaic term "שלמא דמלכותא" instead of the Hebrew term "שלום מלכות" (found in Munich 95, Hamburg 165, Florence II-I-9, Paris 1337, Vatican 115, and the Pesaro and Vilna editions) and, like the Hebrew term, the Aramaic term also appears nowhere else in rabbinic literature. (B.B. Bat. 9a enlists the similar sounding Aramaic phrase "שלמא במלכותא" and Munich 95 there accidentally changed it to "שלמה דמלכותא".)

Once again, Lamentations Rabbati's Casanatense H 3112 and Parma 2559 are exceptions to the rule and they include the phrase "שלום מלכות," "the peace of the kingdom," because their reading was highly influenced by the Bavli.

9. B.B. Bat. 10b–11a according to Hamburg 165.

Just as our story involves an offering sent by the Roman emperor to the Jerusalem temple, this Ifra Hormiz story revolves around charity that the Persian royal house sends to rabbinic sages for them to dispense to the poor. In both stories, moreover, the wisdom of accepting the offering/donation is debated. Whereas Rabbi Ammi refuses to accept the royal charity just as Zechariah ben Avqulas shuns the emperor's blemished calf, both Rava and the sages maintain that the gentile leader's charity/offering should be accepted "for the sake of peace with the kingdom." Since Rava and the sages enroll the very same argument in the context of a very similar predicament, and because the argument does not appear in Lamentations Rabbati's version of the story or in any other rabbinic story, I maintain that Rava's argument from the Persian setting was transformed into the sages' argument in the Roman setting.[10] Indeed, perhaps the story of Rava's argument with Rabbi Ammi inspired not only a legal term in the debate, but even the very debate itself.

What is more, this story of Ifra Hormiz's charity is the second Ifra Hormiz story which conspicuously shares elements with Act 11 of our story. The Ifra Hormiz story from Zevaḥim (discussed above in Chapter 19) has the king's mother send "a three-year-old calf" just as the emperor does in our story, and the Ifra Hormiz story from Bava Batra models the sages' argument that the emperor's offering should be accepted "for the sake of peace with the kingdom." Together, the similarities these two stories share with our story suggest that when a Babylonian editor sought

---

10. Cf. Halevi, *Gates of the Aggadah*, 207–8. Cf. Ben Shahar, "Abolishment of the Sacrifice," 594, who suggests that the sages' desire to sacrifice the blemished calf "for the sake of peace with the kingdom" is a faint echo of the political arguments *The Jewish War* ascribes to the leaders who protested the cessation of the emperor's daily sacrifices. However, since the Bava Batra story is much closer to our story in respect to language, dating, and provenance, there is no need to postulate that a late Babylonian editor was familiar with the details of the argumentation preserved in Josephus's early account. In a related vein, it is unlikely that Zechariah's legal arguments were inspired by the entirely unrelated legal arguments mentioned by Josephus as Ben Shahar argues ("Abolishment of the Sacrifice," 594–96). Zechariah's terminology and reasoning (that is, his concern that people might misunderstand the sages' decisions) reflect a precautionary approach common in the Talmud and are quite unlike the straightforward arguments from precedent cited by Josephus.

to recast the Palestinian story of Bar Qamtza, he refashioned Act II's depiction of the Roman emperor's offering and its reception, perhaps even inventing the ensuing debate, in line with Babylonian stories about comparable contributions from Persian royalty.

Zechariah's First "They will Say" Argument

In line 22 Zechariah ben Avqulas challenges the sages' position, arguing that sacrificing the emperor's blemished animal runs the risk of leading people to accidentally conclude that "blemished animals may be offered on the altar!" Although Zechariah ben Avqulas apparently agrees with the sages that maintaining peaceful relations with the Romans is a sufficiently good reason to sacrifice a calf with a (minor) blemish, he argues nonetheless that the calf may not be sacrificed since sacrificing it would convey a problematic message. Were people to see the sages offer up a blemished calf, says Zechariah, they would wrongly conclude that blemished sacrifices are perfectly acceptable!

In prohibiting a permitted action out of fear that people might interpret it incorrectly, Zechariah ben Avqulas adopts a common rabbinic tack. The rabbis often take precautionary measures and ban otherwise permitted actions when they fear there is a good chance that people might mistakenly draw an incorrect legal conclusion from the actions' permissibility. Moreover, by embedding Zechariah's argument in a sentence starting with the term "יאמרו," "they will say," the Babylonian editor molded Zechariah's argument in typical Babylonian fashion. As Paul Mandel has argued, the "they will say" argument is a distinctly Babylonian formulation.[11]

However, in contrast to typical "they will say" arguments, Zechariah ben Avqulas's position is unusually farfetched.[12] On a practical level, it is hard to imagine how people would actually see the slight blemish on a single calf within the temple precincts, and on a substantive legal level, it would be bizarre for people to conclude "that blemished animals may

---

11. See Mandel, "Tales of the Destruction," 153–54. In the continuation of b. Git. 56a, two "they will say" arguments are similarly attributed to Abba Siqra.
12. See Mandel, "Tales of the Destruction," 154. See also Furstenberg, "Qamtza," 105.

be offered on the altar," since such animals were explicitly prohibited by biblical law. Leviticus 22:17–24 and Deuteronomy 17:1 both forbid the sacrifice of blemished animals, and Leviticus 22:25 even forbids the sacrifice of a *gentile's* blemished animal![13] In addition, when faced with such an explosive situation, worrying over potentially incorrect legal inferences is "a backward sort of thinking. And if people do say these things (which is by no means certain), how serious a problem results?"[14]

The Law of the Informant

Initially intent on sacrificing the emperor's blemished calf "for the sake of peace with the kingdom," the sages are hindered by Zechariah ben Avqulas as they sacrifice moral clarity and political acumen for mere trifles. Seeing no way around Zechariah's objection to their plan to offer up the Roman offering, the sages contemplate eliminating Bar Qamtza "lest he go and say (to the emperor)." Having failed to kill the calf, the sages' intend to raise the stakes and kill the informant. After humiliating Bar Qamtza in Act I in their role as passive onlookers, the sages contemplate putting him to death in Part II.[15]

At first glance, because the notion that an informant may (or must) be executed appears nowhere in Palestinian rabbinic literature, the sages' intention to execute Bar Qamtza might seem surprising. Outside of our story, however, there are two other stories in the Bavli which also tell of sages killing informants. Rav Kahana violently kills an informant on b. B. Qamma 117a–b and Rabbi Shila similarly smites an informant on b. Berakhot 58a. Appearing nowhere in Palestinian sources, the idea that an informant, like Bar Qamtza, forfeited his right to life, was apparently drawn from the social context of Jewish Babylonia.[16] Moreover, whereas the stories of Bar Qamtza and Rav Kahana do not reveal the legal basis for killing an informant, the story of Rabbi Shila does: [17]

---

13. See Deut 15:21; Mal 1:6–9. See also Schwartz, *Studies*, 103.

14. Jeffrey L. Rubenstein, "*Bavli Gittin* 55b–56b: An Aggadic Narrative in its Halakhic Context," *Hebrew Studies* 38 (1997): 26.

15. See b. B. Metz. 58b–59a where the humiliation of another person is likened to murder.

16. Cf. Halevi, *Gates of the Aggadah*, 207.

17. In the story of Rav Kahana, Rav Kahana or Rav, depending on the textual

ר' שילא חזא להההוא דבעל גויה ונגדיה. אזל אכל בי קורציה לבי קיסר, אמ': איכא גברא מיהודאי מאן דעבד דבעי עבר[18] לא ספתא עליה אימתא דמלכותא. שדר קיסר קרייה. א"ל: אמאי תעביד הכי? א"ל: דבעל חמרא. א"ל: אי הכי בר קטלא הוא! א"ל: מיומא דגלינו מארענא לית לנא רשות למקטל, אתון כל מה דבעיתון עבידו ליה. פתח ר' שילא ואמ': "לך יי הגדולה והגבורה והתפארת והנצח וההוד" (דברי הימים א' כט:יא). א"ל: מאי קאמרת? אמ' להו: הכי קאמינא, בריך רחמנא דיהב מלכותא דארעא כעין מלכותא דשמיא ויהב ליה שולטן ורחמי בדינא. א"ל: הואיל וחשבינהו עלייהו כולי האי נותביה אבבא ולידון דינא. יהבו ליה קולפא ואותבוה אפיתחיה דרומי ודאין דינא. כי הוה נפיק אתא ההוא גברא ואמ': עבד רחמנא ניסא לשקרי! א"ל: רשע בקושטא קאמרי! ולא חמרי איקרי דכתי' "אשר בשר חמורים בשרם" (יחזקאל כג:כ)? חזייה דקאזיל למימ' להו דקרנהו חמרי, אמ': האי רודף הוא והתורה אמרה אם בא להורגך השכם להורגו. מחייה בקולפיה דפרזלא וקטליה.[19]

Rabbi Shila saw a man who had sexual intercourse with a non-Jewish woman and lashed him. He (the man) went and informed the emperor's palace against him. He said: There is a man among the Jews who does (or transgresses) as he pleases and the fear of government does not make him afraid. The emperor sent (a messenger) and called him. They said to him: Why did you do this (and lash that man)? He said to them: For he had sexual intercourse with a donkey. They said to him: If so, then he should be put to death! He said to them: Since the day we were exiled from our land we lack the authority to put to death, you may do with him as you please. Rabbi Shila cited and

---

witness, presupposes that an informant who endangers Jewish lives may be killed, and, on the basis of this presupposition, he reasons that just like an informant who endangers Jewish lives may be killed, an informant who only endangers Jewish property may also be killed. In other words, while Rav Kahana expands the scope of the definition of an informant who forfeits his life, he does not reveal the legal rationale for the original notion that an informant may be killed.

18. The phrase "מאן דעבד דבעי עבר" should probably be corrected to "דבעי עבד" (see MS Florence II-I-7).

19. The manuscripts of this story, which differ quite significantly from the printed editions, split into two groups: Munich 95 and Florence II-I-7 versus Oxford 23 and Paris 671. (Cf. Jonah Fraenkel, *The Aggadic Narrative: Harmony of Form and Content* [סיפור האגדה: אחדות של תוכן וצורה], [Tel Aviv: Hakibutz Hameuchad, 2001], 261–62.) The text is cited here according to Munich 95. See also Mokhtarian, *Culture of the Talmud*, 114–16.

said: *Yours, Lord, are greatness, might, splendor, triumph, and majesty* (*– yes, all that is in heaven and on earth; to You, Lord, belong kingship and preeminence above all*) (1 Chr 29:11). They said to him: What are you saying? He said to them: This is what I am saying: Blessed is the Merciful who has given the kingdom of earth the form of the kingdom of heaven and has given it (the kingdom of earth) dominion and lovers of the law. They said to him: Since we are so important to him (Rabbi Shila), let us sit him at the gate and he shall judge the law. They gave him a staff and sat him at the entrance to Rome and he judged the law. When he left, that man (the informant) came and said: The merciful one makes a miracle for liars! He said to him: Wicked one, I spoke in truth for are they (non-Jews) not called donkeys as it is written *whose members were like those of donkeys* (Ezek 23:20)? He (Rabbi Shila) saw that he was going to tell them that he had called them donkeys so he said: This man is a pursuer and the Torah said if someone comes to kill you, rise up and kill him first. So he struck him with his iron staff and killed him.

Rabbi Shila not only kills an informant, he justifies his deed as self-defense.[20] He explains that the informant, who was on his way to have Rabbi Shila put to death, is legally considered a "pursuer" ("רודף") whose life is forfeit so long as he is attempting to commit murder.[21] Like the story of Rabbi Shila, the stories of Bar Qamtza and Rav Kahana also subscribe to a broad definition of the "pursuer," which includes the informant as well, but these two stories do not adduce their underlying rationale – presumably because it already appeared in the story of Rabbi Shila. In other words, I propose that the editors of the stories of Bar Qamtza and Rav Kahana apparently felt no need to justify the execution of an informant since the legal justification had already appeared in the story of Rabbi Shila. In sum, just as the sages' (first) suggestion to sacrifice the blemished animal was apparently inspired by the Babylonian story of Ifra Hormiz, their (second) suggestion to execute Bar Qamtza was apparently inspired by the Babylonian story of Rabbi Shila.

---

20. See Fraenkel, *Aggadic Narrative*, 269n28.
21. See m. Sanh. 8:7.

Zechariah's Second "They will Say" Argument

Rejecting the sages' second suggestion, Zechariah ben Avqulas argues that Bar Qamtza may not be executed since people might misinterpret the reason for his death sentence and mistakenly conclude that blemishing an animal is a capital offense. In conversation with the sages' concern in line 23 that Bar Qamtza "will go and **say** (to the emperor)," Zechariah ben Avqulas contends, in line 24, that if Bar Qamtza were to be executed, people might "**say** that one who inflicts a blemish on a consecrated animal is to be put to death!" Whereas the sages sensibly worry about what Bar Qamtza might "say" to the emperor, Zechariah is needlessly concerned with what the Jewish people might "say" about Bar Qamtza's death sentence.

In addition, just as Zechariah's first claim – "They will say that blemished animals may be offered on the altar!" – sets forth a feeble argument in favor of a precautionary measure designed to prevent an unlikely erroneous inference, his second claim does the same. On a practical level, it seems unlikely that people would learn about the emperor's blemished calf but not about the traitorous Jew responsible for the blemish. On a substantive legal level, since capital punishment is far too severe for the sin and also lacks biblical support, it seems ludicrous to imagine that anyone would ever have concluded that blemishing a consecrated animal could possibly warrant capital punishment. Moreover, when confronted with the near certainty of a national disaster, how important are concerns about what people might mistakenly say? In short, Zechariah ben Avqulas exercises poor judgment a second time, worrying too much about legal minutiae and too little about the welfare of his people.

In light of the weakness of Zechariah ben Avqulas's formal claims, some have viewed them as legal cover for other concerns – such as his support for the Jewish revolt (in line with the rebellious stance Josephus ascribed to Zacharias son of Amphicalleus[22]) or his fear that people unfamiliar with the details of the case might criticize the sages' verdict.[23] Others have persuasively responded, however, that Zechariah's flimsy

---

22. See Rokéaḥ, "Zechariah," 53. See also Alon, *Studies*, vol. 1, 44, 267n63. Cf. Halevi, *Gates of the Aggadah*, 208; Furstenberg, "Qamtza," 107–8.
23. See Schwartz, "Zechariah," 314n5.

contentions condemn Zechariah, along with the sages who accede to him, precisely because they are so absurd.[24] Because the blemish is so slight and not unequivocally forbidden, since it is so unlikely that people would ever view the blemish or mistakenly conclude from seeing it that blemished animals were acceptable offerings, since it is improbable that anyone would infer from Bar Qamtza's execution that blemishing a consecrated animal warrants capital punishment, and since concerns over what people might potentially infer pale in comparison to the severity of the issue at hand, Zechariah's stance reveals terribly poor judgment. Caught up with trivial legal minutiae and unrealistic scenarios, Zechariah and the sages who follow him lose sight of the greater picture, caring more for hypothetical eventualities than the fate of the Jewish people. Rather than seeking to maintain "peace with the kingdom," Zechariah ben Avqulas propounds a foolhardy and myopic legal sophistry, worrying more about hypothetical legal misunderstandings than the welfare of the people.[25] Seen through the lens of the trilogy's preface, Zechariah ben Avqulas was insufficiently "anxious" and immoderately inflexible, lacking the foresight to appraise the calamitous consequences of his hardened heart.

Going Beyond the Letter of the Law

In considering Zechariah ben Avqulas's legal myopia and preposterous application of Torah law, some have linked his arguments to a short discussion in Bavli Bava Metzi'a, yet another tradition which has no parallel in early Palestinian rabbinic literature:[26]

א״ר יוחנן: מפני מה חרבה ירושלם? מפני שדנו בה דין תורה. אלא דינא דמגיסתא נידיינו! אלא מפני שהעמידו דבריהם על דין תורה ולא עבוד לפנים משורת הדין.[27]

Rabbi Yohanan said: On account of what was Jerusalem destroyed? On account of them judging in it the law of Torah. But should they

---

24. See Rubenstein, *Talmudic Stories*, 149; Mandel, "Tales of the Destruction," 154.
25. Cf. Tropper, *Sage Stories*, 29–33. See also Klawans, *Purity*, 185.
26. See, for example, Yisraeli-Taran, *Legends of the Destruction*, 21–22.
27. B.B. Metz. 30b according to Hamburg 165.

have judged the law of the magician?[28] Rather on account of basing their words on the law of Torah and not going beyond the letter of the law.

According to the Talmud's interpretation of the statement attributed to Rabbi Yohanan, the Second Temple was destroyed because the sages were too exacting and inflexible in their administration of Torah law. While at times the judicial process entails following the spirit of the law rather than the strict letter of the law – employing discretionary judgment rather than rule-based legal reasoning[29] – the intransigent sages of the late Second Temple Period obstinately adhered to the letter of the law only. Reading the story of Bar Qamtza through the lens of this Bava Metzi'a sugya, Zechariah ben Avqulas emerges as the perfect illustration of a late Second Temple sage whose stubborn commitment to (what he perceived as) the letter of the law outweighed his devotion to the welfare of the Jewish people and the spirit of the law. Just as Act I, following Lamenations Rabbati, gives narrative form to the Palestinian traditions which claim that senseless hatred and the failure to rebuke triggered the destruction, Act II gives narrative form to the Bavli's claim that the sages' headstrong adherence to the letter of the law led to the fall of Jerusalem.

In the spirit of the statement attributed to Rabbi Yohanan, Act II sets forth, first and foremost, a forceful critique of legal miscalculations.[30] Whereas Lamenations Rabbati's Act II focuses solely on the temple cult, the Babylonian parallel expands the purview to include the law of

---

28. On the term "דינא דמגיסתא," "the law of the magician," see Ezra Spicehandler, "Dina de Magista and Bei Dawar: Notes on Gentile Courts in Talmudic Babylonia," *Hebrew Union College Annual* 26 (1955): 353–54; Sokoloff, *Dictionary of Jewish Babylonian Aramaic*, 640; Secunda, *Iranian Talmud*, 82; Deborah Adèle Barer, "A Judge With No Courtroom: Law, Ethics and the Rabbinic Idea of *Lifnim Mi-Shurat Ha-Din*" (PhD diss., University of Virginia, 2016), 168n196.

29. For the interpretation of "לפנים משורת הדין," "beyond the letter of the law" (or more literally: "within/facing the line of the law") as discretionary judgment, see Barer, "*Lifnim Mi-Shurat Ha-Din*," 1–12, 167–87; "Law, Ethics, and Hermeneutics: A Literary Approach to *Lifnim Mi-shurat Ha-din*." *JTR* 10 (2018): 10–14.

30. See Goldenberg, "Rabbinic Explanations," 521; Yisraeli-Taran, *Legends of the Destruction*, 19.

informants as well. This expanded purview subtly shifts the target of the act's critique from the sacrificial cult to the legal sphere, a shift that is in keeping with the primary concern of the Babylonian rabbinic sages, namely, the study and application of Torah law. By transforming the act into a legal debate not only about the temple cult, the story paints the Jerusalem temple in the image of the Babylonian study house.

THE STRUCTURE OF ACT II SCENE 2

From a bird's-eye view, Act II scene 2's debate between the sages and Zechariah ben Avqulas unfolds within the rubric of an unchanging literary format. The format of lines 21–22: "The Sages thought... Rabbi Zechariah ben Avqulas said to them: They will say... blemished..." ("סבור...אמר להו ר' זכריה בן אבקולס: יאמרו...מומין") – parallels that of lines 23–24: "They thought... Rabbi Zechariah ben Avqulas said to them: They will say... a blemish..." ("סבור...אמר להו ר' זכריה בן אבקולס: יאמרו...מום..."). This repetitive and unchanging format mirrors the unchanging format of the negotiations between Bar Qamtza and the banquet host in Act I scene 2's parallel encounter; in both cases, the repeating format helpfully accentuates the differences between the scene's parts. Accordingly, just as Act I's unchanging format highlights the escalating drama of the negotiations, Act II's unchanging format brings into sharp relief the mounting gravity of the debate. Whereas the sages initially consider only sacrificing a blemished animal, they go on to ponder executing the morally blemished Bar Qamtza.

Act II scene 2 ultimately concludes with Zechariah ben Avqulas's second rebuttal, granting Zechariah the final word in his debate with the sages. The absence of any response to his rebuttal indicates that the sages conceded the case. Although the sages wisely understood that the emperor's calf should have been sacrificed or that Bar Qamtza should have been executed, they nonetheless acceded to Zechariah ben Avqulas, thereby revealing their poor judgment and moral cowardice. Failing to express their solidarity with Bar Qamtza in Act I, the sages did not stand up to the host and rebuke his abusive behavior; failing to express their solidarity with the Jewish people in Act II, the sages did not stand up to Zechariah ben Avqulas and protest his farfetched legal gymanstics. Over the course of the two acts, the silence of the sages condemned Jerusalem.

If we compare the critical thrust of Act II to that of Act I, we find both similarities and differences. On the one hand, both acts critique the weak sense of solidarity amongst rabbinic sages: just as Act I portrays the sages' lack of empathy for a fellow Jew, Act II describes the sages' elevation of legal minutiae over the welfare of the Jewish people.[31] On the other hand, the sages' extreme dedication to the law in Act II contrasts sharply with their callous indifference to Bar Qamtza in Act I, suggesting that ritual piety and strict adherence to the law are worthless if one cares not for one's neighbor.

REVIEWING THE BABYLONIAN IMPACT

Just like the preceding scenes, Act II scene 2 also bears the imprint of Babylonian editing. A particularly notable feature of the Babylonian redrawing of the Palestinian original is the intensified rabbinization of the story. In line with the prominent role of rabbis in the Bavli, the Babylonian editor enhanced the profile of rabbinic sages throughout our story. In Act I scene 3 the Babylonian editor replaced the banqueting Jerusalem elite of Lamentations Rabbati with a group of rabbinic sages and, following suit, in Act II scene 2 he replaced Lamentations Rabbati's priest with rabbinic sages. Whereas Lamentations Rabbati realistically placed a priest in the Jerusalem temple, the Bavli imaginatively envisions that the rabbis determined temple policy. In justifying the Tannaitic tradition which claimed that Zechariah ben Avqulas's meekness prompted the temple's destruction, the Bavli transfers Zechariah to the temple precincts, transforming this minor rabbinic sage into a central figure of the temple administration.

A second notable feature of the Babylonian redrawing of the Palestinian original is the reconfiguration of the Jerusalem temple after the model of Babylonian study houses, that is, as an insular rabbinic institution which prized academic debate and legal argumentation. In lieu of Lamentations Rabbati's negotiation between the Roman officer and the Jewish priest, the Bavli presents a legal debate between the sages and Zechariah ben Avqulas. The sages' argument to offer up the Romans' blemished animals "for the sake of peace with the kingdom" not only

---

31. See Kalmanzon and Fogel, *Legends of the Destruction*, 26–29. See also Baumgarten, "Sages Increase Peace," 231–33.

enlisted a Babylonian legal term, but was also apparently modeled on Rava's legal stance in the Ifra Hormiz story from Bavli Bava Batra. The sages' proposal to execute Bar Qamtza for being an informant not only enrolled a Babylonian legal principle, but was also apparenlty inspired by the story of Rabbi Shila from Bavli Berakhot. For his part, Zechariah ben Avqulas mobilized the Babylonian "they will say" argument twice. In short, from beginning to end Act II scene 2 reflects the academic atmosphere of Babylonian rabbinic study houses and the sage stories they produced.

Furthermore, Zechariah's implementations of the Babylonian "they will say" arguments are caricatures of Babylonian legal dialectics. Although his ludicrous reasoning and preposterous conclusions are perfect illustrations of legal sophistry, they nonetheless persuade the sages. Zechariah's specious legal acrobatics, which extend beyond cultic law to include the law of informants as well, are the fatal flaw of the Jewish leadership in Act II. Rather than critiquing the Jews' excessive cultic or ritual piety only – like Lamentations Rabbati's counterpart act – the Bavli also faults the rabbis for their legal sophistry and hardheaded adherence to the "letter of the law."

Chapter 21

The Destruction of the Temple and the Dispersion into Exile (ACT II SCENE 3)

The cataclysmic consequences of Bar Qamtza's banquet humiliation and the rejection of the Roman calf unfold in Act II scene 3, the final scene of our story.

25 א״ר יוחנן: ענוותנותו של ר' זכר' בן אבקולס

26 החריבה את ביתינו ושרפה את היכלנו והגלתנו מארצנו.

25 Rabbi Yohanan said: The meekness of Rabbi Zechariah ben Avqulas

26 destroyed our temple, burnt our sanctuary and exiled us from our land.

After Bar Qamtza's life was saved by Zechariah ben Avqulas in Act II scene 2, the final stages of his evil plot unfurl in scene 3. The sages' refusal to sacrifice the emperor's calf prompts the Romans to attack and, as a result, the temple in Jerusalem is destroyed, the sanctuary (or central edifice in the temple complex) is burned to the ground, and the Jews are dispersed into exile. From the moment the story's preface proclaimed "On account of Qamtza and Bar Qamtza Jerusalem was destroyed," the audience has been anticipating the devastation outlined here in this final scene. The narrative, in other words, culminates with this portrait of sweeping destruction.

215

An Atypical Finale

The story's finale, however, is not narrated in a typical manner. Rabbinic sage stories usually unfurl in a single running narrative (save for parenthetical asides), and from the preface until now, the story of Bar Qamtza was related, as expected, by a single voice (in Aramaic). The story's final scene, however, appears within a (Hebrew) saying attributed to Rabbi Yohanan. By contrast, the parallel scene in Lamentations Rabbati is narrated as expected: "Immediately he rose up and destroyed the temple." Furthermore, Rabbi Yohanan's saying not only tells the tale's tragic end, it does so in a roundabout way, that is, within the context of a saying which claims that Zechariah ben Avqulas's meekness was responsible for the destruction of the temple and the dispersion into exile. This indirect way of depicting the story's conclusion is most unusual. In short, the final scene in the Bavli omits the original conclusion from Lamentations Rabbati, breaking the smooth flow of the narrative with Rabbi Yohanan's saying. Rather than citing Rabbi Yohanan's saying as an epilogue as Lamentations Rabbati does, the Babylonian editor integrated the saying into the narrative itself.[1] Presumably, the Babylonian editor omitted Lamentations Rabbati's final line because his story of Bar Qamtza is followed by more stories which also take place before the destruction. Therefore, it was premature to narrate the destruction at this point.[2] Nonetheless, the omission of the story's original final scene impairs the literary flow of the narrative.

Rabbi Yohanan's appearance at the end of the story is especially significant because he also appeared in the trilogy's preface. Rabbi Yohanan's presence at both ends of our story forms a literary envelope (or *inclusio*) which frames the story.[3] In addition, the prominent role of moral qualities in Rabbi Yohanan's enveloping sayings, of cautious

---

1. See Mandel, "Tales of the Destruction," 154.
2. See Rubenstein, *Talmudic Stories*, 172–73. In addition, perhaps the Babylonian editor felt that it was superfluous to include two descriptions of the destruction, one in the body of the narrative and a second in a saying about Zechariah, and so he opted to preserve and enhance (see Furstenberg, "Qamtza," 103–4) the description which included a moral lesson as well.
3. See Furstenberg, "Qamtza," 103–4.

foresight, intractable obstinacy, and paralyzing meekness, enwraps our story in the human failings at its very heart.

The Meekness of Zechariah ben Avqulas

The final scene not only describes the devastating consequences of the Bar Qamtza story, it also offers us a new lens through which to interpret the story. The saying ascribed here to Rabbi Yohanan asserts that Zechariah ben Avqulas's "ענוותנות," his "meekness," was responsible for the destruction of the temple and the exile from the land of Israel. The Hebrew term "ענוותנות" has a range of meanings, including humility and patience, though the meaning most appropriate in our context is meekness.[4] Zechariah's meekness as a jurist, his fear of permitting the sacrifice of an animal with a minor blemish and of condoning the execution of an informant, dictates his poor decisions. In order to preemptively avert potentially incorrect legal inferences, Zechariah ben Avqulas knowingly risks the welfare of his people. Unlike Rabbi Shila and Rav Kahana who promptly kill dangerous informants, Zechariah's paralyzing meekness stops him from pursuing the same sensible course.[5] Whereas the lens of Rabbi Yohanan's saying from the preface underlines Zechariah's lack of foresight, the lens of Rabbi Yohanan's final saying brings into sharp relief the underlying meekness which dictates Zechariah's subservience to the letter of the law.[6]

Rabbi Yohanan's saying about Zechariah closely mirrors the parallel saying in Lamentations Rabbati and, as discussed above (in Chapter 7), Lamentations Rabbati's Zechariah saying originated as a Tannaitic saying now preserved in the Tosefta. Since the Tannaitic saying is most

---

4. See Rashi, ad loc. (s.v. *anvetanuto*); Schwartz, "Zechariah," 313–15; Mandel, "Tales of the Destruction," 144–45; Rubenstein, *Talmudic Stories*, 150–51. See also Richie Lewis, "*And Before Honor – Humility* (Proverbs 15:33): Ascending to Lowliness" ("לפני כבוד ענוה' [משלי טו, 33] שבירת מבני החברה כעלייה אל השפלות"), *Daat* 86 (2018): 459–80. Alternatively, if "ענוותנות" also meant cleverness or trickery, perhaps Rabbi Yohanan condemned Zechariah for his excessively clever legal acrobactics. See Chapter 7, n. 22 above.

5. See b. Ber. 58a; b. B. Qam. 117a–b. See also Rubenstein, *Talmudic Stories*, 351n 43 and Chapter 20 above.

6. See the end of Chapter 15 above.

likely the ultimate source of the Bavli's parallel saying, let us consider
how the two sayings differ:

T. SHABB. 16:7:	B. GIT. 56A:
אמ' ר' יוסה:	25 א"ר יוחנן:
ענותנותו של ר' זכריה בן אבקילס היא	ענוותנותו של ר' זכר' בן אבקולס
	26 **החריבה את ביתינו**
שרפה את ההיכל.	**ושרפה את היכלנו**
	והגלתנו מארצנו.

Rabbi Yose said:	25 Rabbi Yohanan said:
The meekness of Rabbi Zechariah ben Avqilas	The meekness of Rabbi Zechariah ben Avqulas
	26 **destroyed our temple,**
burnt the sanctuary.	burnt our sanctuary
	and exiled us from our land.

There are two salient differences between the two sayings. The first
relates to the identity of the tradent: Tosefta Shabbat and Lamentations
Rabbati attribute the statement to (the Tanna) Rabbi Yose, whereas the
Bavli attributes it to (the Amora) Rabbi Yohanan. Some scholars suggest
that the Bavli's Rabbi Yohanan entered the story as a transcriptional error
when the acronym "RY," which stood for Rabbi Yose, was incorrectly
deciphered as Rabbi Yohanan.[7] I suspect, however, that Rabbi Yose

---

7. See, for example, Rokéah, "Zechariah," 56n13; Levine Katz, "Qamtsa" 43;
Kalmin, *Jewish Babylonia*, 207n48. We have encountered on a few occasions the
scholarly reflex to explain change as error. The notion that the Bavli mistakenly
attributed Rabbi Yose's statement to Rabbi Yohanan due to a transcriptional error,
that the Tosefta's Zechariah ben Avqulas was inserted into the story of Bar Qamtza
due to a misunderstanding (see Chapter 7, n. 29) and that Babylonian sages
mistakenly transformed the Romans' perpetual offering into a one-off sacrifice
(see Chapter 19, n. 9) are all examples of change explained as error. Although this
reflex has a long pedigree, our relatively newfound appreciation for the creative
license of rabbinic editors reveals that the change as error approach often under-
estimates the scope of rabbinic literary activity. In all the cases mentioned above

was transformed into Rabbi Yohanan because of the influence of Rabbi Yohanan's earlier appearance in the trilogy's preface. In other words, Rabbi Yohanan may well have entered the story when the Zechariah tradition was adapted for the local literary context of the Bavli's "legends of destruction."

The second substantive difference between the statements is found in their portraits of destruction. Tosefta Shabbat's brief description of the burnt sanctuary is transformed in the Bavli into a longer tripartite description: "destroyed our temple, burnt our sanctuary, and exiled us from our land." This tripartite formulation, which appears on various occasions in rabbinic literature, also appears in the continuation of the "legends of destruction:" [8]

"והידיים ידי עשו" (בראשית כז:כב): זו מלכות הרשעה שהחריבה את ביתינו
ושרפה את היכלינו והגליתנו מארצנו.

Yet the hands are the hands of Esau (Gen 27:22): This is the wicked kingdom which destroyed our house and burnt our sanctuary and exiled us from our land.[9]

Hence, I suggest that our story enriched the Tosefta's brief reference to the burning of the sanctuary with a more expansive formulation

---

it seems likely that the changes were not errors, but were rather the products of the literary freedom enrolled by the rabbis in the reworking of earlier traditions. (It also bears mentioning that abbreviations for sages' names, such as "RY," do not appear in medieval manuscripts.)

8. See Efron, "Bar-Kokhva," 86n188, 92n212. The tripartite formulation, which appears in Pesiq. Rab. 36 (*Pesiqta Rabbati*, ed. Rivka Ulmer, vol. 2 [Lanham, MD: University Press of America, 2009], 834) and on b. Ber. 3a, was truncated in the resumptive repetition on b. Git. 57a (discussed above in Chapter 17) and expanded on b. Sanh. 64a and b. Avod. Zar. 18a. A variation on the tripartite formulation has the third leg refer to exile "among the nations of the world" rather than to exile "from our land." While God, in rabbinic literature, naturally refers to the temple in Jerusalem as his house and sanctuary, I suspect that God tends not refer to the land of Israel as his land since the whole world belongs to him. Hence, perhaps the "exile among the nations of the world" tradition originated in contexts in which God was the speaker, while the "exile from our land" tradition originated in contexts in which God was not the speaker.

9. B. Git. 57b according to St. Petersburg – RNL Evr. I 187.

familiar from elsewhere, that is, with a (common and) more detailed portrait of devastation which lent a more heartrending tone to our story's conclusion.

Having noted above that Act II scene 3 forms a literary envelope with the trilogy's preface, consider how it also forms a literary envelope with our story's preface: "On account of Qamtza and Bar Qamtza Jerusalem was destroyed." Both the preface and the conclusion identify those responsible for the terrible consequences of the first Jewish revolt against Rome, but they pinpoint, or at least emphasize, different consequences and different culprits. Whereas the preface relates only to Jerusalem, the conclusion zooms in on the temple and sanctuary and zooms out so as to include the exile. While the preface mentions Bar Qamtza, the conclusion focuses on Zechariah ben Avqulas.[10]

Furthermore, since the preface's use of the names Qamtza and Bar Qamtza inevitably directs our attention to the banquet fiasco of Act I, while the conclusion explicitly draws our attention to Zechariah's behavior in Act II, it seems that the two declarations should be interpreted sequentially. Namely, once Bar Qamtza's humiliation in Act I spawned his thirst for revenge, Act II reveals how Zechariah ben Avqulas failed to thwart Bar Qamtza's reprisal.[11] In Act I the sages lack the backbone to stand up for a hounded Jew, and in Act II they lack the empathy to safeguard the Jewish people. Too much concerned with legal minutiae and too little concerned with the well-being of their community, the sages wreak havoc and destruction because of their deficient sense of solidarity.

---

10. See Chapter 15, n. 11 above.
11. See Furstenberg, "Qamtza," 102–3.

Chapter 22

Bar Qamtza and the Stories of Tur Malka and Bethar

O n the heels of the story of Bar Qamtza, the Bavli describes the fall of Jerusalem at length, eventually concluding with the statement attributed to Rabbi Eleazar in lines 27–28: "Come and see how great is the power of shame, for God assisted Bar Qamtza and destroyed his temple and burnt his sanctuary." This statement not only serves as the closing bookend of a literary envelope (or *inclusio*), in which all the material about the destruction of Jerusalem is encircled by the story of Bar Qamtza, but it also serves as a resumptive repetition (as noted above), returning us to the trilogy of stories about Jerusalem, Tur Malka, and Bethar.[1] Turning now to the trilogy's final two stories, the stories of Tur Malka and Bethar, let us explore the interpretive lens they supply for the story of Bar Qamtza:

29 אתרנגול ותרנגולתא **חרוב** טור מלכא:

30 **דהוו נהיגי** כי הוה חתנא וכלתא הוו מפקי קמייהו תרנגול ותרנגולתא

31 כלומר פרו ורבו כתרנגולין.

32 **יומא חד הוה חליף** גונדא דרומאי שקלינהו מינייהו.

33 **נפלי עלייהו מחונהו.**

34 **אתאו אמרו ליה** לקיסר: מרדו בך יהודאי!

---

1. See Chapter 17.

35 **אתא עלייהו** . . .

36 **אשקא דדייספק חרוב** ביתר:

37 **דהוו נהיגי כי** איתיליד להו ינוקא שתלי ארזא ינוקתא שתלי תורניתא

38 וכד הוו מינסבי קייצי להו ועביד להו גנאנא.

39 **יומא חד הוה חלפה** ברתיה דקיסר איתבר שקא דדייספק קצו דדייספק ארזא ועיילו לה

40 **נפול עלייהו ומחונהו.**

41 **אתו אמרו ליה לקיסר: מרדו בך יהודאי!**

42 **אתא עלייהו.**

29 **On account of a** cock and a hen Tur Malka (the King's Mountain) **was destroyed:**

30 **It was the custom that when** there was a bride and groom, they would put out before them a cock and a hen,

31 as if to say: be fruitful and multiply like chickens.

32 **One day** a troop of Roman soldiers **passed by** (who) took (the chickens) from them.

33 **They (the Jews) fell upon them and beat them.**

34 **They (the Roman soldiers) came and said to the emperor: The Jews have rebelled against you!**

35 **He (the emperor) came (in battle) upon them (the Jews)** . . .

36 **On account of a** shaft of a litter Bethar **was destroyed:**

37 **It was the custom that when** a boy was born to them they would plant a cedar; a girl, they would plant an acacia,

38 and when they married they would cut them down and make from them a bridal canopy.

39 **One day** the emperor's daughter **passed by** (when) the shaft of her litter broke, so they cut down a cedar tree and brought it to her.

40 **They (the Jews) fell upon them and beat them.**

41 **They (the Romans) came and said to the emperor: The Jews have rebelled against you!**

42 **He (the emperor) came (in battle) upon them (the Jews).**

The twin stories of the fall of Tur Malka and Bethar adhere to a single literary format, sharing a common structure, similar plotline and much of the same language.[2] The stories are introduced with prefaces familiar to us from the trilogy's preface. Echoing the format of the story of Bar Qamtza's preface, "On account of Qamtza and Bar Qamtza Jerusalem was destroyed," the first preface in line 29 ascribes the destruction of Tur Malka to the story of a cock and a hen and the second preface in line 36 ascribes the destruction of Bethar to the story about the shaft of a litter.[3]

Following its preface, each story opens with the identical phrase, "It was the custom that when," "דהוו נהיגי כי," and goes on to describe a local custom related to marriage celebrations. It was the custom in Tur Malka to parade cocks and hens, as live fertility symbols, before brides and grooms on their wedding day, and it was the custom in Bethar to erect bridal canopies out of trees which had been planted at the births of the bride and groom. These customs, which ascribe symbolic value to both chickens and trees, appear nowhere else in all classical rabbinic literature.[4] The wedding feasts mentioned here, however, evoke a festive atmosphere reminiscent of the banquet from Act 1 of the story of Bar Qamtza.

After depicting the local customs, lines 32 and 39 recount that "one day" a group of Roman soldiers passed by. In the case of Tur Malka, the passing Roman troop seized the wedding fowl, and in the case of Bethar, the passing Roman soldiers felled a dedicated cedar in order to replace the broken shaft in the emperor's daughter's litter. From here on out the two stories are identical. In both cases, the Jews attack the passing Roman soldiers who had unwittingly violated their local custom. The Romans, who had no clue that they had breached a venerated Jewish custom, infer from the assault that the Jews are rebelling. They accordingly report back to the emperor "The Jews have rebelled against you!" The repetition of this line, which already appeared in the story

---

2. See Efron, "Bar-Kokhva," 81–82; Mandel, "Tales of the Destruction," 156–57; Watts Belser, *Rabbinic Tales of Destruction*, 138.

3. The similarity of the Aramaic terms for cock and hen, "תרנגול" and "תרנגולתא," echoes the similarity of the names Qamtza and Bar Qamtza, while the parallel line in the story of Bethar includes the similar words "ינוקא" (boy) and "ינוקתא" (girl).

4. See Efron, "Bar-Kokhva," 81; Tropper, "Chickens and Catastrophe," 71–80; Watts Belser, *Rabbinic Tales of Destruction*, 137–43.

of Bar Qamtza, transforms it into a refrain which links all three stories together.[5] Hearing the report, the emperor needs no further proof of the revolt since an assault on Roman troops by provincials is, by definition, a revolt.[6] Hence, the Romans proceed to destroy Tur Malka and Bethar, just as they had earlier demolished Jerusalem.

Before exploring the interpretive lens which emerges from the stories of Tur Malka and Bethar, it bears stressing that, unlike the story of Bar Qamtza, the stories of Tur Malka and Bethar appear nowhere else in all classical rabbinic literature.[7] Furthermore, as excellent illustrations of the rash and stubborn behavior spotlighted in the trilogy's preface, the twin stories fit seamlessly into the immediate literary context. This perfect fit strongly suggests that the stories were fashioned (and perhaps even tailor made) for the local context.

The Story of Bar Qamtza vis-à-vis the Stories of Tur Malka and Bethar

1: FOOLHARDY JEWISH BEHAVIOR

The twin stories of Tur Malka and Bethar illuminate the story of Bar Qamtza in at least four important ways. First, in overreacting to an unintentional breach of a local, relatively insignificant, and otherwise unattested custom, the Jewish inhabitants of Tur Malka and Bethar exemplify the lack of caution and foresight underlined in the trilogy's preface: "What is meant by the verse: *Happy is the man who is anxious always, but he who hardens his heart falls into misfortune*?" Regardless of the symbolic meaning ascribed to the dedicated fowl and cedars, the assaults on the Romans were disproportionate responses to accidental violations of local customs. The Romans were not oppressing the Jews nor were they prohibiting any cardinal precepts. The Jewish violence in Tur Malka and Bethar was rooted in an inordinate sensitivity to the unwitting Roman violation of Jewish customs, a sensitivity which closely

---

5. See Chapter 19, n. 2 above.
6. See Chapter 19 above. Cf. Efron, "Bar-Kokhva," 79, 82, 88.
7. See Mandel, "Tales of the Destruction," 157. On the story's literary backdrop, see Tropper, "Chickens and Catastrophe," 80–86.

resembles Zechariah ben Avqulas's undue fear of the minor blemish on the emperor's calf. Just as the Romans had no intention of cutting down any dedicated trees or eating any dedicated fowl, the emperor was not intent on forcing the Jews to sacrifice a blemished calf. In recklessly rejecting the emperor's offering because of a slight blemish, the inflexible temple authorities pursued a careless course of action that served as the ill-fated paradigm for both Tur Malka and Bethar.[8] Since the impetuous and obstinate provincials of Jerusalem, Tur Malka, and Bethar did not anticipate the likely outcome of an altercation with Rome, their cities fell "into misfortune."[9]

2: A TRIVIAL TRIGGER

Second, scholars have suggested that the Bar Qamtza story's preface, "On account of Qamtza and Bar Qamtza Jerusalem was destroyed," highlights the trivial nature of the ultimate cause of Jerusalem's downfall (by attributing it to a slight difference in name [or to a mere "handful," "קומץ"]) and in this respect served as the literary paradigm for the prefaces of the subsequent twin stories.[10] According to this suggestion, each preface emphasizes that a piddling trigger ultimately led to the destruction of a Judaean city.[11] On account of the miniscule difference between the names Qamtza and Bar Qamtza, Jerusalem was destroyed; on account of a measley cock and hen, Tur Malka was destroyed; and on account of a paltry litter shaft, Bethar was destroyed. The threefold repetition of this preface format reinforces the notion that the Roman-Jewish wars were all triggered by mere trifles.

---

8. See Efron, "Bar-Kokhva," 86; Yisraeli-Taran, *Legends of the Destruction*, 17–18; Furstenberg, "Qamtza," 103–4.

9. Since the Romans responded to Jewish provocations and did not fall "into misfortune," it is unlikely that the prefaces critique Roman behavior. See Yisrael-Taran (1997) 20; cf. Watts Belser, *Rabbinic Tales of Destruction*, 138–39.

10. Cf. Chapter 15, n. 11 above. See Chapter 8, n. 2 above

11. See, for example, Yisraeli-Taran, *Legends of the Destruction*, 18; Duker, "Piety or Privilege," 41, 46. See also Efron, "Bar-Kokhva," 92. The notion that the temple was destroyed because of mere trifles may be related to the rabbinic notion that "the smallest lapse can bring great punishment" (Schofer, *Confronting Vulnerability*, 96).

3: A CULTURAL MISUNDERSTANDING

Third, at the heart of the conflicts at Tur Malka and Bethar stands a cultural misunderstanding highly similar to the pivotal cultural misunderstanding in Act 11 of Bar Qamtza's tale.[12] Just as the Romans did not know that a blemish on the upper lip or white of the eye rendered an animal unfit for sacrifice according to Jewish ritual law, they were similarly unfamiliar with the hallowed status of the dedicated trees at Tur Malka and the dedicated fowl at Bethar. The recurrence of the cultural misunderstanding theme in all three stories not only suggests that it forms a central component of the trilogy, it also brings attention to the other misunderstandings in Bar Qamtza's tale. The host's servant misunderstood his mission when he mistook Bar Qamtza for Qamtza, the host may have misinterpreted Bar Qamtza's presence at his banquet as an intentional provocation, and the Roman authorities mistook a legal decision for revolt.[13] Moreover, I submit that as a group, the gross overreactions, the trivial triggers, and the repeated misunderstandings disclose that the wars between Judaea and Rome were highly contingent (or chance) affairs and not the inevitable results of major political disputes or structural conflicts.

In the study of ancient warfare, modern historians debate the relative weight of contingent factors and events versus structural tensions and conflicts.[14] Historians on one side of the spectrum argue that the

---

12. See Saldarini, "Rabbinic Response," 450; Furstenberg, "Qamtza," 103–4.

13. In addition, Bar Qamtza may have misinterpreted the sages' cowardly silence at the banquet as acquiescence. See Halevi, *Gates of the Aggadah*, 205.

14. Compare, for example, the stances articulated by Martin Goodman and Seth Schwartz in the following studies: Martin Goodman, "The First Jewish Revolt: Social Conflict and the Problem of Debt," *JJS* 33 (1982): 417–27; "A Bad Joke in Josephus," *JJS* 36 (1985): 195–99; *Ruling Class*; "Origins," 39–53; "Current Scholarship on the First Revolt," in *The First Jewish Revolt: Archaeology, History, and Ideology*, ed. Andrea M. Berlin and J. Andrew Overman (London: Routledge, 2002), 15–24; "Trajan and the Origins of Roman Hostility to the Jews," *Past and Present* 182 (2003): 3–29; *Rome and Jerusalem*; Seth Schwartz, "Sunt Lachrymae Rerum," *JQR* 99 (2009): 56–64; *Reciprocity and Solidarity*. See also Greg Woolf, "Provincial Revolts in the Early Roman Empire," in *The Jewish Revolt Against Rome: Interdisciplinary Perspectives*, ed. Malden Popović (Leiden: Brill, 2001), 33–40. (Alternatively, longstanding tensions and conflicts between the Jews and

Roman-Jewish wars were simply bad luck, each one the product of an unfortunate series of events that could have easily unfolded otherwise, while historians on the opposite side of the spectrum contend that deep-seated and structural tensions made the clash of civilizations inevitable. In the framework of this modern debate, it seems that the story of Bar Qamtza and the trilogy as a whole lean towards the idea that the Roman-Jewish conflicts were the outcomes of local events and not deep-seated tensions.[15] Jerusalem fell because of a series of trifling triggers, exaggerated reactions, and avoidable misunderstandings – not because Rome and Jerusalem were at loggerheads. With that being said, it would be wrong to conclude that the trilogy's ultimate goal is to reveal the contingent nature of human affairs and Jewish history.[16] Rather, the trilogy enlists contingent and avoidable events in order to focus our attention on the ethical sphere, teaching us how human failings and moral flaws ultimately bring ravage and ruin.

Korean Air

In order to illustrate this point, consider the case of Korean Air in the late twentieth century. Although the "typical commercial airliner... is about as dependable as a toaster," from 1977 to 1999 an inordinate number of Korean Air planes crashed.[17] The loss rate for Korean Air was many times higher than comparable commercial airliners even though Korean Air planes were well maintained and their pilots highly trained. Moreover, the plague of Korean Air plane crashes is especially puzzling considering

---

their gentile neighbors may well have been a central factor underlying the Jewish revolt(s) against Rome. See Uriel Rappaport, "Jewish-Pagan Relations and the Revolt against Rome in 66–70 CE," *Jerusalem Cathedra* [1981]: 81, 84; Mason, *A History*, 224.)

15. See Halevi, *Gates of the Aggadah*, 205; Efron, "Bar-Kokhva," 78–86. (By placing the blame for the revolt largely on Jewish extremists and lowly Roman administrators, Josephus's *The Jewish War* also seems to argue that there was no inherent conflict between Rome and Jerusalem.)

16. See Chapter 13, n. 17. Cf. Efron, "Bar-Kokhva," 85. (See also Jacob Neusner, *From Politics to Piety: The Emergence of Pharisaic Judaism* [Englewood Cliffs, NJ: Prentice-Hall, 1973], 59.)

17. Malcolm Gladwell, *Outliers: The Story of Success* (New York, NY: Back Bay, 2008), 183.

that plane crashes usually stem from a series of accidents (or contingent events) and not from a design flaw or structural defect:

> The typical accident involves seven consecutive human errors. One of the pilots does something wrong that by itself is not a problem. Then one of them makes another error on top of that, which combined with the first error still does not amount to catastrophe. But then they make a third error on top of that, and then another and another and another *and another*, and it is the combination of all those errors that leads to disaster.[18]

So, if Korean Air planes were not defective and their pilots were not ill prepared, why were so many Korean Air planes crashing? The problem with Korean Air was that Korean culture is a high-power distance culture, a culture in which subordinates, such as first officers and flight engineers, so respect and fear their superiors, such as pilots, that they hesitate to correct or disagree with them. In the fast-paced trying setting of a cockpit, pilots need direct and unmitigated feedback rather than the subtle hints of deferential, lower ranking, social inferiors. So long as Korean flight crews hesitated to disagree with the pilots, Korean Air suffered an excessive number of accidents. In the early 2000s, Korean Air successfully lowered its loss rate by transforming the cockpit culture into a low-power distance setting, in which the pilots' assistants were taught to express themselves in a strong, unapologetic, and direct manner. By replacing the subservient obsequiousness which had plagued Korean cockpits with unmitigated communication, Korean Air managed to reduce pilot error significantly.[19]

Just as the plague of Korean airplane crashes was not due to any design flaw or structural defect, the fall of Jerusalem, Tur Malka, and Bethar, according to the trilogy, was not the outcome of a deep abiding systemic conflict with Rome. Rather, Korea's high-power distance culture wreaked havoc in airplane cockpits just as callous and impetuous Jewish behavior foolishly provoked the Roman authorities. In both cases,

---

18. Gladwell, *Outliers*, 184.
19. See Gladwell, *Outliers*, 177–223. See also Michael Lewis, *The Undoing Project: A Friendship that Changed our Minds* (New York, NY: W.W. Norton, 2017) 316–17.

a flawed cultural setting enabled the series of accidents which led to disaster, though, in the case of Jerusalem, the flaws were not only cultural but also deeply moral. In short, the fall of city after city teaches that while there was no inherent or structural conflict between Judaea and Rome, the systemic Jewish flaws of rash behavior, unbending obduracy, and a poor sense of solidarity triggered calamity after calamity.

4: NO PARALLEL FOR ACT I

Unlike the first three ways in which the twin stories shed light on the tale of Bar Qamtza via their shared features, the fourth and final feature illuminates through contrast.[20] The stories of Tur Malka and Bethar are much shorter than the tale of Bar Qamtza and parallel, for the most part, Act II only. Considering the trilogy's cohesiveness as a literary unit, one wonders why the twin stories include no counterpart to Act I. Although Act II may implicitly condemn the sages' weak sense of solidarity, the overt moral critique of Act I is far more biting than Act II's implied critique. Morally speaking, Act I's public humiliation of Bar Qamtza is much more severe than Act II's legal miscalculation, making Act I more powerful and memorable. Hence, it seems surprising, at first glance, that the twin stories do not parallel the most potent and poignant element of the Bar Qamtza story. If the local context and the story of Bar Qamtza contributed to the formation of the tales of Tur Malka and Bethar (as is likely), why did the moral lesson from Act I leave no imprint on the twin stories?

I suspect that the stories of Tur Malka and Bethar include no counterparts to Bar Qamtza's humiliation due to their relatively modest goals. Whereas the story of Bar Qamtza was supposed to explain the

---

20. Another salient difference between the story of Bar Qamtza and the stories of Tur Malka and Bethar is the role of the sages. The sages play a central role in the story of Bar Qamtza but are entirely missing from the twin stories. It has been suggested that the sages' absence reflects rabbinic reservations about the Bar Kokhva revolt (see Efron, "Bar-Kokhva," 88) or a clash between the Roman Empire and popular Jewish practice (see Mandel, "Tales of the Destruction," 158; cf. Tropper, "Chickens and Catastrophe," 80, 86), although perhaps the Babylonian sages simply did not view Tur Malka and Bethar as centers of rabbinic learning.

destruction of the temple, the fall of Jerusalem, and the dispersion of the Jews into exile, the twin stories were only designed to explain the destruction of relatively minor Judaean cities. Unlike the story of Bar Qamtza, which illustrates the traditions that the Second Temple fell on account of "hating one's fellow before God" and failing to rebuke one another, the cities of Tur Malka and Bethar were not associated with any such moralistic traditions. Although the fall of Tur Malka and Bethar were certainly viewed as awful and tragic events, these cities lacked the religious and national stature of Jerusalem and the temple. Hence, while it was important to emphasize that the moral bankruptcy of the sages ultimately led to the fall of Jerusalem and the exile, no such egregious moral failing was needed to explain the destruction of Tur Malka and Bethar.

Chapter 23

Part II's Conclusion

From the Bavli's perspective, Lamentations Rabbati's story of Bar Qamtza is the road not taken. The Babylonian editor of the story of Bar Qamtza inherited Lamentations Rabbati's story (or some story quite like it) and had he so desired, he could have easily reproduced the Lamentations Rabbati version with no or minimal changes.[1] However, he desired otherwise. Rather than adhering to Lamentations Rabbati's path, the Babylonian editor forged his own path. At times the two paths overlap, but at times the Babylonian editor went his own way. By way of concluding this microhistory of sorts, let us review significant ways in which the Babylonian version diverged from its Palestinian predecessor, showing how the road not taken can help us illuminate the taken road.

The Frames of Reference

Each version's literary context establishes a distinct frame of reference for the story of Bar Qamtza. In Lamentations Rabbati, the genteel banquet practices of the noble Second Temple Jerusalemites sets the stage for a story about a banquet in which the noble Jerusalemites failed to live up to their own elevated banquet etiquette and ethics. In other words, Lamentations Rabbati's context primes the reader for Act I, the banquet act of our story. By contrast, the Bavli's introductory question – "What is meant by the verse: *Happy is the man who is anxious always, but he who*

---

1. See Appendix I.

hardens his heart falls into misfortune?" (Prov 28:14) – in tandem with the Talmud's overarching trilogy, create an entirely different interpretive lens. With the help of a broad historical purview, the Bavli's setting condemns the Jews' repeated lack of foresight and unbending obstinacy. When the Bavli addresses the story of Bar Qamtza alone, it, like Lamentations Rabbati, underlines the banquet travesty: "Rabbi Eleazar said: Come and see how great is the power of shame, for God assisted Bar Qamtza and destroyed his temple and burnt his sanctuary." However, the Talmud's setting as a trilogy directs a floodlight on an entirely different aspect of the story. Rather than drawing our attention to Bar Qamtza's humiliating banquet experience, the trilogy draws our attention to the rash conduct, obstinate behavior, and foolish obsession with ritual minutiae said to have prompted three devastating conflicts with Rome.

Rabbinization

The Bavli intensifies the rabbinization of the story of Bar Qamtza already initiated by Lamentations Rabbati. Whereas Zechariah ben Avqulas is the only rabbinic sage in the Lamentations Rabbati parallel (where he was inserted at a relatively late date), the sages play a far more prominent role in the Babylonian parallel. The Babylonian version assigns Zechariah a leading role within the late Second Temple rabbinic leadership, doubles the number of actions ascribed to him, and relocates him to a legal debate. Moreover, the Babylonian version introduces a group of rabbinic sages into both acts: in Act I the sages replace Lamentations Rabbati's Jerusalem banqueters, and in Act II they, along with Zechariah, stand in lieu of Lamentations Rabbati's temple priest. In rabbinizing the story, the Babylonian editor recruited the fiction that the rabbis dominated the temple administration and high society of late Second Temple Jerusalem. In implicating the rabbinic community in the destruction of the temple, the Babylonian story called upon its contemporary rabbinic audience to mind its ways and avoid the faults of its predecessors.

The Scholastic Culture of Babylonian Study Houses

The scholastic culture of the rabbinic study houses in Babylonia, which pervades the Bavli, had an indelible effect on our story. Over and above the story's thorough rabbinization, the Babylonian editor made the story erudite and academic, packing it with legal minutiae and juristic debates. In contrast to Lamentations Rabbati, which merely notes that Bar Qamtza "secretly" blemished the Roman animals, the Babylonian story describes the blemish in greater detail. Not only identifying the white of the eye or the upper lip as the blemish's location, the Talmud also makes a distinction between Jewish and non-Jewish legal attitudes towards minor blemishes. Mobilizing legal materials from elsewhere in the Bavli, the Talmud's high-resolution account of the blemish is in keeping with the legal orientation of the rabbinic study house. In lieu of the interaction between the Jewish priest and the Roman officer recounted in Lamentations Rabbati, the Bavli presents a legal debate typical of the Babylonian study house and talmudic discourse. The sages and Zechariah dispute whether to sacrifice the Roman emperor's blemished animal "for the sake of peace with the kingdom" and whether to execute Bar Qamtza, and Zechariah twice applies the "they will say" argument in a difficult and farfetched fashion. Once again enlisting legal materials found elsewhere in the Bavli, the Babylonian story transforms the temple into a study house populated and ruled by sages, thereby converting the temple confrontation into an internal rabbinic affair.

One poignant feature of the debate between Zechariah and the sages is that it not only relates to cultic law but also to the law of the pursuer. Unlike Act 11 in Lamentations Rabbati, which faults the Second Temple leadership with excessive cultic or ritual piety, the Bavli's parallel act censures specious legal acrobatics. On top of assigning the rabbis a central role in the story of the temple's destruction and transforming the temple into a rabbinic house of study, the Babylonian story identifies the learned misapplication of Torah law, the failure to go "beyond the letter of the law," as a central cause of the destruction.

The Overarching Cultural Setting

The overarching cultural setting naturally plays a formative role in the composition of any story and, whereas Lamentations Rabbati's version of our story was forged within the cultural climate of Byzantine Palestine, the Babylonian version recast the story within the Persian climate of Sasanian Babylonia. Hence, Greek loanwords, the banquet practices and banquet literature of the Greeks and Romans, proximity to the local Roman administration, familiarity with Roman tribute practices, and knowledge of widespread non-Jewish attitudes towards blemished animals all contributed to the construction of the Palestinian version of our story. In many respects, the Palestinian story of Bar Qamtza would have resonated with the gentiles and Christians of Byzantine Palestine, who would have been well acquainted with the Greek and Roman features of the story.

In contrast, the Babylonian story of Bar Qamtza bears traces of the Persian context in Sasanian Babylonia. Since banquets were widely popular in Persia just as in the Greek and Roman worlds, the Babylonian version preserved the banquet conflict, albeit with adjustments. For example, the Babylonian version removed Lamentations Rabbati's recurring references to reclining, since Babylonian Jews, like their Persian neighbors, did not recline in the Roman fashion.[2] In addition to omitting alien Greek and Roman features of the earlier Palestinian story, such as reclining and Greek loanwords, the Babylonian editor inserted Akkadian loanwords and replaced the local Roman governor with the Roman emperor, a more familiar Roman figurehead in the distant Persian Empire.[3] Moreover, the Babylonian editor introduced into the story entirely new features that were entwined with the local Persian setting. Replacing the daily Roman imperial sacrifices with a one-off offering typical of Persian royalty, projecting onto Roman Palestine the Babylonian sages' willingness to accept a Persian leader's gift "for the sake of peace with the kingdom," and attributing to early Palestinian sages the Babylonian conviction that an informant to the gentile authorities may be put to death as a pursuer all attest to the Persian imprint on the Babylonian version of our story. By reworking the Palestinian story in these ways, the Babylonian editor aligned the Palestinian story of Bar Qamtza with the Persian setting in Babylonia.

---

2. See Herman, "Table Etiquette," 161–64.

3. In addition, the stories about Tur Malka and Bethar use two Iranian loanwords: "גונדא," ("troop") and "דייספק," ("litter"). See Sokoloff, *Dictionary of Jewish Babylonian Aramaic*, 269, 329–330; Mokhtarian, "Iranian Loanwords," 132–33, 145–48.

The Common Core

While the various differences cited underline how the Babylonian editor carved out his own path by revamping the Palestinian story, they crystallize only against the backdrop of a shared common core. In the footsteps of the Palestinian original, the Bavli tells the story of the temple's destruction in two acts: Bar Qamtza's banquet humiliation and Bar Qamtza's revenge. Through the mediation of the earlier Palestinian version, the Babylonian version also ultimately stems from the sources of inspiration enlisted in the formation of the earlier version. The shared core of the parallel versions gives narrative form to traditions which interpreted the temple's destruction as the result of hatred and the failure to chastise one another. The shared core develops the refusal-revolt matrix, which originated from a Josephus-like tradition, and seeks to explain the severe condemnation of Ben Qamtzar and Zechariah ben Avqulas in Tannaitic literature. A striking, and perhaps shocking, feature of the shared core is that the Romans are never at fault. The Roman ruler patiently verifies Bar Qamtza's report of a Jewish rebellion rather than hastily marching off to battle the Jews. He only ventures to attack Jerusalem after hearing that the Jews rejected his tribute and, by implication, his authority. In the rest of the Babylonian trilogy as well, the Romans at Tur Malka and Bethar mean no harm to the local Jews; the emperor only destroys these cities after hearing that the Jews in each locale suddenly attacked his forces for no good reason. In every case, it is the Jews who disrupt the status quo while the Romans merely retaliate to an apparent Jewish revolt.[4] This favorable view of Rome, shared by both versions of the story, promotes a political ideology strongly inclined towards peaceful accommodation with the gentile regime and typical of a colonized or diasporic community with no means of armed resistance. In the centuries after the fall of Jerusalem, Jews in Palestine and Babylonia made their peace living under a non-Jewish and potentially hostile foreign regime.

---

4. After the Jews disrupt the status quo in the story of Bar Qamtza, and war ensues, the Babylonian "legends of destruction" portray Titus as a wicked Roman officer who defiled the temple (b. Git. 56b). However, even in Babylonian eyes the evil Titus does not cause the war, he is merely a general who implements Roman policy in a sacriligeous manner.

In short, the story of Bar Qamtza lays the blame for the destruction of the temple in Jerusalem at the feet of the Jews, not the Romans. In Lamentations Rabbati, the Jerusalemites fail to understand that ritual piety is less important than Jewish solidarity; in the Bavli, the sages fail to understand that legal acrobatics and ritual minutiae are less important than Jewish solidarity. In both cases, the story of Bar Qamtza encourages its audience to care for one another, giving narrative form to the prophetic claim that God desires goodness, not worship, or, in the words of Micah: "Would the Lord be pleased with thousands of rams, with myriads of streams of oil?... He has told you, O man, what is good, and what the Lord requires of you: Only to do justice and to love goodness, and to walk modestly with your God."[5]

---

5. Mic 6:7–8.

Appendix I

From Lamentations Rabbati to the Babylonian Talmud

For a long time, scholars have debated the relationship between the parallel versions of the story of Bar Qamtza. Some have argued for the priority of the Palestinian version, others for the priority of the Babylonian version, and yet others have argued that both versions emerged independently out of a shared (though no longer extant) tradition.[1] Now, we can finally put this debate to rest. A thorough comparison of the *nature* of the differences between the two parallels demonstrates that the Babylonian version reworked the Palestinian one.

First and foremost, the Babylonian version alone bares evidence of Babylonian terms, Babylonian legal thinking, and the Persian cultural context in Babylonia. In other words, the Aramaic term "a three-year-old calf," the Hebrew term "peace with the kingdom," the one-off Persian royal offering, blemishes on the white of the eye and upper lip, the distinction between Jewish and gentile attitudes towards minor blemishes, the "they will say" argument, the debate whether to accept a gift from Persian royalty for the sake of peace with the kingdom, and the notion that an informer may be executed as a pursuer all appear elsewhere in the Bavli, but nowhere in Palestinian rabbinic literature.[2] In a similar

1. See Chapter 1, nn. 12–14 above.
2. On the Aramaic term for "a three-year-old calf," the one-off Persian royal offering, the location of the blemish, and the distinction between Jewish and

237

vein, the debate between Zechariah ben Avqulas and the sages, which appears in lieu of the interchange between the priest and the Roman officer, is best explained as the projection of the scholastic setting of the Babylonian study house onto the temple precincts.[3] In short, the numerous and varied Babylonian features of the Babylonian parallel, none of which appear in Palestinian sources, are best explained as revisions made to Lamentations Rabbati's Palestinian version when it was recast in Babylonia.

Second, various unique features of the Babylonian parallel vis-à-vis Lamentations Rabbati appear to be the clarifications, conflations, and stylistic uniformity typical of secondary revision.[4] The violent expulsion ("He took him with his hand and threw him out") clarifies the end of the banquet fiasco which Lamentations Rabbati did not spell out, and Bar Qamtza's claim – "The Jews are rebelling against you" – makes explicit what Lamentations Rabbati only implied.[5] Bar Qamtza's first offer in the Bavli conflates the substance of his first offer in Lamentations Rabbati with language drawn from his second, and Lamentations Rabbati's unprotesting banqueters are conflated with Zechariah ben Avqulas when they become rabbinic sages in the Bavli.[6] Rabbi Yose was apparently changed to Rabbi Yohanan due to Rabbi Yohanan's prominent appearance at the head of the trilogy.[7]

In addition, some Babylonian revisions naturally prompted omis-

---

gentile attitudes towards minor blemishes, see Chapter 19 above. On the term "peace with the kingdom," the "they will say" argument, the debate over accepting a gift from Persian royalty, and the idea that an informer may be put to death, see Chapter 20 above.

3. See Chapter 20 above.

4. See Shamma Friedman, "The Talmudic Narrative about Rav Kahana and R. Yohanan (Bava Kamma 117a–b) and its Two Textual Families" ("סיפור רב כהנא ור' יוחנן (ב"ק קיז ע"א-ע"ב) וענף נוסח גניזה-המבורג"), *Bar Ilan* 30–31 (2006): 414; Tropper, *Rewriting Ancient Jewish History*, 158n38.

5. See Chapters 18–19 above. In addition, the Bavli probably replaced Lamentations Rabbati's governor with the emperor because, from its distant perspective in the Persian Empire, the Roman emperor, not the local governor, was the most prominent representative of Roman power.

6. See Chapters 17–18 above.

7. See Chapter 21 above.

sions. Jerusalem was omitted from line 1 once it was already mentioned in the preface;[8] the claim that the Jews ate Roman animals was removed as soon as the daily offering became a one-off event; and the Roman official was left unmentioned once his negotiations were replaced with an academic debate.[9]

Third, various literary features of the story of Bar Qamtza were impaired by Babylonian revisions. Whereas Lamentations Rabbati preserves the dramatic tension of the story until the end, the Bavli forfeited this tension when it forecast the temple's destruction in the preface.[10] When the Bavli replaced Zechariah ben Avqulas with the sages in Act 1 scene 3, the price incurred was introducing the sages at a relatively late stage in the story.[11] When the Babylonian editor omitted the final line of the story in Lamentations Rabbati – "Immediately he rose up and destroyed the temple" – because he had more stories to tell, he did not give the story a proper ending.[12]

In short, the distinctive Babylonian and Persian features of the Babylonian version, the signs of editorial revision in the Babylonian version, and the literary flaws of the Babylonian version all indicate that the Babylonian version is secondary to the earlier version preserved in Lamentations Rabbati (or something quite like it).[13] The evidence

---

8. See Chapter 16 n. 8 above.
9. See Chapter 19 above.
10. See Chapter 15 above.
11. See Chapter 18 above.
12. See Chapter 21 above.
13. In light of the potential fluidity of oral traditions (see Martin S. Jaffee, *Torah in the Mouth: Writing and Oral Tradition in Palestinian Judaism 200 BCE–400 CE* [Oxford: Oxford University Press, 2001]; Elizabeth Shanks Alexander, *Transmitting Mishnah: The Shaping Influence of Oral Tradition* [Cambridge: Cambridge University Press, 2006]), one might speculate that the Bavli inherited a version of the story already different in significant ways from the version preserved in Lamentations Rabbati. However, as long as there is no (explicit or implicit) evidence for the existence of such a source, there is no good reason to posit its existence. It is only when we cannot decipher the relationship between parallel sources that "we have recourse to the postulation of a hypothetical source" (Austin M. Farrer, "On Dispensing with Q," in *Studies in the Gospels: Essays in Memory of R.H. Lightfoot*, ed. D.E. Nineham [(Oxford: Blackwell, 1955], 56). See also Shamma Friedman, "Uncovering Literary Dependencies in the Talmudic Corpus," in *The*

undercuts the notion that Lamentations Rabbati revised the Babylonian version, and there are no good reasons to presuppose that both versions independently inherited a shared (and no longer extant) alternative version.[14] Instead, the best explanation for both the extent of the similarities between the two parallels and the nature of their differences is that the Babylonian editor revised the earlier Palestinian version.

Synoptic Problem in Rabbinic Literature, ed. Shaye J.D. Cohen (Providence, RI: Brown Judaic Studies, 2000), 35–57 and the following note.
14. See Tropper, *Rewriting Ancient Jewish History,* 20–28, 121–23.

Appendix II

Identifying the Best Reading of Lamentations Rabbati's Bar Qamtza Story

The Two Branches of Lamentations Rabbati

The textual witnesses of Lamentations Rabbati split neatly into two branches. The complete manuscripts Cambridge 495, Munich 229, as well as the *editio princeps* (or *Defus Qushta*) belong to branch **A**, while the complete manuscripts Oxford 102, Casanatense H 3112, Parma 2559, Parma 2393, and London 27089 belong to branch **B**.[1] In order to simplify the comparison between the branches, I have selected Cambridge 495 to represent **A** and Oxford 102 to represent **B**. Their readings of the story of Bar Qamtza are cited below in full.[2]

Although neither branch is free from errors and interpolations, Paul Mandel has demonstrated that when the branches differ, **B** usually preserves the earlier textual reading. As the more conservative branch,

---

1. See Paul Mandel, "Midrash Lamentations Rabbati: Prolegomenon, and a Critical Edition to the Third *Parsha*" ("מדרש איכה רבתי: מבוא ומהדורה ביקורתית לפרשה השלישית"), (PhD diss., Hebrew University, 1997), 3–6, 68–125 for a thorough analysis of the two branches.

2. My selection of Cambridge 495 follows Mandel's assessment that Cambridge 495 is the best representative of **A**. However, though Mandel views Parma 2559 as the best representative of **B**, Parma 2559 in our case was heavily influenced by the Bavli, and I therefore selected Oxford 102 in its stead. See Mandel, "Critical Edition," 90, 98.

B tends to preserve earlier more authentic readings, while **A**, by contrast, is the more creative branch and tends to produce later secondary readings.[3]

In our case, the two branches, as represented by Cambridge 495 and Oxford 102, are not terribly different, but the slight variations between them confirm Mandel's preference for branch **B**. For example, **A** apparently replaced the rare Aramaic word "תבסרני" ("shame me") in lines 8 and 10 of **B** with the common Hebrew word "תבישני" ("embarrass me"), as well as replaced the unusual Aramaic word "מגוסי" ("my meal") in **B**'s line 8 with the familiar Hebrew word "דסעודה" ("of (my) banquet").[4] **A** elaborated upon Bar Qamtza's brief conclusion in **B**'s line 21 – "ואת ידע" ("and you will know") – clarifying that the ruler will come to know the veracity of Bar Qamtza's words: "ואת ידע מיד שאיני משקר" ("and you will know immediately that I am not lying"). Had **B** been familiar with the clarifying words "מיד שאיני משקר," it seems unlikely that it would have omitted them. Similarly, **A** inserted the messenger's question – "אמ' ליה ?דההוא שליחא דמלכא: למה לית את מקריב אלין קורבניא" ("The messenger of the king said to him (the priest): Why do you not offer up these offerings?") – in order to explain why the priest suddenly addresses the officer in **B**'s line 25 – "אמר ליה: למחר אנא קריב להון" ("He said to him: Tomorrow I will offer them up").[5] By transforming the priest's unprompted explanation into a response to the messenger's query, **A** improved the flow of the narrative. It is also highly unlikely that **B** would have omitted **A**'s account of the messenger's inquiry had it known it.[6] In

---

3. See Mandel, "Critical Edition," 126–78.

4. On the Aramaic word "מגוס" ("my meal,"), see Sokoloff, *Dictionary of Jewish Palestinian Aramaic*, 315. Furthermore, the wordplay created by "תבסרני" ("shame me") and "מסובי" ("recline") is lost once "תבסרני" is replaced with "תבישני."

5. In addition, the officer's question on the first day, which only appears in A, "למה לית את מקריב אלין קורבניא" ("Why do you not offer up these offerings?"), is apparently a copy of his question from the second day, which does have a counterpart in B.

6. The early Genizah fragment, T-S C 1.69 + T-S AS 78.27, which belongs to branch A, also lacks the messenger's query, suggesting perhaps that the query is a relatively late addition to A. In any event, once the query was introduced, the priest's original statement – "למחר אנא קריב להון" ("Tomorrow I will offer them up," according to A) – was apparently shortened to read "למחר" ("Tomorrow").

order to highlight the series of days in Act II, **A** apparently transformed **B**'s "יומא אחרינא" ("the next day") in line 26 into "יום תניינא" ("the second day"). **A** inserted some words for emphasis such as "כל" ("entire") in line 12's phrase "טימי כל הדין סעודתה" ("the cost of the **entire** banquet"), as well as "הוא" ("he") and "כולן" ("all of them") in line 23's phrase "קם הוא בליליא ועשאן כולן" ("**he** got up in the night and **made all of them**"). **A** also seems to have changed the second appearance of the verb "יהיב" ("pay"), found in **B**'s line 10, into the similarly spelled verb "יתיב" ("sit").[7] In sum, the nature of the differences between the two branches strongly suggest that **B**, in the guise of Oxford 102, has preserved an earlier reading of our story than **A**, in the form of Cambridge 495.

In recent decades, however, scholars have learned of another partial reading of **A**, the Genizah fragment, T-S C 1.69 + T-S AS 78.27 (cited below in full alongside Oxford 102 and Cambridge 495). It is often claimed that this fragment's story of Bar Qamtza is the earliest and most original extant reading of the story.[8] This claim rests on two considerations. First, the Genizah fragment dates to the tenth century, a few centuries prior to the earliest extant complete manuscript of Lamentations Rabbati. Second, while the other readings of the story are *mostly* in Aramaic, the Genizah reading is *almost entirely* in Aramaic.[9] These two considerations, however, are not nearly sufficient to establish the fragment's priority. Early documents do not ipso facto preserve pristine readings of their texts, and the greater degree of Aramaic in the Genizah fragment may simply reflect an attempt to enhance the stylistic

---

7. T-S C 1.69 + T-S AS 78.27, which belongs to **A**, consistently, like **B**, enlists the verb "יהב," suggesting perhaps that "יתיב" is a relatively late addition to **A**. (See also n. 26.) In addition, the other traces of **B** in the Genizah fragment, such as the use of the verbal root ב.ס.ר, perhaps the repetition of the final "הכא" in the host's refusals, and the appearance of the phrase "מן דנפיק" followed shortly by "מה" may all attest to original features of the text which predate **A**.

8. See Paul Mandel, "The Story in Midrash Eichah: Text and Style" ("הספור במדרש איכה: נוסח וסגנון") (MA thesis, Hebrew University, 1983), *107; (2004) 145n22; Yisraeli-Taran, *Legends of the Destruction*, 12, 104n2; (Rubenstein, *Talmudic Stories*, 347n23); Furstenberg, "Qamtza," 108n17; Ben Shahar, "Abolishment of the Sacrifice," 567–68n1; cf. Mandel, "Critical Edition," 89–91; Levine Katz, "Qamtsa" 34n5.

9. See Mandel, "Tales of the Destruction," 148n29.

unity of the story. In my opinion, the *nature* of the differences between the textual witnesses is more telling than their dates or languages. By comparing the Genizah fragment to Oxford 102 and Cambridge 495, I hope to show that while the fragment may capture some original features of the text, it is a free and creative rendition of our story in many ways less faithful to the original text than either Oxford 102 or Cambridge 495.

The Three Readings

T-S C 1.69 + T-S AS 78.27	CAMBRIDGE 495 (+ MUNICH 229) (A)	OXFORD 102 (B)
דב׳ אח׳	ד״א	1 ד״א ״בני ציון היקרים״ (איכה ד:ב):
מה היתה יקרותם?	מה היתה יקרותן?	2 מה היתה יקרותן?
שלא היה אחד מהם הולך לסעודה עד [שהיה נקרא][11] וניׁשנה ... דב׳ אחר: מה היתה יקרות[ם][12] בשעה[ש]היה אחד עושה סעודה היה צר כל מיני סעודה בפת, וכל [כך למה?][13] מפני איסתניסין כדי שלא יהא אחד מהם אוכל דבר שרע לו.	לא היה אחד מהן הולך לסעוד[ה][10] עד שנקרא ונשנה.	3 לא היה אחד מהם הולך לסעודה עד שהיה נקרא ונשנה.
מעשה באדם אחד מגדולי	מעשה באחד[14]	4 מעשה באדם אחד
ירושלים שעשה סעודה	בירושלם שעשה סעודה.	בירושלם שעשה סעודה.

---

10. Cambridge 495 is the sole textual witness which reads here "לסעוד," "to dine," rather than "לסעודה," "to a banquet."

11. See Rabinovitz, *Ginzé Midrash*, 152.

12. See Rabinovitz, *Ginzé Midrash*, 152.

13. See Rabinovitz, *Ginzé Midrash*, 152.

14. All other textual witnesses read here "באדם אחד," "about one man."

T-S C 1.69 + T-S AS 78.27	CAMBRIDGE 495 (+ MUNICH 229) (A)	OXFORD 102 (B)
והיזמין את [הכל].		
אמ'[16] לטלייה: [זיל][17] ואייתי לי בר כמצא רחמי; אזל ואייתי ליה בר כמצורא סנא[יה].[18]	אמ' לשלוחו:[15] לך והבא לי לבר קמצא רחמי; אזל ואייתי בן קמצא שנאיה.	5 אמר לשלוחו: לך והבא לי בן קמצא רחמי; אזל ואייתי ליה בר קמצא שנאיה.
[על][19] ואשכחיה דיתיב בין או[ריסטייא].[20]	על וישב בין האורחים, על ואשכחיה ביני ארסיטייא.	6 על וישב בין האורחים, עאל ואשכחיה יני ארסטטיה.
אמ' ליה:	אמ' ליה:	7 אמר ליה:
	את שנאי ואת יתיב בגו ביתי,	[את] שנאי ואת יתיב בגו ביתי,
קום פוק לך מן הכה!	[קום][21] פוק לך מן גוא ביתי!	קום ופוק לך מגו ביתאי!
אמ' לי[ה: לא תפקין] ב[בוסרן].[22] אמ' ליה: לית אפשר דלא נפקת מן הכה.[23]		
אמ' ליה:	אמ' ליה:	8 אמר ליה:
	אל תבישני	לא תבסרני

---

15. Cambridge 495 is in line here with B while Munich 229 and the *editio princeps* read "לבן ביתו," "to his servant/to a member of his household."
16. See Mandel, "Tales of the Destruction," 145.
17. See Rabinovitz, *Ginzé Midrash*, 152.
18. See Rabinovitz, *Ginzé Midrash*, 152.
19. See Mandel, "Tales of the Destruction," 146.
20. See Rabinovitz, *Ginzé Midrash*, 153.
21. Cambridge 495 apparently omitted the word "קום," "Get up," which appears here in all the other textual witnesses.
22. See Mandel, "Tales of the Destruction," 146n24.
23. According to Mandel ("Tales of the Destruction," 146n25), the last two lines – "אמ' ליה לא תפקין בבוסרן אמ' ליה לית אפשר דלא נפקת מן הכה" – erroneously repeat the same lines which follow below.

T-S C 1.69 + T-S AS 78.27	CAMBRIDGE 495 (+ MUNICH 229) (A)	OXFORD 102 (B)
אנה יהב [טימי דסעודה	ואנא יהיב לך טימי דסעוד'.	ואנא יהיב לך טימי מגוסי.
ולא]24 תפקין בבוסרן.		
אמ' ליה: לית אפשר דלא נפקת מן הכא.	אמ' ליה: לית מסובה.25	9 אמר ליה: לית את מסובי הכא.
	אמ' ליה: אל תבישני ואנא יתיב26 לא איכול ולא אשתה.	10 אמר ליה: לא תבסרני ואנא יהיב לך דלא אכיל ולא שתי.
	אמ' ליה: לית את מסובה.	11 אמר ליה לית את מסובי הכא
אמ' ליה: [אנה יהב טי]28מי כל הדין אריצ־טון ולא תפקין בבוסרן. אמ' ליה: לית אפשר דל[א נפקת מן הכא].29 אמ' ליה: אנא יהב בדיפלה ולא תפקין בבוסרן. אמ' ליה: לית אפשר [דלא נפק30]ת מן הכא.	אמ' ליה: אנא [יהיב]27 טימי כל הדין סעודתה. אמ' ליה: קום לך!	12 אמר ליה: אנא יהיב לך טימי הדה סועדתא. 13 אמר ליה: קום פוק ליך!

---

24. See Mandel, "Tales of the Destruction," 146.

25. The final letter of the word "מסובה" ("recline") here and in line 10 seems to be a *resh*. However, the word "מסובר" (with a final *resh*) cannot be right and so I have replaced the *resh* with a *he*.

26. I have omitted the word "לך" ("to you"), which appears here in Oxford 102 but not in Munich 229 or the *editio princeps*, and does not work with the verb "יתיב" ("sit").

27. Cambridge 495 apparently omitted the word "יהיב," "will give," which appears here in all the other textual witnesses (though as "יהב" in T-S C 1.69 + T-S AS 78.27).

28. See Mandel, "Tales of the Destruction," 146.

29. See Rabinovitz, *Ginzé Midrash*, 153.

30. See Rabinovitz, *Ginzé Midrash*, 153.

T-S C 1.69 + T-S AS 78.27	CAMBRIDGE 495 (+ MUNICH 229) (A)	OXFORD 102 (B)
והיה שם ר' זכריה בר אבקליס (שהיה בידו)[33] שהיה ספיק בידו למחות ולא מיחה.	והיה שם ר' זכריה בן אבקולס והיתה ספק בידו למחות ולא מיחה.	14 והיה שם זכריה[31] בן אבקולס והיה ספק בידו למחות ולא מיחה.
מ[ן][34] דנפיק אמ': מה אנה נפק בבוסרן ושביק להון יתבין שליות?	מיד נפק ליה אמ' ליה: בנפשיה אלין מסביין יתבין בשלוותהון?![32]	15 מאן דנפק ליה, אמר בנפשיה: מה אלין מסבין יתבין בשליתהון?!
	מה עבד?	16 מה עשה?
נחת ליה [לגב[35]] מלכה,	הלך אצל השלטון,	17 הלך לו אצל השילטון,
דכל קורבניא דהוון מקרבין מן דכורש מלכא הוון, הדה היא: "ודי להון[36] מהקרביבין ניחוחין לא'י'ל'ה שמיא ומצלן לחיי מלכא ובנוהי" (עזרא ו:י). אזל		
ואמ' ל[יה]: אילין קורבני[37]א דאת משלח להון אינון אכלין להון.	אמ' ליה: אלין קורבניא דאת משלח אינון אכלין להון	18 אמר: אלין קורבניא דאת משלח אינון אכלין יתהון

---

31. Save for Parma 2559, the textual witnesses refer to Zechariah as "Rabbi Zechariah."

32. Since Cambridge 495 along with Munich 229, the *editio princeps*, Casanatense H 3112, and Parma 2559 all enlist the phrase "איכול קורצא," "inform," due to the influence of the Bavli, I have omitted the phrase here.

33. The bracketed words are most probably an error.

34. See Rabinovitz, *Ginzé Midrash*, 153.

35. See Mandel, "Tales of the Destruction," 146; cf. Ben Shahar, "Abolishment of the Sacrifice," 567.

36. See Mandel, "Tales of the Destruction," 146n25.

37. See Mandel, "Tales of the Destruction," 146.

T-S C 1.69 + T-S AS 78.27	CAMBRIDGE 495 (+ MUNICH 229) (A)	OXFORD 102 (B)
	ומקרבין אוחרנין בחילופיהו.	ומקרבין אחרנין בחילופין.
נזף ביה, אמ' ליה: מילא בישא או[מרת, דאת]38 בעי למימר שם ביש עליהון.	נזף ביה;	19 נזף ביה;
	אזל לגבי תוב,	עאל לגביה תוב,
אמ' ליה:	אמ' ליה:	20 אמר ליה:
	כל אלין קורבניא דאת משלח אינון אכלין [להון]39 ומקרבין אוחרנין [בחילופיהו]40	כל אלין קורבניא דאת משלח אינון אכלין להון ומקרבין אחרנין בחלופיהון
	ואם לא תאמין לי	21 ואין לית את מהימן לי, שלח עמי חד אפרכוס וקורבניא עמיה ואת ידע.
שלח עימי קורבניא ו[עימי ברנש מהי]41מן ואת קיים על קושטא. שלח עימיה ברנש מהימן ושלח עימ[יה קורבניא	שלח עמי חד איפרכוס וקרבניא ואת ידע מיד שאיני משקר.42	
	עד דאתין בארחא דמך איפרכוס	22 כי אתי בשבילא עד דאפרכוס דמיך
קם]43 הוא בליליה ויהב בהון מומין דלא מנכרין	קם הוא בליליא ועשאן כולן בעלי מומין בסתר	23 קם בליליא ועשאן בעלי מומין [בסתר]

---

38. See Mandel, "Tales of the Destruction," 147; cf. Ben Shahar, "Abolishment of the Sacrifice," 568.

39. The word "להון," (or "יתהון") "them," appears in all the other relevant textual witnesses and was apparently omitted by Cambridge 495.

40. I have inserted the word "בחילופיהו," "in their stead," according to Munich 229; the *editio princeps*, Oxford 102, and the other relevant textual witnesses also include some variation on this word.

41. See Mandel, "Tales of the Destruction," 147.

42. Munich 229 and the *editio princeps* read here "שקרן," "a liar."

43. See Mandel, "Tales of the Destruction," 147.

T-S C 1.69 + T-S AS 78.27	CAMBRIDGE 495 (+ MUNICH 229) (A)	OXFORD 102 (B)
כיון דחמא יתהון כ[הנא לא קריבינון	כיון שראה אותן הכהן הקריב אחרים תחתיהן	24 כיון שראה הכהן אותן הקריב אחרים תחתיהן
	אמ' ליה ההוא [שליחא][44] דמלכא למה לית את מקריב אלין קורבניא	
אמ' ליה: לית[45] אנה מקריב להון, מחר אנה מקריב להון	אמ' ליה: למחר	25 אמ' ליה: למחר אנא קריב להו
אתא יומא ולא [קריבינון.	[אתא יום תניינא ולא הקריב אמ' ליה: למה לית את מקריב אילין קרבניא אמ' ליה: למחר][46]	26 אתא יומא אחרינא אמר ליה לית את מקריב להון 27 אמר ליה: למחר
אתא יו[47]מא ולא קריבינון מיד	אתא יום תליתא ולא קריבהון	28 אתא יומא תליתאה ולא קריבהון
שלח ואמ' למ[ל]כ[א ההיא מילתא [דאמר][48] לך ההוא [יהודאה][49] קשיט הוא	שלח ואמ' למלכא ההוא מילתא דיהודאה אמ' לך קושטא הוא	29 שלח ואמר למלכא ההיא מילתא דיהודייא קושטא הוא

44. Munich 229 and the *editio princeps* (as well as Casanatense H 3112 and Parma 2559) read here "שליחא," "messenger."

45. See Mandel, "Tales of the Destruction," 147.

46. These bracketed lines cited according to Munich 229 were apparently omitted from Cambridge 495 due to a homoioteleuton.

47. See Mandel, "Tales of the Destruction," 147.

48. See Mandel, "Tales of the Destruction," 147.

49. See Mandel, "Tales of the Destruction," 147.

T-S C 1.69 + T-S AS 78.27	CAMBRIDGE 495 (+ MUNICH 229) (A)	OXFORD 102 (B)
מיד שלה ואחריב היכלה היא דא דבירי|אתא]50 אמרין בין כמצא ובין כמצורא חרב מקדשא	מיד סליק והחריב בית מקדשא הדא דברייתא אמרי בין קמצא ובין בן קמצא חריב בי מקדשא	30 מיד סלק וחרב בי מקדשא 31 הדא היא דבריתא אמרין בין קמצא לבין קמצא חריב בי מקדשא
א׳ ר׳ יוסי בר ר׳ אבון עינות|ונותו]51 שלר׳ זכריה בר אבקליס היא שרפה את ההיכל	אמ״ר יוסי ענותנותו של ר׳ זכריה בן אבקולס שרפה את ההיכל	32 א״ר יוסי ענותנותו של ר׳ זכריה בן אבקולס שרפה את ההיכל
Another teaching:	Another teaching:	1 Another teaching: "The precious children of Zion" (Lam 4:2):
What was their preciousness? That not one of them would attend a banquet until [he was invited] and (then) invited again.	What was their preciousness? Not one of them would attend a banquet until he was invited and (then) invited again.	2 What was their preciousness? 3 Not one of them would attend a banquet until he was invited and (then) invited again.
Another teaching: What was their preciousness? [When] one of them would make a banquet he would wrap up all the courses of the banquet in bread and towards [what end]? Because of the		

---

50. See Mandel, "Tales of the Destruction," 147.
51. See Mandel, "Tales of the Destruction," 147.

T-S C 1.69 + T-S AS 78.27	CAMBRIDGE 495 (+ MUNICH 229) (A)	OXFORD 102 (B)
fastidious ones so that not one of them should eat something distasteful to him.		
A story of one man of the notables of Jerusalem who made a banquet and invited [everyone;	A story of one in Jerusalem who made a banquet.	4 A story of one man in Jerusalem who made a banquet.
He said] to his servant: Go and bring me Bar Kamtza my friend; he (the messenger) went and brought him Bar Kamtzora his enemy.	He said to his messenger: Go and bring me Bar Qamtza my friend; he (the messenger) went and brought him Ben Qamtza his enemy.	5 He said to his messenger: Go and bring me Ben Qamtza my friend; he (the messenger) went and brought him Bar Qamtza his enemy.
He (the host) entered and found him (Bar Kamtzora) sitting among the banqueters.	He (Ben Qamtza) entered and sat among the guests; he (the host) entered and found him (Ben Qamtza) among the banqueters.	6 He (Bar Qamtza) entered and sat among the guests; he (the host) entered and found him (Bar Qamtza) among the banqueters.
He said to him:	He said to him: You are my enemy and (yet) you sit within my home!	7 He said to him: [You] are my enemy and (yet) you sit within my home!
Get up, get yourself out of here!	[Get up,] get yourself out of my home!	Get up and get yourself out of my home!

T-S C 1.69 + T-S AS 78.27	CAMBRIDGE 495 (+ MUNICH 229) (A)	OXFORD 102 (B)
He said to him: Do not make me go out in shame.		
He said to him:	He said to him: Do not embarrass me	8 He said to him: Do not shame me
I will pay you the cost of (my banquet)	And I will pay you the cost of (my) banquet	And I will pay you the cost of my meal.
(just) do not make me go out in shame.		
He said to him: There is no way that you will not get out of here.	He said to him: You are not reclining.	9 He said to him: You are not reclining here.
	He said to him: Do not embarrass me and I will sit without eating or drinking.	10 He said to him: Do not shame me and I will pay you without eating or drinking.
	He said to him; You are not reclining.	11 He said to him: You are not reclining here.
He said to him: I will pay the cost of this banquet and (just) do not make me go out in shame.	He said to him: I will pay the cost of the entire banquet.	12 He said to him: I will pay you the cost of the banquet.
He said to him: There is no way that you will not get out of here.	He said to him: Get yourself up!	13 He said to him: Get up and get yourself out!
He said to him: I will pay double and (just)		

T-S C 1.69 + T-S AS 78.27	CAMBRIDGE 495 (+ MUNICH 229) (A)	OXFORD 102 (B)
do not make me go out in shame. He said to him: There is no way that you will not get out of here.		
Zechariah bar Avqalis was present and he had the opportunity to protest [but did not protest.	Zechariah ben Avqulas was present and he had the opportunity to protest but did not protest.	14 Zechariah ben Avqulas was present and he had the opportunity to protest but did not protest.
When] he (Bar Kamtzora) went out he said: How is that I go out in shame while leaving them sitting at ease?	Immediately he (Ben Qamtza) went out and said to himself: How do they (dare) recline and sit at ease? What did he do? He went to the ruler	15 When he (Bar Qamtza) went out he said to himself: How do they (dare) recline and sit at ease! 16 What did he do? 17 He went to the ruler
He went down [to] the king, since all the offerings which they offered up were Cyrus the king's, as it (is written): [so that they] may offer pleasing sacrifices to the God of Heaven and pray for the life of the king and his sons (Ezek 6:10). He went		

T-S C 1.69 + T-S AS 78.27	CAMBRIDGE 495 (+ MUNICH 229) (A)	OXFORD 102 (B)
and said to [him: These offerings] that you send, they eat them.	He said to him: These offerings that you send, they eat them	18 (and) said: Those offerings that you send, they eat them
	and offer up (inferior) others in their stead.	and offer up (inferior) others in their stead.
He reprimanded him.	He reprimanded him.	19 He reprimanded him.
He said to him: You have said something bad because you wish to give them a bad name.		
	(Nonetheless), he (Ben Qamtza) came to him (the ruler) again.	(Nonetheless,) he (Bar Qamtza) came to him (the ruler) again.
He said to him:	He said to him:	20 He said to him:
	All those offerings that you send, they eat them and offer up others in their stead	All those offerings that you send, they eat them and offer up others in their stead
	and if you do not	
Send with me offerings and send [with me a trustworthy man] and you will establish the truth.	believe me, send with me an officer and offerings and you will know	21 and if you do not believe me, send with me an officer and offerings and you will know.
	immediately that I am not lying.	

T-S C 1.69 + T-S AS 78.27	CAMBRIDGE 495 (+ MUNICH 229) (A)	OXFORD 102 (B)
He sent with him a trustworthy man and sent with [him offerings.		
	While they were traveling on the road, the officer fell asleep.	22 While they were traveling on the path, the officer fell asleep.
He (Bar Kamtzora) got up] in the night and inflicted upon them undiscernible blemishes. When the [priest] saw them, [he did not offer them up.	He (Ben Qamtza) got up in the night and secretly made all of them [the animals] blemished. When the priest saw them, he offered up others in their place.	23 He (Bar Qamtza) got up in the night and [secretly] made them (the animals) blemished. 24 When the priest saw them, he offered up others in their place.
	The messenger of the king said to him (the priest): Why do you not offer up these offerings?	
He said to him: I am not] offering them up (today), tomorrow I will offer them up.	He said to him: Tomorrow.	25 He (the priest) said to him (the officer): Tomorrow I will offer them up.
The (next) day came, and he did not [offer them up.	[The second day came and he did not offer up. He said to him: Why do you not offer up these sacrifices? He said to him: Tomorrow.]	26 The next day came and he (the officer) said to him (the priest): You are not offering them up. 27 He said to him: Tomorrow.

T-S C 1.69 + T-S AS 78.27	CAMBRIDGE 495 (+ MUNICH 229) (A)	OXFORD 102 (B)
The (next) day came] and he did not offer them up. Immediately	The third day came and he did not offer them up.	28 The third day came and he did not offer them up.
He (the officer) sent (a message) to the king saying: The statement which that Jew told you is true! Immediately he sent (an army) and destroyed the sanctuary,	He (the officer) sent (a message) to the king saying: The statement which the Jew told you is true! Immediately he rose up and destroyed the temple	29 He (the officer) sent (a message) to the king saying: The statement of the Jew is true! 30 Immediately he rose up and destroyed the temple
hence people say: Between Katmsa and Kamtzora the temple was destroyed.	hence people say: Between Qamtza and Ben Qamtza the temple was destroyed.	31 hence people say: Between Qamtza and Qamtza the temple was destroyed.
Rabbi Yose bar Rabbi Abun said: The meekness of Rabbi Zechariah bar Avqalis is what burnt down the sanctuary.	Rabbi Yose said: The meekness of Rabbi Zechariah ben Avqulas burnt down the sanctuary.	32 Rabbi Yose said: The meekness of Rabbi Zechariah ben Avqulas burnt down the sanctuary.

Oxford 102 versus the Genizah Fragment

If the Genizah fragment has preserved the earliest reading of our story – a reading which might even have served as the ultimate source for Oxford 102 and Cambridge 495 – a comparison of the variants should reveal how the story evolved over time. In this vein, consider the three different descriptions of the second and third days during which the Roman offerings were not sacrificed:

T-S C 1.69 + T-S AS 78.27	CAMBRIDGE 495 (+ MUNICH 229)	OXFORD 102
אתא יומא ולא [קריבינון;	[אתא יום **תנינא** ולא הקריב.	26 אתא יומא **אחרינא**,
	אמ' ליה: למה לית את מקריב אילין קרבניא? אמ' ליה למחר.[52]	אמר ליה: לית את מקריב להון?
		27 אמר ליה למחר.
אתא יו[ן][53]מא ולא קריבינון.	אתא יום **תליתא** ולא קריבהון.	28 אתא יומא **תליתאה** ולא קריבהון,
The (**next**) day came and he did not [offer them up.	The **second** day came and he did not offer up.	26 The **next** day came;
	He (the officer) said to him (the priest): Why do you not offer up these offerings? He said to him: Tomorrow.	he (the officer) said to him (the priest): You are not offering them up. 27 He said to him: Tomorrow.
The (**next**) day came and he did not offer them up.	The **third** day came and he did not offer them up.	28 The **third** day came and he did not offer them up.

In this case, the Genizah fragment may have indeed preserved a brief and early reading of this literary segment which was subsequently fleshed out in both **A** and **B**. Whereas the fragment does not bother to differentiate between the two days under discussion, **A** and **B** specifically identify each day in the series as the "next"/"second" day or the "third" day. In a similar vein, while the fragment bears no whiff of a second day conversation, both **A** and **B** present the second day's conversation between the priest and officer. In sum, it is quite possible that the

---

52. These bracketed lines cited according to Munich 229 were apparently omitted from Cambridge 495 due to a homoioteleuton.
53. See Mandel, "Tales of the Destruction," 147.

original textual account of the second and third days looked more like the Genizah fragment than did either Oxford 102 or Cambridge 495 (+ Munich 229).

However, most of the variants between the Genizah fragment and the other two readings are not like this segment and indicate that the fragment has not preserved an early and pristine reading of the story. First and most strikingly, the Genizah fragment has carefully integrated into the story terms and ideas drawn from elsewhere. For example, consider the story's opening:

T-S C 1.69 + T-S AS 78.27	CAMBRIDGE 495	OXFORD 102
מעשה באדם אחד מגדולי	מעשה באחד	4 מעשה באדם אחד
ירושלים שעשה סעודה	בירושלם שעשה סעודה	בירושלם שעשה סעודה;
והיזמין את]הכל;		
אמ׳[לטלייה:]זיל[	אמ׳ לשלוחו: לך והבא	5 אמר לשלוחו: לך
ואייתי לי בר כמצא רחמי.	לי לבר קמצא רחמי.	והבא לי בן קמצא רחמי.

A story of one man of the notables of	A story of one	4 A story of one man
Jerusalem who made a banquet	in Jerusalem who made a banquet.	in Jerusalem who made a banquet.
and invited [everyone;		
He said] to his servant: Go and bring me Bar Kamtza my friend.	He said to his messenger: Go and bring me Bar Qamtza my friend.	5 He said to his messenger: Go and bring me Ben Qamtza my friend.

In both Oxford 102 and Cambridge 495 the host is simply called a man of Jerusalem, while the Genizah fragment refers to him as one of the "notables of Jerusalem, "מגדולי ירושלים."[54] In addition, whereas the

----

54. See Levine Katz, "Qamtsa" 37.

host commands his "messenger," "שלוחו," in Hebrew ("לך והבא לי," "Go and bring me") in both Oxford 102 and Cambridge 495, in the Genizah fragment he orders his "servant," "טלייה," in Aramaic ("זיל ואייתי לי," "Go and bring me"). These two distinctive features of the fragment do not appear to be early features of the story since the very same additions, according to other textual witnesses, appear in the opening of a nearby tale:

LAM. RAB. 4:5 (P. 144) ACCORDING TO MUNICH 229:	LAM. RAB. 4:5 (P. 144) ACCORDING TO OXFORD 102:
מעשה באחד מגדולי ירושלים דאמ' לטליא זיל ואייתי לי מיא ...	מעשה באדם אחד שאמר לבן ביתו לך והבא לי מים ...
A story of **one of the notables of Jerusalem** who said to his **servant**: Go and bring me water...	A story of one man who said to his servant (or member of his household): Go and bring me water...

Whereas the Genizah fragment's "notables of Jerusalem" and Aramaic formulations appear within a nearby tale according to Munich 229, they do not appear in Oxford 102. Their consistent absence from Oxford 102 suggests that they are late additions to Lamentations Rabbati.

The phrase "והזמין את הכל," "and invited everyone," in the fragment's opening does not appear in any other textual witness and, at first glance, because the host had no intention of actually inviting "everyone," it seems out of place. However, the very same phrase appears, with just a slight variation, earlier on in Lamentations Rabbati:

א"ר יודן: לעבדו של מלך שעשה סעודה והזמין את כל בני בנאותיו ולא הזמין רבו.

Rabbi Yudan said: (A parable) to the servant of a king who made a banquet and **invited all** the children of his friends but did not invite his master.[55]

---

55. Lam. Rab. Petiḥta 10 (p. 9) according to Munich 229. (See Chapter 5, n. 11 above.) The phrase "והזמין (את) הכל," "and he invited everyone," also appears in Midr. Mish. 16 (p. 131). See also Mandel, "Tales of the Destruction," 145–46n23.

Since Lamentations Rabbati had already enlisted the term "invited all" ("והזמין את כל") in order to highlight the exclusion of a single individual from a banquet, the Genizah fragment apparently inserted the very same phrase into our story in order to emphasize that, just like the servant's master, Bar Kamtzora alone was to be excluded from the banquet. As often happens in the editing, re-editing, and transmission of rabbinic stories, literary material from the local context was woven in.

Second, the Genizah fragment includes explanations and expansions missing from every other textual witness. For example, the fragment apparently transformed **B**'s unfamiliar "לא תבסרני," "Do not shame me," (in lines 8 and 10) into the simpler: "לא תפקין בבוסרן," "Do not make me go out in shame." It inserted a long gloss right after line 17, which enlists Ezekiel 6:10, in order to explain the sacrificial practice presumed by all the other textual witnesses.[56] It elucidated the king's reprimand in line 19 ("נזף ביה," "He reprimanded him") by revealing what the king actually said to Bar Kamtzora. The fragment explicitly states that the king sent Bar Kamtzora with offerings and a trustworthy man (right after line 21), while all the other textual witnesses merely imply as much. In line 23, the word "secretly" in both **A** and **B** explains why Bar Qamtza blemished the animals in the dead of night, but the Genizah fragment interprets it to mean that Bar Kamtzora inflicted unnoticeable blemishes.[57] In line 32

---

56. See Mandel, "Tales of the Destruction," 146n25.

57. In this case, the Genizah fragment seems to represent a transitional stage on the trajectory from Lamentations Rabbati to the Bavli. Whereas the earlier reading of our story in Lamentations Rabbati apparently stated that Bar Qamtza "secretly" blemished the animals during the night, the fragment interpreted the word "secretly" vis-à-vis the blemishes themselves. Developing further the link between the blemishes and "secretly," the Bavli states that Bar Qamtza inflicted minimal flaws which, for all intents and purposes, were invisible to the Romans.

It bears mentioning that the fragment shares some additional similarities with the Bavli's version of the story. Unlike the distinct clauses of line 6 in A and B, "He (Bar Qamtza) entered and sat among the guests; he (the host) entered and found him (Bar Qamtza) among the banqueters," ("על וישב בין האורחים עאל" "ואשכחיה ביני ארסטטיה"), the integrated sentence of the Genizah fragment "He (the host) entered and found him (Bar Kamtzora) sitting among the banqueters" ("על ואשכחיה דיתיב בין אריסטייא"), parallels the Bavli's counterpart sentence. In both the fragment and the Bavli, Bar Kamtzora/Qamtza doubles his offer and the fragment identifies Rabbi Yose as the Amora Rabbi Yose bar Rabbi Abun, but the parallel statement in the Tosefta reveals that the Tanna Rabbi Yose bar Halafta was intended.[58] These sorts of clarifications and interpolations, all of which postdate the emergence of the original tradition reflected in **A** and **B**, give a sense of the freedom with which the fragment's reading of the Bar Qamtza story was rewritten.

Third, the story's literary context in both **A** and **B** is far more natural than its literary context in the Genizah fragment. The context in both **A** and **B**, which records a Jerusalem practice regarding banquet *invitations*, is the perfect setting for a story about an *invitation* to a Jerusalem banquet gone wrong. By contrast, the Genizah fragment's discussion of the fastidious banqueters offers a poor segue into our story. The relatively poor location of our story in the Genizah fragment, in tandem with the differences noted above, highlight the measure of rewriting our story underwent in the fragment.[59]

Fourth, the name Kamtzora, which is paralleled nowhere else, apparently reflects a novel attempt to differentiate between the two Qamtzas, akin to the Bavli's distinction between Qamtza and Bar Qamtza.[60] Hoping to clarify the story by differentiating between the intended guest and the mistakenly invited one, the fragment transformed Bar Qamtza into Bar Kamtzora.

In sum, the Genizah fragment is not a more faithful rendition of the original reading of our story than either **A** or **B**. Though, at times, comparing the fragment to **A** and **B** (or the Bavli) may reveal hints of an earlier reading of the story, the fragment itself has preserved a freely revised rendition of our story – an edited, expanded, and glossed story which incorporated literary elements from elsewhere in Lamentations

---

in neither version does Bar Kamtzora/Qamtza claim that the Jews replaced the Roman animals with inferior ones. These similarities between the Bavli and the Genizah fragment, which are not shared by **A** or **B**, likely refract features of a common tradition.

58. See Mandel, "Tales of the Destruction," 147n27. See also Chapter 7, n. 25 above.

59. Cf. Ben Shahar, "Abolishment of the Sacrifice," 567n1.

60. See Chapters 5 and 16 above. On the Bavli's distinction between Qamtza and Bar Qamtza, cf. the similar distinction (on b. Ḥul. 49b) between the fats called Himtza and Bar Himtza.

Rabbati. Hence, in contrast to much recent scholarship, I opted to focus on Oxford 102 of branch **B**, the preferred branch, rather than on the Genizah fragment.

Bibliography

Ancient Sources

Arnott, W. Geoffrey. *Alexis: The Fragments: A Commentary.* Cambridge: Cambridge University Press, 1996.

Athenaeus. *The Learned Banqueters: Books 1–111.106e.* Edited and translated by S. Douglas Olson. LCL. Cambridge, MA: Harvard University Press, 2006.

Avoth de-Rabbi Nathan Solomon Schechter Edition. Edited by Solomon Schechter. 1886–1887. Repr., New York, NY: The Jewish Theological Seminary of America, 1997.

Barclay, John M.G. *Flavius Josephus: Translation and Commentary: Against Apion.* Leiden: Brill, 2007.

Cicero. *On Old Age, On Friendship, On Divination.* Translated by William Armistead Falconer. LCL. Cambridge, MA: Harvard University Press, 1923.

Clement of Alexandria. *Clementis Alexandrini Paedagogus.* Edited by M. Marcovich and J.C.M. Van Winden. Leiden: Brill, 2002.

Cohen, A., trans. *Midrash Rabbah: Lamentations.* London: Soncino, 1977.

Colluthus. *Oppian, Colluthus, Tryphiodorus.* Translated by A.W. Mair. LCL. Cambridge, MA, 1928.

Danby, Herbert, trans. *The Mishnah.* Oxford: Oxford University Press, 1933.

Dio Chrysostom. *Discourses 12–30.* Translated by J.W. Cohoon. LCL. Cambridge, MA: Harvard University Press, 1939.

Faksimile Ausgabe des Mischnacodex Kaufmann A 50. 1929. Repr., Jerusalem: s.n., 5728 (1967–1968).

Florus. *Epitome of Roman History*. Translated by Edward Seymour Forster. LCL. Cambridge, MA: Harvard University Press, 1984.

Freedman, H., trans. *Shabbath*. London: Soncino, 1972.

Hippolytus (Hippolyte de Rome). *La Tradition Apostolique*. Edited and translated by Bernard Botte. 2nd ed. Paris: Les Éditions du Cerf, 1984.

Homer. *Iliad: Books 1–12*. Translated by A.T. Murray and William F. Wyatt. LCL. Cambridge, MA: Harvard University Press, 1999.

——— *Odyssey: Books 13–24*. Translated by A.T. Murray and George E. Dimock. LCL. Cambridge, MA: Harvard University Press, 2004.

Horace. *Satires, Epistles, Ars Poetica*. Translated by H. Rushton Fairclough. LCL. Cambridge, MA: Harvard University Press, 1929.

Israelstam, J. and Slotki, Judah H., trans. *Midrash Rabbah: Leviticus*. London: Soncino, 1939.

Josephus. *Flavii Iosephi Opera*. Edited by Benedictus Niese. 6 vols. Berlin: Weidmann, 1955.

——— *Jewish Antiquities, Books XII–XIII*. Translated by Ralph Marcus. LCL. Cambridge, MA: Harvard University Press, 1943.

——— *Life, Against Apion*. Translated by Henry St. J. Thackeray. LCL. Cambridge, MA: William Heinemann and Harvard University Press, 1926.

——— *The Jewish War*. Translated by Henry St. J. Thackeray. 2 vols. LCL. Cambridge, MA: William Heinemann and Harvard University Press, 1927–1928.

JPS Hebrew-English Tanakh. Philadelphia, PA: Jewish Publication Society, 1999.

Jung, Leo, trans. *The Babylonian Talmud: Yoma*. London: Soncino, 1938.

Juvenal and Persius. Translated by Susanna Morton Braund. LCL. Cambridge, MA: Harvard University Press, 2004.

Kiperwasser, Reuven. "Addenda: Kohelet Zuta Synopsis" ("סינופסיס נוסחאות של קהלת זוטא"). In "Midrashim on Kohelet: Studies in their Redaction and Formation." 1–80. PhD diss., Bar-Ilan University, 2005.

Krupp, Michael. *Midrash Echa according to the Yemenite Manuscripts with Variants and Introduction*. Jerusalem: Lee Achim Sefarim, 2019.

Livy. Translated by J.C. Yardley. Vol. 11. LCL. Cambridge, MA: Harvard University Press, 2018.

Lucan. *The Civil War*. Translated by J.D. Duff. LCL. Cambridge, MA: Harvard University Press, 1928.

Lucian. Translated by A.M. Harmon. Vol. 1, LCL. Cambridge, MA: Harvard University Press, 1913.

———— Translated by A.M. Harmon. Vol. 3, LCL. Cambridge, MA: Harvard University Press, 1921.

———— Translated by M.D. Macleod. Vol. 7, LCL. Cambridge, MA: Harvard University Press and William Heinemann, 1969.

Luz, Ulrich. *Matthew 21–28: A Commentary*. Minneapolis, MN: Augsburg Fortress, 2005.

Ma'agarim. The Historical Dictionary Project. The Academy of the Hebrew Language. https://maagarim.hebrew-academy.org.il/Pages/PMain.aspx.

Macrobius. *Saturnalia: Books 1–2*. Translated by Robert A. Kaster. LCL. Cambridge, MA: Harvard University Press, 2011.

Martial. *Epigrams*. Translated by D.R. Shackleton Bailey. Vols. 1–2, LCL. Cambridge, MA: Harvard University Press, 1993.

Mason, Steven. *Flavius Josephus: Translation and Commentary: Volume 9: Life of Josephus*. Leiden: Brill, 2001.

———— *Flavius Josephus: Translation and Commentary: Volume 1B: Judean War 2*. Leiden: Brill, 2008.

Mekhilta de-Rabbi Ishmael. Edited by H.S. Horovitz and I.A. Rabin. 1931. Repr., Jerusalem: Shalem, 1997.

Midrash Eikhah Rabbah. Edited by Salomon Buber. Vilna: Romm, 5659 (1898–1899).

Midrash Mishle. Edited by Burton L. Visotzky. New York, NY: The Jewish Theological Seminary of America, 2002.

Midrash Kohelet Rabbah 1–6. Edited by Marc Hirshman. Jerusalem: The Midrash Project of the Schechter Institute of Jewish Studies, 2016.

Midrash Rabbah. Vilna: Romm, 5638 (1877–1878).

Midrash Wayyikra Rabbah. Edited by M. Margulies. 1953–1960. Repr., New York, NY: Maxwell Abbell Publication Fund and The Jewish Theological Seminary of America, 1993.

Mishcon, A. and Cohen, A., trans. *The Babylonian Talmud: 'Abodah Zarah*. London: Soncino, 1935.

Neusner, Jacob, trans. *The Tosefta: Moed*. New York, NY: Ktav, 1981.

Pesiqta Rabbati. Edited by Rivka Ulmer. Vol. 2. Lanham, MD: University Press of America, 2009.

Petronius. *Satyricon.* Translated by Michael Heseltine and E.H. Warmington. LCL. Cambridge, MA: Harvard University Press, 1987.

Philo. Translated by F.H. Colson. Vols. 9–10. LCL. Cambridge, MA: Harvard University Press and William Heinemann, 1941–1971.

Plato. *Lysis. Symposium. Gorgias.* Translated by W.R.M. Lamb. LCL. Cambridge, MA: Harvard University Press, 1925.

——— *Republic: Books 6–10.* Edited and translated by Chris Emlyn-Jones and William Preddy. LCL. Cambridge, MA: Harvard University Press. 2013.

Plautus. Edited and translated by Wolfgang de Melo. Vols. 1–3. LCL. Cambridge, MA: Harvard University Press, 2011.

Pliny. *Natural History: Volume IV: Books 12–16.* Translated by H. Rackham. LCL. Cambridge, MA: Harvard University Press, 1968.

Pliny the Younger. *Letters: Books 1–7, Panegyricus.* Translated by Betty Radice. LCL. Cambridge, MA: Harvard University Press, 1969.

Plisch, Uwe-Karsten. *The Gospel of Thomas: Original Text with Commentary.* Stuttgart: Deutsche Bibelgesellschaft, 2008.

Plutarch. *Lives.* Translated by Bernadotte Perrin. Vols. 2, 6, and 8. LCL. Cambridge, MA: Harvard University Press and William Heinemann, 1914–1919.

——— *Moralia, Volume II: How to Profit by One's Enemies. On Having Many Friends. Chance. Virtue and Vice. Letter of Condolence to Apollonius. Advice About Keeping Well. Advice to Bride and Groom. The Dinner of the Seven Wise Men. Superstition.* Translated by Frank Cole Babbitt. LCL. Cambridge, MA: Harvard University Press and Willlium Heinemann, 1928.

——— *Moralia: Volume VIII: Table-Talk, Books 1–6.* Translated by Paul A. Clement and Herbert B. Hoffleit. LCL. Cambridge, MA: Harvard University Press, 1969.

——— *Moralia: Volume IX: Table-Talk, Books 7–9, Dialogue on Love.* Translated by Edwin L. Minar, F.H. Sandbach and W.C. Helmbold. LCL. Cambridge, MA: Harvard University Press and William Heinemann, 1961.

Polybius. *The Histories: Books 5–8.* Translated by W.R. Paton, Frank W.

Walbank, and Christian Habict. LCL. Cambridge, MA: Harvard University Press, 2011.

Porush, Hillel. *The Babylonian Talmud with Variant Readings: Gittin* (מסכת גיטין עם שינויי נוסחאות). 4 vols. Jerusalem: Yad Harav Herzog and The Institute for the Complete Israeli Talmud, 1999–2013.

Rabinovitz, Zvi Meir. *Ginzé Midrash: The Oldest Forms of Rabbinic Midrashim according to Geniza Manuscripts* (גנזי מדרש: לצורתם הקדומה של מדרשי חז"ל לפי כתבי יד מן הגניזה). Tel Aviv: The Chaim Rosenberg School for Jewish Studies, Tel Aviv University, 1976.

Sallust. *The War with Cataline, The War with Jugurtha.* Translated by J.C. Rolfe and John T. Ramsey. LCL. Cambridge, MA: Harvard University Press, 2013.

Sefer Ben-Sira Ha-shalem. Edited by Moshe Zvi Segal. Jerusalem: Bialik Institute, 1972.

Seneca. *Ad Lucilium Epistulae Morales.* Translated by Richard M. Gummere. Vol. 1, LCL. Cambridge, MA: Harvard University and William Heinemann, 1979.

Seneca the Elder. *Controversiae Books 7–10, Suasoriae.* Translated by M. Winterbottom. Cambridge, MA: Harvard University Press and William Heinemann, 1974.

Sifre on Deuteronomy. Edited by Louis Finkelstein. 1939. Repr., New York, NY: The Jewish Theological Seminary of America, 1993.

Simon, Maurice, trans. *The Babylonian Talmud: Tamid.* London: Soncino, 1948.

Song of Songs Rabbah. Edited by Shimshon Donsky. Jerusalem: Dvir, 1980.

Talmud Bavli. Vilna: Romm, 1880–1886.

Talmud Yerushalmi According to Ms. Or. 4720 (Scal. 3) of the Leiden University Library with Restorations and Corrections. Edited and introduced by Yaacov Sussmann. Jerusalem: The Academy of the Hebrew Language, 2001.

The Dead Sea Scrolls: The Hebrew Writings: Volume 1. Edited by Elisha Qimron. Jerusalem: Yad Ben-Zvi, 2010.

The Greek New Testament. Edited by Kurt Aland, Matthew Black, Carlo M. Martini, Bruce M. Metzger, and Allen Wikgren. Stuttgart: United Bible Societies, 1966.

The Friedberg Jewish Manuscript Society. https://fjms.genizah.org /index.html?lang=eng&UIT=.

The New Oxford Annotated Bible: New Revised Standard Version with the Apocrypha: An Ecumenical Study Bible. Edited by Michael D. Coogan. Oxford: Oxford University Press, 2018.

The Sol and Evelyn Henkind Talmud Text Databank, The Saul Lieberman Institute of Talmud Research of The Jewish Theological Seminary of America. www.lieberman-institute.com.

The Tosefta According to Codex Vienna, with Variants from Codex Erfurt, Genizah Mss. and Editio Princeps (Venice 1521), Zera'im – Nezikin. Edited by Saul Lieberman. New York, NY: The Jewish Theological Seminary of America, 1955–1988; *Tosephta Based on the Erfurt and Vienna Codices.* Edited by M.S. Zuckermandel. Pozevolk: Yissakhar Yitzhak Meir, 5641 (1880–1881).

The Treatises Derek Erez: Masseket Derek Erez, Pirke Ben Azzai, Tosefta Derek Erez. Edited and translated by Michael Higger. New York, NY: "Debe Rabanan," 1935.

Torat Hatannaim. Bar-Ilan University. https://www2.biu.ac.il/JS /tannaim/.

Velleius Paterculus. *Compendium of Roman History.* Translated by Frederick W. Shipley. LCL. Cambridge, MA: Harvard University Press, 1924.

Vitruvius. *On Architecture: Books 6–10.* Translated by Frank Granger. LCL. Cambridge, MA: Harvard University Press, 1931.

Wright, Benjamin G. "Wisdom of Iesous son of Sirach." In *A New English Translation of the Septuagint.* Edited by Albert Pietersam and Benjamin G. Wright, 715–62. New York, NY: Oxford University Press, 2007.

Xenophon. *Memorabilia, Oeconomicus, Symposium, Apology.* Translated by O.J. Todd and Jeffrey Henderson. LCL. Cambridge, MA: Harvard University Press, 2013.

Medieval and Modern Sources

Alon, Gedaliahu. *Studies in Jewish History in the times of the Second Temple, the Mishna and the Talmud* (מחקרים בתולדות ישראל בימי בית שני

ובתקופת המשנה והתלמוד). 2 vols. Tel Aviv: Hakibutz Hameuchad, 1957–1958.

Alter, Yehudah Aryeh Leib. *Sefat Emet: Pesahim* (שפת אמת: פסחים). New York, NY: Mordecai Judah Lubert and Mendel Eiger, 1954–1955.

Altschuler, David and Altschuler, Yechiel Hillel. *Metzudat David* (מצודת דוד). In *Miqra'ot Gedolot Hama'or: Isaiah*. Vol. 2. Jerusalem: Hamaor, 2001.

Amit, Aaron. "The Two Textual Traditions of *Bavli Berakhot* Chapter 11" (שני ענפי הנוסח של פרק 'היה קורא' בבבלי ברכות ותרומתם להבנת תולדות העריכה של הבבלי"). In *Torah Lishma: Essays in Jewish Studies in Honor of Professor Shamma Friedman*. Edited by David Golinken, Moshe Benovitz, Mordechai Akiva Friedman, Menahem Schemlzer, and Daniel Sperber, 223–67. Jerusalem: Bar Ilan University Press, The Jewish Theological Seminary of America, and Schechter Institute of Jewish Studies, 2007.

Ascough, Richard S. "Social and Political Characteristics of Greco-Roman Association Meals." In *Meals in the Early Christian World: Social Formation, Experimentation, and Conflict at the Table*. Edited by Dennis E. Smith and Hal E. Taussig, 59–72. New York, NY: Palgrave Macmillan, 2012.

Azulai, Chaim Yosef David. *Sefer Petah Einayim* (ספר פתח עינים). Livorno: bedefus Eliezer Sa'adon, 1789–1790.

Baer, Yitzhak. "Jerusalem in the Times of the Great Revolt (Based on the source criticism of Josephus and Talmudic-Midrashic Legends of the Temple's Destruction)" ("ירושלים בימי המרד הגדול (על יסוד ביקורת המקורות של יוספוס ואגדות החורבן"). *Zion* 36 (1971): 127–90.

Bakhos, Carol and Shayegan, M. Rahim, eds. *The Talmud in its Iranian Context*. Tübingen: Mohr Siebeck, 2010.

Balberg, Mira. "Imperial Gifts between Romans and Rabbis." *Jews and Empires: Frankel Institute Annual* (2015): 39–41.

Bar-Asher Siegal, Michal. *Early Monastic Literature and the Babylonian Talmud*. Cambridge: Cambridge University Press, 2013.

Barer, Deborah Adèle. "A Judge With No Courtroom: Law, Ethics and the Rabbinic Idea of *Lifnim Mi-Shurat Ha-Din*." PhD diss., University of Virginia, 2016.

———— "Law, Ethics, and Hermeneutics: A Literary Approach to *Lifnim Mi-shurat Ha-din*." *JTR* 10 (2018): 1–14.

Baumgarten, Albert I. "Rabbinic Literature as a Source for the History of Jewish Sectarianism in the Second Temple Period." *DSD* 2 (1995): 14–57.

———— "Sages Increase Peace in the World: Reconciliation and Power." In *The Faces of Torah: Studies in the Texts and Contexts of Ancient Judaism in Honor of Steven Fraade*. Edited by Michal Bar-Asher Siegal, Tzvi Novick, and Christine Hayes, 221–38. Göttingen: Vandenhoeck & Ruprecht, 2017.

Ben Shahar, Meir "The Abolishment of the Sacrifice on Behalf of the Emperor" ("ביטול הקרבן לשלום הקיסר"). In *Josephus and the Rabbis*. Edited by Tal Ilan and Vered Noam, 566–96. Jerusalem: Yad Ben-Zvi, 2017.

———— "The High Priest and Alexander the Great" ("הכוהן הגדול ואלכסנדר מוקדון"). In *Josephus and the Rabbis*, Edited by Tal Ilan and Vered Noam, 91–144. Jerusalem: Yad Ben-Zvi, 2017.

Ben-Shalom, Israel. *The School of Shammai and the Zealots' Struggle Against Rome* (בית שמאי ומאבק הקנאים נגד רומי). Jerusalem: Yad Ben-Zvi and Ben-Gurion University of the Negev Press, 1993.

Benovitz, Moshe. "'It was taught bish 'at herum': The First Act of the Emperor Pertinax (193 CE) and its Impact on Tannaitic Halakha" ("בשעת חירום שנו': המעשה הראשון של הקיסר פרטינקס (193 לספירה) ועקבותיו בהלכה התנאית"). *Sidra* 19 (2004): 7–23.

Bernett, Minika. *Der Kaiserkult in Judäa unter den Herodiern und Römern*. Tübingen: Mohr Siebeck, 2007.

Bialik, Ch. N. and Ravnitzky, Y. Ch. *Sefer Haʾaggada* (ספר האגדה). Edited with a new commentary by Avidgor Shinan. Jerusalem: Avi Chai, Kinneret, Zmora-Bitan, and Dvir, 2015.

Bilde, Per. "The Causes of the Jewish War according to Josephus." *JSJ* 10 (1979): 179–202.

Bokser, Baruch M. *The Origins of the Seder: The Passover Rite and Early Rabbinic Judaism*. Berkeley: University of California Press, 1984.

Boyarin, Daniel. *Socrates and the Fat Rabbis*. Chicago, IL: University of Chicago Press, 2009.

Bradley, Keith. "The Roman Family at Dinner." In *Meals in a Social Con-*

text: *Aspects of the Communal Meal in the Hellenistic and Roman World*. Edited by Inge Nielsen and Hanne Sigismund Nielsen, 36–55. Langelandsgade: Aarhus University Press, 1998.

Brock, Timothy C., Strange, Jeffrey J., and Green, Melanie C., eds. *Narrative Impact: Social and Cognitive Foundations*. Mahwah, NJ: Lawrence Erlbaum Associates, 2002.

Brock, Timothy C., Strange, Jeffrey J., and Green, Melanie C. "Power Beyond Reckoning: An Introduction to Narrative Impact." In *Narrative Impact: Social and Cognitive Foundations*. Edited by Melanie C. Green, Jeffrey J. Strange, and Timothy C. Brock, 1–15. Mahwah, NJ: Lawrence Erlbaum Associates, 2002.

Brody, Robert. "'Rabbinic' and 'Nonrabbinic' Jews in Mishnah and Tosefta." In *The Faces of Torah: Studies in the Texts and Contexts of Ancient Judaism in Honor of Steven Fraade*. Edited by Michal Bar-Asher Siegal, Tzvi Novick, and Christine Hayes, 275–91. Göttingen: Vandenhoeck & Ruprecht, 2017.

Brumberg-Kraus, Jonathan. "Meals as Midrash: A Survey of Ancient Meals in Jewish Studies Scholarship." In *Food and Judaism*. Edited by Leonard J. Greenspoon, Ronald A. Simkins, and Gerald Shapiro, 297–317. Omaha: University of Nebraska Press, 2005.

Brumberg-Kraus, Jonathan, Marks, Susan, and Rosenblum, Jordan D. "Ten Theses Concerning Meals and Early Judaism." In *Meals in Early Judaism: Social Formation at the Table*. Edited by Susan Marks and Hal E. Taussig, 13–39. New York, NY: Palgrave Macmillan, 2014.

Burke, Peter. *History and Social Theory*. 2nd edition. Ithaca, NY: Cornell University Press, 2004.

Calderon, Ruth. *A Talmudic Alfa Beta: Private Collection* (‎־אלפא ביתא תל‎ ‎מודי: אוסף פרטי‎). Tel Aviv: Miskal – Yedioth Ahronoth and Chemed, 2014.

Carroll, Lewis. *Alice's Adventures in Wonderland*. London: Walker Books, 1999.

Clark, Elizabeth A. *History, Theory, Text: Historians and the Linguistic Turn*. Cambridge, MA: Harvard University Press, 2004.

Clayton, Jay and Rothstein, Eric. "Figures in the Corpus: Theories of Influence and Intertextuality." In *Influence and Intertextuality in Lit-*

erary History. Edited by Jay Clayton and Eric Rothstein, 3–37. Madison: The University of Wisconsin Press, 1991.

Cohen, Shaye J.D. *Josephus in Galilee and Rome: His Vita and Development as a Historian.* Leiden: Brill, 1979.

——— "Parallel Historical Tradition in Josephus and Rabbinic Literature." In *Proceedings of the Ninth World Congress of Jewish Studies.* Vol. B, 7–14. Jerusalem: World Union of Jewish Studies, 1986.

Collins, John J. *Beyond the Qumran Community: The Sectarian Movement of the Dead Sea Scrolls.* Grand Rapids, MI: William B. Eerdmans, 2010.

Corner, Sean. "The Politics of the Parasite (Part One)." *Pheonix* 67 (2013): 43–80.

Culler, Jonathan. *Literary Theory: A Very Short Introduction.* Oxford: Oxford University Press, 1997.

Damon, Cynthia. *The Mask of the Parasite: A Pathology of Roman Patronage.* Ann Arbor: University of Michigan Press, 1997.

D'Arms, John H. "The Roman *Convivium* and the Idea of Equality." In *Sympotica: A Symposium on the Symposion.* Edited by Oswyn Murray, 308–20. Oxford: Clarendon Press, 1990.

——— "Slaves at Roman Convivia." In *Dining in a Classical Context.* Edited by William J. Slater, 171–83. Ann Arbor: University of Michigan Press, 1991.

Derenbourg, Joseph. *Essai sur l'histoire et la géographie de la Palestine.* Paris: l'imprimerie impériale, 1867.

Derrida, Jacques. *Adieu to Emmanuel Levinas.* Translated by Pascale-Anne Brault and Michael Naas. Stanford, CA: Stanford University Press, 2000.

——— *Of Hospitality: Anne Dufourmantelle invites Jacques Derrida to Respond.* Translated by Rachel Bowlby. Stanford, CA: Stanford University Press, 1999.

Dohrmann, Natalie B. "Law and Imperial Idioms: Rabbinic Legalism in a Roman World." In *Jews, Christians, and the Roman Empire: The Poetics of Power in Late Antiquity.* Edited by Annette Yoshiko Reed and Natalie B. Dohrmann, 63–78. Philadelphia: University of Pennsylvania Press, 2012.

Douglas, Mary. "Deciphering a Meal." *Daedalus* 101 (1972): 61–81.

Duker, Jonathan. "Piety or Privilege? A Talmudic View of the Fall of the Second Commonwealth." *Milin Havivin* 5 (2010–2011): 41–56.

Dunbabin, Katherine M.D. *The Roman Banquet: Images of Conviviality*. Cambridge: Cambridge University Press, 2004.

———. "Triclinium and Stibadium." In *Dining in a Classical Context*. Edited by William J. Slater, 121–48. Ann Arbor: University of Michigan Press, 1991.

———. "Ut Graeco More Biberetur: Greeks and Romans on the Dining Couch." In *Meals in a Social Context: Aspects of the Communal Meal in the Hellenistic and Roman World*. Edited by Inge Nielsen and Hanne Sigismund Nielsen, 81–101. Langelandsgade: Aarhus University Press, 1998.

Efron, Joshua. "Bar-Kokhva in the Light of the Palestinian and Babylonian Talmudic Traditions" ("מלחמת בר־כוכבא לאור המסורת התלמודית־הארצישראלית כנגד הבבלית"). In *The Bar-Kokhva Revolt: A New Approach*. Edited by Aharon Oppenheimer and Uriel Rappaport, 47–105. Jerusalem: Yad Ben Zvi, 1984.

Ekroth, Gunnel. "Animal Sacrifice in Antiquity." In *The Oxford Handbook of Ancient Animals in Classical Thought and Life*. Edited by Gordon Lindsay Campbell, 324–54. Oxford: Oxford University Press, 2014.

Epstein, Jacob Nahum. *Introduction to the Mishnaic Text* (מבוא לנוסח המשנה). Jerusalem: Hebrew University Magnes Press and Dvir, 2000.

———. "Midiqduqei yerushalmi" ("מדקדוקי ירושלמי"). *Tarbiz* 5 (1934): 252–72.

Farrer, Austin M. "On Dispensing with Q." In *Studies in the Gospels: Essays in Memory of R.H. Lightfoot*. Edited by D.E. Nineham, 55–88. Oxford: Blackwell, 1955.

Fehr, Burkhard. "Entertainers at the *Symposion*: The *Akletoi* in the Archaic Period." In *Sympotica: A Symposium on the Symposion*. Edited by Oswyn Murray, 85– 95. Oxford: Clarendon Press, 1990.

Ferriss Hill, Jennifer L. *Roman Satire and the Old Comic Tradition*. New York, NY: Cambridge University Press, 2015.

Fish, Stanley. *Is There a Text in This Class? The Authority of Interpretive Communities*. Cambridge, MA: Harvard University Press, 1980.

Fischel, Henry A. "Studies in Cynicsm and the Ancient Near East: The Transformation of a *Chria*." In *Religions in Antiquity: Essays in*

Memory of Erwin Ramsdell Goodenough. Edited by Jacob Neusner, 372–411. Leiden: Brill, 1968.

Flusser, David. *The Josippon (Josephus Gorionides): Edited with an Introduction, Commentary and Notes* (ספר יוסיפון: יוצא לאור סדור ומוגה על פי כתבי יד בלוויית מבוא, ביאורים וחילופי גרסאות). Jerusalem: Bialik Institute, 1978.

Fox, Michael V. *Proverbs 10–31*. New Haven, CT: The Anchor Yale Bible, 2009.

Fraenkel, Jonah. *The Aggadic Narrative: Harmony of Form and Content* (סיפור האגדה: אחדות של תוכן וצורה). Tel Aviv: Hakibutz Hameuchad, 2001.

Freudenberg, Kirk. "Introduction: Roman Satire." In *The Cambridge Companion to Roman Satire*. Edited by Kirk Freudenberg, 1–30. Cambridge: Cambridge University Press, 2005.

Friedman, Albert B., Doughtie, Edward, and Brogan, T.V.F. "Incremental Repetition." In *The New Princeton Encyclopedia of Poetry and Poetics*. Edited by Alex Preminger and T.V.F. Brogan, 580–81. Princeton: Princeton University Press, 1993.

Friedman, Shamma. "A Good Story Deserves Retelling: The Unfolding of the Akiva Legend." *JSIJ* 3 (2004): 55–93.

———— "'History and Aggadah': The Enigma of Dama Ben Netina" (דמא בן נתינה – לדמותו ההיסטורית: פרק בחקר האגדה התלמודית"). In *Hiyagon L'Yona: New Aspects in the Study of Midrash, Aggadah and Piyut in Honor of Professor Yona Fraenkel*. Edited by Joshua Levinson, Jacob Elbaum, and Galit Hasan-Rokem, 83–130. Jerusalem: Hebrew University Magnes Press, 2006.

———— "Now You See It, Now You Don't: Can Source-Criticism Perform Magic on Talmudic Passages about Sorcery?" In *Rabbinic Traditions between Palestine and Babylonia*. Edited by Ronit Nikolsky and Tal Ilan, 32–83. Leiden: Brill, 2014.

———— *Talmud Ha-Igud: Babylonian Talmud Gittin IX*: Edition with Commentary (תלמוד האיגוד: המגרש, גיטין פרק תשיעי מן התלמוד הבבלי עם פרשנות על דרך המחקר). Jerusalem: The Society for the Interpretation of the Talmud, 2020.

———— "The Talmudic Narrative about Rav Kahana and R. Yohanan (Bava Kamma 117a–b) and its Two Textual Families" ("סיפור רב כהנא

"ור' יוחנן (ב"ק קיז ע"א-ע"ב) וענף נוסח גניזה-המבורג"). *Bar Ilan* 30–31 (2006): 409–90.

———— "Uncovering Literary Dependencies in the Talmudic Corpus." In *The Synoptic Problem in Rabbinic Literature*. Edited by Shaye J.D. Cohen, 35–57. Providence, RI: Brown Judaic Studies, 2000.

———— "Untangling Branches of Transmissions of the Babylonian Talmud" ("אחת דבר אלהים שתים זו שמעתי:' בירור מנגנון הפילוג לענפים' בנוסח התלמוד הבבלי על פי פרק תשיעי במסכת גיטין"). In *Professor Meir Benayahu Memorial Volume*. Edited by Moshe Bar Asher, Yehudah Liebes, Moshe Assis, and Yosef Kaplan, vol. 1, 103–73. Jerusalem: Yad Harav Nissim, 2019.

Funkenstein, Amos. *Perceptions of Jewish History*. Berkeley: University of California Press, 1993.

Furstenberg, Yair. "Qamtza and Bar Qamtza, 55b–56a," ("קמצא ובר קמצא, נה ע"ב - נו ע"א"). In *Five Sugyot from the Babylonian Talmud*. Edited by Shamma Friedman, 95–114. Jerusalem: The Society for the Interpretation of the Talmud, 2002.

Gafni, Isaiah M. *Babylonian Jewry and its Institutions in the Period of the Talmud* (יהדות בבל ומוסדותיה בתקופת התלמוד). Jerusalem: Zalman Shazar Center, 1986.

———— "Jerusalem in Rabbinic Literature" ("ירושלים בספרות חז"ל"). In *The History of Jerusalem: The Roman and Byzantine Periods (70–638 CE)*. Edited by Yoram Tsafrir and Shmuel Safrai, 35–59. Jerusalem: Yad Ben-Zvi 1999.

———— *The Jews of Babylonia in the Talmudic Era: A Social and Cultural History* (יהודי בבל בתקופת התלמוד: חיי החברה והרוח). Jerusalem: Zalman Shazar Center, 1990.

Gallagher, Catherine and Greenblatt, Stephen. *Practicing New Historicism*. Chicago, IL: University of Chicago Press, 2000.

Geertz, Clifford. *The Interpretation of Cultures: Selected Essays*. New York, NY: Basic, 1973.

Ginzberg, Carlo. "Microhistory: Two or Three Things that I Know about It." *Critical Inquiry* 20 (1993): 10–35.

Gladwell, Malcolm. *Outliers: The Story of Success*. New York NY: Back Bay, 2008.

Goldenberg, Robert. "The Destruction of the Jerusalem Temple: Its Meaning and Its Consequences." In *The Cambridge History of Judaism: Volume IV: The Late Roman-Byzantine Period*. Edited by Steven T. Katz, 191–205. Cambridge: Cambridge University Press, 2006.

Goodman, Martin. "A Bad Joke in Josephus." *JJS* 36 (1985): 195–99.

———— "Current Scholarship on the First Revolt." In *The First Jewish Revolt: Archaeology, History, and Ideology*. Edited by Andrea M. Berlin and J. Andrew Overman, 15–24. London: Routledge, 2002.

———— "Early Rabbinic Explanations of the Destruction of Jerusalem." *JJS* 33 (1982): 517–25.

———— *Rome and Jerusalem: The Clash of Ancient Civilizations*. London: Penguin, 2008.

———— "The First Jewish Revolt: Social Conflict and the Problem of Debt." *JJS* 33 (1982): 417–27.

———— "The Origins of the Great Revolt: A Conflict of Status Criteria." In *Greece and Rome in Eretz Israel: Collected Essays*. Edited by A. Kasher, U. Rappaport, and G. Fuks, 39–53. Jerusalem: Yad Ben Zvi and Israel Exploration Society, 1990.

———— *The Ruling Class of Judaea: The Origins of the Jewish Revolt Against Rome A.D. 66–70*. Cambridge: Cambridge University Press, 1987.

———— "Trajan and the Origins of Roman Hostility to the Jews." *Past and Present* 182 (2003): 3–29. Gosbell, Louise A. *"The Poor, the Crippled, the Blind, and the Lame:" Physical and Sensory Disability in the Gospels of the New Testament*. Tübingen: Mohr Siebeck, 2018.

Gowers, Emily. *The Loaded Table: Representations of Food in Roman Literature*. Oxford: Clarendon Press, 1993.

Graetz, H. *Geschichte der Juden von den ältesten Zeiten bis auf die Gegenwart*. Vol. 3. Leipzig: Oskar Leiner, 1906.

Greatrex, Geoffrey. "Introduction." In *Shifting Genres in Late Antiquity*. Edited by Geoffrey Greatrex and Hugh Elton with the assistance of Lucas McMahon, 1–7. Burlington, VT: Ashgate, 2015.

Hacham, Noah. *"Bigthan and Teresh* and the Reason Gentiles Hate Jews," *VT* 62 (2012): 318–56.

———— "3 Maccabees and Esther: Parallels, Intertextuality, and Diaspora Identity." *JBL* 126 (2007): 765–85.

Halevi, Elimelekh E. *Gates of the Aggadah* (שערי האגדה). Tel Aviv: 1963.

Harland, Philip A. "Banqueting Values in the Associations: Rhetoric and Reality." In *Meals in the Early Christian World: Social Formation, Experimentation, and Conflict at the Table*. Edited by Dennis E. Smith and Hal E. Taussig, 73–85. New York, NY: Palgrave Macmillan, 2012.

Hasan-Rokem, Galit. *Web of Life: Folklore and Midrash in Rabbinic Literature*. Translated by Batya Stein. Stanford, CA: Stanford University Press, 2000.

Herman, Geoffrey. "Table Etiquette and Persian Culture in the Babylonian Talmud" ("פרסאי בצרכי סעודה בקיאי מינייכו': נימוסי שולחן' ותרבות פרס בתלמוד הבבלי"). *Zion* 77 (2012): 149–88.

Hidary, Richard. *Dispute for the Sake of Heaven: Legal Pluralism in the Talmud*. Providence, RI: Brown University Press, 2010.

Hooley, Daniel M. *Roman Satire*. Oxford: Blackwell, 2007.

Horden, Peregrine and Purcell, Nicholas. *The Corrupting Sea: A Study of Mediterranean History*. Oxford: Blackwell, 2000.

Hudson, Nicole Anne. "Food: A Suitable Subject for Roman Verse Satire." PhD diss., University of Leicester, 1991.

Humphreys, W. Lee. "A Life-Style for Diaspora: A Study of the Tales of Esther and Daniel." *JBL* 92 (1973): 211–23.

Hurovitz, Victor Avidgor. *Proverbs: Introduction and Commentary* (משלי עם מבוא ופירוש). Vol. 2. *Mikra Leyisraʾel*. Tel Aviv: Am Oved and Hebrew University Magnes Press, 2012.

Ilan, Tal. *Lexicon of Jewish Names in Late Antiquity: Part I: Palestine 330 BCE–200 CE*. Tübingen: Mohr Siebeck, 2002.

——— *Lexicon of Jewish Names in Late Antiquity: Part IV: The Eastern Diaspora 330 BCE–650 CE*. Tübingen: Mohr Siebeck, 2011.

Jaffee, Martin S. *Torah in the Mouth: Writing and Oral Tradition in Palestinian Judaism 200 BCE–400 CE*. Oxford: Oxford University Press, 2001.

Jastrow, Marcus. *A Dictionary of the Targumim, the Talmud Babli and Yerushalmi, and the Midrashic Literature*. London: Luzac and G.P. Putnam, 1903.

Johnson, Scott Fitzgerald. "Introduction." In *Greek Literature in Late*

Antiquity: Dynamism, Didacticism, Classicism. Edited by Scott Fitzgerald Johnson, 1–8. Burlington, VT: Ashgate, 2006.

Jones, Bruce William. "Antiochus Epiphanes and the Persecution of the
Jews." In *Scripture in Context: Essays on the Comparative Method.* Ed-
ited by Carl D. Evans, William W. Hallo, and John B. White, 263–90.
Eugene, OR: Pickwick, 1980.

Joseph Hayyim ben Elijah. *Sefer ben Yehoyada: Gittin* (ספר בן יהוידע:
גיטין). Jerusalem: Hatzvi, 1997.

Jost, I.M. *Geschichte der Israeliten seit der Zeit der Maccabaer bis auf unsre
Tage.* Vol. 2. Berlin: Schlesingerschen Buch- und Musikhandlung, 1821.

Justi, Ferdinand. *Iranisches Namenbuch.* Marburg: N.G. Elwert'sche,
1895.

Kalmanzon, Beni and Fogel, Shimon. *Why the Land is in Ruins: Investigations into the Legends of the Destruction* (על מה אבדה הארץ: עיונים
באגדות החורבן). Otniel: Giluy, 5769 (2008–2009).

Kalmin, Richard. *Jewish Babylonia between Persia and Roman Palestine.*
Oxford: Oxford University Press, 2006.

———— *The Sage in Jewish Society of Late Antiquity.* New York, NY:
Routledge, 1999.

Kaminka, Armand. *Studies in Bible, Talmud and Rabbinic Literature:
Book 2: Studies in Talmud* (מחקרים במקרא ובתלמוד ובספרות הרבנית:
ספר שני: מחקרים בתלמוד). Tel Aviv: Dvir, 1951.

Kim, Chan-Hie. "The Papyrus Invitation." *JBL* 94 (1975): 391–402.

Klawans, Jonathan. "Josephus, the Rabbis, and Responses to Catastrophes Ancient and Modern." *JQR* 100 (2010): 278–309.

———— *Purity, Sacrifice, and the Temple: Symbolism and Supersessionism in the Study of Ancient Judaism.* Oxford: Oxford University
Press, 2005.

Klein, Gil P. "Torah in Triclinia: The Rabbinic Banquet and the Significance of Architecture." *JQR* 102 (2012): 325–70.

Klein, Samuel. "Anshei yerushalayim, yaqirei yerushalayim, neqiyei-ha-
da'at shebeyerushalayim, benei-tzion" ("אנשי ירושלים, יקירי ירושלים,
נקיי־הדעת שביְרושלים, בני־ציון"). *Jewish Studies* 1 (1926): 72–78.

————. "Leheqer hashemot vehakinuyim" ("לחקר השמות והכינויים").
Lĕšonénu 1 (1929): 325–50.

Klinghardt, Matthias. "A Typology of the Communal Meal." In *Meals in* the Early Christian World: Social Formation, Experimentation, and Conflict at the Table. Edited by Dennis E. Smith and Hal E. Taussig, 9–22. New York, NY: Palgrave Macmillan, 2012.

———— Gemeinschaftsmahl und Mahlgemeinschaft: Soziologie und Liturgie frühchristlicher Mahlfeiern. Tübingen: A. Francke, 1996.

Kloppenborg, John S. and Ascough, Richard S. Greco-Roman Associations: Texts, Translations, and Commentary: I: Attica, Central Greece, Macedonia, Thrace. Berlin: Walter de Gruyter, 2011.

Koller, Aaron J. Esther in Ancient Jewish Thought. Cambridge: Cambridge University Press, 2014.

König, Jason. Saints and Symposiasts: The Literature of Food and the Symposium in Greco-Roman and Early Christian Culture. Cambridge: Cambridge University Press, 2012.

Kraemer, David C. "Food, Eating, and Meals." In The Oxford Handbook of Jewish Daily Life in Roman Palestine. Edited by Catherine Hezser, 403–19. Oxford: Oxford University Press, 2010.

———— Jewish Eating and Identity through the Ages. London: Routledge, 2007.

———— Responses to Suffering in Classical Rabbinic Literature. Oxford: Oxford University Press, 1995.

Kuhn, Thomas S. The Structure of Scientific Revolutions. Chicago, IL: University of Chicago Press, 1962.

Kulp, Joshua. "The Origins of the Seder and Haggadah." CBR 4 (2005): 109–34.

Kutscher, Edward Yechezkel. "Addenda to the Lexicographical Section" ("נוספות למדור המילוני"). ANDRL 1 (1972): 83–105.

———— "Some Problems of the Lexicography of Mishnaic Hebrew and its Comparison to Biblical Hebrew" ("מבעיות המילונות של לשון חז"ל"). ANDRL 1 (1972): 29–82.

Lapin, Hayim. Rabbis as Romans: The Rabbinic Movement in Palestine, 100–400 c.e. Oxford: Oxford University Press, 2012.

Lau, Binyamin. Sages – Volume 1: The Second Temple Period (חכמים - כרך ראשון: ימי בית שני). Jerusalem: The Jewish Agency for Israel – Eliner Library and Beit Morasha, 2006.

Lee, Jae Won. Paul and the Politics of Difference: A Contextual Study *of the Jewish- Gentile Difference in Galatians and Romans.* Eugene, OR: Pickwick, 2014.

Lévi Strauss, Claude. *The Naked Man.* In *Introduction to a Science of Mythology.* Vol. 4. New York, NY: Harper & Row, 1981.

———— *The Story of Lynx.* Chicago, IL: University of Chicago Press, 1995.

Levick, Barbara. "Morals, Politics, and the Fall of the Roman Republic." *Greece and Rome* 29 (1982): 53–62.

Levine, Lee I. "Jews and Judaism in Palestine (70–640 CE): A New Historical Paradigm." In *The Faces of Torah: Studies in the Texts and Contexts of Ancient Judaism in Honor of Steven Fraade.* Edited by Michal Bar-Asher Siegal, Tzvi Novick, and Christine Hayes, 395–412. Göttingen: Vandenhoeck & Ruprecht, 2017.

Levine Katz, Yael. "'Because of Qamtsa and Bar Qamtsa Jerusalem was Destroyed' – Studies in the Traditions of the Story" ("על קמצא ובר קמצא חרבה ירושלים' - עיונים במסורות הסיפור"). *Pathways through Aggadah* 3 (2000): 33–58.

Levinson, Joshua. "Literary Approaches to Midrash." In *Current Trends in the Study of Midrash.* Edited by Carol Bakhos, 189–226. Leiden: Brill, 2006.

Lewis, Michael. *The Undoing Project: A Friendship that Changed our Minds.* New York, NY: W.W. Norton, 2017.

Lewis, Richie. "*And Before Honor – Humility* (Proverbs 15:33): Ascending to Lowliness" ("לפני כבוד ענוה' (משלי טו, 33): שבירת מבני החברה' כעלייה אל השפלות"). *Daat* 86 (2018): 459–80.

Liddell, Henry George and Scott, Robert. *A Greek-English Lexicon.* Oxford: Clarendon Press, 1966.

Lieberman, Saul. "Notes on Chapter I of Midrash *Koheleth Rabbah*" ("הערות לפרק א' של קהלת רבה"). In *Studies in Mysticism and Religion.* Edited by E.E. Urbach, R.J. Zwi Werblowsky, and Ch. Wirszubski, 163–79. Jerusalem: Hebrew University Magnes Press, 1967.

———— *Tosefta Ki-Fshuṭa* (תוספתא כפשוטה). 12 vols. New York: The Jewish Theological Seminary of America, 1955–1988.

———— *Yemenite Midrashim: A Lecture on the Yemenite Midrashim, their Character and Value* (מדרשי תימן: הרצאה על מדרשי תימן על מהותם וערכם). Jerusalem: Shalem, 1962.

Lintott, A.W. "Imperial Expansion and Moral Decline in the Roman Republic." *Historia* 21 (1972): 626–38.

Loew, Judah ben Bezalel. *Sefer Hidushei Agadot Maharal Miprag* (ספר חידושי אגדות מהר"ל מפראג). Vol. 2. London: Honig and Sons, 1960.

Macuch, Maria. "Jewish Jurisdiction within the Framework of the Sasanian Legal System." In *Encounters by the Rivers of Babylon: Scholarly Conversations between Jews, Iranians and Babylonians in Antiquity.* Edited by Uri Gabbay and Shai Secunda, 147–60. Tübingen: Mohr Siebeck, 2014.

Mader, Gottfried. *Josephus and the Politics of Historiography: Apologetic and Impression Management in the Bellum Judaicum.* Leiden: Brill, 2000.

Mandel, Paul. "Midrash Lamentations Rabbati: Prolegomenon, and a Critical Edition to the Third *Parsha*" (מדרש איכה רבתי: מבוא ומהדורה ביקורתית לפרשה השלישית). PhD diss., Hebrew University, 1997.

———— "'Tales of the Destruction of the Temple': Between the Land of Israel and Babylonia" (אגדות החורבן: בין ארץ ישראל לבבל). In *Center and Diaspora: The Land of Israel and the Diaspora in the Second Temple, Mishna and Talmud Periods.* Edited by Isaiah M. Gafni, 141–58. Jerusalem: Zalman Shazar Center, 2004.

———— "The Story in Midrash Eichah: Text and Style" (הספור במדרש איכה: נוסח וסגנון). MA thesis, Hebrew University, 1983.

Manuwald, Gesine. "Tragedy, Paratragedy, and Roman Comedy." In *The Oxford Handbook of Greek and Roman Comedy.* Edited by Michael Fontane and Adele C. Scafuro, 580–98. Oxford: Oxford University Press, 2014.

Marks, Susan. "Introduction." In *Meals in Early Judaism: Social Formation at the Table.* Edited by Susan Marks and Hal E. Taussig, 1–12. New York, NY: Palgrave Macmillan, 2014.

Martin, Joseph. *Symposion: Die Geschichte einer literarischen Form.* Paderborn: Ferdinand Schöningh, 1931.

Mason, Steven. *A History of the Jewish War* A.D. 66–74. Cambridge: Cambridge University Press, 2016.

Meinhold, Arndt. "Die Gattung der Josephsgeschichte und des Esterbuches: Diasporanovelle I." *ZAW* 87 (1975): 306–24.

———— "Die Gattung der Josephsgeschichte und des Esterbuches: Diasporanovelle ii." *ZAW* 88 (1976): 72–93.

Miles, Deri Pode. "Forbidden Pleasures: Sumptuary Laws and Ideology of Moral Decline in Ancient Rome." PhD diss., University College London, 1987.

Miller, Stuart S. "The Study of Talmudic Israel and/or Roman Palestine: Where Matters Stand." In *The Faces of Torah: Studies in the Texts and Contexts of Ancient Judaism in Honor of Steven Fraade.* Edited by Michal Bar-Asher Siegal, Tzvi Novick, and Christine Hayes, 433–54. Göttingen: Vandenhoeck & Ruprecht, 2017.

Milne, A.A. *Winnie-the-Pooh.* London: Methuen, 2000.

Mintz, Alan. *Ḥurban: Responses to Catastrophe in Hebrew Literature.* New York, NY: Columbia University Press, 1984.

Mitchell, T.N. "Cicero on the Moral Crisis of the Late Republic." *Hermathena* 136 (1984): 21–41.

Mokhtarian, Jason Sion. "Clusters of Iranian Loanwords in Talmudic Folkore: The Chapter of the Pious (b. Ta'anit 18b–26a) in Its Sasanian Context." In *The Aggada of the Bavli and Its Cultural World.* Edited by Geoffrey Herman and Jeffrey L. Rubenstein, 125–48. Providence, RI: Brown Judaic Studies, 2018.

———— *Rabbis, Sorcerers, Kings, and Priests: The Culture of the Talmud in Ancient Iran.* Oakland: University of California Press, 2015.

Morford, Mark. "Juvenal's Fifth Satire." *AJP* 98 (1977): 219–45.

Muecke, Frances. "Rome's First Satirists: Themes and Genres in Ennius and Lucilius." In *The Cambridge Companion to Roman Satire.* Edited by Kirk Freudenberg, 33–47. Cambridge: Cambridge University Press, 2005.

Murray, Oswyn. "Sympotic History." In *Sympotica: A Symposium on the Symposion.* Edited by Oswyn Murray, 3–13. Oxford: Clarendon Press, 1990.

Murray, Shirley Anne. "Quis Ego Sum Saltem? An Investigation of Plautus' Captiui, Menaechmi and Amphitruo with Special Reference to Problems of Identity." MA thesis, University of KwaZulu-Natal, 2007.

Neusner, Jacob. *A History of the Jews in Babylonia: Part 2: The Early Sasanian Period.* Leiden: Brill, 1966.

———— *A History of the Jews in Babylonia III: From Shapur I to Sha-pur II*. Leiden: Brill, 1968.

———— *A History of the Jews in Babylonia IV. The Age of Shapur II*. Leiden: Brill, 1969.

———— *From Politics to Piety: The Emergence of Pharisaic Judaism*. Englewood Cliffs: Prentice-Hall, 1973.

Niditch, Susan. *Underdogs and Tricksters: A Prelude to Biblical Folklore*. San Francisco: Harper & Row, 1987.

Noam, Vered. "Introduction" ("מבוא"). In *Josephus and the Rabbis*. Edited by Tal Ilan and Vered Noam, 1–90. Jerusalem: Yad Ben-Zvi, 2017.

Novick, Tzvi. "Charity and Reciprocity: Structures of Benevolence in Rabbinic Literature." *HTR* 105 (2012): 33–52.

Noy, David. "The Sixth Hour is the Mealtime for Scholars: Jewish Meals in the Roman World." In *Meals in a Social Context: Aspects of the Communal Meal in the Hellenistic and Roman World*. Edited by Inge Nielsen and Hanne Sigismund Nielsen, 134–44. Langelandsgade: Aarhus University Press, 1998.

Paul, George. "Symposia and Deipna in Plutarch's *Lives* and in other Historical Writings." In *Dining in a Classical Context*. Edited by William J. Slater, 157–69. Ann Arbor: University of Michigan Press, 1991.

Pniel, Menashe. "The Text of Tractate Gittin Chapter VIII in the Babylonian Talmud" ("נוסח פרק 'הזורק גט' בבבלי: על-פי כתבי-יד, קטעי גניזה, קטעי כריכה ודפוס ראשון, בצירוף מבוא ודיון בענייני נוסח"). MA thesis, Bar-Ilan University, 2014.

Porter, Patrick. "Unlawful Passions: Sumptuary Law and the Roman Revolution." *MHJ* 28 (2000): 1–18.

Price, Jonathan. "Josephus' Reading of Thucydides: A Test Case in the *Bellum Iudaicum*." In *Thucydides – A Violent Teacher?: History and its Representations*. Edited by Georg Rechenauer and Vassiliki Pothou, 79–98. Göttingen: V & R Unipress, 2011.

Quine, Willard V.O. "Two Dogmas of Empiricism." *The Philosophical Review* 60 (1951): 20–43.

Rappaport, Uriel. "Jewish-Pagan Relations and the Revolt against Rome in 66–70 C.E." *Jerusalem Cathedra* (1981): 81–95.

Rawson, Beryl. "Banquets in Ancient Rome: Participation, Presentation and Perception." In *Dining on Turtles: Food Feasts and Drinking in*

History. Edited by Diane Kirkby and Tanja Luckins, 15–32. New York, NY: Palgrave Macmillan, 2007.

Reed, Annette Yoshiko and Dohrmann, Natalie B. "Rethinking Romanness, Provincializing Christendom." In *Jews, Christians, and the Roman Empire: The Poetics of Power in Late Antiquity*. Edited by Annette Yoshiko Reed and Natalie B. Dohrmann, 1–21. Philadelphia: University of Pennsylvania Press, 2013.

Relihan, Joel C. "Rethinking the History of the Literary Symposium." *ICS* 17 (1992): 213–44.

Rimmon-Kenan, Shlomith. *Narrative Fiction: Contemporary Poetics*. London: Routledge, 1983.

Rindge, Matthew S. "Jewish Identity under Foreign Rule: Daniel 2 as a Reconfiguration of Genesis 41." *JBL* 129 (2010): 85–104.

Rokéaḥ, David. "Comments on the Revolt of Bar Kokhba" ("הערות כוזביות"). *Tarbiz* 35 (1966): 122–31.

——— "Word-Play Nonetheless: A Rejoinder" ("בכל זאת משחק מלים: תגובה"). *Zion* 53 (1988): 317–22.

——— "Zechariah ben Avkules: Humility or Zealotry?" ("זכריה בן אבקולס: ענוותנות או קנאות?"). *Zion* 53 (1988): 53–56.

Roller, Matthew B. *Dining Posture in Ancient Rome: Bodies, Values, and Status*. Princeton: Princeton University Press, 2006.

Rosen-Zvi, Ishay. "Is the Mishnah a Roman Composition?" In *The Faces of Torah: Studies in the Texts and Contexts of Ancient Judaism in Honor of Steven Fraade*. Edited by Michal Bar-Asher Siegal, Tzvi Novick, and Christine Hayes, 487–508. Göttingen: Vandenhoeck & Ruprecht, 2017.

Rosenberg, Yehoshua. "Mishna 'Kippurim' (Yoma): A Critical Edition with Introduction" ("משנה 'כיפורים': מהדורה ביקורתית, בצרוף מבוא"). 2 vols. PhD diss., Hebrew University, 1995.

Rosenblum, Jordan D. *Food and Identity in Early Rabbinic Judaism*. Cambridge: Cambridge University Press, 2010.

——— "Inclined to Decline Reclining? Women, Corporeality, and Dining Posture in Early Rabbinic Literature." In *Meals in the Early Christian World: Social Formation, Experimentation, and Conflict at the Table*. Edited by Dennis E. Smith and Hal E. Taussig, 261–74. New York, NY: Palgrave Macmillan, 2012.

Rubenstein, Jeffrey L. "*Bavli Gittin* 55b–56b: An Aggadic Narrative in its Halakhic Context." *Hebrew Studies* 38 (1997): 21–45.

———— "Criteria of Stammaitic Intervention in Aggada." In *Creation and Composition: The Contribution of the Bavli Redactors (Stammaim) to the Aggada.* Edited by Jeffrey L. Rubenstein, 417–40. Tübingen: Mohr Siebeck, 2005.

———— *Talmudic Stories: Narrative Art, Composition, and Culture.* Baltimore, MD: Johns Hopkins University Press, 1999.

———— *The Culture of the Babylonian Talmud.* Baltimore, MD: Johns Hopkins University Press, 2003.

———— "The Story-Cycles of the Bavli: *Part 1.*" In *Studies in Rabbinic Narrative: Volume One.* Edited by Jeffrey L. Rubenstein, 227–280. Providence, RI: Brown Judaic Studies, 2021.

Rubenstein, Richard L. *The Religious Imagination: A Study in Psychoanalysis and Jewish Theology.* Lanham, MD: University Press of America, 1968.

Sacchi, Paola and Viazzo, Pier Paolo. "Honour, History, and the History of Mediterranean Anthropology." *JMS* 22 (2013): 275–91.

Safrai, Shmuel. "Home and Family." In *Compendia Rerum Iudaicarum ad Novum Testamentum: The Jewish People in the First Century: Volume Two.* Edited by Shmuel Safrai and Menahem Stern, 728–92. Philadelphia, PA: Fortress Press, 1976.

———— *In the Times of Temple and Mishnah: Studies in Jewish History* (בימי הבית ובימי המשנה: מחקרים בתולדות ישראל). Vol. 1. Jerusalem: Hebrew University Magnes Press, 1994.

Safrai, Shmuel and Safrai, Ze'ev. *Haggadah of the Sages: The Passover Haggadah* (הגדת חז"ל: הגדה של פסח). Jerusalem: Carta, 1998.

———— *Mishnat Eretz Israel: Tractate Shabbat* (משנת ארץ ישראל: מסכת שבת). Vol. 2. Jerusalem: E.M. Liphshitz, 2008.

———— *Mishnat Eretz Israel: Tractate Yoma* (משנת ארץ ישראל: מסכת יומא). Jerusalem: E.M. Liphshitz, 2010.

Safrai, Ze'ev. "Har hamelekh adayin hidah" ("הר המלך עדיין חידה"). *JSRS* 19 (2010): 69–82.

Saldarini, Anthony J. "Good from Evil: The Rabbinic Response." In *The First Jewish Revolt: Archaeology, History, and Ideology.* Edited by

Andrea M. Berlin and J. Andrew Overman, 221–36. London: Routledge, 2002.

———— "Varieties of Rabbinic Response to the Destruction of the Temple." *Society of Biblical Literature 1982 Seminar Papers*, 437–58. Chico, CA: Scholars Press, 1982.

Sarason, Richard S. *The Talmud of the Land of Israel: A Preliminary Translation and Explanation: Demai*. Chicago, IL: University of Chicago Press, 1993.

Satlow, Michael. "Beyond Influence: Toward a New Historiographic Paradigm." In *Jewish Literatures and Cultures: Context and Intertext*. Edited by Anita Norich and Yaron Z. Eliav, 37–54. Providence, RI: Brown University Press, 2008.

Schäfer, Peter. "Introduction." In *The Talmud Yerushalmi and Graeco-Roman Culture*. Edited by Peter Schäfer. Vol. 1, 1–23. Tübingen: Mohr Siebeck, 1998.

Schank, Roger C. and Berman, Tamara R. "The Pervasive Role of Stories in Knowledge and Action." In *Narrative Impact: Social and Cognitive Foundations*. Edited by Melanie C. Green, Jeffrey J. Strange, and Timothy C. Brock, 287–313. Mahwah, NJ: Lawrence Erlbaum Associates, 2002.

Schofer, Jonathan Wyn. *Confronting Vulnerability: The Body and the Divine in Rabbinic Ethics*. Chicago, IL: University of Chicago Press, 2010.

Schürer, Emile, Vermes, Geza, Millar, Fergus, and Black, Matthew. *The History of the Jewish People in the Age of Jesus Christ (175 B.C. – A.D. 135)*. Edinburgh: T.&T. Clark, 1979.

Schwartz, Daniel R. *Agrippa I: The Last King of Judaea*. Tübingen: Mohr Siebeck, 1990.

———— "From the Maccabees to Masada: On Diasporan Historiography of the Second Temple Period." In *Jüdische Geschiche in Hellenistisch-römischer Zeit*. Edited by Aharon Oppenheimer and Elisabeth Müller Luckner, 29–40. Munich: Oldenbourg, 1999.

———— *Judeans and Jews: Four Faces of Dichotomy in Ancient Jewish History*. Toronto: University of Toronto Press, 2014.

———— "More on 'Zechariah ben Avkules: Humility or Zealotry?'" ("עוד לשאלת 'זכריה בן אבקולס: ענוותנות או קנאות?'"). *Zion* 53 (1988): 313–16.

————— *Studies in the Jewish Background of Christianity*. Tübingen: Mohr Siebeck, 1992.

————— *2 Maccabees*. Berlin: Walter de Gruyter, 2008.

Schwartz, Seth. *Imperialism and Jewish Society 200 b.c.e. to 640 c.e.* Princeton, NJ: Princeton University Press, 2001.

————— "No Dialogue at the Symposium? Conviviality in Ben Sira and the Palestinian Talmud." In *The End of Dialogue in Antiquity*. Edited by Simon Goldhill, 193–216. Cambridge: Cambridge University Press, 2008.

————— "Sunt Lachrymae Rerum." *JQR* 99 (2009): 56–64.

————— *Were the Jews a Mediterranean Society? Reciprocity and Solidarity in Ancient Judaism*. Princeton: Princeton University Press, 2010.

Secunda, Shai. *The Iranian Talmud: Reading the Bavli in Its Sasanian Context*. Philadelphia: University of Pennsylvania Press, 2013.

Shahar, Yuval. "Har Hamelekh – A New Solution to an Old Puzzle" ("הר המלך - לפתרונה של חידה"). *Zion* 65 (2002): 275–306.

Shaked, Shaul. "'No talking during a Meal': Zoroastrian Themes in the Babylonian Talmud." In *The Talmud in its Iranian Context*. Edited by Carol Bakhos and M. Rahim Shayegan, 161–77. Tübingen: Mohr Siebeck, 2010.

Shanks Alexander, Elizabeth. *Transmitting Mishnah: The Shaping Influence of Oral Tradition*. Cambridge: Cambridge University Press, 2006.

Shero, L.R. "The Cena in Roman Satire." *Classical Philology* 18 (1923): 126–43.

Shinan, Avigdor. "R. Yannai, the Peddler and the Well-Dressed Man: A Study of the Structure of Two Stories from Leviticus Rabbah" ("רבי ינאי, הרוכל והאדם המשופע: עיון בתשתיתם של שני סיפורים במדרש ויקרא רבה"). *Criticism and Interpretation* 30 (1994): 15–23.

Shoval-Dudai, Nurit. *A Glossary of Greek and Latin Loanwords in Post-Biblical Jewish Literature* (גלוסר המילים השאולות מן היוונית ומן הרו־מית במקורות היהודיים הבתר־מקראיים). Israel: The Academy of the Hebrew Language, 2019.

Slater, William J. "Sympotic Ethics in the *Odyssey*." In *Sympotica: A Symposium on the Symposion*. Edited by Oswyn Murray, 213–20. Oxford: Clarendon Press, 1990.

Smallwood, E. Mary. *The Jews under Roman Rule: From Pompey to Diocletian*. Leiden: Brill, 1976.

Smelik, Willem F. *Rabbis, Language and Translation in Late Antiquity*. Cambridge: Cambridge University Press. 2013.

Smith, Dennis E. *From Symposium to Eucharist: The Banquet in the Early Christian World*. Minneapolis, MN: Fortress Press, 2003.

———— "Next Steps: Placing this Study of Jewish Meals in the Larger Picture of Meals in the Ancient World, Early Judaism, and Early Christianity." In *Meals in Early Judaism: Social Formation at the Table*. Edited by Susan Marks and Hal E. Taussig, 175–81. New York, NY: Palgrave Macmillan, 2014.

———— "The Greco-Roman Banquet as a Social Institution." In *Meals in the Early Christian World: Social Formation, Experimentation, and Conflict at the Table*. Edited by Dennis E. Smith and Hal E. Taussig, 23–33. New York, NY: Palgrave Macmillan, 2012.

Sofer, Abraham Samuel Benjamin Wolf. *Hidushei ketav sofer hashalem al hashas: Gittin* (חידושי כתב סופר השלם על הש"ס: גיטין). Jerusalem: Mehon Da'at Sofer, 2006–2007.

Sofer, Moses. *Hidushei hatam sofer: Gittin* (חידושי חתם סופר: גיטין). Jerusalem: s.n., 5730 (1969–1970).

Sokoloff, Michael. *A Dictionary of Jewish Babylonian Aramaic of the Talmudic and Geonic Periods*. Ramat-Gan: Bar Ilan University Press and Johns Hopkins University Press, 2002.

———— *A Dictionary of Jewish Palestinian Aramaic of the Byzantine Period*. Ramat-Gan: Bar Ilan University Press, 2017.

Sperber, Daniel. *Greek in Talmudic Palestine*. Ramat Gan: Bar-Ilan University Press, 2012.

———— "Melilot 5" ("מלילות ה"). *Sinai* 91 (1982): 270–75.

Spicehandler, Ezra. "Dina de Magista and Bei Dawar: Notes on Gentile Courts in Talmudic Babylonia." *Hebrew Union College Annual* 26 (1955): 333–54.

Stein, S. "The Influence of the Symposia Literature on the Literary Form of the Pesah Haggadah." *JJS* 8 (1957): 13–44.

Stern, Menahem. "Aspects of Jewish Society: The Priesthood and Other Classes." In *Compendia Rerum Iudaicarum ad Novum Testamentum: The Jewish People in the First Century: Volume Two*. Edited by Shmuel Safrai and Menahem Stern, 561–630. Philadelphia, PA: Fortress Press, 1976.

Storey, Ian C. and Allan, Arlene. *A Guide to Ancient Greek Drama*. Chichester: Wiley Blackwell, 2014.

Strack, H.L. and Stemberger, Günther. *Introduction to the Talmud and Midrash*. Translated by Markus Bockmuehl. Minneapolis, MN: Fortress Press, 1996.

Streett, R. Alan. *An Analysis of the Lord's Supper under Roman Domination during the First Century*. Eugene, OR: Pickwick, 2013.

Taussig, Hal E. *In the Beginning was the Meal: Social Experimentation and Early Christian Identity*. Minneapolis, MN: Fortress Press, 2009.

——— "Introduction." In *Meals in the Early Christian World: Social Formation, Experimentation, and Conflict at the Table*. Edited by Dennis E. Smith and Hal E. Taussig, 1–5. New York, NY: Palgrave Macmillan, 2012.

The Comprehensive Aramaic Lexicon. cal.huc.edu.

Todd, Alan William. "Feasts and the Social Order in Early Jewish Society (ca. Third Century B.C.E. – Third Century C.E.)." PhD diss., Duke University, 2014.

Tropper, Amram. *Like Clay in the Hands of the Potter: Sage Stories in Rabbinic Literature* (כחומר ביד היוצר: מעשי חכמים בספרות חז"ל). Jerusalem: Zalman Shazar Center, 2011.

——— "On Children, Cypresses, Chickens and Catastrophe" ("על ילדים, ארזים, תרנגולים וחורבן"). *JSJF* 24–25 (2006–2007): 69–86.

——— *Rewriting Ancient Jewish History: The History of the Jews in Roman Times and the New Historical Method*. London: Routledge, 2016.

——— *Simeon the Righteous in Rabbinic Literature: A Legend Reinvented*. Leiden: Brill, 2013.

——— "'Teach Me the Whole Torah while I Stand on One Foot': On the Formation of a Story" ("על מנת שתלמדני כל התורה כולה כשאני 'עומד על רגל אחת': להתהוותו של סיפור"). In *Between Babylonia and the Land of Israel: Studies in Honor of Isaiah M. Gafni*. Edited by Geoffrey Herman, Meir Ben Shahar, and Aharon Oppenheimer, 267–86. Jerusalem: Zalman Shazar Center, 2016.

———— "The Economics of Jewish Childhood in Late Antiquity." *HUCA* 76 (2005): 189–233.

Veyne, Paul. *Bread and Circuses: Historical Sociology and Political Pluralism.* London: Allen Lane, 1990.

Visotzky, Burton L. *Aphrodite and the Rabbis: How the Jews Adapted Roman Culture to Create Judaism as We Know It.* New York, NY: St. Martin's Press, 2016.

Watts Belser, Julia. *Rabbinic Tales of Destruction: Gender, Sex, and Disability in the Ruins of Jerusalem.* Oxford: Oxford University Press, 2018.

Weinfeld, Moshe. *The Organizational Patterns and the Penal Code of the Qumran Sect: A Comparison with the Guilds and Religious Associations of the Hellenistic Period.* Fribourg: Éditions Universitaires, 1986.

Weiss, Abraham. *Studies in the Literature of the Amoraim* (על היצירה הספרותית של האמוראים). New York, NY: Horeb, Yeshiva University, and The Lucius N. Littauer Foundation, 1961–1962.

Weiss, Haim. "'From that Hour the Doom Was Sealed': On Class Reversals in the 'Legends of Destruction'" ("ועל אותה שעה נחתם גזר הדין': על היפוכים מעמדיים וחורבן הבית"). *JSJF* 31 (2018): 3–17.

Weiss, Ruhama. *Meal Tests: The Meal in the World of the Sages* (אוכלים לדעת: תפקידן התרבותי של הסעודות בספרות חז"ל). Tel Aviv: Hakibutz Hameuchad, 2010.

Wilkins, John. *The Boastful Chef: The Discourse of Food in Ancient Greek Comedy.* Oxford: Oxford University Press, 2000.

Wimsatt, William K. and Beardsley, Monroe C. "The Intentional Fallacy." *Sewanee Review* 54 (1946): 468–88.

Wisse, Ruth R. *Jews and Power.* New York, NY: Schocken, 2007.

Woolf, Greg. "Provincial Revolts in the Early Roman Empire." In *The Jewish Revolt Against Rome: Interdisciplinary Perspectives.* Edited by Malden Popović, 27–44. Leiden: Brill, 2001.

Yassif, Eli. *The Hebrew Folktale: History, Genre, Meaning.* Translated by Jacqueline S. Teitelbaum. Bloomington: Indiana University Press, 1999.

Yisraeli-Taran, Anat. *The Legends of the Destruction* (אגדות החורבן: מסורות החורבן בספרות התלמודית). Tel Aviv: Hakibutz Hameuchad, 1997.

Yuval, Israel J. "'The Lord will take Vengeance, Vengeance for his Tem-

ple' – historia sine ira et studio" "(היסטוריה :'נקמת ה' היא נקמת היכלו
ללא חרון וללא משוא פנים"). *Zion* 59 (1994): 351–414.

———— *Two Nations in Your Womb: Perceptions of Jews and Christians in Late Antiquity and the Middle Ages* Translated by Barbara Harshav and Jonathan Chipman. Berkeley: University of California Press, 2006.

Ziegler, Ignaz. *Die Königsleichnisse des Midrasch beleuchtet durch die römische Kaiserzeit*. Breslau: Schlesische Verlags-Anstalt v. S. Schottlaender, 1903.

Index

Ancient Sources Index

Hebrew Bible

7:36–50, 18n11
11:37–54,18n11
14:1–24, 18n11
14:7–11, 32n46
14:12–14, 49n22

14:17, 38n1
15:1–2, 18n11

1 Corinthians
10:17, 30n37
11:20–22, 33n46

Rabbinic Literature

Mishnah

SHABBAT
21:3, 81n19

PESAḤIM
4:8, 180n3

YOMA
3:9, 98n32
3:10–11, 90–91, 94
6:4, 17n10

SHEQALIM
5:1–2, 92–95

TAʿANIT
4:6, 151n5

KETUBBOT
1:5, 180n3

SOṬAH
9:12, 151n5
9:14, 151n5, 163n15

GITTIN
5:1, 151n5
5:5, 151n5
5:6, 150–52
5:8–9, 151n5

MENAḤOT
10:8, 180n3

Tosefta

BERAKHOT
4:8, 18–20, 26n12, 55
4:9–10, 16
5:5–6, 20–21, 24, 32n46

SHABBAT
16:7, 80n15, 81–83, 202n6, 218

PESAḤIM
3:19, 180n3

KIPPURIM
2:8, 91n13, 92–4

KETUBBOT
1:1, 180n3

SOṬAH
15:8, 163n15

MENAḤOT
13:22, 63–64

ARAKHIN
2:2, 17n10

Talmud Yerushalmi

BERAKHOT
2:2, 4c, 180n3
6:1, 10d, 18n13
8:2, 12a, 20n16

PEʾAH
1:1, 16a, 78n11

DEMAI
4:4, 24a, 14–15

SHABBAT
5:4, 7c, 78n11

ERUVIN
10:1, 27a, 180n3

YOMA
1: 1, 38c, 63n21
3:9, 41a–41b, 92–95

Inscriptions

The Rule of the *Iobakchoi*

Greek and Roman Literature

Athenaeus

Cicero

Colluthus

Dio Chrysostom

Florus

Homer

Horace

Juvenal

Livy

Lucan

Lucian

Macrobius

Martial

EPIGRAMMATA
7.86, 44–45

Petronius

SATYRICON
26–79, 61n15
46, 44n5
65–66, 68
74, 70

Plato

RESPUBLICA
8.545A ff, 142n16

SYMPOSIUM
174A, 43n5
174A–175A, 67–68
212D–213A, 68
223B, 68

Plautus

BACCHIDES
489–525, 51–52
539–640, 52

MENAECHMI
355–477, 52

PERSAE
777–858, 68

Pliny

NATURALIS HISTORIA
14.28, 61n15

Pliny the Younger

EPISTULAE
2.6, 33n46

Plutarch

BRUTUS
34.4, 68

CATO MAJOR
25.3, 30

QUAESTIONUM CONVIVIALUM
1.612D, 30n35
1.612D–615C, 33n46
1.614E–615D, 30n35
1.615D–617A, 32n46
1.621C, 33n46
2.629E–631C, 33n46
7.708A–D, 30n36,
7.708D, 43
7.697C, 24n4
7.697C–E, 30n35

SEPTEM SAPIENTIUM CONVIVIUM
147F–148A, 43n.4
147F–148B, 30n36
148A, 30
148F–149B, 32n46
160D, 67

Polybius

HISTORIES
6.7–9, 142n16
6.57, 61n15

Sallust

BELLUM IUGURTHINUM
4.5–9, 61n15

Seneca

AD LUCILIUM
19, 10, 30n36

Seneca the Elder

SUASORIAE
7.13, 60n11

Tacitus

HISTORIES
2.38, 61n15

Velleius Paterculus

HISTORIAE ROMANAE
2.1.1–2, 138–39

Vitruvius

DE ARCHITECTURA
6.5.1, 42

Xenophon

SYMPOSIUM
1.3–4, 43n5
1.11–16, 68

Subject Index